Bridging the Pacific

San Francisco Chinatown and Its People

Bridging the Pacific

San Francisco Chinatown and Its People

Thomas W. Chinn

Chinese Historical Society of America
San Francisco

Library of Congress Cataloging-in-Publication Data

Chinn, Thomas W.
    Bridging the Pacific: San Francisco Chinatown and its people /
  Thomas W. Chinn.
       p.   cm.
  Bibliography: p.
  Includes index.
  ISBN 0-9614198-3-0 — ISBN 0-9614198-4-9 (pbk.)
  1. Chinese Americans—California—San Francisco—History.
2. Chinese Americans—California—San Francisco—Social conditions.
3. Chinatown (San Francisco, Calif.)—History. 4. Chinatown (San
Francisco, Calif.)—Social conditions. 5. San Francisco (Calif.)—
History. 6. San Francisco (Calif.)—Social conditions.   I. Title.
II. Title: Chinese Historical Society of America.
F869.S39C52   1989
979.4´61004951—dc19   89-926
                                                    CIP

Printed in the United States of America

9 8 7 6 5 4 3 2

Dedicated to my wife,
Daisy Lorraine.

Contents

Foreword

When I was a little girl, visiting Chinatown was an adventure. Grant Avenue was one long colorful pageant of oriental splendor: narrow sidewalks thronged with busy people, tiny shops with fragrant odors of incense and herbs, fish and crabs and turtles in tanks and tubs, live fowl stacked up in cages, all manner of restaurants, and the exotic buildings with iron balconies and turned-up roofs.

Bridging the Pacific describes the real people who lived behind the exotic sounds and smells and colors of my childhood memories. Confined for a long time to an overpopulated ghetto, hemmed in by prejudice and denied the right to enter mainstream American life, the people of San Francisco Chinatown have stories to tell that can touch any American of any race. Thomas Chinn tells their stories with sympathy and humor, and gives us a new look at San Francisco's early years. Chinatown's churches, the Six Companies, traditional festivals and parades, and the first merchants and business enterprises come alive again. How refreshing it is to read these accounts, and how different from the nonsense of the typical Caucasian clichés about the Chinese I heard when I was a child! The honest fact is that the Chinese have always been as busy as any other people in pursuing the basic needs of life: food, clothing, and shelter. And, it might be added, a good education and a decent salary, when they could get a chance.

Many of the first generation of Chinese immigrants set sail as little more than boys, risking everything for the chance of striking it rich. San Francisco was the destination of these young fortune hunters. It was the gateway to the gold fields, where they hoped to find the means to a better life. Instead, Chinese miners were barred from the rich strikes until the white miners had exhausted the find. Most of the original fortune hunters ended up working as common laborers, ranch hands, cooks, or at whatever odd jobs they could find, until they were suddenly in demand to help build the Central Pacific Railway. But after the railway was completed, they drifted back to the cities. Shunned by their white neighbors, they withdrew into their tight ghettos and dwelt among themselves.

By the end of World War I Chinatown was bursting at the seams. Chinese could not rent or buy property anywhere else in the city. Signs in places of public amusement warned "Oriental and Negro patronage not solicited." This is a period with which Mr. Chinn is very familiar, for he has not only spent nearly a lifetime in Chinatown, he was active in many of the community organizations that helped break through the barriers between Chinatown and the rest of American society. He tells us about the YMCA and the first attempts to organize American-style athletic events in Chinatown; the clubs and contests and political organizations; and the Chinese Hospital, the Chinese Playground, and other familiar places and institutions that took years of struggle and careful planning to create. And he gives us glimpses into the lives of dozens of his contemporaries, men and women who ended up dwelling in every corner of the city, side by side with people of many different nationalities—despite the fact that, as children, they could not walk beyond the borders of Chinatown without risking a beating.

This book is a valuable contribution to our city's history. In my work as archivist for the City and County of San Francisco I find such personal details about days gone by woefully lacking, especially with regard to the lives of common folk. We have very few records of people's daily lives, of how they worked, shopped, and entertained themselves. Thomas W. Chinn has addressed an urgent need.

I sincerely hope that other people will be encouraged to put their own stories of San Francisco's past in writing.

Much credit is due Mr. Chinn for his efforts in founding the Chinese Historical Society of America and for his energetic editorship of the society's *Bulletin* for the first fourteen years it was published. He has devoted a major part of his life to the history of San Francisco Chinatown and its people, and his efforts have done much to overcome the many falsehoods and myths about the Chinese. This book continues that worthy task.

Gladys Cox Hansen
Archivist, City and County of San Francisco

Acknowledgments

Chinatown's many tea houses help perpetuate a ritual that is enjoyed by all who take part in it: a gathering of friends to have coffee or tea together early in the morning (or sometimes at noon) before they set off for work or play. For me, the place is usually Sun Wah Kue, at 848 Washington Street. My good friend Chingwah Lee and I met there often, even as far back as the 1920s, when the restaurant was only a year or two old. In those days we were usually talking about the activities planned for Boy Scout Troop 3. In 1935 we shook hands at Sun Wah Kue on our agreement to become partners and copublishers of the *Chinese Digest*, the first English-language publication for Chinese-Americans. Chingwah began his studio for Oriental art just half a block away, and that same studio became the office for the *Digest*. The staff met at the restaurant often, individually and collectively. And still later, I used to spend a lot of time having breakfast or lunch there when I had my own typography business.

More recently, over ten years ago, a group of my friends started to meet for lunch every Tuesday at Yuen's Garden Restaurant on Grant Avenue. They included Albert Lim, owner of the Mow Fung produce company, started in 1911 by his father, who began by shipping Chinese and other vegetables all over the country; Jackie Wong Sing, an immigration lawyer since 1945; Gabriel Gock, retired manager of the international Wing On Department Store and wholesale import-export corporation; James Hom, dentist; Buddie Huen, a former general in the Nationalist Chinese Army; Ernest Yao, travel agency owner; Herbert Chew, retired Social Security branch manager and now a travel agent; Hem Locke, a former colonel in the Chinese Nationalist Army and now a consultant for a local bank; Tommy Fong, owner of the Wax Museum at Fisherman's Wharf and the Movieland Wax Museum in Buena Park, Southern California; Franklin Sing, insurance agency owner; and myself. I joined them after I retired in 1980. Most are longtime friends. On other weekdays, most of us meet for morning coffee at Sun Wah Kue, where we share a waffle and converse on any subject that is interesting to us. Throughout the restaurant, other smaller groups gather and engage in similar coffee chatter. One can expect to find anyone from well-known businessmen to city hall officials such as Jeffrey Lee, public works director; or Melvin Lee, president of the Civil Service Commission; or Sinclair Louie, the prominent bazaar baron.

Due to time and space limitations, I have not been able to describe all my friends in this book. However, I would like at least to mention some of them here. For me, recollections of pleasant associations with friends of long standing make living worthwhile.

Kem Lee, premier Chinatown photographer, was to work with me on this book. Unfortunately, he passed away within the first month after the project was started.

Henry Shue Tom—how can I forget him! He always liked to remind people of my beating him in the mile run in the mid-1920s, when he was the favorite among the runners. He later became Executive Director of the

Chinatown YMCA, and served as secretary of the Chinese Historical Society of America in 1965 and 1966. He also helped me do some of the interviewing regarding churches for this book before he passed away in 1988.

Pardee Lowe is the author of the book *Father and Glorious Descendant* (1943). Jade Snow Wong is the author of *Fifth Chinese Daughter* (1950). The Ong brothers are all good friends: Woodrow was a member of Boy Scout Troop 3, and later married Jade Snow Wong. George and I served in the California State Militia together in Chinatown's 17th Infantry Company A during World War II. Gilbert is a banker; Ronald, an accountant.

Leon Shew of San Jose, John Lee of San Mateo, Fred Mah of Berkeley, and my son Walter were my tennis partners during the years I played competitive tennis, from 1929 to 1950, and we won many trophies.

The Yoke Choy Club of the 1920s and 1930s included some of my closest friends: Thomas A. Wong, M.D., football halfback, accomplished tenor vocalist, and the best man at my wedding; Yee Wong, fullback, portrait photographer, and florist; Ton Wong Lee, film laboratory and photography expert; Ira C. Lee, stringer for the Central News Agency, banker, and in U.S. Government service in Washington, D.C., and Taiwan; Wing Wy, pharmacist, singer in the San Francisco Municipal Men's Chorus, and composer of the words and music to "Miss Chinatown USA"; Myron Chan, a Stanford man and tennis player; James R. Lee, UC Berkeley, an architect involved in the design of the San Francisco Bay Bridge; and J. K. Chen,

tennis player and banker, whose father was one of the founders of a Shanghai bank.

Many people have worked with me on this book. For their help with typing and research, I would like to thank Deborah W. Chinn, Frances L. Chinn, Louis W. Chinn, Walter W. Chinn, Jeffrey Frediani, Sherryl C. Frediani, Sally Joe, William Joe, Deborah C. Shealy, and Philip Shealy; and for assistance with research, Rose C. Loo, Edward M. Loo, Ernest M. Loo, Marian Loo; Norbert Woo; Frank Lem; Eva Tom Lim, who helped me with data on Chinese Opera; Jennifer Larson of Yerba Buena Books; Jean Moon Liu; and especially Herbert Chew.

I would also like to thank the many individuals who have helped me reconstruct the family histories described in this book: Willa K. Baum; Balfour Chinn, Jr.; Candy Q. Chinn; Carole Chinn; George Chinn; Ruth F. Chinn; Flora Hall Chong; Vyolet L. Chu; Dr. Collin Dong; Bill Fong; Rev. Matthew Fong; Elizabeth Hall; Gloria Sun Hom; Fay Jin Lee; Edmund D. Jung, M.D. and Haw C. Jung, M.D.; Florence Kwan; Pauline K. Lee; Thomas and Fawn Leong; Alice and Ronald Louie; Charlie Low; Helen Wong Lum; Howard Ah Tye; Dr. Edwin Owyang; Jeanette Quan; Jane M. Seid; Ling-Gee Tom; Albert E. Wong; Annie, Warren, and Wilson Wong; Rose Wong Lee; Honey Q. Wong; Bessie K. Woo; Stella Yep; Arthur Yick; Andrew and Nellie Young; and Betty Louie Chin.

I am most grateful to the following individuals, who helped me with information on some of Chinatown's clubs, institutions, and other organizations: Mrs. Peng Van

Etten; Fay Jin Lee; Flora Lee; Ruby Gwen Lee; Lillian and Thomas Lym; Ernest M. Loo; Lorraine Pon; Rev. Timothy Tam; Ling-Gee Tom; Harry Q. Wong; Stella Yep; and Benita Yu. Thanks also to Bill Fong, Bessie K. Woo, Richard Springer, Sandra Yung Lee, Arthur Yick, Robert C. Stevenson, Violet Wong, Pauline K. Lee, Vyolet L. Chu, Mei Ling Sander, and Dr. Albert Shumate for providing me with specialized information about Chinatown; and to the Henry Ford Museum, Greenfield Village, and Howard Seeto.

Unless otherwise indicated, photographs in the book are from my own collection. I would like to thank the following for the loan or use of other photographs: Enid Ng Lim; Arthur Yick; Alice Louie; Edwin Owyang, M.D.; Fawn and Thomas Leong; Thomas Tong; Hattie Dong Kwong; Paul Chow; Charlie Low; Stella Yep; Howard Louis; Hubert Lew; Ruth Fong Chinn; Marian Chinn Loo; Bew Tong; Robert Dunn Wu; Kaye Hong; Fred Wong; Thomas T. Fong; Chinatown YMCA; Milton Shoong Foundation; Andrew Young; Elizabeth Hall; Florence Haw Jung; Howard Seeto; William Jack Chow; Mrs. H. K. Wong; John Yehall Chin; Kee Joon; Mrs. Alice Louie; On Lok; Chinatown Neighborhood Improvement Resource Center; Rose Wong Lee and Annie, Warren, and Wilson Wong; and Joseph Yick. Alton Chinn of the Chinatown Resource Center kindly provided me with the maps of Chinatown reproduced in Appendix F.

Several organizations have also provided me with invaluable assistance by giving me access to their files and permitting me to use photographs and other material: the Bancroft Library, the California Historical Society, the Chinese Historical Society of America, the Mechanics Institute Library, the Special Collections Department of the San Francisco Library, and the Society of California Pioneers.

The publication of this book was made possible by a grant from Bei Shan Tang Foundation in Hong Kong. Mr. J. S. Lee, chairman of the foundation, made the grant as a tribute to the Chinese in America and their role in American society. Mr. Lee's grandfather, Mr. Lee Liang Yick, lived and worked in San Francisco Chinatown in the late nineteenth century; and his father, Mr. Lee Hysan, attended school there. A donation by Mr. Chien Lee, son of Mr. J. S. Lee, provided for a computer that improved flexibility in writing and editing the manuscript.

I especially want to thank my panel of advisors, who have given so wholeheartedly of their time since this project first started on January 2, 1986:

Gladys C. Hansen, Archivist, City and County of San Francisco.

Lim P. Lee, San Francisco Fair Political Practices Commissioner, State of California, 1985–1988; San Francisco Postmaster, Retired.

The author's panel of advisors in 1989. Back row: *Alan S. Wong, William F. Strobridge, Albert C. Lim, Jackie Wong Sing.* Front row: *Gladys C. Hansen, Lim P. Lee, and Sylvia Sun Minnick.* [Photo by Nancy Warner.]

Albert C. Lim, Past President, Chinese Historical Society of America; Past President, Chinese Consolidated Benevolent Association; Past Vice President, Chinese Chamber of Commerce; Former Member, San Francisco Asian Art Commission.

Sylvia Sun Minnick, President, City of Stockton Cultural Heritage Board, 1988–89; author of *Sam Fow: The San Joaquin Chinese Legacy.*

Jackie Wong Sing, attorney; Past National President, Wong Family Association; Past Chairman, National Chinese Welfare Council.

William F. Strobridge, Historian, Wells Fargo Bank History Department; Colonel, U.S. Army, Retired; formerly Chief, Army Historical Services.

Alan S. Wong, Executive Director, Chinatown YMCA; Past President, San Francisco Community College Governing Board.

Introduction

As far back as I can remember, I've had a strong desire to learn more about Chinatown—not so much from historical records, but from the point of view of the Chinese themselves: their everyday lives, their joys and sorrows, their work and thoughts and personal experiences. I looked hard, but never found one book that described what I wanted to learn. Slowly, over the years, I began collecting stories and other information for my own benefit. Then, a few years ago, I was approached about writing just such a book. I decided to give it a try, and persuaded a few friends to advise me—people who had spent much of their lives in Chinatown or in San Francisco, and who knew a great deal about some of the things I wanted to describe. I wanted to make sure that my own conceptions of Chinatown would be shared by others.

Now, as the book approaches completion, I must confess that the job I thought I was setting out to do has taken many twists and turns. Chinatown is constantly changing, and it is difficult to describe one part without taking all the other parts into consideration at the same time. For example, I wanted to include an up-to-date directory of Chinatown businesses. This was accomplished by means of a street-to-street survey, counting only activities that were obvious at ground level; we did not go inside any buildings or conduct any interviews. However, as we worked up and down each street, we discovered that businesses on one side were closing, and new ones were opening, by the time we came back down the other side of the street. As a result, the summary of our survey, Appendix E, gives only an approximate indication of the pattern of business activity at the time we made the survey.

This kind of problem was compounded when I tried to describe the history of specific organizations or the lives of individual Chinese. Much of the information is missing, or varies depending on the source, or cannot be properly understood without taking many other considerations into account at the same time. Any ideas I had of being able to make an exhaustive survey of Chinatown and its people quickly fell by the wayside. Instead, I have had to settle for a series of sketches, divided into parts and chapters for the convenience of the reader. Each of the book's five parts begins with a brief description of the historical context for the stories it contains. Each chapter begins with a few general comments about the person or events it describes.

Parts I and II deal mainly with the period before World War I. Part I, "Early San Francisco Chinatown," describes some of early Chinatown's institutions, cultural activities, and business enterprises. Part II, "The First Generation," gives brief accounts of some individual Chinese immigrants who decided to stay in this country—and of Chew Fong Low, one of the few Chinese women born in the United States before 1870.

There were very few Chinese women among the early immigrants. Most men came to the United States alone and sent what money they could save back to China to support their families. Some, however, like my father, decided to bring their families over when they could afford to do so and to take their chances in this country. These pioneers chose to make their home in the United States in spite of the discrimination they faced on a daily basis. They saw a better life for their children here than in China, and they hoped that some day their descendants would find a greater degree of acceptance. These Chinese who chose to remain in this country and raise their families thus began the fight for equal rights for themselves and their children.

Chinese-Americans today owe a great debt to these pioneers, as well as to the many American businesses and service organizations that did so much to help the early arrivals. We are also indebted in large measure to the churches that, from the very beginning, established missions in Chinatown and took many Chinese under their wings, providing much practical help in the form of English classes and other aid.

Much has been written about the struggles of the first generation of Chinese to make their home in the United States, and I see no need to repeat such stories here. One piece of anti-Chinese legislation stands out from all the rest, however. On May 6, 1882, Congress passed a bill called the Chinese Exclusion Act. This law prohibited Chinese laborers from entering the country, although merchants and their families were still allowed to come

in. It was the first and only time that the United States government has enacted legislation to exclude a specific nationality from immigration. The act had a profound effect on the Chinese in the United States. From a peak of more than 125,000 before the act was passed, the number of Chinese dwindled to 61,000 by 1920. The act was not repealed until 1943. By then the number of Chinese-Americans had begun to increase again as more children were born to the Chinese already in America.

Prejudice against the Chinese, which was building before the Exclusion Act was passed, increased after it became law. Chinese were not welcome outside of Chinatown in those days, and many people lived, attended school, worked, and died within its confines without ever having much contact with the outside world.

The first priority for most of the early immigrants with families was to educate their children. They saw education as the means to a brighter future, and they would sacrifice a great deal to put their children through school. At the same time, however, in the early days after China became a republic in 1912, it was common practice among families that could afford it to send one boy—generally the eldest—back to China for a Chinese education. There were several reasons for this, as I discovered many years after I was sent to China myself to be educated. The Chinese in America were seldom able to find jobs outside of Chinatown. Even the well-educated were reduced to taking jobs as waiters, dishwashers, janitors, or clerks in

Chinatown stores, earning only a few dollars a week. Many people felt that the new Republic of China, which had replaced the Manchu dynasty in 1912, might offer their children better opportunities—provided they could read, write, and speak Chinese.

Parts III and IV of the book focus on the period between World War I and World War II, although many of the stories that begin in that period continue into the present. Part III, "Chinatown Comes of Age," describes how times were changing for Chinese-Americans, and how they improved their lot through their own organizations as well as making use of existing institutions such as the Boy Scouts, the YMCA and YWCA, veterans' organizations, and still later the Lions, Masons, and Optimists, to mention just a few. Although there were still hardships and obstacles to assimilation, the generation described in Part IV, "Breaking Through the Barriers," was finally able to go beyond Chinatown and find acceptance in the mainstream of American society. These stories describe many firsts for Chinese Americans. The hard work and sacrifices of their parents paid off, and the new generation achieved success in fields their elders never dreamed of entering.

Finally, Part V, "Contemporary Chinatown," reveals some of the organizations that have come into being since the 1960s that are helping to shape the Chinatown of today. As the influence and well-being of the Chinese community grows, an increasing amount of energy is going into providing health services for the elderly and needy, helping new arrivals in this country become established, and preserving the cultural heritage of Chinese-Americans. In addition, a major effort is under way to persuade eligible Chinese to register to vote. The increase in the Chinese population is gradually making the Chinese voter an important factor in American politics.

The appendixes contain material that some people may find helpful while reading the rest of the book. Appendix A contains charts of the major clans and clan organizations in Chinatown. Looking down the clan chart, one can almost visualize some instances in which disaffection led to secession from the original groups. Appendix B lists some of the early Chinese newspapers in America. Appendixes C, D, and E contain business directories for Chinatown from 1876, 1931, and 1988, respectively. The two maps in Appendix F show the core area of Chinatown and the gradual spread of Chinese homes into adjoining areas. Appendix G contains some brief notes on the transliteration of Chinese names used in this book.

757 - 大益 - 757
TIE YICK LUNG KEE & CO.

大益記隆

收各號貨

A CORNER IN CHINATOWN SAN FRANCISCO CALIFORNIA

PART I

Early San Francisco Chinatown

*C*hina was an unhappy and impoverished country during the latter half of the nineteenth century. Droughts, floods, famine, bandits, and ruthless warlords wrought havoc in the countryside and the cities. The land was poor and poorly managed, and the last ineffective rulers of the Manchu dynasty were plagued by intrigues and warring factions. The people of South China, particularly in the vicinity of Canton, were generally not as well educated or as well off as people in the north, and were hardest hit by the political and economic hardships of the times. So when news arrived of a gold strike in a place called California, many of them were prepared to gamble their all on a long and difficult journey, with no guarantee of success when they reached their destination.

But they were always reluctant immigrants. Their strong ties to their families and villages were not broken by the trip to America. They came as sojourners, seeking only to find gold in Gum Shan, the Golden Mountain, and return home. Even those who eventually decided to stay and make their homes here were dependent on their family and district associations for guidance and assistance. Chapter 1 describes the important role these organizations played in early San Francisco Chinatown.

One of the first problems addressed by both the early church missions and the Chinese associations was the need for education. The churches provided the first (and for many years the only)

A street scene in San Francisco Chinatown, ca. 1900. Tie Yick Lung Kee & Co. was a general merchandise store located at 757 Dupont Street (now Grant Avenue) at Clay Street. Note the cable car tracks in the cobblestone street; a cable car line once ran down Clay Street. The men across the street are studying notices pasted on the brick wall. Several such "bulletin boards" were scattered throughout Chinatown; one was discovered behind boards in 1987 by workers remodeling a building. [Photo courtesy of California Historical Society; FN-24740.]

English-language classes for residents of Chinatown. The associations, which existed in some form almost from the time the first Chinese immigrants reached the shores of California, helped establish Chinese-language schools and provided leadership in the long battle against discrimination by the board of education and most of the Caucasian residents of the city.

In addition to the churches and associations, traditional Chinese customs and festivals and Chinese opera helped maintain the morale of the early residents of Chinatown. Although most of the early immigrants to this country came from South China, near Hong Kong, they hailed from many different parts of China and spoke many different dialects. Local customs varied widely from district to district, as did the spoken language. My family is from the Toishan district; from 1850 to around 1930, the Toishan people were one of the largest groups of Chinese in America. So when I reminisce about early customs and culture, it is Toishan culture and Toishan customs, by and large, that I remember. Chinese-Americans whose ancestors came from different districts will have slightly different recollections.

But there was much more to early Chinatown than the benevolent associations, traditional customs and festivals, and the constraints of ghetto life in San Francisco after the gold rush. The seemingly insurmountable barriers to learning English, obtaining a good education, and succeeding in American society only led the Chinese to turn their energies elsewhere. Most of Part I describes institutions, cultural activities, and business enterprises that were important to the residents of San Francisco Chinatown during the years before World War I.

Whenever the Chinese perceived a need or an opportunity, they were quick to make the best of it. They received some help from American institutions such as the churches, Wells Fargo Bank, the telephone company, and the San Francisco Gas & Electric Company; and they met with success in the shrimp industry, journalism and publishing, and the banking, retail, and manufacturing industries, all the while building and strengthening their own clubs and organizations. More and more of the early immigrants came to believe that America would provide a brighter future for their descendants than China, and they were willing to make almost any sacrifice that would help their children get a good education and advance themselves.

1 Chinese Associations

In its early days, the Chinese community in San Francisco tended to be very self-contained. Widespread discrimination, differences in language and culture, and the threat of physical violence confined most Chinese to Chinatown for virtually all their activities. As a result, the Chinese usually took care of their own. Instead of seeking help from the American social services and charities, a Chinese person in need of assistance would turn to his or her family or district association. Similarly, disputes were usually handled by a district association or by the Chinese Six Companies rather than by the American court system; and the tongs, rather than the police department, often provided protection.

J. S. Tow, a secretary with the rank of consul-élève at the New York Chinese Consulate General, described the function of the associations as follows in his booklet The Real Chinese in America *(1923):*

> *If a Chinese is in need, he naturally goes first to the society of the same family name as his. If he cannot find one, he can go to the society of the district whence he has come. If he still finds none, he may resort to the consolidated or united benevolent association, the central organization for assistance, unless he belongs to a protective society. Thus he can avoid becoming a public charge.*
>
> *Among the Chinese people domestic troubles are usually settled in the family by the elders or by the relatives assembled. Small commercial disputes are usually settled by the parties themselves, but in case they cannot agree, they appeal by mutual consent to the consolidated association or their respective trade associations for arbitration.*

The Chinese Six Companies

The Chinese Consolidated Benevolent Association, popularly known as the Chinese Six Companies, is the watchdog association that oversees the affairs of the Chinese community. To fully comprehend the role of the Chinese Six Companies, one must know a little about the historical setting in which it was founded.

In the 1850s the Chinese population in California was increasing rapidly, and San Francisco, the principal port of entry, became the hub of Chinese economic, social, and cultural activities. According to William Hoy's monograph *The Chinese Six Companies* (1942), "The first bona fide Chinese immigrants to arrive in [California] did so in 1849." By the end of that year, the number of Cantonese in California had reached 791. This number rapidly rose to 4,025 in 1850 and 12,000 in 1851, according to Hoy.

Sources differ slightly as to the year in which the first Chinese organization was founded in San Francisco and as to the name of the organization. In his article entitled "Historical Development of the Chinese Consolidated Benevolent Association/*Huigan* System" in *Chinese America: History and Perspectives 1987*, Him Mark Lai reports that

> by 1849 Chinese merchants in the city apparently had formed a *gongsi*, or company, to maintain internal order and to facilitate dealings with the larger community. In that year, they met to select an advisor, and in 1850 they organized Chinese participation in some civic events. However, the name of this *gongsi* still has not been found in historical documents.

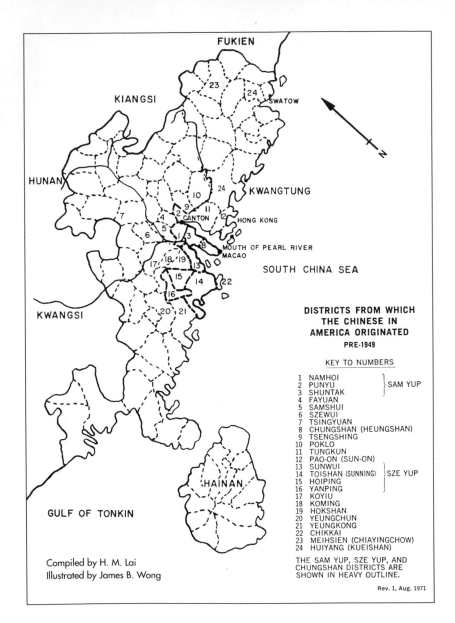

FUKIEN

KIANGSI

SWATOW

KWANGTUNG

HUNAN

10

24

9
2
4 CANTON 11
5
6
7
3
8
12 HONG KONG

MOUTH OF PEARL RIVER
MACAO

SOUTH CHINA SEA

17 18 19 13
15 14 22
16

KWANGSI

20 21

HAINAN

GULF OF TONKIN

N

**DISTRICTS FROM WHICH
THE CHINESE IN
AMERICA ORIGINATED
PRE-1949**

KEY TO NUMBERS

1	NAMHOI	
2	PUNYU	} SAM YUP
3	SHUNTAK	
4	FAYUAN	
5	SAMSHUI	
6	SZEWUI	
7	TSINGYUAN	
8	CHUNGSHAN (HEUNGSHAN)	
9	TSENGSHING	
10	POKLO	
11	TUNGKUN	
12	PAO-ON (SUN-ON)	
13	SUNWUI	
14	TOISHAN (SUNNING)	} SZE YUP
15	HOIPING	
16	YANPING	
17	KOYIU	
18	KOMING	
19	HOKSHAN	
20	YEUNGCHUN	
21	YEUNGKONG	
22	CHIKKAI	
23	MEIHSIEN (CHIAYINGCHOW)	
24	HUIYANG (KUEISHAN)	

Compiled by H. M. Lai
Illustrated by James B. Wong

THE SAM YUP, SZE YUP, AND
CHUNGSHAN DISTRICTS ARE
SHOWN IN HEAVY OUTLINE.

Rev. 1, Aug. 1971

Hoy's monograph states that the first real organization among the early California Chinese was the Kong Chow Association, which, he says, appeared in 1851. However, Liu Pei-chi's *History of the Chinese in the United States, 1848–1911* (1976) indicates that the Kong Chow Association was established in 1849.

The group that formed this association included Chinese immigrants from six districts of a geographic region in Kwangtung province known as Kong Chow. Next to organize were the Cantonese from the area called Sam Yup, encompassing the three districts of Namhoi, Punyu, and Shuntak. They founded the Sam Yup Association in 1850. Before the end of that year, a third organization, the Sze Yup Association, with a constituency of people from the Yanping, Hoiping, Sunning, and Sunwui districts in Kwangtung province, also came into being.

The year 1852 saw the establishment of the fourth and fifth district associations as a result of internal disagreement, rivalry, and schism. The Young Wo Association consisted of immigrants from the Heungshan area, and the Hip Kat Association (Yan Wo Association) was formed exclusively by Hakka compatriots. And in 1854 a sixth district organization, the Ning Yung Association, which was to become one of the largest and the most powerful of the district associations, was formed.

Each association would settle disputes among its members and represent the general interests of the people from its district or districts. Membership in each association was open to all who had emigrated from that district.

As disputes among members of different associations became more frequent, a neutral party was needed to settle matters. Thus, around 1862, a *kung saw*—literally a "public hall" but more accurately a public association—

consisting of members of the various associations was established to resolve disputes.

The importance of safeguarding common community interests was not realized until after the passage of the Chinese Exclusion Act in 1882. It was then, at the height of anti-Chinese sentiment, that the six district associations of Kong Chow, Ning Yung, Sam Yup, Young Wo, Hop Wo, and Yan Wo were first urged by Chinese Consul General Huang Tsun-hsien to form a comprehensive association to look after their common interests. According to the *San Francisco Call*, a new association patterned after the *kung saw*, or public association, came into being on November 19, 1882. The Chinese envoy in Washington, Tseng Tzao-ju, gave it the name Chung Wah Hui Guan, while the Chinese in San Francisco referred to it as the Chung Wah Kung Saw, or "public association of the Chinese," aptly reflecting its social function as mediator and voice of the Chinese community. Its presidency rotated among the heads of its member associations, but no member of any feuding association could become its president, nor could he serve on the board of presidents. On January 25, 1901, the organization was incorporated under the laws of the State of California as the Chinese Consolidated Benevolent Association.

Although the number of member associations belonging to the organization has varied over the years, its popular name of Chinese Six Companies has never changed. In the 1890s, for example, the organization actually consisted of eight district associations. According to J. S. Tow's 1923 booklet, the Chinese Consolidated Benevolent Association "is composed of eight subsidiary associations, namely, the Ning Yung, the Yan Wo, the Sam Yup, the Young Wo, the Shew Hing, the Kong Chow, the Hop Wo and the En Kai." In 1942 William Hoy listed seven, omitting the En Kai Association from his list.

Since its inception, the Chinese Consolidated Benevolent Association has played a unique role as an ethnic Chinese organization looking after the interests of the Chinese people living in a hostile western world. It has provided guidance and assistance to Chinese in the United States, Canada, and Latin America. Encouraged by Chinese diplomatic officials, Chinese Consolidated Benevolent Associations began to spring up in all large Chinese communities around the world. In New York, for example, a similar communal association founded in 1871 became the Chinese Consolidated Benevolent Association in 1883; others were founded in Honolulu and in British Columbia in 1884; a Lima, Peru, benevolent association was founded in 1885; and one in Portland, Oregon, was established some time before 1887.

Between the late 1880s and the early 1900s, the Chinese Consolidated Benevolent Association worked successfully within the American judicial system to nullify and modify anti-Chinese legislation and hostile measures. It helped Chinese victims of discrimination during the Mexican revolution in 1913 and again in 1916, as well as helping victims of anti-Chinese measures promulgated in Guatemala in 1920, the Philippines in 1921, El Salvador in 1925, Ecuador in 1926, Mexico in 1930 through 1932, and the Dominican Republic in 1932.

Before 1911 the Chinese Consolidated Benevolent Association supported the policies of the Manchu emperor, even though popular sentiment at the time was sympathetic toward the Chinese reformists and Dr. Sun Yat-sen, who called for the overthrow of the Manchu dynasty and the establishment of a republic. After the

The Chinese Consolidated Benevolent Association, popularly known as the Chinese Six Companies, was first organized in the 1850s and is still an active force today. This photo shows members of the Chinese Six Companies during a business session in 1938. [Photo from the Chinese Digest, *Vol. 4, No. 2.]*

Republic of China came into being on January 1, 1912, the Chinese Consolidated Benevolent Association in effect helped to implement the policies of the republican Chinese government, which sought to abolish all unequal treaties with China and all anti-Chinese legislation in the United States and Latin America. The members of the board have traditionally been merchants, who hold the title of merchant-directors, and Chinese merchants have always supported free enterprise.

Even today, the sponsorship role of the Chinese Consolidated Benevolent Association is important. It still represents the Chinese community in many ways. Its

president is the spokesman for all the Chinese in the community, and the social functions he attends are indicative of the political stance of the majority of the community. (In recent years, however, many Chinese have broken with custom and do not regard the Chinese Six Companies as representing them in any way.) The Chinese Consolidated Benevolent Association has been actively involved in local and national politics and, with the Chinese-American Citizens Alliance (see Chapter 23), exerts a certain amount of influence in getting votes for candidates for various local and state offices.

The Chinese Consolidated Benevolent Association

has also undertaken a number of community welfare projects. It established the present Chinese Central High School in 1905 to teach Chinese language and culture to Chinese children; was one of the fifteen founding members of the Chinese Hospital, which replaced the dilapidated Tung Wah Dispensary; hired night watchmen to protect Chinatown against nocturnal prowlers; and raised funds for many social and community projects. The association has also acted as witness to the transfer of business ownership and property.

Family and District Associations

The basic unit of Chinese society is the family, and all of the various associations established by the Chinese began with the household or extended family association, which included all relatives and anyone remotely related by blood or marriage. Those with the same surnames joined the extended family associations, such as the Wong Family Association or the Lee Family Association. These expanded quickly to become what are now known as the *tsung ch'ing hui*, or "kinship associations." The use of the word "clan" to describe such family associations is misleading, because a majority of their members do not claim to be from the same village or district or of common descent.

At about the same time as the family associations were forming in the United States, village or district associations were also being established. The members of these associations not only claimed a common village or district origin but also spoke the same subdialect. These proliferated, mostly because of feuds among members, into what

The Chinese Consolidated Benevolent Association building at 843 Stockton Street, 1988. The lions on either side of the main stairway scrutinize visitors as they enter the central doorway, which is flanked in turn by two dragons. The entrance on the right leads to a Chinese language and culture school on the upper floor. [Photo by Nancy Warner.]

are known today as the *hui guan*, or district associations. As the district associations grew, they became more heterogeneous and eventually developed into "benevolent associations," "public associations," and literally "fellow villagers associations."

As the Chinese population increased, separate benevolent organizations were created to provide lodging, medical care, and financial assistance to help the feeble to return to China, to bury the dead, and to disinter and ship remains for reburial in China. As early as 1855 and 1856, the Fook Yum Benevolent Society, founded by immigrants from Namhoi, and several other associations established by the Young Wo company were involved in sending remains back to China for reburial.

The Role of the Merchant Class

The merchant class has traditionally been the one sector of Chinese society able to foster unity and bring about social change. The merchant-directors of the Chinese Consolidated Benevolent Association must be well-established businessmen in the local community as well as outstanding members of their own family associations. They have already played a leading role in their own social circles before becoming merchant-directors, and they enjoy a great deal of respect.

Yet the real power to mobilize social change still lies in the family and district associations headed by local merchants. Thus the friendly corner grocer may simultaneously be the president of both his family association and his district association as well as a merchant-director or even the president of the Chinese Consolidated Benevolent Association.

Protective Societies and the Tongs

Some of the associations formed by the Chinese, called *tongs*, were based on self-defense. In 1852 the first of the so-called "fighting tongs," the Kwong Duck Tong, appeared; by 1854 another one, the Hip Yee Tong, was active. As the strong preyed on the unprotected and the weak, many family associations formed their own tongs to protect their members. The Bow On Tong, for example, was formed to defend members of the Kong Chow Association. Feuds among the associations thus quickly turned into the tong wars of the late 1800s and early 1900s.

Some of the tongs became involved in organized crime. For example, one tong controlled the gambling clubs, another exacted tribute from the brothels, and still another trafficked in Chinese slave girls.

Although the tongs are often described as secret societies, their activities were far from clandestine. They did their utmost to protect the interests of their own members and affiliate associations and to look after their own businesses. The tongs retained individuals as hatchet men (so called because they often used cleavers as weapons), who were usually members of the secret Triad Society, which was active from the late 1880s until shortly after 1906.

As more and more disputes were resolved peacefully through arbitration and mediation, the frequency of tong wars gradually diminished, and none have occurred since the mid-1920s.

Other Brotherhood Associations

The tongs were relatively small brotherhood associations whose members did not share any kinship or common geographic heritage, but rather had a common goal of mutual help and protection. Other brotherhood associations are based on kinship. One of the largest of these, dating back to 1827, is the Lung Kong Tien Yee Association, made up of Chinese with the four surnames Lau (Lew or Liu), Quan (Kuan), Jeong (Chang), and Chew (Chao). This brotherhood is based on that formed by the four historical figures Liu Pei, Kuan Kong, Chang Fei, and Chao Yun in the Chinese classical novel *Romance of the Three Kingdoms*.

Political Associations

During the first decade of the 1900s, when Dr. Sun Yat-sen was calling for the overthrow of the Manchu Dynasty and Chinese scholars such as reformists Liang Chi-tsao and Kang Yu-wei were advocating westernization for China, some brotherhood associations split into small political groups and rallied support either for Dr. Sun and his revolutionary cause or for the imperial Chinese monarchy. These groups called themselves political parties, and some launched vigorous campaigns to propagate their views. They included the Chinese Imperial Reform Association, founded on June 13, 1899, and the secret revolutionary association Tung Meng Hui, founded by Dr. Sun Yat-sen in New York on November 3, 1909. (A San Francisco branch was established on January 18, 1910.) Then there was the Ning Yeung Association (a splinter group of the original association of the same name), which was established mainly to help enforce a nationwide boycott against the San Francisco Kuomintang newspaper *Young China Daily* during the late 1920s and early 1930s. All were short-lived, however.

2   Festivals and Parades

The Chinese who came to America in the nineteenth century brought with them many of the customs and festivals of their homeland. Most of them were superstitious, and lived according to a philosophy that included reverence for ancestors, filial piety, and a hearty enjoyment of life. Traditions were very important, and they enjoyed all manner of celebrations. This chapter describes some of the early festivals and customs as well as the part the Chinese played in the 1909 Portola Parade, one of the most spectacular parades that San Francisco has ever seen.

Although very few Chinese women traveled to the United States, it was largely the women who perpetuated the old customs. The color and pageantry of Chinese festivals in America, particularly in San Francisco, home of the largest Chinese community in the country, was provided by the mothers, wives, daughters, and sisters of the Gum Shan *hak* (Gold Mountain sojourner). Most of these women had been taught from childhood the dates, customs, and minute details of the rituals necessary for each occasion. They made all of the festival food and cakes; they wore the colorful ceremonial silks and brocades and tiny, silk-embroidered slippers; and they took care of the myriad religious details so necessary to many festivals.

For the San Francisco religious festivals, or *da chew*, large sums of money would be collected by popular subscription, and the names of the donors would be posted on the street "bulletin board"—the side of a centrally located brick building. The long list would be surrounded by a colorful border of celestial beings, such as Kuan Yin (goddess of mercy for Taoists and Buddhists alike) pouring blessings from her magic bottle, the deer of long life, and so forth. Huge images of the door gods, or *san dai low*, made of bamboo and paper, would be erected. Colorful in dress and fierce in expression, their purpose was to prevent evil spirits from entering the building they guarded. One such image, placed on Spofford Alley near Washington Street, was two stories high.

Vacant stores were rented for the exhibit of religious paintings. Many of these paintings, some 12 feet high, portrayed various gods and goddesses, such as Wah Tou, Ommi To Fu, Kuan Yin, and Tieh Quai Li, all of whom represent various desirable qualities: valor, mercy, trustworthiness, financial skill, political acumen, and so forth. Other paintings depicted the punishment meted out to sinners by the nine judges of Hades. They showed devils busy pulling out the tongues of gossipers and boiling sinners in oil, gouging out their eyes, sawing them in two, and impaling them. Other wrongdoers were shown being ground by iron rollers or thrown into shark-infested waters or roaring furnaces. There were also displays of calligraphy, consisting of proclamations by high officials, bits of sacred writings, and mottoes, such as "May the heavens produce good men; may men produce good deeds."

Orange-robed priests conducted public services at which they read sacred passages, burned incense and prayer papers, displayed sacred signs (sayings and drawings meant to ward off evil), and chanted prayers to the accompaniment of gongs and cymbals. The parade of the gods and the purging of the evil spirits of Chinatown was the most colorful event of the year.

The services were followed by the distribution of sacramental buns and the presentation of charms, or *wus*. These charms were taken home, folded into compact triangles, encased in a cloth bag, and worn as protection against evil spirits.

Public kitchens were established to serve free incarnate meals (meatless food that has been blessed). These meals generally consisted of bean curd soup, or *lohan jai* (disciples' meal); preserved melons, or *qua ying*; cold bean custard; rice; and tea. These religious festivals have long since faded from memory. The last one was held in 1908, although many of the more secular holidays and celebrations survive in some form to this day.

Traditional Festivals

Certainly the most important and best known of the traditional Chinese festivals is Chinese New Year, the only holiday still celebrated today by most Chinese in China and America. It is generally celebrated for seven to fourteen days. A few days before New Year's Day, everyone is busy with *dah faw hom muy*, or general housecleaning. The floors of homes and buildings are swept clean, not to be swept again until the celebration is over. This is said to avoid misfortune, as sweeping floors during this period is akin to sweeping away all the good luck that has just arrived with the new year. Also, meeting halls and head-

Unidentified Chinese parade in the 1880s or 1890s, probably in San Francisco. Chinese wore queues and Chinese jackets; Americans wore bowler hats. Note streetcar tracks, probably along Kearny Street.

quarters of fraternal, district, family, and other associations are brightly lit for the arrival of the new year.

Chinatown is always busy, noisy, and crowded the last few days before Chinese New Year. The sidewalk tables in front of the food markets are piled high with the choicest delicacies—sharks' fins, birds' nests, dried fish and meat, pressed duck, and dried oysters—and the flower vendors amass their best blooms during this period. Flowers represent growth to the Chinese, and when a blossom opens on New Year's Day, it is a sign of a prosperous year.

Red paper scrolls containing blessings and wishes for good fortune for all who come and go are hung on door frames, and visits are paid to relatives and teachers. (Respect for teachers is second only to that due one's father and mother.) The devout honor their departed ancestors, the household god, and heaven and earth during this time.

New Year's Eve is "watch night," when everyone stays up all night. The entire family is on hand for New Year's Eve dinner, the most sumptuous meal of the year. Toasts are given, and the atmosphere is festive. Later, the youngsters play games and light firecrackers outdoors, while the adults chat, sing, or play mah-jongg.

On New Year's Day, no knife, cleaver, or other sharp instrument is used, lest it cut luck. Cooking is also avoided, food having been prepared in advance. Parents and elders wrap coins in small pieces of red paper and distribute them to all the children and young unmarried men and women of their acquaintance on New Year's Day. This *li shee*, or good luck money, is supposed to bring the giver good luck and prosperity for the coming year.

The seventh day of the New Year, known as the Day of Man, is considered to be everyone's birthday and is traditionally celebrated with an exotic raw fish salad.

The dragon dance traditionally closes the New Year celebration in San Francisco Chinatown. The Chinese dragon is not the monster of western mythology but is instead a beneficent creature of strength and goodness. It is said to carry out the will of the gods and to guard their treasures. A round, red object precedes the dragon; it is variously described as the sun, the moon, a symbol of rolling thunder, an egg emblem representing the dual influences of nature, the pearl of potentiality, or a ruby.

The *Pure Brightness Festival* (Ching Ming) is the Chinese version of Memorial Day. Visits to family tombs are a formal rite in China. Because the Chinese in America were far from the family tombs of their native villages, they would visit the local Chinese cemetery area on this day. Various associations erected "spirit" shrines for those who had no loved ones buried in the area.

In the San Francisco area, Ching Ming is generally celebrated on a Sunday early in April. Before World War II, Chinese could not be buried in Caucasian cemeteries, so Chinese cemeteries were established near Colma, California, south of San Francisco. Buses and carloads of Chinese would travel to Colma on Ching Ming to visit the shrines or the graves of loved ones.

At the tomb, the elder of the family would carefully sweep the graves with willow branches to repel evil spirits. Then the family would clean and pull weeds from the grave. The final ritual involved laying cooked food in dishes before the graves for the deceased to "eat." After a while, the roast pig, chicken, buns, and so on would be eaten as a picnic lunch at the site. Following lunch, wine would be poured on the ground, after which the remaining food was removed and taken to different families. No food was wasted.

During the course of the ceremony a spirit offering would be made, consisting of lighted incense sticks and red candles, which, together with paper money and paper clothing (sold in certain stores in Chinatown), were burned and thus transmitted to the deceased for their comfort and needs in the spirit world. While these offerings were being burned, firecrackers were exploded to confuse evil spirits and keep them from pursuing the deceased.

These same rituals are still observed by most of the

older generation of Chinese in America, although offerings of food and incense and the exploding of firecrackers are not as common today.

The *Dragon Boat Festival* occurs on the fifth day of the fifth month. The customary food for this festival is the *tsung*, a dumpling made of glutinous rice and wrapped in plantain leaves. *Tsung* are made with a wide variety of sweet or salty fillings. This festival honors Chu Yuan, a scholar and official in the third century B.C. who drowned himself in protest against his monarch's degenerate court. The people, who revered him, established boat races in his memory, symbolizing the search for his body. The *tsung* was originally a food offering to Chu Yuan in his watery grave, which is why, even today, it is wrapped in waterproof leaves.

The *Spirits Festival* (Shao-I, or "burning paper clothing") occurs on the fifteenth day of the seventh moon of the lunar calendar. Like Ching Ming, it is connected with the dead. On this day the family makes its second and last formal visit to the family tombs for the year.

Traditionally, this is the day the dead are believed to return to roam at will or to visit living relatives. Since the spirits must have money in order to travel, more paper money and paper clothing are transmitted by burnt offerings than at the Ching Ming festival.

The *Moon Festival* (Chung Chow, or mid-autumn festival) occurs on the fifteenth day of the eighth moon, when the moon is brightest. It is a women's festival, the moon being the symbol of yin, the feminine principle.

Traditionally, on the night of the festival, while the women of the family took part in the ritual, the men would discreetly leave home and repair to a local store for a talk with their friends. The women would then bathe in

Colma Chinese cemetery, ca. 1890 or 1900. Offerings of food, incense, paper money, and paper clothes were made for the deceased. At right a roast pig on a wooden tray is set beside the grave. Later it will be carved and eaten by family members. [Photo by Louis J. Stellman, courtesy of the Society of California Pioneers.]

The Chinese Lunar Calendar

Most Chinese in America during the nineteenth century still observed traditional Chinese festivals, whose dates were determined by the Chinese lunar calendar. Nowadays Chinese whose families have lived here for several generations tend to observe the usual American holidays, and most of the old festivals (except Chinese New Year) have taken a subordinate role. But a strong minority of older people and recent immigrants still keep the old festivals alive, and with them the Chinese lunar calendar.

The Chinese calendar originated thousands of years ago, when tillers of the soil first learned to time their activities by the positions of the sun, moon, and stars. In 2637 B.C. a prime minister under the "Yellow Emperor" Huang Ti discovered that the centuries-old calendar, which was based on the lunar month, did not work out to an even number of days for each year. There was always a fraction left over. So he devised a new system that compensated for the leftover fraction by adding an extra month (or "moon") to the year at regular intervals. Thus the Chinese lunar calendar is divided into twelve moons of either twenty-nine or thirty days, plus a thirteenth moon at specific intervals. The Chinese have always considered the year with the extra moon the "complete year" because it takes in all the fractions of previous years.

The animal year in which you are born is believed to influence your personality as follows:

RAT: Open, honest, thrifty, hardworking, generally successful.
OX: Patient, stubborn, not talkative, with an uncontrollable temper.
TIGER: Sensitive, courageous, but short-tempered, suspicious, unfinished.
HARE: Talented, ambitious, lucky in finance, but leaves projects unfinished.
DRAGON: Soft-hearted, healthy, respected and energetic, eccentric.
SNAKE: A deep thinker, good at finances, vain and selfish.
HORSE: Cheerful, talented and perceptive, rarely heeds advice.
SHEEP: A worrier, reserved, artistic, seldom a leader, but wise.
MONKEY: Ingenious, excellent memory, a go-getter but easily bored.
FOWL: A loner who likes to keep busy, leads an exciting life.
DOG: A good leader, loyal, honest, but selfish, emotionally distant.
PIG: Honest, ambitious, well-informed, but quick tempered.

The first few weeks of each western year belong to the previous Chinese year. The western year 1990 is the Chinese year 4688.

The Chinese day is also divided into twelve two-hour watches, each of which corresponds to one of the twelve animals.

Calendar

RAT	OX	TIGER	HARE	DRAGON	SNAKE	HORSE	SHEEP	MONKEY	FOWL	DOG	PIG
1948	1949	1950	1951	1952	1953	1954	1955	1956	1957	1958	1959
1960	1961	1962	1963	1964	1965	1966	1967	1968	1969	1970	1971
1972	1973	1974	1975	1976	1977	1978	1979	1980	1981	1982	1983
1984	1985	1986	1987	1988	1989	1990	1991	1992	1993	1994	1995
1996	1997	1998	1999	2000	2001	2002	2003	2004	2005	2006	2007

Add or subtract increments of twelve years chronologically to calculate years not shown.

Watches

RAT	OX	TIGER	HARE	DRAGON	SNAKE	HORSE	SHEEP	MONKEY	FOWL	DOG	PIG
11 P.M.–1 A.M.	1–3 A.M.	3–5 A.M.	5–7 A.M.	7–9 A.M.	9–11 A.M.	11 A.M.–1 P.M.	1–3 P.M.	3–5 P.M.	5–7 P.M.	7–9 P.M.	9–11 P.M.

water perfumed with blossoms, dress themselves neatly but without ostentation, and put flowers in their hair. They would place the table that would serve as an altar near a window, so that the moon could see it. On the table they would arrange incense and candles, and they would fill vases with chrysanthemums, a flower associated with the moon because of its round shape. Bowls of grapes and other fruits, lichee, peanuts, and buffalo nuts, as well as plates of steamed taro, lotus roots, and moon cakes were also placed on the table.

When the full moon came into sight, the candles and incense were lit, and the women would take turns bowing and praying before the altar. The children were then called in from the street to repeat the rituals.

The women would then tell the children the story of the moon. The moon, they said, is a silvery chamber inhabited by a toad, who is really Chang O, the moon goddess, in disguise. Chang O is the wife of Hou Yi, god of the sun. Her companion is a rabbit who is constantly pounding the elixir of immortality in a large mortar. The moon is also inhabited by a woodcutter who tries to cut down the cassia tree, giver of life. But as fast as he cuts into the tree, it heals itself, and he never makes any progress. The Chinese use this image of the cassia tree to explain mortal life on earth—the limbs are constantly being cut away by death, but new buds continually appear.

Today these rituals are very rarely performed, and the moon festival is instead a day of relaxation and feasting. The tradition of serving moon cakes still continues. These small cakes, round like the full moon, about 1½ inches thick, are stuffed with a variety of delicacies, such as whole salted duck egg yolks, shelled melon seeds, sweetened soybean paste, and so on.

The *Chung Yang Festival* originated, claims one source, in ancient days when a fortune teller predicted calamity for a farmer on the ninth day of the ninth moon. To escape disaster, the farmer took his family to the top of a high hill on that day. When they returned home the next day, they discovered that their domestic animals had all died mysteriously. After hearing of this, people would follow his example and go to the highest place they could find on that day. To while away the time, they fashioned kites of all kinds to fly on the windy hills. To this day, the Chinese fly beautiful kites at this time of the year.

The *Festival of the Winter Solstice* (Tung Chih) usually occurs a few days before Christmas. In the early days, the business houses closed and a general holiday was declared. Family members came home, offerings were placed on family ancestral altars, and food offerings were made to the deceased.

The festival dish, then and today, is *tong yuan*, small, round, bite-sized dumplings made of glutinous rice and cooked in a rich, heavy broth.

The 1909 Portola Parade

After the 1906 earthquake and fire, San Franciscans spent the next couple of years rebuilding. To celebrate the rebirth of the city, the first Portola Festival was held in 1909. The highlight was the parade, and all of Chinatown took part with great enthusiasm. The festival became a San Francisco tradition, and was held annually for several years. It gradually became less popular, although it continued sporadically until the 1950s.

Chinatown's early parades were spectacular, featuring

some of the most colorful floats San Francisco has ever seen, and the Portola Parade of 1909 was one of the best. Although San Francisco was still pulling itself together after the earthquake and fire, a feeling of great optimism was in the air. In addition, the residents of Chinatown sensed that the downfall of the old empire in China was imminent. Nostalgic for the pomp and color of the old China, they put their souls into one glorious display. Ten thousand dollars was raised for the general fund, in addition to smaller funds collected by separate organizations such as the district associations, the family associations, the tongs, and the bazaars (shops selling Asian goods and souvenirs).

The organizers of the event were among the most prominent and influential people of Chinatown, including Wong Lo You, local millionaire; Look Tin Eli, founder of the first Bank of Canton; and Tong Bong of Sing Fat Bazaar. Equipment, props, and costumes were ordered from Canton. To ensure that the parade would have something to fall back on should the items fail to arrive on time, the organizers also arranged to borrow all the available props from Marysville, Los Angeles, and Portland. The Wells Fargo Express bill for the Los Angeles shipment alone was $200, a large sum in those days. The goods arrived from China just one week before the parade. A special exemption from Washington enabled them to land duty-free. All of the shipping was handled by Suey Chong Tai Company, a large import-export company.

For the assembling of the floats, Chinatown was organized like a Hollywood studio. A huge empty lot at 1044 Stockton Street (where the Chinese-American Citizens Alliance now stands) was divided among the various organizations putting floats together. Days in advance, each group pulled the truck upon which its float would be built into its assigned spot, and the carpenters and decorators got busy. Each organization also maintained a makeup stand close to its truck.

Special committees chose the various characters to be portrayed on the floats. Each participant received $3 for the day, in addition to three meals and money for either a hair dressing or a haircut. Women with suitable costumes of their own received a pair of slippers as a rental fee. Other participants were given an order slip for a complete outfit from any of the five *so-hong-po* (silk houses), which were temporarily turned into costume departments.

On the day of the parade, each participant reported to the makeup stands, where he or she was given a *sui-fon*, or liquid facial makeup. Then deft artists added the finishing touches. Some were given thick eyebrows, others false beards, and still others the *fa-min*, or masklike makeup. Soon the lot became a colorful assembly of *niu-ying* (heroines), *ta-cheung* (generals), *fa-don* (stars), *siu sung* (leading men), *hwang ti* (emperors), *po ping* (soldiers), *ma ping* (cavalry), *wo sheung* (priests), *chou* (clowns), *ta chok* (bandits), *singyan* (sages), and so on.

The parade marshal was a young woman, as is usually the case with Chinese parades. She was called a *fah muk lan*, a sort of Joan of Arc. The *fah muk lan* was always carefully chosen, as she represented the fiery spirit of victory. She was selected as much for her aristocratic bearing as for her beauty. Her costume was a red silk *peh gop* (ornamental chest "armour"), heavily decorated with tiny mirrors and gold cable appliqués. On her chest she wore a huge bow cluster of vermilion satin ribbon, and four handkerchief-sized silk flags waved from her shoulders, each bearing the word "victory."

At the head of the parade, the *fah muk lan* was preceded by two pages bearing huge gooseberry-shaped lanterns. Immediately following the *fah muk lan* were the bearers of the *min pei po* (civil and military insignia). The civil insignia consisted of the eight precious symbols of the Buddhists, the eight mystic symbols of the Taoists, the imperial fans, and the various signs of rank and honor. The military insignia included the fighting weapons of old, badges of authority, and imperial standards.

The floats, representing legendary and historical events, were arranged chronologically. Thirty floats, or *sic*, were assembled. The sacred dragon was easily the most impressive float in the parade. The Association of Heung Shan fishermen sponsored it, and they numbered about a hundred, each one strong as an ox. All wore sea-green brocade jackets and trousers, with red silk sashes, white socks, and black slippers. Red silk cords were braided into their queues. Nearly three-quarters of a block long, the dragon all but breathed fire as it moved with a sinuous, majestic sweep toward a flaming pearl manipulated by a dancer. The head of the dragon was 2 yards in length, and the eyes were as large as basketballs. After the parade, the dragon was sold by the Sing Chong Company to an American in Menlo Park.

Other colorful floats depicted *chut che kwo kiu* (seven maidens crossing the bridge of magpies), *muk ying ha san* (heroine descending a cliff), and *san ying jin Louie Po* (Louie Po encountering three generals). A *pa lung sheun* (paddling the dragon boat) float featured ten young women on each side of a boat, assuming the position of

REMEMBER WHEN?

Chinatown Barbers

Instead of barber poles, the early Chinatown barbershops displayed a red and green stand holding a basin as a sign of their trade. The Chinese barber did not really give haircuts, only shaves. He would start by wrapping a hot towel over the customer's head, and then he would shave the forehead a full inch beyond the hairline, since all Chinese desired to be "highbrows." He would also shave an inch from the sides and back. In so doing, he might "accidentally" remove a few of the long strands, to be recovered later and sold at a high price to a toupee maker.

Next, the eyebrows and what little beard and whiskers the customer had were trimmed. This was followed by a shave of the entire face "to remove the fuzz, lest one look like a foreigner." Then the ears and sometimes the nostrils were given an elaborate cleaning—a process that all customers enjoyed. Finally, he gave the customer a mild massage from behind the ears to the back of the neck.

In braiding the queue, a long pigtail that hung down a man's back, a black silk cord was wound around the hair for half an inch just where the braiding started. The rest of the cord was braided into the queue and terminated in a tassel. Queues came in many different styles. Dignified scholars would have tightly braided, inconspicuous queues hanging straight down their backs. Working men would coil their queues around their heads. The town rake might have a loosely braided queue that hung in front of him, sometimes necklace fashion. When an attractive woman passed, he would twirl his snaky "whip."

Queues were imposed on the Chinese as a sign of their subjugation to the horse-loving Manchus. They were formally abolished shortly after the establishment of the Republic in 1912.

paddlers but remaining motionless. In the middle of the boat, on a slightly raised platform, another row of young women assumed the position of musicians but also remained motionless. Overhead hung lighted lanterns. Two musicians, hidden from view, struck a gong and a drum softly in slow cadence.

There were several floats of the type known as *pui yan sic*, which portrayed battles, heros, and heroines of ancient legends. The characters participating in these floats were generally perched high in the air and assumed many flying positions. Their perches had a saddle and a footrest, and the characters were bound in place by bandages. One such float, representing *jin kwok* (warring nations), depicted a bloody battle. A general was shown shot through the head with an arrow, and another was being decapitated by a *kwan tu* (a curved knife mounted on a long pole). Still others had swords thrust through their chests. Great emphasis was placed on the postures assumed and on the liveliness of the scenes.

Another float of the *pui yan* type was *hai lung wang yiu din*, or "travel of the sea king." The aged king was seated on a chariot drawn by lovely maidens. He was shown engaged in a swordfight with two warriors, played by lightweight children, who appeared to be floating on air. Chingwah Lee was chosen to represent the sea king. This float, sponsored by the Sing Chong Company, won a first-prize trophy.

To be chosen for the Queen of the Mountain float was equivalent to being acknowledged the most beautiful girl in Chinatown, and many of Chinatown's young women vied for this honor. Yang Kuei Fei, one of China's great beauties and a legend to this day, won this role in the 1909 parade. She was almost completely surrounded by pages carrying lanterns mounted on staffs.

All along the procession route, workers carried *sic cheung* or *cha bang sheung*. These were boxes containing tea, cookies, cigarettes, candies, and soft drinks for the people on the floats. Interposed among the floats were *lo ko che*, or orchestra cars. Musicians played huge gongs, large cymbals, three kinds of drums, and various flutes, horns, and fiddles. Preceding each was a huge banner. Always seen in pairs, the *lo san*, or sacred umbrellas, denoted the presence of royal figures. The bearers positioned themselves to protect royalty from the rays of the sun.

After the revolution of 1911, such colorful parades were considered passé. Many of Chinatown's revolutionists and converted Christians considered them pagan and old-fashioned. In place of the elaborate floats depicting ancient legends, school cadets marched snappily, carrying wooden rifles. The occasional float showed scenes such as "Uncle Sam shaking hands with young China" (the latter in a tuxedo), or "Young China defying the Manchus," with the hero wearing a Civil War uniform.

Gradually, however, some old traditions began to creep back into the Chinatown parades. The first of the old symbols to return was the lion, used for a charity drive. The lion is not indigenous to China. Introduced around the beginning of the Christian era, it was a Buddhist symbol, the defender of law and protector of sacred buildings. The stone lion found in pairs in front of official buildings is sometimes referred to as the "Lion of Corea" or "Dog of Fu," and was intended to scare off demons. The dragon, which had been all but forgotten because it was a symbol of imperial power, first made its comeback in America during the Diamond Jubilee Parade in 1925, allegedly only to please the American spectators. The dragon is the fifth of the symbolic creatures corresponding to the Twelve Terrestrial Branches (the Chinese signs of the Zodiac). The eastern dragon is not the gruesome monster of medieval imagination, but the genius of strength and goodness. It represents the spirit of change and therefore of life itself. Today, of course, the dragon is the main feature of the annual Chinese New Year parade in San Francisco.

3   Chinese Opera

By the time performances began in the United States, Chinese opera was centuries old. Henry Burdon McDowell, in an article entitled "The Chinese Theater" published in the November, 1884 issue of Century Magazine, *observed that*

> *It is safe to say that no stage is, or ever has been, so completely overlaid and encrusted with conventions as that of the Chinese. Even to Chinese who have been educated to the theatre from their youth, a dramatic performance must often be a vivid pantomime—a dazzling spectacle, if you will, of color and light. For all the characters in the drama, except perhaps the comedian, who may, to save his joke from falling flat, occasionally drop into the vernacular, speak a dialect unfamiliar to the mass of the audience. The costumes, again, from the humblest person on the stage to the emperor, are taken from an early period of Chinese history; and the gestures, instead of being the free and natural expression of emotion, are the studied product of a narrow school of art.*

On October 18, 1852, only three years after the first Chinese arrived in California to search for gold, the first performance on record by Chinese actors took place in San Francisco. The Hong Fook Tong company of China, made up of 123 performers, presented an opening performance at the American Theater at prices ranging from $2 to $6 per seat. By December of that year the first Chinese theater had been built in Chinatown; six others appeared in the course of time, all of which prospered.

The Chinese recognized seven different types of plots: Fu-Cheng (historical play or tragedy); Fai-Wood (comedy); Oi-Yue (platonic-love play); Tai-Mong (court play); Hong Koi (chivalry play); Yuen-Wang (persecution play); and Po-Yeng (merit-rewarded play). The last two are types of melodrama.

An actor who threw his leg into the air was supposed to be mounted on horseback. A change of scene was indicated in one of two ways: If the change was from one part of a house to another, the characters would indicate their entrance into another room by pantomime (at times the comedian, or *dop doy*, would stumble over the imaginary threshold). If a change of scene was required that could not adequately be acted out, the whole cast would walk rapidly three times around the stage.

The stage of the early theaters was an elevated platform with a door on each side. There were no wings, flaps, drops, or set pieces, nor any curtain. The two doors were hung with curtains of red cloth or elaborately embroidered silk. The only props were chairs and tables, used to simulate mountains, bridges, doorways, and so on.

Sometimes the back wall of the stage would be decorated with paintings, hangings, or banners embroidered

The interior of a Chinese theater on Jackson Street in San Francisco, ca. 1885. Balconies and loges surround the stage. The curtained loges on the right were reserved for women. [Photo by Taber Photo, courtesy of the California Historical Society, San Francisco; FN-13018.]

or painted with Chinese characters. The actors' dressing rooms, behind the stage, were narrow and poorly lit. Tea was kept ready for members of the troupe in a small kitchen area.

The orchestra was an important part of the show. The musicians, sitting on three-legged stools, were placed in the center of the stage, behind the actors and in full view of the audience. The instruments usually included an oxhide drum, a Chinese guitar, a moon guitar, a gong, and cymbals.

Over the years, in America (and more recently in China), footlights and an occasional spotlight came into use, and women began to appear in female roles that had previously been played by men. The stories, the acting method, the music, and many of the costumes remained unchanged, however.

The seating for the audience consisted of plain wooden benches. In the early days, the main floor of the auditorium would be filled exclusively with men, wearing black, felt-brimmed hats or skull caps and smoking cigarettes or cigars. A section of the gallery was set aside for women. In later years, women and men in the audience were allowed to mix freely.

During the performance, boys carrying napkin-covered baskets passed constantly through the audience, selling mandarin oranges, Chinese melon seeds, candies, and other delicacies.

About twenty years after Chinese actors began performing in San Francisco, the *San Francisco Chronicle* for September 25, 1879, described a Chinese theater that was just being built:

> It is a three-story brick building, 92 feet deep, with a frontage of 52 feet. The height of the ceiling from the floor in front of the stage is 35 feet. It has an iron front, a large main gallery in the center of the auditorium, and two hanging side galleries. Its seating capacity is to be for 2,500 people, and the total cost of the building . . . will be upward of $15,000. The interior is furnished with plain wooden benches and no stage scenery. Thirty-five cents is the price of admission to all parts of the house except the private boxes, which will be rented at $4 each. The ground floor will be occupied by stores, and the garret is to be used as a lodging-house for the actors and other attachés.

This large theater with its modern amenities reflected the popularity of Chinese opera in San Francisco at the time. From the very beginning, all the actors and actresses who appeared in Chinese operas in San Francisco were imported from Canton, China. A few native sons and daughters traveled to China to study for the stage, but no local school of Chinese theater arts was ever established.

The Mandarin Theater, built on Grant Avenue in 1924, featured for a year the "Mary Pickford of Southern China," Cheung Sook Kun (or Jung Shook Kan), at that time the highest-paid actress on the Chinese stage. The Great China Theater was built on Jackson Street at about the same time, and a professional rivalry soon developed that culminated in the brief appearance of the Pekingese Mei Lan-fang as guest artist at the Great China in 1930, followed by the presentation of Mah See Don at the Mandarin in eighteen months of fine Cantonese-style drama. These were two of the most famous actors in all of South China. The Chinese in America considered fine actors well worth the high prices they commanded.

Many American actors were greatly impressed by the talents of their Chinese counterparts. Broadway actress Pauline Frederick once said of a Chinese actress, "I can't make out what she's driving at, but if I could swing my hands like she does I'd make a million dollars a year." The famous actor Edwin Booth is said to have studied in San Francisco the art of a Chinese tragedian named Ah Chic, and Sarah Bernhardt, during one of her early visits to the city, said of a popular Chinese actor that he was the greatest she had ever seen on any stage.

Although Chinese theaters sprang up at different times in Los Angeles, Sacramento, New York, Portland, Seattle, Chicago, and Boston, San Francisco was always the center of Chinese dramatic activity in America.

Today Chinese opera in America is a thing of the past, although a couple of the old theaters are still standing.

The Mandarin, on Grant Avenue, has been converted into a miniature mall. Others are now movie theaters, showing movies made in Taiwan or Hong Kong that vary from ancient dramas to kung fu specials.

4   Wells Fargo Bank and the Chinese

The John Parrot Building, the very first granite-faced building in San Francisco, was erected on the corner of Montgomery and California streets in 1852. The granite for its construction was cut, polished, and fitted in old granite quarries in China before being shipped to San Francisco. But the quarrying of the granite was not to be the end of Chinese involvement with this building. And Wells Fargo Bank, as it turned out, had good reason to be glad about that.

A great fire had swept through San Francisco in 1851. The building housing the offices of the flourishing Adams & Company, express agents who handled the major portion of gold shipments from the mines, was among those destroyed, and they planned a brand new style of building to replace their old quarters. The firm engaged John Parrot to build a new, three-story office building on the northwest corner of Montgomery and California streets.

To save time and money, because heavy timber would need to be cut, sawn, seasoned, and then transported to the site, Parrot devised another plan. He decided to import granite, cut to specification, polished, and ready for assembly, from China.

When the stones arrived in San Francisco, however, the markings indicating their placement were found to be in Chinese. Caucasian workmen, of course, could not understand the markings, and so Chinese laborers were recruited from the city's Chinatown to put together the first stone building in San Francisco.

When the Chinese masons arrived to assemble the huge granite pieces, they looked at the Chinese words on the finished stone, looked at the spot on which the building was to be put up, and refused to work on the project. The stones sat there until a builder from China could be hired and brought over to do the job. When the builder arrived, he and his crew went straight to the site. A local group watched as he examined the stones, the markings, and the site, which he went over with compass and tape measure. Finally he told them, "You are placing the building on the wrong corner of the street. It must be erected on the opposite side. The stones are all cut and marked for the other corner, where no evil influences will be encountered. Building here will bring you bad luck."

The American contractors wouldn't listen, however. They decreed that the building would be built as planned, evil spirits or no evil spirits. The Chinese builder said that no good would come of the undertaking, and he refused to have anything to do with it, as did all of the local Chinese. They knew, as for many centuries their ancestors

The John Parrot Building, the first granite-faced building in San Francisco, built in 1852 after a great fire in 1851 destroyed this section of the financial district. Because of the scarcity of seasoned lumber, the building was built of granite from stone quarried and cut to specification in China and shipped to San Francisco. [Photo courtesy of Wells Fargo Bank.]

had known, that going contrary to these ancient beliefs would lead to calamity.

The Chinese had always done all they could to protect themselves from evil spirits. They suggested that, if John Parrot and his builder insisted on going ahead with their foolish plan, they should exorcise the evil spirits by preparing a tray with some rice and three cups of tea, placing a lighted incense stick at each corner, burning some yellow or gold paper, and emptying the three cups of tea on the burning paper while scattering the rice. This, they said, would have the effect of drawing away the evil spirits and appeasing the good ones. But the Americans refused to perform the ceremony.

After spending much time and labor to determine the placement of each stone, Parrot completed the structure, which finally cost $117,000. It was occupied immediately by Adams & Company. Over the entrance hung huge signs that read "Adams & Company, Bankers and Express" and "Page, Bacon & Company, Bankers." The latter occupied part of the first floor and was closely related to Adams & Company. Each day, the bulk of the state's newly mined gold was stored here before being shipped by boat to the U.S. mint in Philadelphia.

From the very beginning, no Chinese ever went into the building, nor would they ship their gold through the Adams & Company express. They seemed to favor a thriving little express company called Wells, Fargo & Company, located farther down Montgomery Street, dwarfed by larger buildings.

Adams & Company seemed to do well in its new building and gradually became the most widespread express agency on the West Coast. It had an office in every camp and town of importance in California. Page, Bacon

& Company also grew to become the largest banking concern on the coast.

The smaller Wells, Fargo & Company was not far behind, however. It soon occupied a large stone building across from Adams & Company, on the very corner on which the Chinese builder had wanted to erect the Parrot building. When Wells Fargo moved into its new building, there was much burning of incense and paper before the temples and buildings in Chinatown, as well as in their mining camps. They seemed to be making every effort to prevent evil spirits from interfering with the progress of their favorite express company and bank.

When Wells, Fargo & Company opened up its new building, a long file of Chinese walked in one door of the banking house and out the other. They did not conduct any business on this first day; they came to pay their respects to their god, who had blessed their favorite bank. The new Wells Fargo building seemed of great interest to the Chinese. Some time later, the banking people learned that a certain local Chinese man had made a neat sum by setting up a stall not far from the bank's entrance and charging his fellow countrymen a small fee for the privilege of walking through the building for good luck.

By 1855 the competing firms occupying the two buildings seemed to be doing so well that the dire predictions directed toward Adams & Company and Page, Bacon & Company seemed ill-founded. One morning, however, into the Golden Gate came the ship *Oregon*, and with it news that shocked the financial foundation of California's banking system. Page, Bacon & Company, leading bankers of St. Louis, had suspended operations.

The news started a panic as depositors began a run on Page Bacon's San Francisco branch. Before the day was out, the panic included all the other banks in the city, and it soon spread to the mining camps.

Wells Fargo closed its doors for two days to accumulate additional funds. When it reopened, it began paying all its depositors on demand. No Chinese came to take out their gold during the panic, and their mines continued without interruption to ship their gold to Wells Fargo, as if nothing exceptional were happening.

After the panic of 1855 had receded, more than 200 San Francisco firms had failed. Their liabilities exceeded 8 million dollars, and their assets were estimated at less than 20 percent of that amount. Of all the city's banks, only Wells Fargo managed to maintain its integrity. The Chinese population in the closing months of 1855 became a major factor in helping to maintain Wells Fargo's position as the leading bank in the city.

In time the doors of the granite building opened wide once again. But it was not Adams & Company waiting to greet its old customers; Wells Fargo had taken over the John Parrot Building. Before the reopening of the building, Wells Fargo and its Chinese friends had spent much time and made many prayers and offerings to their god of wealth, Choy Pak Sing Kung, to bless the building and look after the welfare of Wells Fargo in its new home.

These efforts must have done the job, because today, more than 130 years later, Wells Fargo is one of the leading banks in the state. And many Chinese are still among its most loyal customers.

REMEMBER WHEN?

Shoe Factories

At one time the Chinese dominated the shoe industry in California, and custom-made shoes could be had for as little as $3 a pair. At the height of the boom, more than 5,000 men were said to be in the business. They operated machinery brought in from the East Coast but still had to do some tasks by hand, the machines being rather primitive. Later, the unions, by agitation and legislation, forced the shoe business out of Chinese hands; only a few Chinese shoe factories managed to stay in business to meet the Chinese demand.

Besides making regular shoes, the Chinatown shoe factories also featured the half boot. These shoes had an elastic web on each side, thus dispensing with laces and buttons. They were extremely durable and, being custom made, were form-fitting as well. The younger generation was becoming style conscious, however, and flocked to Broadway or Kearny Street to buy American-style patent leather, pointed-toe ("New York cut") shoes.

After the fire of 1906, shoe factories were located at 937 Stockton Street, 949 Stockton Street, 742 Washington Street (all two-story buildings), and 902 Stockton Street. With the decline of the Chinese population in California, these factories finally degenerated into repair shops. The last one closed its doors around 1930.

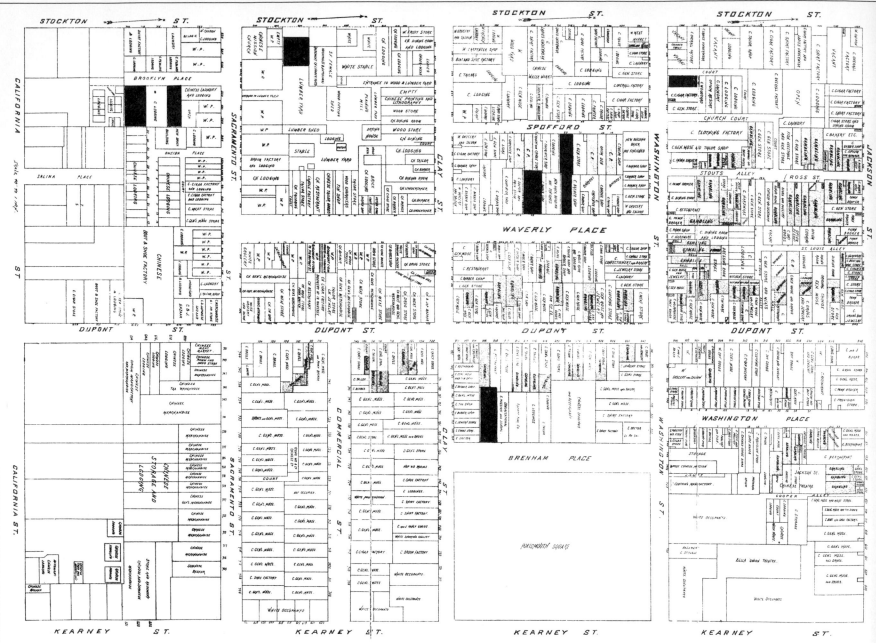

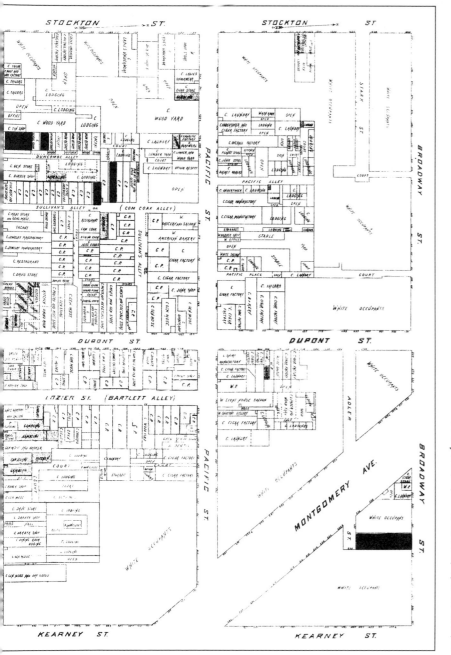

The San Francisco Municipal Reports *for the fiscal year 1884–85, ending June 30, 1885, a 340-page book, was published by order of the Board of Supervisors. It contains a section on the Chinese quarter and the Chinese in San Francisco with great detail on three main subjects: Mongolian Leprosy, the Immigration Act of 1882 (U.S.), and the Amendatory Chinese Restriction Act.*

The Chinese section, containing 101 pages, opens with a six-color Official Map of Chinatown prepared under the supervision of the Special Committee of the Supervisors in July of 1885: W. B. Farwell, John E. Kunkler, and E. B. Pond. The map shown here is a slightly reduced black and white copy of the original. It shows only the occupant or business on the ground floor of each building. The areas shown in solid black indicate joss houses. "C.P." indicates Chinese prostitution, and "W.P." white prostitution. Note "Kearny Street" incorrectly spelled as "Kearney Street" at the bottom. Street names that have changed since this map was made include Grant Avenue, formerly Dupont Street; Columbus Avenue, formerly Montgomery Avenue; Walter U. Lum Place, formerly Brenham Place; and Wentworth Place, formerly Washington Place.

5   Some Early Churches
of Chinatown

The Presbyterian Church of Chinatown
925 Stockton Street

In the 1850s, when thousands of Chinese began to come to California to seek their fortunes, many churches sent missionaries to San Francisco to build missions and introduce the Chinese to Christianity. The first step was usually to conduct English language classes and Sunday school. Some missionaries also provided rescue homes and other social services that provided care for the sick and protection against racial discrimination.

These activities were of great importance to many Chinese. The only English classes to be found in Chinatown at the time were those offered by the missions. In this way the churches gained widespread respect as well as new converts.

The churches of Chinatown continue to provide essential services right up to the present. During the 1930s and 1940s, the increasing number of Chinese children spurred the creation of organizations to meet their needs. Many churches sponsored Chinese language schools to teach students in first grade through high school the language of their homeland. During and after World War II, as attendance at these schools decreased, a great deal of emphasis was placed on youth work.

After the change in the immigration laws in 1965, the Chinese population experienced great growth, and English classes once again proved popular for the new immigrants. The large numbers of Asian immigrants in recent years has provided a new focus for the churches of the community.

This chapter describes only a few of the oldest churches among more than forty that are active, in one form or another, in and out of Chinatown today.

The first mission to be established in San Francisco Chinatown was organized in 1853 by Dr. William Speer at the request of the Presbyterian Board of Foreign Missions. Dr. Speer, who had spent five years in China as a missionary, started his church at 911 Stockton Street, with the help of four Chinese members who had been converted in China and who joined Dr. Speer when he moved to San Francisco.

From the beginning, the church conducted day and night schools that taught English to Chinese immigrants. Dr. Speer resigned after four years because of poor health. He was succeeded by Reverend A. W. Loomis, who devoted thirty-two years to the church. He was joined in 1870 by Reverend Ira M. Condit, whose work at the mission lasted until 1904. Another highly respected minister was Reverend Ng Poon Chew, who had graduated from the San Francisco Theological Seminary (see Chapter 20). He served the church from 1892 to 1898.

The congregation eventually outgrew the original mission quarters, and in 1882 another building, also on Stockton Street, was purchased for the church. This building was destroyed by the earthquake of 1906, and the following year the present building at 925 Stockton Street was built.

By 1938 the church had 278 members. Today, under the direction of Reverend Harry Chuck, the church still has an active congregation and offers services in Chinese and English.

The Reverend Nam Art Soo-Hoo and family, San Francisco, 1902. He was the first ordained Chinese pastor of the Presbyterian Church of Chinatown. Left to right: Lily, Clara (in back), Lincoln, Mother Quan Shee Soo-Hoo, Andrew (standing), Peter, Reverend Nam Art Soo-Hoo, Pauline, *and* Antoinette.

Choir practice of the Presbyterian Church of Chinatown at the home of one of the members, 1941. Back row, left to right: *Benjamin Chung, Edward Tom, Wing Wy, George Jung, Benton Tully.* Front row: *Theodore Hopkins, pianist, Faye French Tully, director, Mary Lee Chung, Alice Lum Wy, Hazel Tom Kwok, Nora Ng Wong, Pearl Lowe Chung, Jenny May Louie Lee.*

Chinese United Methodist Church
920 Washington Street

In 1868 the Reverend Otis Gibson, a Methodist minister, returned to America after ten years of missionary work in China to became a missionary for the Chinese community in California. He felt that it was important to build a permanent mission building in San Francisco Chinatown to combat the climate of racial prejudice that existed at that time. His efforts resulted in the establishment in 1870 of the Mission House on Washington Street. It was dedicated to furthering the cause of Christian missions among the Chinese in America. A central, graded evening school was opened shortly after the dedication.

In the next few years local sentiment against the Chinese grew, and in 1877 "Riot Night" occurred in

The Reverend and Mrs. Bing Y. Leong, 1930. He was acting minister of the Chinese Congregational Church from 1913 to 1917, and minister from 1917 to 1920 and from 1927 to 1953. [Photo courtesy of Thomas and Fawn Leong.]

Chinatown. Several homes and businesses were destroyed and looted, but Dr. Gibson stood his ground. The Mission House was spared, but was later destroyed during the 1906 earthquake and fire. The church was finally rebuilt in 1911 at the corner of Washington and Stockton streets, where it still stands.

At the turn of the century a Japanese Christian group began meeting in the basement of the church; it later acquired its own building and became the first Japanese Methodist Church. The first Korean group met in the church in the 1920s and went on to establish a Korean

Methodist Church with its own church building. Also in the 1920s, the Chinese Congregational Church became a joint sponsor with the Chinese United Methodist Church of the Hip Wo Chinese Language School, which can still be found at 1600 Clay Street.

The San Francisco Chinese United Methodist Church is looked upon as the hub of the Pacific Chinese Methodist missions because of its many activities and annual conferences. It continues these activities today under the direction of Reverend Timothy Tam.

Chinese Congregational Church
21 Walter U. Lum Place

In 1873 Reverend Dr. William C. Pond, pastor of the Third Congregational Church of San Francisco, invited the Chinese to attend Sunday school classes at his church. It was very rare in those days for churches outside Chinatown to extend such an invitation. Later, Reverend Pond wished to baptize his Chinese converts and receive them into his church, but the board of directors rejected the idea. As a result, Dr. Pond and seventeen of his supporters left the Third Congregational Church and formed the Bethany Congregational Church of San Francisco.

Following the devastation of the 1906 earthquake, a new church building was erected at 21 Walter U. Lum Place (formerly Brenham Place). In 1913 Mr. Bing Y. Leong arrived from China and became associated with the church. He was ordained in 1917. He left in 1920 to become a pastor in Bakersfield, California, and later went to Chicago, Illinois. In 1927 he returned to the Chinese

Congregational Church in San Francisco, where he served as pastor until his retirement in 1953.

The church is now under the direction of Reverend Wilson Chan. Services are held in both English and Chinese each Sunday, and a Chinese school serves the community's needs. The church currently has more than 200 active members.

First Chinese Baptist Church
15 Waverly Place

On October 3, 1880, Dr. J. B. Hartwell, a former missionary to China, led in the formation of the First Chinese Baptist Church in San Francisco Chinatown. The congregation, which initially consisted of nine members, met in rented quarters on Washington Street. Janie Sanford was the first of a number of missionaries sent to the mission to work with the children, teach young men English, and provide programs for women. In 1886 the Reverend Tong Kit Hing came to serve as the first Chinese pastor of the church, a position he held for fourteen years.

The first location was soon found to be inadequate for the needs of the church, so Hartwell raised funds to purchase land at the corner of Waverly Place and Sacramento Street. A church building was constructed on the site in 1888, but was destroyed by the earthquake and fire of 1906. Like several other churches in San Francisco, the First Chinese Baptist Church moved to a location in Oakland until the new San Francisco building was completed on the same site in 1908.

Over the years the church has offered English and Chinese language classes and other programs for Chinese children and youth. Since the late 1970s it has provided outreach programs for immigrant children. The First Chinese Baptist Church continues these activities today under the direction of Reverend James Chuck.

The Salvation Army Chinatown Corps
1450 Powell Street

Major Alfred Wells of the Salvation Army arrived in San Francisco in 1883 with the intention of helping the Chinese. Three years later the Salvation Army Chinatown Corps officially opened on Turk Street. The first commanding officers of the Corps in San Francisco were Lieutenants Maud Sharp, L. M. Simonson, and Helen Rutherford.

Like other Christian churches, the Salvation Army found that the most practical way to attract the Chinese to Christianity was through English night classes. Evangelistic teams also helped in this effort. Fong Foo-Sec, a member of an evangelistic team under General William Booth, was well known for his dedication and success at reaching the Chinese.

The earthquake and fire of 1906 drove thousands of Chinese to Oakland, where they sought refuge in the army's tent camp. An Oakland Chinese Corps was formed to serve the people there. When the rebuilding of San Francisco was completed in 1909, the Corps moved back into a rented building on Jackson Street.

During the period from 1883 until 1943, when the Chinese Exclusion Acts were repealed, the Corps was active in aiding women who were being mistreated. Many young women during this time were sold and put to work in brothels. Captain Violet Roberts, commanding officer in 1932, served as a social worker to help these women take care of health and family matters.

The current commanding officer of the Salvation Army Chinatown Corps, Major Check-Hung Yee, and his wife, Major Phyllis Yee, have succeeding in increasing interest in the Corps among the Chinese.

Cumberland Presbyterian Church
865 Jackson Street

The Cumberland Presbyterian Church began in the Cumberland Mountains of Tennessee in 1810, and spread branches across the nation. The Cumberland Presbyterian Mission in San Francisco was organized by J. J. Sitton in 1894. As part of his work, Sitton cared for dying children in Chinatown, since at this time some Chinese believed that having a baby die in their home would bring bad luck. He also taught English and organized a Sunday school.

In 1900 Reverend Gam Sing Quah established the Cumberland Presbyterian Church, the successor to the mission. The San Francisco earthquake and fire destroyed the church building in 1906, and many members moved to Oakland until it was rebuilt.

In 1921 the church moved to a new building. English classes continued, and in the evenings children attended Chinese language school. The congregation continued to grow, and in 1958 it moved to its present site. It currently sponsors many educational and social service programs. Reverend Roy Low is in charge of English programs, and Reverend Lawrence Fung and Reverend Peter Wang are in charge of Cantonese and Mandarin programs.

Saint Mary's Chinese Catholic Center
902 Stockton Street

Saint Mary's Catholic Center was established by the Paulist Fathers, who came to the West Coast in the 1870s to set up missions. Father Henry Ignatius Stark began the Paulist Fathers Chinese Apostolate in San Francisco in 1903. His initial efforts were met with indifference by the Chinese. But Stark was determined, and he persuaded some Chinese to join him in the mission's basement for instruction in the Catholic faith.

Mrs. Bertha Welch is credited with arranging for nuns to come to San Francisco and assist the mission and the people it served. Under the direction of Mother St. Ida, the Sisters of Holy Souls arrived in 1904.

The 1906 earthquake and fire destroyed the mission, and it was forced to take a minor role until the building was restored in 1909. The same year, the mission began its first night school for Chinese in its basement.

In 1920 Anthony Chan, a native Catechist, came from Canton to preach in Chinese, and his efforts helped attract new members. At about the same time, Father Charles Bradley decided that Chinatown needed another Asian grade school, because the only one available to Chinese students was the Oriental School (see Chapter 8). California law did not allow Asian and Caucasian grade school students to attend the same schools. As a result of Bradley's efforts, the Holy Family Catholic Chinese School and Social Center opened in 1921 with 212 students. Today the school attracts some 350 students from all over San Francisco.

Shortly after the opening of the grade school, Dr. Chu Shin Shong founded the Chinese Language School.

Ever since, it has continuously provided instruction in the Chinese language on weekends and evenings after students' regular school hours. The Chinese Language School has been under the direction of John Yehall Chin since 1931 (see Chapter 58).

True Sunshine Episcopal Church
1430 Mason Street

The True Sunshine Episcopal Church became a mission in 1905 under the organization of Deaconess Emma Drant, who had formerly worked among the Chinese in Hawaii. In the first year of its existence, True Sunshine made good progress; however, the 1906 earthquake and fire destroyed the building that housed it. Following this disaster, an Oakland branch of the church was established to serve the homeless who had sought refuge across the bay. Following the rebuilding of the San Francisco mission, the Oakland branch remained to serve the people who had decided to stay on that side of the bay.

After Deaconess Drant's retirement in 1913, Mr. Daniel Wu became the priest at True Sunshine. He had received his theological training at the Church Divinity School of the Pacific. Reverend Wu served for thirty years; after he retired, the Oakland branch came under the pastoral care of Reverend Stephen Ko, while Reverend Clarence Lee of Canada served the San Francisco church.

In the 1950s the mission's property on Clay Street was taken over by the San Francisco School District for the purpose of expanding the Commodore Stockton School. The congregation sought temporary shelter at Grace Cathedral until it was able to purchase the property on Mason Street.

The choir of the True Sunshine Episcopal Church in 1937. The church was then located at 966 Clay Street. Reverend Daniel Wu is in the front row at the extreme right. [Photo courtesy of Jackie Wong Sing.]

In 1965 Bishop James Pike decided to encourage integration by having True Sunshine's ethnic congregation worship at Grace Cathedral. He sold part of True Sunshine's property on Mason Street to the San Francisco Housing Authority.

In 1968 Reverend James Pun, a senior priest from Hong Kong, became the director of the Chinese ministry for the diocese and also took charge of the True Sunshine congregation. Canon Pun is credited with organizing the Chinese Newcomers' Association and the Chinese Newcomers' Service Center. He also received permission to build on the property the church still held at Mason Street. The new building was designed to serve as a church on weekends and as a day care center on weekdays. Bishop Kilmer Myers consecrated the new building in

1972, and in the next year True Sunshine was accepted by the diocese as a self-supporting parish. Reverend Donald Fox is the current pastor.

The Chinese Christian Union

The Chinese Christian Union is thought to have been formed well before 1900, but a written constitution was not drawn up until after 1916. According to its revised constitution of 1924, the Union was founded by ten churches: the Presbyterian, Congregational, Baptist, Methodist, Independent Baptist, Cumberland Presbyterian, Episcopalian, Disciples, First Disciples, and the Salvation Army. It was formed to assist with social, spiritual, and physical problems that one denomination alone could not solve.

One of the first problems the Union tackled was the need for a Chinese Christian cemetery. The Chinese had to establish their own cemeteries because they were not permitted to bury their dead in Caucasian cemeteries. The first Chinese cemetery in the San Francisco Bay Area was the Ning Yung Cemetery near Colma. Only Chinese from the district of Toishan were permitted to be interred there. Later, the Luk San Cemetery, also near Colma, was established for immigrants from six other Chinese districts.

The Chinese Christian Cemetery was established by the Chinese Christian Union. It accepts all Chinese Christians and their spouses, regardless of their home district. Even a few Caucasian missionaries who were very close to the Chinese community are buried there. The caretakers at this cemetery discourage the use of incense and traditional Chinese offerings, but they are not able to stop the practice completely (see Chapter 2). Originally, another difference between the Chinese Christian Cemetery and the other Chinese cemeteries was that the former did not permit disinterment.

Before World War II the remains of individual Chinese were often disinterred and shipped back to China for burial in their home districts. This reflected the Chinese concern with proper burial (which could only take place on ancestral soil) and the need for living members of a family to care for ancestral graves. Many early Chinese immigrants were determined to return to China eventually, even after death if necessary. It was the duty of the family and district associations that maintained the cemeteries to arrange for disinterment.

To help immigrants without family or savings to finance a funeral and burial, the Ning Yung Cemetery maintained an area of free plots. Every decade or so this area would be dug up and the remains collected to be returned to Hong Kong to be interred again. This type of large-scale disinterment ended around World War I.

During World War II the disinterment and shipping of remains proved impossible. After the war ended, a few plots were dug up, and the bones were cremated and sent to Hong Kong to be inurned in mausoleums. No such shipments were made after the Communist revolution in 1949.

The Chinese Christian Cemetery is only one of many important projects the Chinese Christian Union has undertaken over the years. The Union is now sponsored by ten Chinese churches and is still going strong. Most recently it has made special efforts to help the large number of recent Asian immigrants and refugees who now make their homes in San Francisco.

6

The Chinese Shrimp Industry

No one remembers the names of the cook and the tong leader who, according to an old story, gave the Chinese shrimp industry its start. What is remembered is that from the early 1870s until the 1950s the tiny San Francisco Bay shrimp caught by the Chinese were a delicacy sought after by gourmets and common laborers alike. The Chinese dominated the region's shrimp industry for more than eighty years.

In the late 1860s a story made the rounds that went something like this. A Chinese cook, out of work because of the closing of the mines near Nevada City, came to San Francisco and, walking near Hunters Point, saw an Italian man netting shrimp nearby. He asked for a handful of the shrimp and cooked them, with his last bit of rice, in a tin can over a driftwood fire. When they were done, he took his first taste of shrimp, and then stopped.

He hurriedly put out his fire and walked toward Chinatown with his tinful of shrimp and rice. There he located the head of his tong and respectfully asked him to try the food in the can. The leader did and agreed that the cook had discovered a new source of the tasty crustaceans. The Chinese shrimp industry was born.

Bay shrimp have always been picked, or shelled, by hand, a job that was generally handled by Chinese housewives or children because of their dexterous hands. They were paid approximately 25 to 35 cents per pound. It takes about 350 shrimp to make a pound of shelled meat, which means that they had to shell twelve or thirteen shrimp to earn a penny.

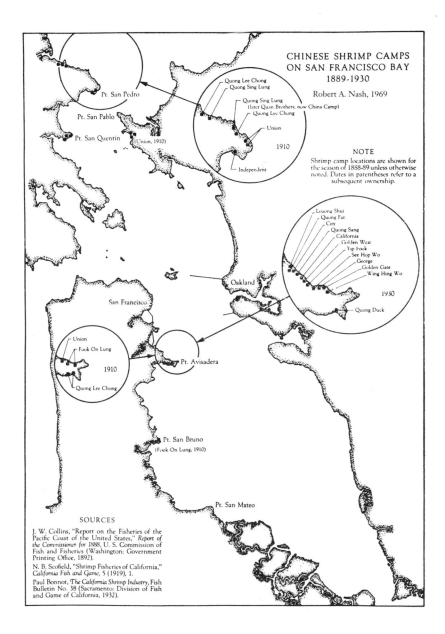

CHINESE SHRIMP CAMPS
ON SAN FRANCISCO BAY
1889-1930

Robert A. Nash, 1969

NOTE

Shrimp camp locations are shown for the season of 1888-89 unless otherwise noted. Dates in parentheses refer to a subsequent ownership.

Pt. San Pedro

Quong Lee Chong
Quong Sing Lung

Quong Sing Lung
(later Quan Brothers; now China Camp)
Quong Lee Chong

Union

1910

Independent

Pt. San Pablo

Pt. San Quentin

(Union, 1910)

Lcuong Shui
Quong Fat
City
Quong Sang
California
Golden West
Yip Fook
See Hop Wo
George
Golden Gate
Wing Hing Wo

1930

Quong Duck

Oakland

San Francisco

Union
Fook On Lung

1910

Quong Lee Chong

Pt. Avisadera

Pt. San Bruno

(Fook On Lung, 1910)

Pt. San Mateo

SOURCES

J. W. Collins, "Report on the Fisheries of the Pacific Coast of the United States," *Report of the Commissioner for 1888*, U. S. Commission of Fish and Fisheries (Washington: Government Printing Office, 1892).

N. B. Scofield, "Shrimp Fisheries of California," *California Fish and Game*, 5 (1919), 1.

Paul Bonnot, *The California Shrimp Industry*, Fish Bulletin No. 38 (Sacramento: Division of Fish and Game of California, 1932).

Shrimp fishermen aboard their boat, ca. 1900. [Photo courtesy of San Francisco Maritime Museum.]

To the women pickers, being paid to shell shrimp was like earning money to sit and chat. They sat around a table, where baskets of shrimp were dumped in a big pile. Each woman had a washbasin in her lap to catch the shells and another on the table to hold her shelled meat. Holding a shrimp between the thumb and forefinger of one hand, she would twist the shrimp to break the shell and then reverse the twist and pull the meat out whole. Skilled pickers did this so effortlessly that they could carry on a conversation as though their hands had eyes of their own. They could work for hours at a stretch, and the time would pass pleasantly enough once the beginner got used to the odor of cooked shrimp and developed her skill.

The shrimp catch gradually started to dwindle in the 1950s. Many blamed the growing amount of sewage and pollution spilling into the bay. That and the building of the Golden Gate, San Francisco Bay, and Richmond bridges were big factors in the disappearance of the bay shrimp. By the end of the 1950s there were only three Chinese shrimp companies left, the Lincoln Shrimp Company, the Hunters Point Shrimp Company, and the China Camp Shrimp Company in Marin County.

The Hunters Point Shrimp Company closed its doors in 1960. It had been started on a shoestring in 1946. One of its six partners, Jennie Lim, was the guiding light. She was able to raise her three sons and see them through college with the profits from her share of the shrimping enterprise and from the Shrimp Boat Restaurant, which she also ran, even after the bay shrimp disappeared and she had to buy Mexican shrimp. Today, Jennie is still living in San Francisco, near Chinatown. The China Camp Shrimp Company survives only by taking fishing parties out on deep-sea fishing excursions.

Of all the shrimp companies of the past hundred years, only Lincoln, a fringe operator (contracting with independent fishermen), is still thriving today. Located at 708 Commercial Street, the company is owned by David Chan. His father, Chan Hoy, started the Lincoln Shrimp Company in 1912. He didn't operate his own boats; instead, he would travel by buggy to the various Chinese shrimp camps at Hunters Point and buy the shrimp they had caught. His workers would then process the shrimp, which would be delivered to restaurants the next morning. Later, he had plants at Hunters Point and Point San Pablo (North Bay camp). Until the mid-1960s the company was still able to scour all the fishing areas and round up enough shrimp to satisfy its customers. With the demand for shrimp growing, however, the company was finally forced to buy and distribute shrimp, first from Mexico and then from Louisiana. Today, Lincoln receives shellfish from both national and international sources and distributes it wholesale to restaurants and stores.

7   The China 5 Exchange

The Chinatown Telephone Exchange was a familiar part of daily life in Chinatown for many years. Known locally as the "China 5 Exchange" because of the prefix (CH5-) for every phone number it handled, its headquarters from 1896 until the earthquake and fire in 1906 was famous for its sumptuous Oriental ornamentation. When the new headquarters was built in 1909, Chinatown had 800 phones, and the China 5 Exchange became the nerve center of the community's communication system. By 1949, when the dial telephone came into widespread use and the exchange was no longer necessary, it had over 2,200 subscribers.

The first Chinese in the world to become a telephone subscriber was Quong Lee, a merchant living in San Francisco Chinatown. When the first San Francisco telephone directory was issued on June 1, 1878, with the names of the first 150 telephone subscribers on the Pacific Coast, Quong Lee's name was among them. He continued to be listed in the directory for many years, even after he had passed away and his business on Grant Avenue had been taken over by his descendants.

It was not until years after Quong Lee became a subscriber that the Chinatown Telephone Exchange, a switchboard devoted to Chinatown, was established by a Marysville-born man named Loo Kum Shu.

Loo Kum Shu's father had been among the early Chinese to come to America, and he was able to realize a small fortune in mining. Later, Kum Shu's father drowned at sea while he was employed by the Pacific Mail Steamship Company, and the eight-year-old boy became the charge of Mrs. Marian Bokee, a teacher at a Chinese mission school sponsored by the First Congregational and Presbyterian churches in San Francisco. He received his first-grade education at the school, which was then located at Dupont (now Grant Avenue) and Jackson streets.

After graduating from high school, Loo Kum Shu attended the University of California and then, at the age of twenty-one, was hired as managing editor of the *Oriental Daily News*, one of San Francisco's first Chinese newspapers. It had been founded in the 1890s, when there were something like 85,000 Chinese on the Pacific Coast.

Several years after Loo Kum Shu was hired, the first public telephone in Chinatown was installed in his office, although not for the convenience of editor Loo. It was done in response to a long-felt need on the part of the telephone company. In the late 1880s Chinese labor contractors from adjacent agricultural districts and railroad centers would call up the San Francisco main telephone office, then on Pine Street, when they needed laborers

Loo Kum Shu, founder of the Chinatown Telephone Exchange, in 1902. [Photo courtesy of Ling-Gee Tom.]

and ask to have some Chinese merchant or labor contractor called to the telephone. A messenger boy would be sent hustling into Chinatown to summon the requested party. When the person was found, he would have to go to the main office to answer the call. There was seldom an hour in those days that a Chinese was not called to the telephone in this manner.

Finally, when the telephone calls became too numerous for the main office to handle conveniently day after day, a public phone was installed in Loo Kum Shu's newspaper office. At that time the young editor could not have dreamt that the strange-looking instrument in his office would later be the chief interest of his life.

In 1894 the telephone company installed a switchboard in a building on the northeast corner of Washington and Dupont streets. Almost at once, thirty-seven Chinese firms became subscribers, despite the fact that the service was limited to calls within Chinatown, since it was not connected to the main city telephone system. Loo

Kum Shu became the manager of this first switchboard, which had three male operators, and Chinese journalism lost a capable editor for good.

Within two years, in 1896, a larger switchboard capable of connecting 200 telephones was put in, this time at the southeast corner of Washington and Dupont streets, and it was connected with the main city system. As business grew, Loo Kum Shu prospered. He solicited his own subscribers, kept and collected his own accounts, and hired and paid his own operators. The telephone company kept the lines in good repair and advised manager Kum Shu on various aspects of his business.

That same year, the telephone company purchased a piece of property next to the existing location on Washington Street and made it the permanent site of the Chinatown Telephone Exchange. Its exterior was remodeled in a sumptuous Oriental manner. There were chairs of carved teakwood inlaid with mother-of-pearl; black, glistening teakwood tables, gilded and lacquered; wood carvings on every side; and windows of imitation Chinese oyster-shell panes. Near the entrance was a beautiful shrine, giving the place a touch of religious splendor. The switchboard, too, was elaborately designed, made of ebony and ornamented with wood carvings of gold-yellow hue. A carved dragon seemed to wind sinuously in and out of the plug-holes.

In its sheer beauty, the Chinatown Exchange at that time could not have been rivaled by any other business house in the community. Unfortunately, its beauty was not to last. The earthquake and fire of 1906 completely destroyed the building.

A three-tiered pagodalike structure, much less elaborate than its predecessor, was built to replace the old

Second-floor office of the Chinatown Telephone Exchange, 1902. [Photo by Gabriel Moulin Studios, courtesy of Ling-Gee Tom.]

exchange building, and it opened for service in August of 1909. By that time Chinatown had 800 phones, and a small force of women operators had replaced the men. Thereafter, the busy switchboard at 743 Washington Street became the nerve center of the community's com-munication system. It became part of Chinatown's grow-ing business community, and the increase and decrease in its number of subscribers was as much a barometer of the community's prosperity as the figures representing im-ports and exports from the Far East.

Chinatown Telephone Exchange switchboard, 1935. Loo Yee Kern, manager and son of founder Loo Kum Shu, is standing at right. The switchboard was staffed around the clock. [Photo courtesy of Ling-Gee Tom.]

By 1911 the Chinatown Telephone Exchange had 474 business subscribers and 660 residential subscribers. Because anyone could use the telephone to order cooked food for a midnight supper, the restaurants' delivery service began to boom. Chinese housewives also began to do their food shopping in this manner, and "telephone bargaining" kept the exchange operators' nimble fingers busy

day and night. By 1919 the exchange was handling close to 10,000 calls each day.

Loo Kum Shu died in 1926, thirty-two years after he started the exchange. His son, Loo Yee Kern, who had been studying the business since he graduated from high school in 1923, took over. The exchange was handling 17,000 calls per day.

By the mid-1930s the Chinatown Exchange had twenty-one operators, with Mrs. Florence Chan, Loo Yee Kern's sister, as chief operator. All were proud of the fact that it was the only Chinese telephone office outside of China. An average of 13,000 calls were handled per day, 30 percent of them calls between Chinese and Caucasians. (The drop in the number of calls per day from 17,000 in 1923 to 13,000 in the mid-1930s was due to the Depression. Many businesses had closed, and others had canceled their telephone service in order to save money.) The operators memorized the names and numbers of the exchange's subscribers, since the average Chinese would invariably make a call by asking for a person or store by name instead of by number.

Two of the exchange's pioneer operators retired in 1935. Ho Lee had served for twenty-five years, and Bow Lau for twenty years. Ho Lee had been taught to operate the switchboard by her own father. When she retired her daughter, Elizabeth, filled the place she vacated. As the other operators retired, their daughters also took their places.

The Chinese Telephone Directory, a list of Chinese telephone subscribers, was published twice a year, and the residents and merchants of the community always looked forward to its appearance. The 3,000 or so copies that were printed would be gone within a few days, distributed to subscribers or taken by people who dropped in at the exchange to pick one up. The names and telephone numbers for the directory, which were written in Chinese, were drawn by hand—each character and numeral was written on paper with Chinese ink, which is thick and jet-black. The lettering, done with the traditional Chinese brush, took about two weeks. Engravings were then made from the written pages, and the directory was ready for printing.

The March 1936 issue was a thirty-two-page booklet with a somber green paper cover. It contained the names of 1,450 Chinatown telephone subscribers, in addition to some 300 Chinese telephone users in Oakland. This list did not represent the total number of telephone users in the community, as there were at least several hundred homes using "outside" stations. Some 2,200 phones were actually in use in the community at the time.

In 1949 the Chinese Telephone Exchange became part of Pacific Telephone and Telegraph, a victim of progress in the form of dial phoning. The building that had housed the exchange was acquired by the Bank of Canton and is now a branch of the bank. Some of the Chinese operators transferred to the Pacific Telephone and Telegraph office at 444 Bush Street, but the custom of passing the job on from mother to daughter became obsolete.

REMEMBER WHEN?

Horse and Buggy Days

After the fire of 1906, bicycling to Palo Alto or San Jose was a favorite pastime. But on Chinese New Year, when money was plentiful, the youngsters would bicycle out to riding academies in Golden Gate Park, hire horses for $3 per day, and ride back to Chinatown, where they would go galloping down Grant Avenue like cowboys. Some would even sport sombreros, leather gloves, brass-studded belts, and bandannas. The elders would look on, shaking their heads, with the comment *"San fun meng,"* which is the Chinese equivalent of "One foot in the grave."

A horse and buggy, another favorite means of locomotion, could be rented for $5 a day. The young people would roam the city in them, even entering the North Beach district, despite a feud raging between Chinese and Italian youth.

Families, too, often hired *kwan yin chee*, or horsedrawn sedans, to visit Golden Gate Park or the Cliff House. Both horses and driver would be correctly attired, the latter in a top hat. The whip, a 5-foot affair, was always flourished gracefully in the air before it descended lightly on the horses, as if to flick off a fly. At the park the family would take out a favorite picnic lunch typically consisting of barbecued duck, steamed layer bread, bananas, oranges, tea, and chocolate éclairs.

Above: *Postcard showing a class at the Chinese Primary School, 920 Clay Street, sometime before 1910. [Photo by Britton & Rey, San Francisco, courtesy of California Historical Society; FN-23272.]*

Above left: *Chinese vegetable garden in San Francisco's Western Addition/Cow Hollow, ca. 1885. Today this is near the intersection of Union and Pierce streets. [Photo courtesy of California Historical Society, San Francisco; FN-12616.]*

Below left: *The Chinese Primary School, 916 Clay Street, San Francisco, ca. 1898. Chinese children were not allowed to enter regular public schools until well into the 1920s. (Many addresses changed after the earthquake and fire, which may explain why the address given with this photo differs from that given with the photo above.)*

Opposite: *Dr. Sun Yat-sen (third from left in second row) in San Francisco on one of his several trips to the United States to raise money to overthrow the Manchu monarchy, ca. 1890s. His life was in constant danger, and the fact these men espoused his cause put them in jeopardy also. In 1912 he became the first president of the Chinese Republic. Everyone else in the photo was a resident of the United States. Back row, left to right: Wong Git Ting, Wong Yum Yu, Chong Chew Kun, Lee Mow Ming, Soo Hoo Mun Fong. Third row: Low Guk Haw, Tong King Chong, Wong Wai Ting, Gee Sam Jun, Wong Sam Dock, Low Dun Yee. Second row: Jung Oy Wun, Wong Bok Yew, Dr. Sun Yat-sen, Lee She Nom, Wong Wun Soo. Front row: Ng Yet Ping, Jow Yuk. [Photo courtesy of Thomas Tong, whose father, Tong King Chong, is in the third row.]*

黃傑亭　　黃任賢　　鄭超羣　　李務明　　司徒文晃

劉鞠可　　唐琼昌　　黃衛廷　　朱三進　　　　黃三德　　羅敦怡

張露蘊　　黃伯耀　　孫中山先生　　李是男　　黃芸蘇

伍一平　　　趙煜

8 Commodore Stockton School

Commodore Stockton School, at 929 Clay Street, was built at a time when racial discrimination was being institutionalized in San Francisco. It was originally named the Oriental School, with the intention that all Asian students should be sent there, not just the Chinese. From the beginning, however, most of the school's students were Chinese, and efforts by the Chinese community to change the name were soon under way.

The first city-run school for Chinese children in San Francisco began operating in 1859, and was known simply as the Chinese School. By 1886 the Chinese Primary School had been established as part of an attempt by the Board of Supervisors to continue the segregation of Chinese children from white children in San Francisco's public schools. The Chinese Primary School received only half-hearted support from the city, however, and few of the eligible Chinese children attended it. After its building was destroyed in the earthquake and fire of 1906, the school was housed in a temporary shack that drew criticism from both the Chinese and the city health officer. Nothing was done, however, for another eight years.

The Chinese Republic was officially founded in 1912, an event of great significance for the Chinese in America. By that time almost every male Chinese had cut off his queue, the long braid that symbolized the oppression of the Chinese by the Manchus. Just as the queue was a symbol of inferiority in China, the flimsy wooden shack that housed the Chinese students in San Francisco was a reminder of pervasive discrimination in the United States.

REMEMBER WHEN?

Chinese Scholars

The earliest wave of Chinese reaching California were true pioneers and, like pioneers the world over, they were not noted for their scholastic achievements. However, many proved great organizers, and all of them were adventurous. As they formed lodges, tongs, and business firms, they had a growing need for administrators and clerks, so they brought scholars (*sin-soung*) over from China and put them to work at fat salaries.

Soon the missions established night schools, and years later the Yuen Tung Siu Hok (Oriental Public Grammar School) was founded, with a handful of pupils attending. Those with two or three years of study were looked upon with awe. The parents of some of the first grammar school graduates had photographs taken of their diplomas for framing and then put the original in a safe. Photographic copies were sent to China to be placed in the village temples, and banquets were held both here and abroad to celebrate a graduation. Even as late as 1915, fewer than fifty Chinese were attending high schools, and no more than a dozen were enrolled in the universities (not counting foreign students from China).

The city finally approved construction of a new Oriental School—intended for all Asian students, not just the Chinese—in 1913, and a contract for its construction was awarded in April of 1914. On October 20, 1915, the school was officially dedicated. The ceremony was attended by Mayor James Rolph; Superintendent Alfred

A class at the Oriental School (later renamed the Commodore Stockton School), ca. 1920. The teacher in the center was Mr. Tremayne. Nearly all of the men in the last row were born in China and came to San Francisco without knowing any English. They were put into a grade commensurate with their language level. [Photo courtesy of Jimmy (Fay) Lee.]

Roncovieri; several prominent Chinese leaders, including the Chinese Consul General, S. C. Shir; and the school's teachers and its principal, Miss Newhall. The Cathay Club Boys Band provided the music. The same building, along with an annex built in 1924, was to serve generations of Chinese boys and girls, and is still in use today.

From the day it opened, nearly all the school's students were Chinese. Members of the Native Sons of the Golden State (a predecessor of the Chinese-American Citizen's Alliance) disliked the name Oriental School, which was a reminder of the discriminatory policies in effect at the time of its construction. They immediately began a campaign to change the school's name, but it was nine years before they got their way. On April 1, 1924, the school and its annex were officially renamed the Commodore Stockton School, after an early military leader who had promoted the construction of public schools when California declared its independence from Mexico.

The first Chinese teacher in San Francisco, Alice P.

Fong, started teaching at the school in 1927. By 1936 it had a faculty of thirty-one, including three Chinese teachers, three nurses (one Chinese), and a doctor.

Today, in accordance with the Consent Decree mandating integration of all San Francisco's public schools, students from many different cultures attend Commodore Stockton School. In 1988 Chinese students made up only 42 percent of the more than 800 children enrolled. Other racial groups were represented at the school as follows: Hispanics 40 percent, Blacks 6 percent, Whites 2 percent, Filipinos 1 percent, and other groups 9 percent. Those of the school's first students who are still alive might be surprised to see how much it has changed.

9   Chinese Journalism on the West Coast

Since the arrival of the first Chinese forty-niners, the Chinese in America have always been eager readers of every Chinese-lanquage newspaper or magazine published about China and the Chinese community in America. Events in China will probably always be interesting to them, not only because China is their ancestral home, but also because in many cases they have relatives and friends who are still in China. The printed word keeps them abreast of events, good and bad, that might affect loved ones or friends.

This chapter is adapted from an article written by Lim P. Lee for the November 13, 1936, issue of the Chinese Digest. *It mentions only a few of the important early Chinese newspapers, as well as some of the more recent ones. A more detailed list can be found in Appendix B.*

The first known journalistic endeavor by the Chinese in America was the *Chinese News Paper*, a weekly published by Mon Kee at 821 Washington Street, San Francisco. The only existing copy of that paper is dated December 16, 1884, recorded as issue number 428. No other issues or records of the paper survived the San Francisco fire of 1906. Ten years later, in 1894, the *Oriental Daily News* made its first appearance; it was edited by Loo Kum Shu, who later became the first manager of San Francisco's Chinatown Telephone Exchange (see Chapter 7). These two publications can be said to be the forerunners of Chinese journalism on the West Coast, if not in America.

It was the venerable Dr. Ng Poon Chew, however, who was the true father of Chinese journalism on the Pacific Coast. As described in Chapter 20, he started the *Wah Mei Sun Bo* (*Chinese-American Morning Paper*) in Los Angeles in 1898, and in 1900 he started the *Chung Sai Yat Bo* (*Chinese Western Daily*) in San Francisco.

Organs of Political Reform

At about the same time that Ng Poon Chew was establishing his daily newspaper, another newspaperman and statesman was attempting modern reforms in China. In 1898 Kang Yu-wei was able to convince Emperor Kang Hsu of the Manchu regime to map out a program of modernization in China. The famous "Hundred Days Reform" gave rise to a coup d'etat by the Empress Dowager Tzu-Hsi and caused Kang Yu-wei to flee for his life. In 1899, while he was a political refugee in San Francisco, Kang Yu-wei started the *Mon Hing Yat Bo* (*People's Recovery Daily Paper*), which advocated constitutional government and a limited monarchy. After 1906 the name was changed to *Chinese World*, and the paper was published under that name until it closed in the 1960s.

If the reforms preached by Kang Yu-wei had been heeded by the Empress Dowager, there would perhaps have been no need for a Sun Yat-sen. However, the reaction and conservatism of the empress gave Sun Yat-sen the impetus he needed to carry out his revolution and bring about the downfall of the Manchu dynasty. Sun Yat-sen made three visits to America before the revolution, and each time his following increased. During his third visit, in 1909, he felt he had sufficient strength in America to organize the San Francisco chapter of the Tung Meng Hui (the forerunner of the Kuomintang), and he started a daily paper called *Young China* to spread his revolutionary ideas. After the 1912 revolution, when the Tung Meng Hui became the Kuomintang, *Young China* was made the official organ of the party in America, and today it is still recognized as the voice of the party here, although it is now controlled by the Kuomintang in Taiwan.

The *Chinese Times* was started in 1924 by Walter U. Lum, Thomas U. Jung, Lee Bock Yin, and other members of the Chinese-American Citizens Alliance (CACA; see Chapter 23). The primary aim of the *Chinese Times* was to convince American citizens of Chinese ancestry of the need to exercise their political rights. Walter U. Lum was one of the early pioneers in encouraging the Chinese-American citizens to vote and to fight discrimination against the Chinese people. In August of 1988 the paper was sold to an independent group. It is no longer connected with the CACA.

The *Kuo Min Yat Bo* (*Chinese Nationalist Daily*) was started in 1927 after dissension in the ranks of the Kuo-mintang in China resulted in a left wing and a right wing. D. Y. Mah and his colleagues organized the *Kuo Min Yat Bo* to rally behind the left-wing or Hankow group, which was led by Wang Ching-wei. When the breach was healed during the Japanese invasion of China in 1932, Wang Ching-wei became the premier of China, and he recognized the *Kuo Min Yat Bo* as the official organ of the Kuomintang in America. The paper closed in the 1960s.

English-Language Publications

Chinese journalism on the Pacific Coast took on a new slant with the inauguration in 1935 of the *Chinese Digest*, a weekly published in English (see Chapter 33). The *Digest* was preceded by three mimeographed English-language papers, in which two of the people who would eventually work on the *Digest* gained their first experience. The *Tri Termly Toots*, a publication for Chinese high school students, had its start in 1921. The *Scout Wig Wag* came out in 1927, and the *Y-World* made its initial appearance in 1929. These pertained to scouting and the YMCA, respectively, and occasionally referred to the Chinatown community.

After the *Chinese Digest* stopped publication in 1940, I started the *Chinese News*, a monthly published from 1940 to 1942, when I entered government service. Other papers that followed were the *Chinese Press*, published by Charles L. Leong and William Hoy, which began in the mid-1940s and closed in the early 1950s; *East West*, published beginning in 1967 by Gordon Lew; and *Asian Week*, published by John Fang, which began in 1979. The latter two are still published weekly.

Above: *Sing Chong Co., a prominent Chinese general merchandise store and butcher shop at the northeast corner of Grant Avenue and Clay Street, ca. 1915. The man with the cleaver at the butcher block was the owner, Louie Dick Chuen. His store operated for over sixty years at this location.* [Photo courtesy of Sally Joe.]

Above right: *An altar in the Kong Chow Temple, the oldest Chinese temple in North America. It was originally built in 1857 on Pine Street near Kearny. In the 1960s it was moved to the fourth floor of the Kong Chow building at 855 Stockton Street. It is one of the most ornamental temples, with nearly all of the original pieces over a century old still in place. This photo was taken in 1988.* [Photo by Nancy Warner.]

Right: *Young devotees of Chinese opera, ca. 1936. In front of these four young girls is a miniature stage scene of a typical Chinese opera. The owner of the miniature scene had it made when Chinese opera began to disappear in the United States.* Left to right: *Stella Yep, Ruby Fung, Lorraine Wong, and Daisy Yep.* [Photo courtesy of Stella Yep.]

Opposite: *Hang Far Low Restaurant, ca. 1885. The first banquet-size Chinese restaurant in San Francisco, Hang Far Low was founded prior to 1875 and operated continuously until the 1970s, when new owners changed the name to the Four Seas Restaurant.*

10 San Francisco Gas & Electric Company

In July of 1852 James Donahue applied for and received a franchise to erect a gasworks, lay pipes in the streets, and install street lamps to light the city with gas at a cost of 32.5 cents per lamp per night. Gas was to be supplied to householders "at such rates as will make it to their interest to use it in preference to any other material." The company was incorporated on August 31, 1852, as the San Francisco Gas Company. Gas lights were introduced to the city on February 11, 1854. The last of San Francisco's gas street lights were not extinguished until December 27, 1930, long after electricity had proved more efficient for providing this service.

Like other early contacts between American businesses and the residents of Chinatown, that between SFG&E and its customers was based on mutual need: The company wanted the business, and the Chinese wanted gas and electricity.

In the late 1800s the San Francisco Gas & Electric Company (SFG&E) was the main supplier of power and gas in the city. Because many residents of Chinatown couldn't speak English, the company had always found it necessary to employ an interpreter, for its own benefit as well as for the convenience of its customers. For a number of years the company's Chinese representatives had no office in Chinatown; they would make their rounds and return to the main office.

Finally, because of stiff competition from the Equitable Gas Light Company from 1900 to 1903, SFG&E decided that a Chinatown office was necessary to maintain close ties with its Chinese customers. As Dupont Street (now Grant Avenue) near Jackson seemed to be the center of Chinese business activity, the company chose the street floor of the old Globe Hotel, which in the early 1850s had been San Francisco's most fashionable hotel. It was later remodeled for Chinese occupancy.

The office was brilliantly lighted at night, inside and out, with both gas and electricity, and became an excellent advertisement for the company. It was a favorite place to congregate and attracted many of the locals. In March of 1906 that office was supplanted by one of the company's regular branch offices that served the entire North

---

REMEMBER WHEN?

Business Altars

In the back of nearly every shop in Chinatown there used to be an altar, before which the most venerable or senior member of the firm would offer incense every morning and before dinner. The altar was always a simple one, dedicated either to the Earth God (*t'u ti shen*) or to the God of Prosperity (*choy shen*), represented by a written inscription. In front of the altar would be an incense urn, candlesticks, and three cups of tea. On important occasions there would also be three thimbles of wine, flowers, fruit, and other food.

Most of these altars disappeared after 1911, the revolutionists having decreed that the gods and the ancient religion were old-fashioned. Many present-day businesses have revived the custom, however, generally placing an altar at the rear of the business, facing the entrance, to welcome your presence.

This Chinese notice was translated by the San Francisco Gas and Electric Co. in 1908 and appeared in PG&E Magazine in 1910: "Our company having been established a number of years and having expended a great deal of money in San Francisco, it should be patronized by the Chinese people, and this patronage will be much appreciated. We now have a special office in Chinatown at 752 Sacramento Street. This notice is to suggest that you pay the accompanying bill there to Lee Hing Sue or Lee Yuk Sue, the company's agents at that address if you do not care to go to the main office—445 Sutter Street."

本公司開創數十餘年歷蒙華友光顧銘感五內現
爲華友利便起見如本公司收銀西人到來收銀時
適有事外出不遇請將此原單卽携到唐人街七百
五十二號廣生和內交代理華人
李崇瑚
李崇登　簽收便可電話差拿八百五十七號
或交總公司在所打街四百四十五號
舊煤氣電燈公司謹識

telephone were always available for the company's business. Later, another of the company's growing force of Chinese representatives, Hing S. Lee, a native son and merchant, offered the use of his store and clerical office for customers wanting to place orders for SFG&E services and pay bills. This store was located at 752 Sacramento Street and operated under the firm name of Kwong Sang Wo.

Lee's store served the SFG&E in this capacity for many years. In 1905, shortly after the Pacific Gas and Electric Company (PG&E) was incorporated, PG&E purchased the outstanding stock of the San Francisco Gas and Electric Company, although SFG&E retained its corporate identity. The Kwong Sang Wo company continued to handle the community's gas and electric business for some time following the acquisition.

Beach district as well as Chinatown. It was located at the triangle formed by Stockton Street and Montgomery Avenue (now Columbus Avenue) and extended from one street to the other. The next month, on April 18, 1906, the famous earthquake and fire destroyed most of San Francisco, including the branch office that had just been opened. The office was never reconstructed.

After the earthquake the company had in its employ an old Chinatown representative named Sam Lock. Although he had no company office to work from, he informed his Chinatown customers that his residence and

11　The Canton Banks in San Francisco

The name Canton Bank or Bank of Canton has actually been used by three separate financial institutions in the course of San Francisco's history. This chapter mainly concerns the first one, the Canton Bank of San Francisco. The Bank of Canton of California, the only one of the three that still exists, celebrated its fiftieth year of business in 1987.

The first Canton Bank of San Francisco was organized shortly after the San Francisco earthquake and fire of 1906 and was incorporated on October 1, 1907. This was before the enactment of California's Bank Act of 1909.

After the passage of the Bank Act, the bank received a certificate—number 41—from the State Banking Department, authorizing it to operate under state law.

According to its state certificate, the principal founder of the Canton Bank was a man named Look Tin Eli. However, William K. Luke, (the "historian of the Lukes of Hawaii and a nephew of Look Poong-shan") expressed a different opinion in the following article, entitled "The First Chinese Bank in the United States," published in the *Chinatown News* of Vancouver, British Columbia, on July 3, 1974:

> The first Chinese bank in the United States was founded by Look Poong-shan of San Francisco, California, in 1906. Located on the corner of Clay and Kearny Streets, facing a small park, it was a state-registered institution called the Canton Bank.

Look Poong-shan was born in Mendocino, California, and had a unique racial background. His mother was an American Indian woman. He was the youngest in the family of four children, three boys and a girl. When they reached school age his father sent them back to China, along with his mother, to study Chinese.

After they all had acquired a fair Chinese education, they came back to America, settled in San Francisco, and attended American schools there. Poong-shan was a brilliant student and completed his high school education in due time with good grades.

At that time, the Russo-Asiatic Bank of San Francisco was looking for a talented Chinese boy with a fair knowledge of Chinese to join their foreign exchange department. This bank, with headquarters in Russia and branch banks throughout the Far East, handled a large volume of foreign exchange from South America. They were mostly Chinese remittances being sent back to Hong Kong and funneled through the San Francisco office.

The 1906 earthquake, which destroyed a large area of the San Francisco business section, also destroyed the Russo-Asiatic Bank. After the quake this bank did not resume normal operation but established only a correspondent. The resultant effect was the entire bank staff had to look for new jobs, including Look Poong-shan.

Isaac P. Allen, a bank executive, suggested to Poong-shan the possibility of starting a Chinese bank. The Chinese transactions formerly done by the Russo-Asiatic bank were sufficient to sustain a bank. This was a tempting factor, and Poong-shan immediately took action by calling a meeting of the Chinese Chamber of Commerce, of which he was a member. A resolution was passed and the required capital was fully subscribed by the members of the Chamber. The bank was named The Canton Bank of San Francisco. Action was completed to legalize the bank, and the first Chinese bank in the United States came into existence with Poong-shan as general manager and I. P. Allen as assistant manager. A number of the old staff from the Russo-Asiatic Bank also joined the new bank.

Business prospered and the board of directors voted to establish a branch bank in Hong Kong. Problems came up because under the U.S. banking law no state-registered banks were allowed to establish branches outside the country. This was a privilege accorded to national banks only.

Poong-shan and I. P. Allen went to Hong Kong to look into the possibility of establishing a bank there. They found no trouble complying with the Hong Kong banking law. Within a year's time, the Bank of Canton in Hong Kong was in business. The name differed slightly from the one in San Francisco. Business was good, and great progress was achieved within a decade. Branch banks were established throughout the main cities of China and Southeast Asia.

Not long after the bank was well established in the Far East, World War I started. When the war ended, the bank came out on top. Following World War I, there was a worldwide depression and depreciation in the price of gold took place.

When the price of gold dropped to its lowest ebb, Poong-shan took steps to convert the bank's capital from Hong Kong dollars to British pound sterling. He consulted several top lawyers in Hong Kong. They all told him that no such thing had ever happened in British banking history. They could see no way to help him realize his wild dream. Not satisfied with their opinions, Poong-shan wrote to London to seek advice from the most prominent barrister of law who was an authority in colonial affairs. The answer was most surprising. It shook the Hong Kong legal community with the same impact as a bomb explosion.

Poong-shan's program was absolutely valid, because Hong Kong was a British colony and the Hong Kong dollar, although of silver standard, is a crown currency.

There was one point, according to British law: that for the Bank of Canton to convert its capital into pound sterling, the bank's registration must be transferred to London. This proved to be a simple legal procedure.

Steps were taken, and the transfer was finally completed. Business prospered and the world economic situation gradually improved. Within a few years' time, the British pound sterling regained its full value. A decade later the Bank of Canton converted its capital back to Hong Kong dollars. This brilliant movement by Look Poong-shan increased the bank's capital tremendously. Through this single achievement, which had never been attempted by anyone in the history of banking in the Far East, Poong-shan became an acknowledged authority of modern banking, particularly in international exchange.

Of particular interest to me is that he happened to be my uncle. He and my father were third cousins. I was with the Canton Bank of San Francisco for several years before I went to China. It was in this institution that I gained a good knowledge in banking, particularly in international exchange.

On July 15, 1908, after operating for approximately nine months, the Canton Bank of San Francisco issued its first financial statement. In this time it had become the principal bank for nearly 100,000 Chinese scattered throughout the United States and Mexico. The statement listed I. P. Allen as manager and cashier and showed the following directors, as well as the number of shares held by each: Look Poong-shan, 60; Lew Hing, 40; Look Tim [sic] Eli, 40; Lew Hing Gang, 30; Lee Fay, 20; Tom Yuen, 20; Yee Dan Young, 10; Tang Ching Hing, 10; Ng Hee Wing, 10; Fung Hing, 10; Chun Kew, 10; Hoo Janson, 10; Sei Wah Low, 6; Yee Wah Hen, 6; Loui Sang, 4; Chin Yuen Yee, 2; Lee Chan, 2; Chun Yook Gee, 2.

The files of the California State Banking Department

also show I. P. Allen as manager. Thus, if Look Poong-shan was ever manager, as Luke's article states, he could only have held the title in the early period after the bank was founded, turning responsibility for day-to-day management over to Allen some time in the first nine months of operation. Look Poong-shan was, however, the largest individual stockholder. He also shows up in financial reports as being on the board of directors from 1907 until 1913, after which his name does not appear at all. It can be surmised that he moved to Hong Kong to run the Bank of Canton of Hong Kong and gradually became less involved in the affairs of the Bank of Canton of San Francisco.

Look Tin Eli also served on the bank's board of directors from the beginning until his death in 1919, and he was president of the bank from 1910 to 1919. Although there is no evidence, it is distinctly possible that Look Poong-shan and Look Tin Eli were related in some way, perhaps even brothers; both were born in Mendocino.

It is odd that Luke's article states that Look Poong-shan was the bank's founder, while other sources claim this role for Look Tin Eli. In all of the community's various activities, the name of Look Tin Eli is the only one known. In *Financing an Empire: History of Banking in California*, Ira. B. Cross writes: "The bank owed its origin to the initiative of Look Tin Eli, a member of the local Chinese community. Eli was a man of broad education . . . served on the staff of the International Banking Corporation . . . in 1907 he brought about the organization of the Canton Bank." It is possible that the two men were cofounders of the bank or that Look Poong-shan was the principal investor in the enterprise.

On July 21, 1926, about six years after Look Tin Eli died, the Canton Bank of San Francisco failed and was closed by the state superintendent of banks.

A second Bank of Canton, the Bank of Canton, Ltd., of San Francisco, was chartered on October 11, 1924. It was a branch of a foreign institution and was in no way connected with the original Bank of Canton of San Francisco.

The present Bank of Canton of California was incorporated on April 27, 1937. It was authorized to do commercial and savings business and was licensed and opened for business May 15, 1937. It celebrated its fiftieth year of business in 1987 by issuing a brochure entitled "Fifty Years . . . And Onward!" showing the 1937 and 1987 financial statements. Construction of the nineteen-story Bank of Canton of California building was completed in 1984, and in 1986 the bank had become the twenty-third largest in California.

12   The Cathay Club

Thomas L. Lym, ca. 1919. He served as conductor of the Cathay Club Band for nearly fifty years. Note the cadet uniform. [Photo courtesy of the Cathay Club.]

Promptly at opening time each work day, the Emporium department store on Market Street used to reverberate to the sound of a bugle playing reveille. The bugler was Thomas L. Lym, performing one of his duties as an employee of the Emporium. He was also one of the musicians in the store's concert band, which played regularly under the dome a long time ago; and he was one of the thirteen founders of the Cathay Club Band. Soon after the club was founded, when he was seventeen years old, he was appointed conductor by acclamation— a volunteer post he held for nearly fifty years.

At its peak, the Cathay Club had more than a hundred members, with sixty to seventy-five of them playing in any one event. The band played all over the United States and won numerous prizes and trophies.

One day in 1911 a group of thirteen young boys, aged eleven to sixteen, met near the Chinese Six Companies building on Stockton Street. They had just heard a concert given by the Columbia Park Boys Band, an Italian band from North Beach, which had recently returned from a triumphal tour abroad, and their eyes sparkled as they talked of forming a band of their own. Their names were Edward Dong, Quong Gong, James Hall, Thomas Kwan, Quong Lee, Cheong Yoke Liang, Hugh Kwong Liang, Francis Lym, Frank Lym, Herbert Lym, Thomas Lym, Charles Mar, and Frank Quon. None of them had much experience playing musical instruments.

As the boys eagerly discussed ways of accomplishing their goal, it became clear that they couldn't do it alone; they would need a sponsor. They decided to approach the Chinese Six Companies to ask it to provide instruments and to hire a teacher who would instruct them and mold them into a performing group.

The Six Companies met and discussed the pros and cons of such an action. The boys all attended the Six Companies Chinese Language School, and therefore the Six Companies felt some obligation to help them. Everyone agreed that the band would attract other boys and

The New Cathay Boys' Band (later renamed the Cathay Club Boys Band) in front of the Chinese Six Companies building, 1913. [Photo courtesy of Thomas L. Lym.]

help keep truancy levels down at the Chinese school. Furthermore, after some discussion, the representatives decided that such a band would benefit the Chinatown community, which had not previously known anything but the music of Chinese opera. The band would play American music. The idea was accepted, to the great joy of the thirteen boys.

The young man who had initiated the idea of going to hear the Columbia Park Boys Band was a student at UC Berkeley named Hugh Liang (see Chapter 44). A bit older than the other boys, he had been hired by the Chinese Six Companies to teach the boys from the Chinese Language School how to march, something he had learned through serving in the ROTC at the university. Liang also found the band's first musical director, Mr. Thomas Kennedy, a retired U.S. Navy concertmaster.

The club, the first Chinese band in America, was officially organized on October 9, 1911, with thirteen members. By the following year the boys were giving concerts, and over the years they played throughout the United States.

When Thomas Kennedy retired as conductor a couple of years after the club was formed, Thomas Lym, then only seventeen, succeeded him by acclamation. He held the volunteer post for nearly a half century, until the band stopped playing in 1962. During most of this period, he was also president of the club. Lym's ability and dedication made his name almost synonymous with that of the

"The Conquering Cathayans" march, written by the band's musical director and conductor, Thomas L. Lym, in 1930. [Courtesy of Thomas L. Lym.]

"THE CONQUERING CATHAYANS" MARCH

Conductor

T. L. LYM

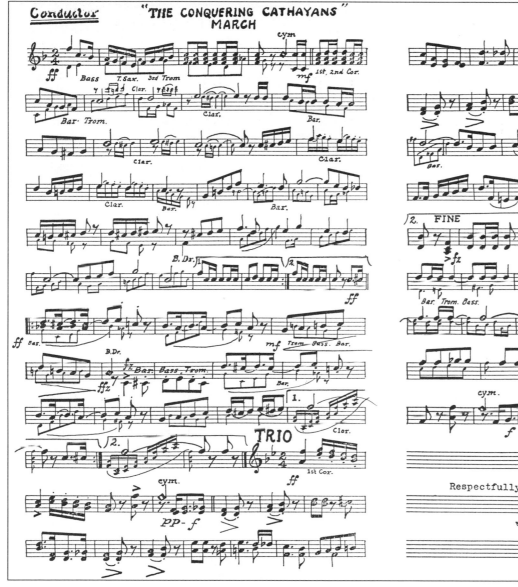

Respectfully dedicated to the members of Cathay Club

Cathay Club. The clubroom quickly became studded with trophies, almost all for first or second prize, including one awarded at the San Francisco Panama Pacific International Exposition in 1915.

In 1919 the band won a contract with the Orpheum Theatre circuit for a five-month, fourteen-city tour from San Francisco to New Orleans. This marked the club's first step into the big time. Wherever they went, they received generous applause. The band was also offered an opportunity to perform abroad, but turned it down reluctantly because some of the boys were anxious to return home to finish their schooling.

In 1928, when Los Angeles celebrated the opening of its new city hall with a parade, the Cathay Club was awarded first prize out of a field of seventy bands. As it marched along the parade route, the band had received its share of applause. When they approached the reviewing stand, however, director Lym, noticing the large number of Hispanics in the audience, cancelled the piece he had originally planned to play before the judges and substituted "La Paloma." The crowd burst into deafening applause, and the judges voted accordingly. In addition to its paid performances, the band gave a free concert once a year, either at the CACA auditorium or at the Chinese Playground after it opened in 1927.

In 1930 Lym wrote a march, the earliest known Western-style piece of band music written by a Chinese-American. The title of the march was "The Conquering Cathayans," and it was played publicly for the first time on May 4, 1931, during a National Music Week concert given by the Cathay Club and the Chinese-American Citizen's Alliance at the CACA hall.

By tradition in Chinatown, most prominent Chinese

Thomas L. Lym, age ninety-one, and wife Lillian, eighty-five, in 1987.

who passed away were accorded elaborate funerals. A typical funeral procession was led by a band, after which came the hearse carrying the departed, followed by the family, relatives, and friends, sometimes numbering in the hundreds, and then conveyances to carry the walking procession to the cemetery. Originally, Caucasian bands were used. It is not clear exactly when the Chinese overcame their reluctance to hire the Cathay Band for funerals, but once they did, the band was hired to play in nearly every funeral procession. This custom continued until 1962, when the Musicians' Union required the Cathay Band to join the union or be picketed. Since the dues each member would have to pay to the union greatly exceeded the small fee received for each performance, the club decided reluctantly not to play for funerals or, for that matter, to make any further public performances. The club continued to meet, however, mainly as a social group to enjoy the friendships begun so long ago.

13 The Fat Ming Cookbook

I have known the Wong family, especially the nine children, since the 1920s. The children's names are Daisy K., Pearl, Rose, Bertha, Beulah, Ann, Laura, Wilson, and Warren. Mr. Wong Foon Chuen passed away in 1924. Wilson, Warren, Ann, and Rose gave me portions of the family history, most of which is centered on the Fat Ming store. Wilson, Warren, and Ann still operate the store today. The eldest daughter, Daisy K. Wong, who passed away in 1970, worked for the Bank of America after graduating from UC Berkeley. Wilson has been a member of the Cathay Club since the 1930s.

The cookbook published by the Fat Ming Company was truly a family enterprise: The entire Wong family moved to Shanghai for two years to supervise the typesetting, which was done in both Chinese and English, and the printing.

In the early 1900s an enterprising and practical man by the name of Wong Foon Chuen started a small stationery store at 903 Dupont Street (now Grant Avenue). It was called the Fat Ming Company. Ever observant of the needs of his Chinese customers, Wong Foon Chuen was particularly interested in the requests of those wishing to learn more about the recipes and menus in American books and magazines. He discovered that people would take such materials to friends who were fluent in both English and Chinese. From these sources, they would develop a file of recipes that enabled an intelligent and enterprising Chinese to learn to cook American food for American consumption.

Learning to cook American-style food was a long process, even for those experienced in Chinese cookery. Some took menial jobs in American restaurants, where they would wash dishes, peel potatoes, and cut vegetables, all the while watching the chefs prepare each dish. After doing this for a period of time, such a worker would feel confident enough to seek employment in a residence or inn where he could further refine his cooking skills. His patience would ultimately pay off in a job as the cook for an affluent family, where he would earn better wages than he could in Chinatown.

Realizing all this, Wong soon decided that a cookbook printed in both Chinese and English would be a profitable enterprise for his store, and he immediately started to hire people who could compile such a book for him. It was a tedious process, but he persisted.

The cookbook was carefully planned. A great deal of research and correspondence was necessary. After the book had been compiled in English, it had to be translated into Chinese— and not just any version of the language (such as classical), but the euphonic tones ordinarily used by the Cantonese, who predominated in the United States. In addition, the words used couldn't be too scholarly; they had to be common ones used by semiliterate Chinese.

Wong Foon Chuen had the book printed in Shanghai, China, and in due time received his first supply of books. The first edition quickly sold out, as did a hastily enlarged second edition.

Wong Foon Chuen and his family in Chinatown, 1910. Left to right: Mrs. Foon Jum Wong, Foon Jum Wong, Foon Yook Wong, Foon Kum Wong, daughter Rose Wong, Shee Jing Wong, daughter Daisy Kim Wong, Ting Gung Wong, daughter Pearl Wong, Wong Foon Chuen, and Mrs. Wong Foon Chuen. Note the slippers worn by Mrs. Foon Jum Wong. They were embroidered Manchu slippers with a "heel" in the arch area, and they required considerable dexterity to walk in. [Photo courtesy of Wilson Wong and Rose Wong Lee.]

In 1917, when the third edition of the book was ready for typesetting, Wong and his wife and family of six children left for Shanghai and laid the job before the Commercial Press, which had also published the first two editions. The family lived in Shanghai for two years, reading and correcting proofs as they were typeset by hand, matching up each recipe in English with the Chinese, and finally approving the material for printing. In December of 1919 they at long last returned to San Francisco. Two more children had been born while they were in Shanghai.

The following excerpt is from the preface to the third and last edition:

> In America, and in the foreign settlements in China, many Chinese are employed as cooks in various hotels, inns and private houses. The constantly increasing wage and the large demand for reliable and efficient Chinese help attracted many young men, especially Cantonese, to this vocation. Hitherto, such young men were compelled to serve long apprenticeships under more or less skillful preceptors in order to learn the preparation of foreign dishes. There were no reliable books to aid the beginner, so that much time was wasted. Not only was this a loss to the employee, but also to the employer. To be sure, there were a few attempts published heretofore, but they have proven inadequate and impractical. Some contained only a few common recipes, while others, more complete, proved valueless to the majority of Cantonese cooks because of the peculiar provincial terms used in the translation.
>
> The present work is the first thorough compilation of recipes of foreign cookery, designed especially for the use of Cantonese. . . . Local and provincial phrases have been eliminated and more universal terms used instead. A large majority of the recipes have been contributed by successful Chinese masters of the art of foreign cooking, others have been contributed by several famous American and European chefs and still others have been culled from reliable foreign authorities on culinary art.

The third edition of the cookbook, printed in the Chinese style, from back to front, contains nearly a thousand pages. Its fifty-page table of contents is divided into several dozen types of food. Included are recipes for wild game, instructions for pickling fruits and vegetables, and even a description of how to make tea (American style, of course). Everything is printed in Chinese as well as in English; an American employer could select the recipes to be served for dinner and then simply point them out to the Chinese cook. The cook would then prepare the meal according to the Chinese wording accompanying each recipe.

In addition, the book provided typical English conversations between an employer and a cook or waiter, with the appropriate Chinese translations. It also gave English and Chinese phrases for use when traveling by train and steamship.

The book undoubtedly enabled many an aspiring chef to reach his goal. All of the cookbooks were sold, but the Fat Ming Company kept one copy of the last edition as a memento.

Right and overleaf: *Three pages from the third edition of the* Chinese and English Cook Book, *published by the Fat Ming Company in 1920. The first edition was published around 1912. This bilingual cookbook was of great practical help both to Chinese cooks and to their employers.*

廚書摘要

食餐肉類

食餐	Meal.	美路
朝餐	Breakfast.	巴力化士
大餐	Dinner.	典拿
晚餐	Supper.	濕巴
小餐	Lunch.	蘭治
牛肉	Beef.	比扶
牛肉耙	Beefsteak.	比扶士的
局牛肉	Roast Beef.	魯士比扶
凍牛肉	Cold Beef.	哥路比扶
鹹牛肉	Corned Beef.	銀比扶
牛仔肉	Veal.	威路
牛肝	Ox Liver.	握士尼化
牛肚	Ox Tripe.	握士杜拉
牛腦	Ox Brain.	握士巴連
羊肉耙	Mutton Chops.	蔑頓揷士
羊脾	Leg of Mutton.	力柯扶蔑頓
羊腰	Sheep Kidney.	什揭利
猪肉	Pork.	撲
猪肉耙	Pork Chops.	撲揷士
猪脚	Pig's Feet.	脬士域
火腿肉	Ham and Eggs.	坎晏咽士
烟肉	Bacon.	壁建
煎魚	Fried Fish.	扶拉啡士
牛乳	Milk.	苗路
牛乳皮	Cream.	咕廉
牛乳油	Butter.	畢打
牛乳餅	Cheese.	矢士
餅食	Pastry.	披士杜利
麵包	Bread.	巴烈
麵包仔	Biscuit.	比士杰
炕黃麵包	Toast.	都士
派	Pie.	派
布剪	Pudding.	布典

飲物類
BEVERAGES

(一) 烹茶之法

如欲烹製好茶，須用滾水。為一人用茶葉一羹、滾水一杯。將茶葉放入壺內，隨將滾水加入，俟二三分鐘便可。飲者如用糖，先將糖放在杯處，然後用茶。亦當奶皮係先放牛奶方料在杯內，其味必佳。

(1) Tea

To make good tea, the water must be boiling. Allow one teaspoon of tea and one cup of boiling water to each person. Put the tea in the teapot, and pour the boiling water over it. Stand two or three minutes before pouring. If sugar is used, put the sugar into the cup before the tea is poured; also, cream, if used, should precede the tea.

(二) 烹咖啡之法

凡人所飲之最要者，是晨早咖啡也。倘所飲之咖啡係凍或淡及所烹製不佳，不樂者必須注意如下。烹製之咖啡者是濃與新鮮及熱者，令飲者精神及歡樂，且可在於朝餐席上暢談以半。常為廚夫者而論，似有難烹好咖啡。但現有新發明之隔壺，如以為烹咖啡之用，斷未有不佳者。

(2) Coffee

The most important beverage to many of us is our morning coffee. If the coffee is weak, cold, and badly made, gloom descends upon the whole family. On the other hand, if the coffee is strong, fresh, and hot, it cheers and braces us up, and even a little conversation may be attempted at the breakfast table. To make good coffee seems to be a very difficult feat for the average cook. I do not know why, for with the modern percolator, one need never go wrong.

以隔壺而烹咖啡之法

凡烹咖啡為一人，以一磨幼之咖啡一羹零半，凍水調一杯。將咖啡放咖啡袋在壺底，放水在壺底。將隔壺載上火，使蒸煮。火滾當要凡新鮮。烹製咖啡過時，飲製當為佳。分鐘使十五咖啡。係烹製必失原咖啡味，須為注意。

Percolator Coffee

Allow one and one-half tablespoons of finely ground coffee and one cup of cold water to each person. Put the coffee in the container and the water in the bottom. Place the percolator on the fire and allow it to come to a boil. Let it percolate for fifteen minutes after it has started to boil, and then the coffee is made. Make the coffee fresh whenever needed, because it loses its flavor when kept.

烹咖啡之常法

凡烹咖啡所用為一人，及水一杯。其數惟要如上。咖啡滾開放入而已，先將雞蛋一只放在壺內，打開殼放入咖啡，中以攪勻在其加水。滾之水以開即烹，火上滾俟放，分鐘之久但不可有。滾太速如否則浮雲之咖啡。將沉濁諸如，至二三分鐘後轉將咖啡。於擺底之壺然後載咖啡，斟飲其味甚佳。

REMEMBER WHEN?

Chinese Fruits

Citrus fruits and sugarcane imported from China were favorite treats among the residents of early Chinatown. Sweet, thin-skinned oranges arrived packed in rattan baskets called *law*. Their color was a deep orange bordering on red, and each was stamped with a trademark in bold, black Chinese characters. Because the best oranges were always the first to be chosen, those at the bottom of the basket were generally sold for a cent less (hence the age-old Chinese saying "bottom of the basket").

Shaddock or pomelo fruit, similar to grapefruit but very sweet and mild, was another favorite import. They could be peeled and eaten just like oranges. They were especially popular during New Year's and were often used to decorate altars. After the fruit had been eaten, the skin was used to perfume bathwater or was dried and used as an herb.

Sugarcane arrived in coffinlike boxes a foot wide and tall and about 5 feet long. The ends of the canes were sealed with red clay to keep them from drying out. About 2 inches in diameter and deep emerald-green in color, they made the modern brownish cane seem sickly in comparison. The fruit dealers would sell them for 5 cents a foot, slicing the bark off the section purchased. The customer would then cut the cane into 3-inch lengths, quarter them, and chew the individual quarters to extract the juice.

Sidewalk fruit and vegetable stand in San Francisco Chinatown, 1926. Leaning against the wall to the right of the stand is a bundle of sugar cane. Next to the sugar cane are two bundles of boards, each with a crosswise piece nailed on to prevent warping. At closing time, after the merchant had tucked all protruding merchandise away, he would slide these boards into grooves in the stand and padlock the end of each groove. [Photo by Gabriel Moulin, courtesy of California Historical Society; FN-28876.]

PART II

The First Generation

*T*he birth dates of the people described on the following pages range from 1840 to 1889. What they had in common (with the exception of Chew Fong Low, who was one of the first Chinese women born in America) was that they came to this country as sojourners and decided to stay. Like countless other first-generation immigrants to America, they gambled everything on the chance for opportunity in an unknown land.

Only a few of the people whose stories I have told here had much luck as miners. Like other Chinese of that era, they worked at all kinds of jobs: as common laborers, gardeners, cooks, merchants, labor contractors, journalists, and ranch hands. Two of them, Lew Hing and Thomas Foon Chew, ended up running successful canneries, years after arriving in this country as young boys with no money and no knowledge of English.

I have also described the lives of my parents, Chinn Wing and Chinn Lee Shee Wing. They did not accumulate great wealth or become important community leaders, but in some ways they were typical of many other families in Chinatown, struggling to give their children a chance in a new America they believed in but did not find for many years.

Developments in China during the first years of the twentieth century were followed closely by all Chinese in America, but especially by the first generation. The weakened Manchu dynasty finally collapsed in 1911, and was replaced in 1912 by the new Republic of China, which abolished

Chew Fong Low (left foreground) with some of her children and their playmates, ca. 1907. Her McDermitt, Nevada, store is in the background. The other adults are probably residents of McDermitt. Chew Fong Low's story is told in Chapter 21. [Photo courtesy of Charlie Low.]

the long pigtail or queue worn by Chinese men to symbolize their subjection by the Manchus. By that time almost every male in Chinatown had already cut off his queue, and women were beginning to give up the painful practice of foot-binding. Early Chinese-American journalists as well as relatives and friends who still lived in China kept everyone in Chinatown informed as events unfolded.

Communication across the Pacific was not one-sided. The Chinese in America raised funds for relief and other purposes in China, and leaders such as Sun Yat-sen found some of their most ardent supporters in the Chinatowns of America. Every Chinese person felt keenly the impact of the political and social changes taking place in China at the time; and China relied on her emigrés in many different ways, ranging from the small cash payments the sojourners sent back for their families to the considerable political and moral support they provided throughout the crises that accompanied the establishment of the Chinese Republic.

Ah Louis was a merchant, adviser, labor contractor, brickmaker, banker, herbalist, and owner of a quicksilver mine. During his long life he also took up seed farming, vegetable growing, race-horse breeding, and dairy farming. But he was most famous for his store and the role he played in the development of San Luis Obispo. The site where he first built his store was declared a state historical monument in 1965. The plaque that can be found there today tells only part of his story:

> *Here in 1874 was established Ah Louis' store. The first Chinese store in the county, it sold general merchandise and herbs and served as a bank, counting house, and post office for the numerous Chinese coolies who dug the eight tunnels through the mountains of Cuesta for the Southern Pacific Railroad, 1884 to 1894.*

I first became interested in Ah Louis (his English name; his Chinese name was Wong On) through Howard Louis, his youngest son. Howard and I became friends in the mid-1920s when he joined the Yoke Choy Club. We were on the club's football and track teams, and "Toby" (Howard's nickname) was the star. Through Toby, I learned about his family and especially his father.

Ah Louis arrived in San Francisco in 1861, at the age of twenty-one. Like many other young Chinese men at the time, he quickly discovered that gold could not just be picked up off the ground. He managed to follow the trail to the gold fields, but met with only modest success. Finally he turned to work as a common laborer, traveling from place to place in search of work. He was also looking for a climate that would help relieve his asthma. In 1870 he found a job as cook in the French Hotel in San Luis Obispo, and decided to stay.

Ah Louis worked hard and became the leader of the Chinese community in San Luis Obispo. His ability to set an example and lead soon came to the attention of John Harford, a leading citizen of the town. So when Harford began planning a narrow gauge railroad leading from Avila to the wharf (called Port Harford then, but now known as Port San Luis), he suggested that Ah Louis contract the labor for constructing the railroad. Ah Louis took his friend's advice, and brought in over 160 Chinese from San Francisco by schooner to work for Harford's San Luis Obispo Railroad Company. After Harford's company merged with the Santa Maria Valley Railroad, he contracted the labor for the construction of that railroad as well.

By 1872 Ah Louis had established his own brickyard. This proved to be a shrewd move. His sturdy bricks were used in many of the buildings put up during the next few years, including the County Courthouse, the Hall of Records, and the Southern Pacific roundhouse terminal. Some of these buildings are still standing today.

In 1874 Ah Louis built his first store, which was also intended to serve as the headquarters for his contracting business. By the following year, his ad began to appear in the *San Luis Obispo Tribune*. It read as follows:

> Ah Luis's [sic] Chinese Labor Agency and Store. Dry goods, Black Teas, Sugars, Rice, and all kinds of Chinese Provisions. Chinese Labor Contracted for on short notice. Satisfaction guaranteed in All Business Transactions. Office on Palm Street, San Luis Obispo.

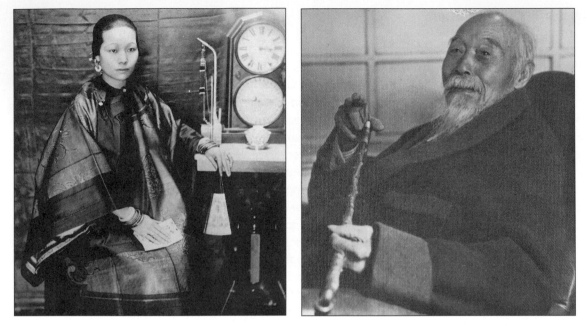

Ah Louis' wife Lee Gon Ying in 1908, and Ah Louis in 1936. They were married in the late 1880s. Both photos were taken in San Luis Obispo. [Photos courtesy of Howard Louis.]

Two years later he was bidding successfully for road-building labor contracts. In 1882 he took on the enormous task of draining large portions of the Laguna area in San Luis Obispo for cultivation after the contract had been abandoned by a previous contractor. In 1885 he had a brand new brick store built on the corner of Palm and Chorro streets. The bricks, of course, came from the kilns in his own brickyard. Ah Louis was acclaimed the "Mayor of Chinatown" by the city in general as well as the Chinese.

In May of 1889, while in San Francisco, Ah Louis met nineteen-year-old Lee Gon Ying, and they were

married after a brief acquaintance. Their first son, Young Louis, was born in 1891, followed over the next several years by Lena, Mae, Walter, George, Helen, Fred, and Howard. Howard was only a year old when their mother died in 1909.

The years passed, and Ah Louis continued to prosper. After he opened his store, his activities increased in scope. Ah Louis' crews went to work for the Southern Pacific Railroad on a difficult section of Cuesta Pasa, the mountainous region through which the railroad had to pass to connect San Francisco and Los Angeles. The railroad reached the eastern side of the pass in 1889, but not until

Above left: *This Pai Lor, a temporary two-story feasting pavilion, was built by Ah Louis in 1933 to accommodate guests he invited from several neighboring villages as well as his own. They were celebrating his return visit to his ancestral home. [Photo courtesy of Howard Louis.]*

Above center: *A Buddhist priest blesses the food before the four-day celebration of Ah Louis' return visit to his ancestral home in 1933. Before the year was out he couldn't wait to return to San Luis Obispo and his family. [Photo courtesy of Howard Louis.]*

Above right: *In 1933 a committee celebrating the completion of the quarter-mile Pearl River bridge in Kwangtung invited the four oldest men on the committee to be the first to walk across the bridge. Ah Louis was the first of the four to do so, and received a silver medal to commemorate the event. From left to right their ages were 90, 90, 92, and 102. Ah Louis is the one with the cane. [Photo courtesy of Howard Louis.]*

Right: *The children of Ah Louis and Lee Gon Ying, 1976. Left to right: Walter, George, Helen, Mae, Young, Lena, Howard, and Fred. They were born between 1891 (Young) and 1908 (Howard). [Photo courtesy of Howard Louis.]*

American-born Taft Fong (left) and Howard Louis were sent back to China in 1932 to acquire a Chinese education. Here they are on holiday, "somewhere in Canton." [Photo courtesy of Howard Louis.]

1894 was it completed over the mountains to San Luis Obispo. On the way, eight tunnels had to be carved with dynamite and hand tools; when one section caved in, it was converted into an open cut. Over two thousand Chinese had worked on the project when railroad service between San Francisco and Los Angeles finally began on March 31, 1891.

In 1933 Ah Louis decided to retire and to live out his days in the little village in China where he was born. He had visited the village twice before, in 1868 and 1886, but this time he thought he would stay. He took along Fred and Howard, his two youngest boys, to accompany him. Upon arriving in the village, he had a two-story *Pai Lor* gate and pavilion built, which was a special feasting quarters for the guests he invited from several neighboring villages as well as his own. The celebration lasted for days, with guests dining in relays.

After the celebration, Ah Louis thought he was ready for his retirement. He was—but not for long. Life went on much as before after the feasting was over. No progress had been made in the villages since his previous visits. Worst of all, he found himself with nothing to do. He had been an active businessman and community leader all his life, and the reality of China in the 1930s began to get to him—and to his sons, who were supposed to be studying Chinese.

Before the year was out, Ah Louis had had enough. He moved to Canton, but everyone there was a stranger to him. He finally had to return to his adopted country—back to his beloved San Luis Obispo. On arrival in San Luis Obispo he was greeted by his family and crowds of townspeople, all very happy to see him again.

Ah Louis took up where he had left off, except that he did manage to take things a bit easier. He turned 93 in 1933, but his counsel was still sought by many, and even in San Francisco his activities were duly reported in the Chinese newspapers. Some people in Chinatown still remember that Wong Bock Yue, who was with the local newspaper *Young China*, was a cousin of Ah Louis' children. And for many years Wong Bock Yue's brother, Wong Bock Dun (Frank Dun), operated the Wing Sun mortuary at 19 Brenham Place (now Walter U. Lum Place) and the China Drayage Company a few doors away.

Ah Louis passed away in December 1936. Friends from far and near came to pay homage to him; the town's schools closed, and the big funeral was broadcast by radio nationwide.

15   Moy Jin Mun

Moy Jin Mun was a man who made friends easily. By the time he passed away at the age of eighty-seven, he was one of the most popular and respected people in Chinatown. His life included several stints as a gold miner and labor contractor as well as a long and successful career as a merchant. As a young man he got to know Mrs. Leland Stanford, whose husband later became one of the Big Four of the Central Pacific Railroad. He spoke English well and was appointed the first official Chinese interpreter for the U.S. District Court in California, which led to friendships with most of the judges in the district. He was also a valued leader in the Chinese community, both within the Chinese Six Companies and in various emergencies related to the tong wars, which he helped end permanently.

In 1848, the year that gold was discovered in California, a second son was born to a schoolteacher and his wife living in the small rural village of Hoy Young On Fun in the Toishan district of Kwangtung province, in South China. To choose a name for his new son, the child's father, following ancient custom, consulted the village elders and the departed spirits of his ancestors, whose names were inscribed in red and gold on the family altar. The name chosen was Jin Mun.

At the time he was born, no one in Moy Jin Mun's village had yet heard of America, or Gum Shan (Golden Mountain), as the Chinese would call it after the first wave of Chinese gold seekers returned to China. But Jin Mun was to follow the call of gold to the New World, where he would play a prominent role in the early history of San Francisco Chinatown.

Jin Mun began his education at an early age. As soon as he was able to talk, his father taught him the Three Character Classic, a 2-inch-thick primer on how to conduct oneself that had been compiled and refined over thousands of years. These moral teachings had a profound influence on Jin Mun; he learned them by heart and they were to serve as his philosophy throughout his life.

News of the California gold rush soon reached Jin Mun's village, and his older brother and one of his paternal uncles, whose names have been lost, decided to join the many Chinese traveling to California to seek their fortunes.

When Jin Mun's uncle returned to the village several years later he was a rich man, and he fired the imaginations of the youths of the village with stories of the fabulous wealth to be found under the ground in America. He was planning to return to California soon, and he asked Jin Mun's father if he could take the twelve-year-old boy along. Jin Mun's father consented.

In August of 1860 Jin Mun and his uncle set sail on a schooner bound for America. He was not to see his parents again for nine years. During the six-and-a-half-month boat trip across the Pacific, Jin Mun and the others on board lived through fierce storms and sighted whales that were as big as the ship. It was a grueling experience, but it was also an adventure for the young boy.

Finally, in the latter part of February, 1861, the ship arrived in San Francisco. Jin Mun disembarked somewhere between Montgomery and Battery streets, where the waterfront was located in those days.

The boy went to live with his cousins, who had been in the country for several years and had prospered. He helped his cousins in their business (the type of business is not known) and strove to become acclimated to his new home. A mission school had already been established in Chinatown, and Jin Mun studied English there for half an hour every Sunday.

In the meantime, Jin Mun's older brother had become a cook for the family of Leland Stanford, Senior, who later became one of the California railroad barons, at his home in Sacramento. When Jin Mun was fifteen his brother decided that he was old enough to earn his keep, and sent for him to come to Sacramento. Jin Mun went to work as a garden boy in the Stanford home. During the three years that he worked for the Stanfords, the boy won the affection of Mrs. Stanford, who later even asked to adopt him. Jin Mun's brother objected to this on the grounds that the racial and social differences between Jin Mun and the Stanford family were simply too great, and so in 1866, after three years, Jin Mun left the Stanford home to join in the search for gold. Before he left, Mrs. Stanford gave him a gold ring with his name engraved on the inside as a remembrance. He treasured the ring and wore it until his death seventy years later.

In those days, thousands of Chinese followed the trails of the white miners, who would often impatiently abandon a gold vein before it was exhausted. The Chinese would painstakingly rework the beds, finding much gold without fear of persecution from the often-hostile miners. Along with some other Chinese, Jin Mun traveled to Moss Platt and began to comb the region for gold. He prospected old claims, finding many flakes of gold that the white miners had left behind.

After doing this for three years, Jin Mun had accumulated what seemed to his young mind a fortune, and he decided to take a trip back to China. Great was the rejoicing several months later when he returned to the village of his birth. He was then twenty-one years old, the age at which young Chinese men traditionally married and assumed their family responsibilities. His parents asked a local matchmaker to find a suitable bride, and he was soon married to a young woman from another village.

A year later Jin Mun returned to America, leaving his wife behind. He went back to the business of reworking old mines, traveling across California and Nevada to do so. As an old man, Jin Mun was fond of telling stories of this period. Once, when he was traveling on a stagecoach, he was held up and robbed of everything of value except for his watch. The robber, examining the timepiece he had just taken from Jin Mun, apparently thought that the black-looking object would be hard to sell, and he placed the watch back in Jin Mun's pocket with a gesture of disdain.

Some of Jin Mun's anecdotes involved the American Indians. Although the white men often encountered hostility from the Indians in the 1870s as they blazed the trail to make way for the railroad, he said that the Indians never molested the Chinese. He thought that their features and the long queues they wore caused the Indians to assume that the Chinese were another Indian tribe. Whatever the reason, the Indians tended to leave the Chinese alone.

Jin Mun's knowledge of English was a valuable asset to him during these years. The railroad companies were in desperate need of laborers to lay tracks throughout the West. When he was not panning for gold, Jin Mun acted as an agent for the railroads, hiring Chinese crews. This proved to be a profitable sideline, and it also brought him the respect of Chinese and whites alike.

This was the era of persecution of the Chinese in California. Sparked by the virulent rhetoric of Denis

Kearney of San Francisco, anti-Chinese sentiment, often resulting in violence against the Chinese, spread rapidly throughout the state and the nation. Late in 1874 Jin Mun was in Truckee, in northern California, when he was caught in an anti-Chinese riot. The crowd had been incited to violence by white labor unions, the members of which were primarily Irishmen who feared that they would lose their jobs to Chinese workers. Not all of the Irish sympathized with the rioters, however. Jin Mun was saved from injury and possible death by an Irish police officer with whom he had become friends. The man let Jin Mun stay at his home until the riots had subsided and it was safe to leave.

Most of the Chinese in the region were not so fortunate. Some 4,000 Chinese were in Truckee and the neighboring mining towns at the time. They were driven out of the area en masse, and wherever they sought refuge they encountered anti-Chinese demonstrations and harsh treatment.

After a few more years of mining for gold and hiring railroad crews, Jin Mun, now fairly wealthy and becoming well known among the Chinese, moved back to San Francisco. He found Chinatown crowded with his countrymen. The days of the gold rush and the building of the railroads were over, and many immigrants returned to San Francisco, where they had begun their American sojourn. From there, many made the trip back to China with their money belts full of Mexican dollars and gold dust. But more than 50,000 remained. In addition, thousands of Cantonese were still arriving from China, traveling 10,000 miles to seek a better life for their families, possible only if they could find gold or a way to earn money to send home.

Jin Mun had come to cherish his new country, and he decided to settle in the United States permanently. In 1881 he made a second trip to China. When he returned, his wife was with him. He opened an import-export store on Dupont Street (now Grant Avenue) and also organized a mining company with several other wealthy Chinese to mine what gold was left in the California gold country. His scrupulous honesty, together with his ability to do business in English, soon made him a highly respected figure in the community. His voice was heard often in the chambers of the Chinese Consolidated Benevolent Association (the Chinese Six Companies).

In 1884 Jin Mun was appointed the first official Chinese interpreter for the U.S. District Court in California. This was a post of great importance to the Chinese, and he became good friends with several of the judges on the court, including Judges Fields, Sawyer, Hoffman, Cooks, and Murasky.

Not long after his appointment to the court Jin Mun's wife, who had borne three sons, died. In time Jin Mun remarried, this time choosing as his wife an American-born woman of the Wong clan. In Chinatown, great feasting and the explosion of countless firecrackers celebrated the marriage of this wealthy merchant to a bride from a large and powerful clan. There was no traditional sedan chair to bring the bride to her new home; a car sumptuously draped in vermilion cloth served in its place.

Jin Mun's fortune and family grew. Chinatown was also growing, becoming a prosperous community. It became a small version of the cities of China, full of people bustling about their daily lives. It was the gay nineties—a time of freedom and plenty throughout San Francisco.

Moy Jin Mun wrapping li shee *for children at New Year's, ca. late 1920s.* *[Photo from the* Chinese Digest, *1936.]*

Even as late as the turn of the century, Jin Mun's knowledge of English was invaluable among the Chinese of his age, and he became a minor political power in Chinatown, gaining many friends among the city officials. Court and treasury officials were numbered among his acquaintances, and he later became a close friend of Mayor James J. Rolph, who was to become governor of California. To Jin Mun's credit, he never misused his influence and was never unfair in any of his dealings. He followed to the letter the Confucian teaching that the superior man is one who puts sincerity and honesty above all other principles in his relations with his fellow man.

At the peak of his success, however, came tragedy.

Everything that Jin Mun owned was destroyed by the fire following the earthquake of 1906. Standing amid the smoldering ruins with his family, he watched the work of half a lifetime crumble into ashes. But Moy Jin Mun was a pioneer. In August of 1906 he set out once more in search of his fortune. He took up mining again, working the gold country of northern California. The pickings were meager, but there was still some gold to be found. Later he took a job as an interpreter at the U.S. Immigration Service office at Angel Island. Jin Mun soon had enough money to establish himself in the import/export business again.

At the same time, Jin Mun had become increasingly active in community affairs. He was constantly being called in as a Six Companies elder to settle legal matters as well as disputes involving the fighting tongs, which were then at the height of their power. The fighting tongs had begun as protective organizations, but by this time they had degenerated into criminal groups. Tong warfare had cropped up in almost every city in the United States with a large Chinese population, threatening the lives of innocent people, hurting business, and giving the Chinese community as a whole a bad reputation.

In 1918, in hopes of putting an end to the violence and criminal activity, a General Peace Association was formed to arbitrate disputes and promote law and order. Jin Mun became an enthusiastic participant in this new movement and, volunteering his services, traveled up and down the coast soliciting contributions for the new organization. It took years of work, but Jin Mun and other association members finally achieved a binding peace in 1924. Since then, no tong wars have occurred.

During one of these campaign trips, he visited San

Luis Obispo, where immigration officers were on a campaign to find Chinese who had entered the country illegally. Jin Mun was accosted by the officers and was asked for his *chak chee*, or immigration certificate. Unfortunately, he didn't have it with him, and so he was detained for hours. Finally, he managed to give the officers the name of a federal judge in San Francisco who would vouch for him. After calling the judge, the officers released Jin Mun in a hurry, with profuse apologies.

Between 1910 and 1920, Jin Mun was one of the most active members of the Chinese community in the state. Representing the General Peace Association, he traveled from one area of tong conflict to another, often at considerable risk to his safety. He continued his mining operations also, and once he was nearly buried in an avalanche at one of his mining camps.

The stock market crash of 1929 once again brought Jin Mun to the brink of financial ruin. Now at the zenith of his life, the proud father of nine sons and four daughters, he saw the wealth he had built up over a quarter of a century vanish. It was a bitter blow, one from which he never recovered. He was eighty-one years old; even a hardy pioneer like Jin Mun could not start again at that age. He went into retirement, and his sons carried on. Even in retirement friends often sought his advice, for he was known as a wise man. Jin Mun died on May 1, 1936.

Lew Hing and Lew Chin Shee

I never knew Lew Hing personally. As a boy I was not considered important enough to talk to important people—and Lew Hing was important! But one day my father took me over to Oakland to visit Lew Hay Gum, who was Lew Hing's brother. Lew Hay Gum took a liking to me, and before I knew it, father told me that I would soon be his godson. Sure enough, Lew Hay Gum became my godfather; but I didn't realize at the time that I had become a distant relation of sorts to a whole bunch of other people I was not to see or visit for many decades.

My father passed away in 1924, and the friendship between the two families waned. I did not learn of the important part that Lew Hing played in the Chinese communities of San Francisco and Oakland until quite recently, when I met Lew Hay Gum's son, Hubert Lew, and his wife Helen unexpectedly in a restaurant. This chapter grew out of our subsequent meetings, and includes much material kindly provided by Jean Moon Liu, Lew Hing's granddaughter.

Lew Hing's family came from a small village made up of the Liao clan in the South China district of Sunning, Toishan, Kwangtung province. Early on, they moved to the city of Canton and had practically no further ties with the village. As early as the mid-1850s, Lew Hing's father had journeyed to San Francisco, where he spent two months, traveling alone and unable to speak English. Finally deciding that this life was not for him, he had returned to Canton.

Lew Hing was the third son in a family of five children, four sons and a daughter. He was born in May of

1858. In 1868 Lew Hing's oldest brother, the first son, came to San Francisco to try his luck. (His name has been lost.) He established a small business on Commercial Street, between Dupont (now Grant Avenue) and Kearny. After two years he decided to return to China to visit his wife and son, and he wrote home to urge his younger brother, Lew Hing, then twelve years of age, to come to America to assist him in his growing business.

Before Lew Hing embarked on his journey, his mother betrothed him to a girl of ten named Chin Shee. Her father was an herbalist, and the family lived on the same street as Lew Hing's family. Although they had grown up in the same neighborhood, the two children had never met, because girls were kept close to home and were not allowed to go to school. Lew Hing was attending school in Hong Kong at the time of his engagement, so he didn't meet his bride-to-be before leaving for San Francisco. The wedding was set for some time in the future.

Lew Hing arrived in San Francisco in 1871. His brother soon left for China, leaving the boy in charge of the business. As his sailing ship neared Japan, however, it became engulfed in a fire that spread so rapidly that the passengers could not escape. The ship sank, and only a few people were saved. Lew Hing's brother was not among them.

For a while Lew Hing, then thirteen years old, tried to carry on his brother's business. He was a bright boy, and after putting in a full day at the store he would hasten to a church mission school in the evening to study English. The burden soon became too much for the young man to handle, however, and he disposed of the store a short time later.

Lew Hing soon found a job in a metal shop helping to make storage containers—work he would do for many years. By 1877 Lew Hing was earning enough to support a family, but he was too busy with his work to return to China to marry Chin Shee, so his mother brought his bride to America. Before Chin Shee left Canton, a wedding ceremony was held for the young couple. Standing in for Lew Hing, in keeping with Chinese custom, was a rooster.

On board the ship, one of the first steamers to make the journey, Lew Hing's mother would not permit Chin Shee to leave her cabin, for fear that she would find another suitor. Chin Shee thus was confined to her tiny cabin throughout the month-long voyage. When they arrived in San Francisco, a small wedding was held, followed by a dinner party attended by a few friends. Lew Hing was twenty and Chin Shee was seventeen at the time of their wedding. Lew Hing's mother returned to China a month later. The couple lived at first on Commercial Street, where, in 1878, their first daughter, Lew Yuet-Yung, was born.

In time Lew Hing's work with metal containers led him to become interested in canning foodstuffs as a way of preserving them. After saving for many years, he was able to establish a small cannery in San Francisco, on the first and second floors of a building on the northeast corner of Sacramento and Stockton streets. The family lived on the third floor of the building.

At first Lew Hing went through a period of trial and error in his canning. Sometimes food would ferment in the tin cans. Finally, after much experimentation, he succeeded in perfecting a method for canning perishables on a large scale, and his cannery went into operation.

Between 1885 and 1902 seven more children, four

sons and three daughters, were born to the family, all on the third floor of the cannery building. Their sixth child, a son named Ming Lew, died in 1900, when he was four. Chin Shee, a tiny woman not more than 4 feet 10 inches tall and weighing about 90 pounds, had had her feet bound when she was a baby, as was the custom in good families, and she did the same with her daughters. She was an accomplished seamstress and was very meticulous in everything she did.

In 1902, when he was in his mid-forties, Lew Hing returned with his family, which by then included his oldest daughter's husband, Quan Yick-Sun, to Canton, intending to settle there permanently. He purchased a large home on a street named Fung Yuan Nam in a wealthy part of town. The house surrounded a courtyard large enough to hold four sedan chairs, the primary means of transportation in those days. There was room for the whole family plus seven or eight servants, and an entire room was set aside for smoking opium, a fashionable pastime in those days.

In Canton, distant relatives of Lew Hing's began to come forward to ask for assistance, and he soon had invested in about ten different businesses—stores selling such items as fabric, china, furniture, and drugs. Of these, the drugstore was the most successful. It was run by a nephew by marriage, P. C. Lau, and featured some of Lew Hing's own medicinal recipes, including one for a pill called *Bit Tak Sin Dan*, said to be good for many ailments.

In 1903, for unknown reasons, Lew Hing decided that they should return to the United States. Three of his children—Quai, a son, and Yuen-Hing and Wai Hing, both daughters—remained behind in Canton to attend school, and they continued to live in the family home. In 1905

Quai came down with an illness known as *Lin Gee Lect*, characterized by high fever and swollen neck glands, and he died. Yuet-Yung, the oldest daughter, and her husband had also stayed in China; they returned to San Francisco in 1907.

Upon returning to San Francisco, Lew Hing bought a house for the family on the south side of Sacramento Street, between Kearny Street and Grant Avenue. In September of 1903, shortly after they moved in, their last child, Ralph, was born.

Wanting to get back into the cannery business, Lew Hing looked around San Francisco Chinatown for a site suitable for a large cannery, but he couldn't find a location large enough for what he had in mind. He finally found what he was looking for in Oakland, at Twelfth and Pine streets, and he established the Pacific Coast Canning Company at this location in 1904. Anticipating a growing business, he purchased two blocks of land. The machinery installed was of the very latest type, geared for mass production. He justified the move to Oakland because he was able to place the cannery next to the railroad tracks for efficient transportation of his canned products. Under his "Buckskin" label, Lew Hing's canned goods were soon being shipped throughout America and Europe.

When more room was needed, he expanded onto his vacant land, building the first concrete building in that part of Oakland. It still stands there today. Although his business was in Oakland, Lew Hing and his family continued to live in San Francisco.

The canned goods produced by the Pacific Coast Canning Company included asparagus, cherries, apricots, peaches, pears, grapes, and tomatoes. The cannery soon required hundreds of employees. Besides the Chinese,

Lew Hay Gum (Lew Hing's brother) and his family, 1923. He worked for years at the Pacific Coast Canning Company in Oakland. Left to right: *Harry, Charlie, mother Wong Shee, Henry, Chuck, father Lew Hay Gum, Hubert, Rose, Shang Fong, King, George, and Kay. [Photo courtesy of Hubert Lew.]*

jobs were found for Portuguese and Italians who lived in the area. By 1911 Lew Hing was the largest employer of Chinese in the area, and his company was one of Oakland's largest businesses. During peak periods, there were as many as 1,000 employees.

Two of Lew Hing's relatives—an older brother and that brother's son—came to Oakland from China to work at the cannery, but it was said that the brother gambled too much for his own good and the nephew caused other problems; eventually Lew Hing had to fire them. Another nephew, the son of Lew Hing's sister, also came to work at the cannery. He married a Caucasian woman who worked there and remained to make his home in the United States. Two of Lew Hing's sons also worked in the cannery. His oldest son, Lew Gin-Gow, served as treasurer of the company, and the youngest child, Ralph Ginn Lew, worked at both the Pacific Coast Canning Company and the West Coast Canning Company, which Lew Hing established years later.

In 1905 Chin Shee left for an extended visit to China with three of her children—Lew Gin-Gow, Rose, and Ralph. It would be her last trip to China. They lived in the family home in Canton with the children who had stayed in China to attend school. While they were abroad, the earthquake and fire of 1906 destroyed their San Francisco home, burying all of their possessions under tons of rubble. Lew Hing, who had remained behind in the United States, moved immediately to Oakland, where he purchased a furnished three-story home on Eighth Street between Alice and Harrison streets (now the site of the recreation room of the Chinese Presbyterian Church). He paid $3,000 cash for the dwelling.

After the earthquake, many Chinese took refuge across the bay in Oakland. Lew Hing arranged to have temporary tents set up on the cannery grounds for housing, and he hired people to cook meals for the refugees during the adjustment period. Many Chinese remained in Oakland, forming a larger nucleus in the growing Oakland Chinatown.

In 1907 Lew Hing's family returned from China, and they all moved into the Oakland house, where they would live for several years. Three of his daughters and their husbands lived on the first floor of the house. Lew Hing, Chin Shee, son Lew Gin-Gow, and his new wife, whom he had married in China, lived on the second floor, and the family servants lived on the third floor.

As Lew Hing's business prospered, he began to look for other investment possibilities. In 1906 he purchased a fruit ranch in Winters, California. Presumably, the fruit produced by the ranch was canned at the Pacific Coast Canning Company. One of Lew Hing's nephews came over from China to help supervise the ranch.

From 1907 to 1912 Lew Hing became involved in several new business ventures. He helped to build the Republic Hotel on the northeast corner of Grant Avenue and Sacramento Street; the building is still standing today. In 1910 he purchased an herb store in Oakland called Hong Yin Tong and two import/export companies, one in San Francisco and one in Canton, that dealt in wholesale Chinese food products. The San Francisco business was called Hop Wo Lung, and its Cantonese counterpart was Hop Wo Cheung. Hop Wo Lung occupied the ground floor of the Republic Hotel. In 1912 Lew Hing, with a partner named Look Yuen Hing, established the first Chinese-owned hotel in Chinatown. Called Mun Ming Lue Kwan, the building was at 858–870 Clay Street, between Grant Avenue and Stockton Street. Today it is known as the Lew Hing Building.

By 1913, 80 percent of the canned goods produced by the Pacific Coast Canning Company were being distributed in Europe, due primarily to the efforts of distributor William Rolph, brother of San Francisco Mayor James Rolph. During World War I Herbert Hoover headed a food rehabilitation program in Belgium for the

Hubert Lew and his wife Helen in 1988.

Europeans. Rolph and the Pacific Coast Canning Company contributed greatly to the success of this program, which was vital to the war effort.

Lew Hing's prominence in the business community grew immensely during this period. In 1913 he became president of the Canton Bank of San Francisco, and from 1915 to 1921 he was chairman of the board of the China Mail Steamship Lines.

A proud moment in Lew Hing's life arrived when a San Francisco women's society chose his daughter, Rose Soon-Hing Lew, to be the first San Francisco Chinatown Queen. This event coincided with the 1915 Panama Pacific International Exposition, which took place in the present Marina district of San Francisco from February 20 to December 4, 1915. The coronation of the queen took place at the Grand Ballroom of the Fairmont Hotel. During her reign, Queen Rose christened two new ships, *China* and *Nanking*, for the China Mail Steamship Line.

From 1916 to 1921 Lew Hing was the largest stockholder in a cotton plantation in Mexicali, Mexico.

Chinese workers were brought from China to Mexicali via San Francisco. A special arrangement with the U.S. government allowed the laborers to land in San Francisco and board trains for Mexicali. Hundreds of Chinese workers came to the plantation in this way. Near the plantation, Lew Hing developed a street several blocks long on which he started Chinese businesses to serve the needs of the workers. Remnants of this small Chinatown exist in Mexicali to this day.

Lew Hing also invested in a cannery on Cannery Row in Monterey, California, and in 1928 he started another cannery in Antioch, California, on the shore of San Pablo Bay. It was called the West Coast Canning Co.

In 1911 the family had moved from their Eighth Street home to a large house on Stow Avenue, on the shore of Oakland's Lake Merritt. Lew Hing wanted his entire family, including his children and their families, to live together under one roof. This arrangement proved unworkable, however, and he ended up purchasing a house for each of his children in the Lake Merritt area. In 1928 he had a smaller house built on Lakeshore Avenue for himself, Chin Shee, and Ralph, who had continued to live with them.

As his wealth grew, Lew Hing became an important contributor to many community projects. He became a benefactor to the Lung Kong Tien Yee Association, the family association for members of the Lew, Quan, Jung, and Chew clans, contributing heavily to a new building for the association, which was completed in 1926. Of all his philanthropic contributions, however, Lew Hing was proudest of his gift of a swimming pool for the new Chinatown YMCA built on Sacramento Street in 1925. In recognition of his generosity, he was asked to participate in the ground-breaking ceremony for the building, an event that he relished. More than sixty years later it is still the only swimming pool in Chinatown, and today men of many different nationalities swim there.

Lew Hing died in Oakland on March 7, 1934, at the age of seventy-six. After his death Chin Shee moved to a smaller home on Clarendon Crescent in Oakland, where she lived with Ralph and his second wife, Dean. Chin Shee died on July 10, 1947, at the age of eighty-seven.

17   Chin Quong, Contractor

Chin Quong's first job in San Francisco, when he arrived from China at the age of sixteen, was as a domestic servant. Sixty years later he had made a million-dollar fortune. His wealth came from a number of sources—his import/export business, affiliations with packing companies in Alaska, investments in land, and many interests in Chinatown, including the old Mandarin Theatre, of which he was a major stockholder. His home at 738 Washington Street is still "headquarters" for his children, who are all well-known members of the community. I got to know them when I was a young man, and it was from them that I learned some of the details of Chin Quong's story.

Chin Quong (also known as Chin Gow and Chin Jeung Weay) was born in 1861 in the Toishan district (formerly Sunning) of Kwangtung province, China. Not much is known about his young boyhood. However, since all of his district had subscribed heavily in sending their young men to seek their fortune in the gold fields of California, it would have been impossible for young Quong not to know about it. And when a few returned with small fortunes, Quong, who was adventurous and full of similar dreams, began planning for his turn.

In 1877, when Quong turned sixteen, he took the long and tedious voyage by sailing ship to California. Upon his arrival in San Francisco, his first job was as a domestic servant, a position he held for several years. But he became restless and yearned for more responsibility. Finally, in 1882, he signed up with a Chinese labor contractor to work in the canneries of the Alaska Packing Company as a salmon cannery worker.

The treacherous sea voyage on his first trip from San Francisco to Alaska was made on a sailing ship. This had always proved hazardous, and shortly thereafter the Alaska Packing Company began providing larger vessels to transport the laborers.

Work at the cannery was highly seasonal, normally lasting from April to August. The hours were long, wages were low, and living conditions were inadequate. But Quong was industrious, dependable, and a hard worker, and he was eventually promoted to foreman.

Quong was ambitious, however, and had still higher goals. He wanted to become an independent labor contractor. Chinese labor for the canneries was supplied by Chinese contractors based in San Francisco, Seattle, Portland, and Vancouver. The contractor would make an agreement with the canning company to do all of the work, from the time the fish were delivered at the wharf until they were ready to be shipped at the end of the season. In return, the owner would pay a certain fixed sum per case of fish and would promise to pack a certain number of cases.

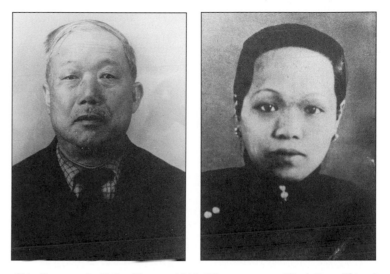

Chin Quong and wife Lee Shee, ca. 1910. [Photos courtesy of Ruth Fong Chinn.]

Quong soon became a highly successful labor contractor. From his own headquarters in San Francisco, he supplied laborers for the Alaska Packing Company. The packing company provided the workers with free round-trip transportation from San Francisco to Alaska and supplied their room and board. Quong obtained the necessary Chinese foodstuffs, which he purchased from local grocery stores. When the local stores cut off his Chinese supplies (it is not known why they did this), he opened his own import store, Quong Kee Jan & Company, and imported Chinese goods from Hong Kong. He thus turned his adversities into profits.

The Chinese played an important role in the Alaska fish canneries. Mr. R. D. Hume was the first salmon cannery owner to use Chinese laborers; he hired them to work in his plant on the Rogue River beginning in 1871. In 1872, when the industrious labor and capability of the Chinese workers at Hume's cannery became known, they were brought into the Columbia River canneries. Before long, Chinese laborers were used almost exclusively in salmon canneries in Washington, Oregon, British Columbia, and Alaska. This went on for many years. Following the passage of the Chinese Exclusion Act in 1882, the number of Chinese cannery workers began to decrease, while the number of workers of other nationalities, such as Japanese and Filipinos, increased.

Chinese workers predominated in the early days of the salmon industry because other laborers were not attracted to the long hours and hard work. The short season also appealed more to the Chinese, who often had difficulty finding steady work, than to other racial groups. John Hittel, in *The Commerce and Industries of the Pacific Coast of North America* (1882), described work at the canneries in the 1870s as follows:

> The salmon, when taken to the cannery, are placed on a long table, where the head, tail, and fins are cut off, and the entrails removed by a few flashing strokes of a large knife, in the hands of an expert Chinese worker, the average time for each of these large fish being less than half a minute. They pass to a tank of fresh water, where other men take off the scales; in a tank of salt water where they are thoroughly washed. A gang knife, with six blades, at one stroke divides the meat into pieces just long enough to fill a can. These sections are cut lengthwise into strips of suitable size, ready for the cans, which are filled by hand or by machine. The top of the can is put on and soldered by hand or by machines. The can is now put into a crate and lowered until the tops of the cans are half an inch under the surface of a pan of boiling water.

The remainder of the cooking and testing process was all done by Chinese.

It is interesting to note that the same year the Chinese Exclusion Act passed and became law, Quong decided to go to Alaska to work for the Alaska Packing Company. Although the Chinese labor force began to dwindle in that year, there were still a number of Chinese working in the canneries. The following table gives an idea of the numbers, up until the mid-1930s.

Number of Cannery Workers in Alaska

	Chinese	Total		Chinese	Total
1907	2,217	6,809	1925	1,242	14,239
1913	2,050	10,891	1931	662	11,081
1919	2,770	16,390	1934	872	13,716

On the eve of Chinese New Year, Quong always advanced wages to prospective workers, who would repay their debt from future earnings.

In 1896, when he was thirty-five, Chin Quong married; his bride, Lee Shee, born in San Francisco, was seventeen. Their marriage was arranged by a matchmaker, and they had fourteen children, seven sons and seven daughters. The sons were Chin Bing Gay, Chin Bing Bun, Chin Bing Soon, Stanley Bing Foo Chinn, Robert Bing Yit Chinn, Vincent Bing Sun Chinn, and Arthur Bing Chun Chinn. The daughters were Chin Hung King, Rose Chin Lee, Chin Hung Mui, May Chin Tong, Ann Chin Jay, Chin Hung Joa, and Minnie Chinn.

In a traditional Chinese family, a son was called a "pillar of the house." Chin Quong was truly that and more. He provided not only for his family in America but also for his family in China. He was deeply devoted to his

Iron Chink
at work in
E. Cannery
Bellingham.

1905

Machine with the derogatory name "Iron Chink," Pacific American Fisheries' Cannery, Bellingham, Washington, 1905. This was one of the early machines designed to replace human labor in processing fish for canning. [Photo courtesy of the San Francisco Maritime Museum.]

mother, whom he had left behind in China. As a dutiful son, he naturally sent money home to care for her. But he went beyond just sending money. On one trip back to China, Chin Quong took a second wife so that she could care for his aged mother. From this marriage he had three children, one son and two daughters.

In the late 1930s, when labor unions organized the cannery workers, Quong's position as a labor contractor for the Alaska Packing Company was terminated, and he retired. He passed away in 1938. His wife, Lee Shee, died in 1953.

Chin Quong lived in San Francisco nearly all his life

after arriving in 1877, except for a brief period after the 1906 earthquake and fire, when he moved to Oakland. One of his sons, Vincent, became a well-known local tennis player, and Vincent's son, also named Vincent, with partner Myron Tong, became Chinese national doubles champion in the late 1960s.

18   Chin Quong, Church Elder, and Yee Shou

Another man by the name of Chin Quong, born in the same year and in the same district as the Chin Quong described in Chapter 17, also emigrated to America as a young boy. In addition to his selfless service for his church and the students to whom he taught English, Chin Quong managed to raise and educate his six children on an income of $50 per month. His and his wife's devotion to their family was typical of many hard-working Chinese who made daily sacrifices to ensure that their children would receive a good education.

I obtained most of the details in this chapter from several long interviews with Chin Quong's daughter-in-law, Helen Tong Chinn, M.D.

Born to a poor family in the village of Sam Gop in the Toishan district of Kwangtung province in 1861, Chin Quong converted to Christianity when he was twelve years old. His inspiration for doing so was the Rev. Dr. C. R. Hager, a missionary in the Kwangtung area. Dr. Hager had been sent to China in the late 1860s or early 1870s by the American Board of Commissioners for Foreign Missions. The first church he set up was in Hong

Kong. Dr. Hager was also the minister who baptized Dr. Sun Yat-sen in China in 1885.

The same year that he became a Christian, Quong left his family to travel with Dr. Hager to America. The journey by clipper ship took several months. Having learned English from Dr. Hager, Quong found upon his arrival that he was one of the few Chinese in America who could speak the language. The young boy helped Dr. Hager in his missionary work at the Chinese Congregational Church, located at 21 Brenham Place (now Walter U. Lum Place), and also did domestic work for various employers, including the Ehrmans, an old San Francisco family.

During his youth, Quong was able to return to China several times. On one of these visits he married a woman named Yee Shou, and he subsequently became the father of two boys, Arthur and Gordon. Because the immigration laws at that time were so strict, Yee Shou and the boys stayed behind in China, where they lived on funds sent home by Quong as well as what they could earn by selling the produce they grew on their own small plot of ground.

Quong continued to support himself and his family in China by doing domestic work and serving as a lay preacher for the Chinese Congregational Church. He was also active in teaching English to newly arrived Chinese immigrants. At that time the churches were the only ones offering English classes to the older Chinese immigrants, most of whom were beyond school age.

Finally, in 1898, when Yee Shou was almost forty years old, Quong was able to bring her and the two boys to the United States. Four more children were born after their arrival—Florence; Alfred, who lived only a year;

William (Bill), born on the day William McKinley was elected, and named accordingly; and Alexander Balfour, who came to be known as Balfour, named for a valued sponsor of the Chinese Congregational Church.

Soon after he arrived in the United States, Arthur began attending the College of Physicians and Surgeons in San Francisco, where he studied dentistry. The year he was to graduate, however, the 1906 earthquake and fire destroyed most of the city. School was interrupted for Arthur; the college never did become reestablished, and he never received his diploma. He had three children: Philip, Silas, and Elaine.

The Chinese Congregational Church was one of the buildings that was destroyed during the fire that followed the earthquake of 1906, leaving the family homeless. They evacuated across the street to Portsmouth Square, and the U.S. military took them from there to the beach, where they lived in empty cable cars for a while. Finally they were brought to Oakland.

After the dust settled, the family returned to San Francisco and lived in a wooden shack on Laguna Street, in the affluent Pacific Heights district. Temporary headquarters had been set up there for the Chinese Congregational Church while a new building was being erected on the Brenham Place site. They lived on Laguna Street for three or four years. Church worship was conducted there, with Quong continuing to serve as a lay preacher and to conduct English classes for many Chinese houseboys. The Laguna Street site actually proved more convenient for many of the pupils than the Chinatown church had been because they worked in the Pacific Heights area and did not have to travel all the way to Chinatown for the nightly classes.

All the young children—Florence, Bill, and Balfour—helped out with the classes. Balfour remembers falling asleep a lot because he was so young and the classes ran so late. There were only a few Chinese women in San Francisco at that time, but Yee Shou taught cooking, sewing, and embroidery to all who were interested.

Once the new church was built, the family moved back to Chinatown and lived in the upper floors of the church building for many years. Finally they were able to save enough money to buy a house on Trenton Street, and they later bought the property at 1037 Washington Street, between Mason and Powell, becoming the first Chinese family to live on that block.

Although Arthur never officially received his diploma and his license to practice dentistry, he worked for many years as a dentist before going into the insurance business. Gordon entered dental school but left after a short time to start his own business making trunks and luggage. He had a store for many years on the southeast corner of Jackson and Stockton streets, where he sold trunks and suitcases. Business was brisk in those days because of all the travel and commerce between the United States and China. Gordon married a San Francisco–born girl, Maude Wong, sister of John and Peter Wong. They had two girls, Lorraine and Doris. Maude passed away within months of Doris' birth. Later, Gordon married Emily, who bore him three more children: Irene, Richard, and Daniel.

Because the family income had risen with the help of Arthur and Gordon (Quong never made more than $50 per month), it was decided that the three youngest children should go to college. Florence became the first Chinese woman to graduate from Mills College, and later

Helen Tong Chinn, M.D., and husband A. Balfour Chinn, M.D., 1974. He was the youngest son of Chin Quong. [Photo courtesy of Balfour Chinn, Jr.]

earned her master's degree at the University of Chicago. She worked for a while for the Chinatown YWCA, and married S. T. Kwan, a brain surgeon, in 1923. They later moved back to Peking, China, where S. T. was one of only two brain surgeons in the country. After World War II they returned to San Francisco, and S. T. resumed practice for a while before retiring. In 1988 Florence was still living in Berkeley, at the age of ninety-one, the only surviving child of Chin Quong.

Bill studied dentistry briefly, but a bad back prevented him from continuing, and he went to work for the U.S. Immigration Service as an interpreter. He later became an insurance agent in Fresno and got married. He passed away some years ago, leaving his widow Lily and a son.

Balfour is believed to have been the first Chinese to enter the UC Medical School in San Francisco, where he finished second in his class. He was the youngest person to have graduated from the school, earning his doctorate

in medicine at the age of twenty-two. While he was in school he received some assistance from the family, but he had to work to make up the rest, and he held jobs as a waiter, fruit picker, assistant to a fur manufacturer, and quarry worker, among others, before receiving his degree. After graduating he did a two-year surgical residency at the Peking Union Medical College in Peking, China, and returned to San Francisco to establish a private practice.

Helen Tong Chinn, Balfour's wife, knew him when he was at the University of California. When she completed medical school, they were married and she joined him in private practice; he had a general practice, and she specialized in obstetrics. In 1935 they left for Peking, Helen for the first time, to put in a stint at Peking Union Medical College before coming back to San Francisco to resume practice.

Helen's father, Tong Bong, was the well-known proprietor of the Sing Fat Company. The Sing Fat Company, which was one of the earliest stores in Chinatown to sell oriental antiques and art goods, occupied the building on the southwest corner of California and Dupont (now Grant Avenue). The company was severely affected by the Depression because of Tong Bong's large overhead and inventory. Tong Bong finally decided to close the business in the early 1930s and return to China. He had contributed generously to his home village before the crash and still had many relatives there.

Tong Bong's letters to his children, who all remained in the United States, were full of descriptions of the primitive conditions in China, and he urged Helen to come and run a hospital that he proposed to build for her. Helen replied that the need for women doctors on the part of Chinese women in America was also great, that she was

Chinn Wing and Chinn Lee Shee Wing

Chin Quong's children in the 1970s. Left to right: *granddaughter Carole, son A. Balfour Chinn, M.D., son-in-law S. T. Kwan, M.D., daughter-in-law Helen Tong Chinn, M.D., daughter Florence Chinn Kwan, granddaughter-in-law Candace Quan Chinn, grandson Balfour Chinn, Jr.* [Photo courtesy of Balfour Chinn, Jr.]

My parents, I believe, were typical of those early Chinese immigrants who saw beyond the curtain of ignorance and bigotry they first found in America and decided to make their home here. Like so many others, they sacrificed a great deal to survive. I am sure there are omissions in their story as I have tried to tell it in this chapter. To begin with, I know little about the period before we were born; or the many little things that they deemed "not worth telling"; or the state of their finances on the many occasions when we asked for money to buy some little knickknack. And there are many other things I don't know.

When Don Canter of the San Francisco News (later the News-Call Bulletin) interviewed mother for his Chinese New Year edition, he called on me to interpret her answers to his questions. Pretty soon, he realized that I was answering him without putting his questions to mother.

"But I know the answers to all your questions, Don," I said.

"Never mind. I want her answers, not yours," he retorted.

So I quit answering for her and repeated his questions. That's when I learned that my mother's first name was Chrysanthemum. I also learned that my father was not the first of our family to come to America. He came in 1877. My maternal grandfather, Lee Man Bien, Chrysanthemum's father, had arrived here with the first wave of Chinese forty-niners. Astonished, I asked her, "But why didn't you tell me all this?"

Her answer: "You never asked!" It was true. And that must be the reason so many of us never realize what a treasury of memories our elders have to share—we never asked!

Despite the inevitable omissions, I feel lucky to be able to offer this much of my parents' history.

sure that her husband Balfour would not be able to leave with her, and that she would therefore be unable to go.

Balfour and Helen had two children: Balfour Jr. and Carole. Balfour Jr. attended local schools and received a bachelor's degree in business from the University of Nevada and a law degree from the University of Michigan. In 1970 he joined the San Francisco City Attorney's office. He is currently managing attorney for the San Jose branch of the USF&G, a national insurance company. Carole is a teacher for the San Francisco Unified School District.

My father, Chinn Wing, was born in 1861 in South China, in the village of Gop Sak in the Toishan district of Kwangtung province. Times were hard for the farmers in the countryside. The land was overworked, the crops poor, and bandits and thieves infested the area. In addition, there were intermittent uprisings and armed conflicts, the most recent of which, between the Pun-ti people who had lived in the area for centuries and the Hakkas, a northern tribe that moved south rather than submit to the Manchus, had left many men dead. It is little wonder that when word of the discovery of gold in California reached Canton in 1848 and quickly spread to Sunning City (now called Toishan City) and from there to the small villages, including Gop Sak, many men left to seek their fortunes in America.

Wing's family had, generations earlier, founded the village of Gop Sak and was thus its leading family. His father was the village elder and was responsible for settling disputes and maintaining law and order. The family was expected to look after the poor, to see that the men of the village found suitable matches, and to help pay for weddings. In 1877, twenty-nine years after the discovery of gold, Wing became one of the first members of the village to travel to California. He was sixteen years old. When he arrived in San Francisco, Wing found that none of the established Chinese mining companies were interested in taking on a young boy. Times had changed since the early days of the Gold Rush; partnerships had been formed years back and were not open to newcomers. Too young and inexperienced to strike out on his own, Wing ended up doing odd jobs for a restaurant where an acquaintance worked. Eventually one of the cooks there taught him the rudiments of cooking, an opportunity he

was grateful for. He knew that he needed to learn a trade, and in exchange he was willing to work for 5 or 10 cents a day and a place to stay. He was anxious to begin earning money so that he could send some home to his family, who had made great sacrifices to pay his way to the United States.

Wing soon discovered that his countrymen usually banded together with their kin in their endeavors. He sought out men from his village area who would show him the ropes and help him get on his feet. But those he found in San Francisco had decided to move north, to Oregon. Leaving his job at the restaurant, Wing began building stone fences for ranchers in the towns surrounding San Francisco, earning 50 cents a day. A hundred years later, local residents would still point with pride to the beautiful stone fences and bridges built without mortar by Chinese laborers during that period, as well as to limestone tunnels in which wine was stored for aging. Wing performed this work for only a short time.

He then joined a crew clearing land for agricultural use along the delta in the San Joaquin Valley. Competition for jobs was becoming increasingly fierce, however, and he decided to follow his kinsmen north. Still quite young, he journeyed to Oregon, determined to help his older relatives in any way he could.

He ended up working in North Bend and Marshfield, two towns a few miles apart in Coos County in southern Oregon. They were clearing land to expand the towns, removing tree stumps, felled trees, and underbrush. Wing did this work and then helped to build the town. He and the other men lived in lean-tos while they were helping to put up the dwellings. The only jobs the Chinese were allowed to do were laborers' jobs, such as fetching and carrying lumber and shingles and assisting the white carpenters as directed. They also dug trenches for water pipes and did minor sewage work.

While he was doing this heavy work, Wing also did whatever he could to refine his cooking skills. Eventually, through a stroke of good fortune, he found a cousin who worked as a cook for a lumber camp in the Coquille-Bandon-Myrtle Point area. He was hired to help in the camp kitchen, a job that meant being out in the forest for weeks at a time. In time he learned the art of cooking the rough fare of the lumberjacks, and after a while he was hired away to be the head cook at another lumber camp. This promotion made him very happy, because it meant that he would be receiving one $20 gold piece as his pay each month, a grand sum to him. He was able to send money steadily to his family in China.

Now that he had a steady job, Wing wanted to return to China, marry, and start a family. A few years after his arrival in America, however, the Chinese Exclusion Act had been passed. If he traveled to China, he knew that he would have to prove to the U.S. immigration authorities that he was a former resident of the country before he would be allowed to return. This was becoming increasingly difficult, and many Chinese men had been denied reentry to the United States.

Finally he hit upon a plan. He decided to buy some land; that, he concluded, would prove his residence. He found and purchased a small piece of property on the outskirts of North Bend. He was not aware, however, that he had to record the deed, and when he tried to sell the parcel at a nice profit a few years later, the deal fell through because he did not have clear title to the land. It reverted to the seller, and he lost his investment. After a while he was able to save enough to buy another piece of land, and this time he was careful to record it.

In the early 1890s, after he had spent nearly fourteen years in California and Oregon, Wing had saved enough to return to China and marry. He took a leave of absence from his job and embarked on the journey. Upon his return to his village, he received a typical greeting: "Aie! So you have returned home, oh Wing daughter!" This gender switch was to fool any evil spirits within hearing distance into thinking that he was a young woman and so to be ignored, rather than a young man, whom they might wish to harm.

His family soon found him a bride, named Lee Suey Ho, from a nearby village. He married her and then, his leave being up, returned to Oregon while his new wife remained behind. In due time he received a letter informing him that a son had been born. After a second trip to China he became the father of a daughter, but his wife became ill shortly thereafter and died. Upon learning of his wife's death, Wing left immediately for China. It was 1896, and he was thirty-five years old.

With two small children to care for, Wing knew that he needed to marry again and that he needed to find someone who was mature enough to be a capable stepmother to his children. He found her in a village of the Lee clan, located a short distance from his own. Her name was Ah Guk, or Chrysanthemum, and she was twenty-seven years of age. They were married in 1897.

Although they had grown up not far from each other, Wing and Chrysanthemum had never met as children. Chrysanthemum's father, Lee Man Bien, had been one of the first to make the journey to California when gold was discovered. Traveling with his five brothers, Man Bien

Like many other early Chinese immigrants, Chinn Wing joined the Equal Rights League of America, which billed itself as "The First Voice of the Americanized Chinese of the United States to the Public." He was given this receipt for a contribution of $2 in 1897.

had arrived in San Francisco early in the fall of 1849, and together they began to search for gold. They did not know anything about prospecting or how to stake a claim, however, and they were unable to find others to learn from. Discouraged, the brothers returned to China, but Man Bien decided to stay in the United States and work as a common laborer. He took what jobs he could find, moving between San Francisco and the Sacramento-Stockton area. He returned to China every five to eight years, eventually marrying there and fathering two daughters, the younger of whom was Chrysanthemum.

Like Wing himself and many other Chinese men, Lee Man Bien returned to America to work after each of his visits, leaving his family behind in China.

Chrysanthemum had been raised according to the traditional values of the time, and these values dictated that the feet of young girls should be bound to keep them small, a practice that had been followed for more than a thousand years. Small feet were thought to be beautiful, and only peasant women had large, unbound feet. Thus, when she was very young, Chrysanthemum's feet had been wrapped in cloth bandages about 2 inches wide and nearly 10 feet long. One end started at the instep and from there was brought over the small toes, forcing them in, toward the big toe, which was not bound. The bandage was then brought tightly around the heel, pressing the toes toward the heel. The wrapping continued in this way until the bandage had been used up. As she grew older, her feet were not only compressed but the small toes became bent under, so that she walked on the knuckles. Women with bound feet could not walk very far without suffering a great deal of pain. The practice of foot binding was abolished in 1912, when the monarchy in China was overthrown and replaced by the Chinese Republic.

Fortunately for Chrysanthemum, her mother had decided to bind her feet in only a token manner. Some girls had their feet bound so tightly that they lost all feeling in them after a while and the feet became deadened stumps. Many girls lost toes as a result of this extreme form of foot binding.

After their wedding Wing again returned to America to work, not to return to China until 1906. Soon after he arrived back in Oregon, he learned that he was a father for the third time; he had a new daughter named Ngon.

In his countless evenings of solitude at the lumber camp, Wing had time to reflect on his situation. For many generations, his family's meager successes in China had been wiped out periodically by reverses, as had the fortunes of most people. They depended entirely on the rice crops from their overworked land, a few miserable acres, for their livelihood. No other source of income was available, unless one hired out as a common laborer, doing "coolie" work, or became apprenticed to a tradesman. But apprenticeships were almost impossible to get unless one was somehow related to a tradesman. China was basically an agricultural country, with no other meaningful industry.

In America, however, he had found something new — opportunity. He had learned a trade, and he could earn more money in one month than he could make from years of toil in China. Although he had to learn new customs and the rudiments of a new language, his new life was far better than the lives of those who had stayed behind in China.

Wing made up his mind. On his next trip to China, he would bring his family back to America and settle here permanently. It took him some time to save enough money for the voyage, particularly since, as the village chief's eldest son, he was expected to send money and goods back to China and to advance the cost of transportation to young men of the village who wanted to come to California. By the latter half of the nineteenth century, a village counted among its assets the number of men it had abroad. Each person was considered a source of income.

By 1906 Wing had saved enough to move his family to Oregon, and he traveled to China to fetch them. Once he arrived, they were not able to return to the United States right away, however. Word had reached China of the earthquake and fire that had devastated San Francisco, the port for ships arriving from China. Their voyage was delayed for nearly a year. Finally, in 1907, Wing, Chrysanthemum, and Ngon embarked for San Francisco aboard the S.S. *Siberia*. (Woon, Wing's first daughter, had married by this time. His son Sing stayed behind because he had no papers.) Chrysanthemum was seven months pregnant with her second child, and the trip, which involved more than a month of rough traveling, must have been very hard on her.

When they arrived in port, Chrysanthemum and the children were detained briefly because of the increasingly strict immigration laws. Chinese women in particular were treated with suspicion because many were brought over and forced into prostitution until they had paid for their passage. Wing was free to come and go, having established himself as a property owner in Oregon. Finally Chrysanthemum and Susie (as her daughter Ngon was now called) were released into the custody of Donaldina Cameron. Known as *Lo Mo*, or Mother, to her large brood of Chinese "daughters," Miss Cameron was the superintendent of a home for rescued Chinese prostitutes, or slave girls, as they were called, and she was a legend in San Francisco Chinatown.

Chrysanthemum and Susie spent two weeks at the mission home run by Miss Cameron while Wing attended to some business. They then left for Marshfield, Oregon, where they rented a house for a brief period while their own house was being built for them on one of Wing's lots on McPherson Street in North Bend. On December 15, 1907, just a few weeks after they arrived in Marshfield, Marian was born.

Two views of the author's home in North Bend, Coos County, Oregon, taken in 1936, a number of years after the family moved to San Francisco. Chinn Wing built two houses in 1908 and also owned commercial property in North Bend. [Photo courtesy of Marian Chinn Loo.]

Soon after Marian's birth, Wing returned to his work as a lumber camp cook. He would come home on his infrequent days off to see his family. The Marshfield house was not in a very good neighborhood, and drunken men often roamed the streets at night. One night, when Wing was away, Chrysanthemum was awakened by loud noises outside, and then someone began banging at the

door. She had Susie crawl through the window to get the police while she, all of 5 feet tall, barricaded the door to keep the men out. Nothing came of it, however. Whoever it was left, and she never knew what they were after.

It must have been a relief to move away from that house to North Bend. There Wing had had two houses built; one was rented and the other was occupied by the family. They had a big yard in which Chrysanthemum planted vegetables and raised chickens. When there were too many vegetables, she would dry some in the sun and pickle others in brine so that they would last all winter. Five more children were born after the move to North Bend: myself, Edna, James, William, and Mae. Chrysanthemum, helped by Susie, did all of the work of the household, from chopping firewood to the most delicate embroidery. She learned to use a sewing machine and began to make clothes for the family.

Her stepson Sing had managed to come to the United States, using papers with the name Sam Soo Hoo. However, he soon left to make his own way, and was later killed in action in France during the last days of World War I. Susie also left after a few years, marrying a hop farmer named Ngon Dy Foon who lived near Aurora, Oregon. With Wing away for weeks at a time, Chrysanthemum had to be both father and mother to the smaller children.

Only a handful of Chinese lived in North Bend. An elderly Chinese couple rented the smaller residence behind the Chinn house, half a dozen men ran a laundry nearby, and the Chan Jing-hing family ran a small grocery on the other side of town. There was thus no Chinese community for Chrysanthemum to rely on, and she had to communicate with the American townspeople as best she could, mostly through Marian, who spoke some English. Although she did not speak English, Chrysanthemum earned the respect of the neighbors. North Bend was hit hard by the influenza epidemic of 1918, and the entire family was stricken, including Chrysanthemum. Wing was summoned home to care for them. A kind neighbor across the street, Mrs. Charles King, made pots of soup during the family's illness. She would leave the pot near a window, knock on the window to let them know it was there, and hastily retreat to avoid the disease.

Chrysanthemum was able to command respect from the neighborhood children as well. Once, when we were being beaten up by some older boys, she heard our cries, ran over, and from an adjoining hillside called out sternly to the youthful tormentors, "No! No!" The boys stopped at once, saying, "Yes ma'am, we were only teasing."

For years after she moved to the United States, Chrysanthemum continued to bind her feet, as she had done since she was a child. Walking was difficult for her, however, and after James was born in 1913 she decided to begin the long and painful process of gradually loosening the bindings and massaging her feet to allow them to regain some feeling. She was forty-three years old. Bound feet were only a hindrance to her in this country, she reasoned, and all of her neighbors had large feet. Because her feet had not been wrapped as tightly as they might have been, she still had some feeling in her toes. Her feet would never return to a completely normal shape, and she would never wear a shoe larger than size 4, but eventually she was able to walk with very little pain.

Wing was pleased to see his children growing up knowing the English language and American customs, but he also wanted them to retain some of the culture and language of the motherland. There was still much discrimination against the Chinese in the West, and many feared that if things became worse they might be forced to return to China. If that happened, he thought, his children would certainly be at a loss because they would not know the language well and would not even know about Chinese customs and culture. In addition, China had become a republic in 1912 after being ruled by monarchs for thousands of years, and its future looked bright. Wing wondered whether there would be a place for his children to help build a revitalized China. He did not want them to be strangers in their own homeland. Wing was not the only one who felt this way. All of the Chinese of any substance wanted their children to learn Chinese, to speak it and, if possible, to read and write it so that they might be able to make a living in China if they had to return there.

These concerns prompted Wing to ask the elderly man who lived behind our house and who had been well educated in China to teach the children the rudiments of the Chinese language. The older children began studying Chinese with him after school for two hours every day. It wasn't easy. We had become used to speaking English away from home.

In 1919 Wing decided to move the family to San Francisco. It was a big decision. He had a good job in Oregon, and he was not sure how he would earn a living in San Francisco. Further, he would have to leave behind the bulk of his assets—the property that he owned. But in North Bend he felt isolated from his countrymen, and despite the after-school Chinese lessons, his children were losing touch with their language and heritage.

Wing wound up his affairs in Oregon, entrusting his property, which consisted of four houses and a commercial building that he rented out, to a real estate agent to manage for him. The family left North Bend in 1919 by ship for San Francisco—the Mecca in the United States for Chinese seeking rapport with their countrymen. The weather was very rough during the trip, and waves pounded the small coastal vessel. Nearly everyone was seasick, including some of the crew. I was the only one to avoid getting sick, and I was kept busy running all over the ship, tending to my family and others.

Wing had asked clansmen in San Francisco to find the family a place to live. Housing in Chinatown was very tight, but that was the only area where we could live. Landlords outside Chinatown would not rent to us. After much searching, the only place that could be found was a storefront on the ground floor of a small three-story building at 24 Spofford Alley. Wing arranged to rent it, planning to look for better accommodations as soon as he was able. He partitioned the large back room of the store into three bedrooms, divided only by 8-foot-high wooden partitions, with curtains serving as doors, leaving a long hallway the rear section of which served as bathroom and kitchen. The storefront became the family living room. Wing and Chrysanthemum occupied the back room, the girls used the middle room, and the boys had the front room, next to the storefront.

Wing never regretted moving to San Francisco. His children were enrolled in both public and Chinese schools. And Chrysanthemum was happy to be among Chinese women, many of whom would be her lifelong friends. Just about the only thing she sorely missed was her garden.

Wing found a job as a cook for the Southern Pacific Railroad, feeding the maintenance crews as they traveled along the tracks making repairs. His kitchen was an old railroad boxcar with a makeshift kitchen at one end and a few tables at the other, where a dozen or so men had breakfast, lunch, and dinner. This was a rough job, and it kept Wing constantly on the go. He was rarely home. Eventually he found the work too strenuous, and he quit.

Wing soon found work as a cook, and after a while had saved enough to open his own restaurant on the edge of Chinatown at 653 Clay Street, just below Kearny. It was not profitable, however, perhaps because it served only American food, and Wing closed it a year later. He then puttered around in Chinatown for a while, working as a relief cook for friends or relatives who wanted to visit their loved ones in China.

One of the reasons that Wing had to work so hard was that besides having to provide for his family, he felt it was his duty to send some money back to his destitute relatives in his village in China. Nearly all of the young men whose passage he had paid had become dazzled by the glitter of the fast life and soon forgot their obligations to the folks at home. As the "elder" in America to these young fellows, Wing was burdened with the moral obligation of keeping an eye on them. Letters from their parents were always directed to Wing. In them, the families asked about their sons, and they always requested money. He would send each family a few dollars occasionally, telling them that it was from their sons. He dunned the men for the money when he could find them, but he never got anywhere. This was a great disappointment to both Wing and Chrysanthemum.

Chrysanthemum's influence with Wing was great. The two never quarreled, and he always sought her advice in matters concerning the family and its future. Her calm, reasoned mind helped Wing over many a crisis. For example, at one time Wing's friends wanted him to join the Triads, or Free Masons, a Chinese organization that did some good for the community but that also tended to become embroiled in factional controversies. Chrysanthemum was adamantly against Wing's joining, and he heeded her objections.

In 1924 Wing became ill, and after several months he died. The doctors said it was heart trouble. I had been sent to school in China and had been there only a few months when I learned of his death; I left immediately for home.

While Wing was alive, Chrysanthemum had earned extra money by taking in mending and alterations, but now she was forced to look for full-time work. She found a job in a basket factory on Merchant Street below Sansome that employed many Chinese women. The work involved making clusters of clay fruit and adorning bamboo baskets from China with them. The clay shapes were then hand-painted in the appropriate colors. She and her friend Yung Moo would walk to work together every day, rain or shine. Yung Moo was a tall, friendly woman, a little younger than Chrysanthemum, whom she called "godmother." She and the short (5-foot), slender Chrysanthemum were often called "Mutt and Jeff," after an old-time cartoon pair of similar stature.

When she was at home, Chrysanthemum and the girls would crochet net bags called *mong oy* out of light cord and sell them to Chinese laundries. The bags were used to hold people's clothes together when they were washed, as a way of keeping each customer's laundry separate.

Chrysanthemum was eventually made forelady of the factory. Her daughters Marian and Mae helped out after school in the factory during busy times, working for 15 cents an hour. The owner, a tall, thin, hawklike man named Lee Gok Yew, promised Chrysanthemum an extra bonus if the Christmas orders exceeded their expectations. She and the women working under her put in many long hours over that season, with only a short snack for lunch. Although the factory prospered, Chrysanthemum never received her bonus. The owner told her that he was expanding the business and didn't have any extra money. She was very disappointed and eventually left that job.

All this time the family lived in the storefront on Spofford Alley. After leaving the basket factory, Chrysanthemum became the janitor and manager of the building where we lived. There were two stores on the ground floor and eight or nine tiny rented rooms on the upper two floors, and she would clean the stairs and hallways on Sundays and collect rent once a month. In return for this work the family lived rent-free, and Chrysanthemum was also paid a few dollars per month. Collecting the rent was not always an easy job. Sometimes tenants would disappear owing several months' back rent, and she would then have to make up the difference herself. When she told one tenant, a member of one of the tongs, that the rent was going up a dollar per month, he refused to pay it and said, "A dollar couldn't buy enough poison to kill someone." She was furious but was not able to collect the extra money.

Some of the people who drifted in and out of the building and neighborhood were less than admirable. For example, Oscar, who lived in the neighboring storefront, was a gambler. Hong Gor, a clean-cut, well-dressed young man in the neighborhood turned out to be a contract hit man for one of the tongs. Rumor had it that he eventually went mad with remorse and jumped into the bay.

Chinn Lee Shee Wing (at far end of table) working in the basket factory, 1925. Workers in the factory, located on Montgomery near Pacific Street, made flowers, fruits, and leaves of clay, glued them onto spray-painted baskets from China, and then hand-painted the clay objects in suitable colors. Chinn was forelady of about a dozen women, who were seated at a distance from one another to diffuse the paint fumes.

Chrysanthemum managed to raise honest and upstanding children despite their surroundings, however.

On Sundays Chrysanthemum and Marian would do the family laundry in the big galvanized tub that doubled as a bathtub. They heated pots of water on the gas burners and, stationing themselves with washboards on opposite sides of the tub, scrubbed the clothes up and down. After rinsing the clothes in more hot water, they used a pulley on the wall to lower the clothesline from the ceiling. Once they had hung the wash, they would haul the rope up again so that the clothes dangled near the ceiling to dry.

Always industrious, Chrysanthemum also began to make homemade rice wine for her friends. She set up a small still and labored over it patiently, watching the wine slowly drip into the jug. She couldn't charge her friends much for the wine, so eventually she stopped making it.

For a while after Wing died, rent money for the property in Oregon came in regularly and was an important source of income for the family. Gradually, however, letters from the real estate agent arrived instead, complaining about vacancies and tenants who wouldn't pay their rent. Eventually, after he found out that Wing had passed away, even these stopped coming, and Chrysanthemum received no response to her letters asking about the status of the property. She later discovered that the property had been sold, that it had all been lost. It isn't clear how this could have happened; it is possible that Wing had to give the real estate agent power of attorney, which he took advantage of for his own profit.

One by one Chrysanthemum's children left home, married, and started families. She became the matriarch of the Chinn and Lee clans, giving freely of her wisdom and counsel to all who asked. In 1937, when my wife Daisy and I moved to a larger home in San Francisco, she left Spofford Alley and came to live with us, and she moved with us to San Mateo in 1942, shortly after Pearl Harbor. There, despite her more than seventy years, she took tremendous pleasure in transforming a wild, unfenced backyard into a huge victory garden and in supervising the building of a chicken shack (allowable during the war years, when meat was rationed). Everything grew for her; she had a remarkable green thumb, and she greatly enjoyed having the family come down from the city to reap the benefits of her labor.

After living with us for eighteen years, she returned to San Francisco in 1955 and moved in with James. Although she was eighty-four by then, she still enjoyed puttering around the house, cooking and washing, and sewing her own dresses.

Finally, at the age of eighty-nine, Chrysanthemum decided that it was time for her to become a citizen, since her family was nearly all in America. She studied hard to learn about the American system of government and, although she had never learned to read and write, in Chinese or English, she insisted upon learning to write her own name in English. At her naturalization examination, with an interpreter translating for her, she was asked, among other things, the name of the mayor of San Francisco. Stuck on the pronunciation for a moment, she finally blurted out, "The milkman!" referring to Mayor George Christopher, who owned a dairy company.

She passed the examination and in due time received a notice asking her to appear before a federal judge for the swearing-in ceremony. James took her to the Federal Building, where a large crowd had assembled for the cere-

Chinn Wing (1861–1924) in 1919; and Mrs. Chinn Lee Shee Wing (1871–1969) in 1958. [Photo by Kem Lee.]

mony. Suddenly James remembered the notification letter and, thinking that it might be required to identify those being sworn in, he seated Chrysanthemum in a chair in the waiting room, admonishing her, "Don't move a step until I come back." Hurriedly he dashed home to get the letter. When he returned, the waiting room was empty. In a near panic, he asked someone where the ceremony was to take place and was directed to a certain courtroom. There he found the assemblage, hands raised, being sworn in. In the group was Chrysanthemum, going through the ceremony with all the solemnity of the others. After it was over, when James was able to get to her, he scolded, "Why didn't you wait for me, as I told you? It's dangerous for you to go around in a strange building by yourself!" She replied, "Well, everyone was directed to go to this courtroom to be sworn in, and I didn't want to be left out, so I joined them."

Three years later, in 1962, she was invited to the official opening of Chinatown's Portsmouth Square Garage, and found herself, as a community "elder," riding into the garage at its ribbon-cutting ceremony in a motorized rickshaw. By her side, sharing her rickshaw, was her milkman, the mayor of San Francisco. By nature a shy, retiring person, she nevertheless enjoyed this particular incident.

In her last dozen or so years, Chrysanthemum admitted to being a self-converted Christian. After seeing most of her children embracing the faith and finding in her later years greater time for meditation, she declared to herself that she would become a Christian in her own mind. Thereafter, unbeknownst to most of the family, she often said her prayers to "Our Father, who art in Heaven. . . ." She had not been to more than half a dozen church services in her life.

Now in her nineties, Chrysanthemum was still alert and sharp mentally, but the years had taken their toll on her 86-pound frame. Near the end of May 1966, after a lifetime without complaint, she was diagnosed as having an intestinal blockage. Surgery would be necessary. She refused the operation, however, saying that she had had a full and happy life, that her children were all settled and that her job was done. Her health declined rapidly until finally her doctor, Dr. Frank Choy, said she had only three or four days to live. The children, grandchildren, and great-grandchildren were one by one asked in to say good-bye to her. She blessed each one and then gathered them all together and said, "To you all, I admonish you to act uprightly. Do not let anyone look down on you."

It wasn't her time to go, however. After suffering intensely, at times barely conscious, Chrysanthemum finally consented to the operation. She weighed less than 70 pounds. Within a week of the surgery, she was bright-eyed and smiling; she was released from the hospital on July 2, 1966, and went to live with Edna.

Chrysanthemum continued to be active, crocheting afghans for "the children" and riding into the suburbs to visit them on weekends when the weather was good. On October 2, 1966, she joined city and state officials in cutting the ribbon to dedicate the headquarters and museum of the Chinese Historical Society of America in San Francisco, which I had helped to found.

In May of 1969, although she was failing, Chrysanthemum participated in another ceremony that meant a great deal to her. A bronze plaque was unveiled at the Chinese Historical Society of America commemorating the centennial of the transcontinental railroad and honoring the countless Chinese laborers who had built it. She and other VIPs were photographed holding the plaque. This was the last of her community services. Later that year she was diagnosed as having cancer of the stomach and chest. Rather than place her in a nursing home, her children rented an apartment for her on Mason Street and hired a companion to care for her. She passed away at the age of ninety-seven on the morning of July 11, 1969, and was buried at Olivet Memorial Park in Colma, in the small family plot.

20 Ng Poon Chew

"The best known, most honored, and most brilliant Chinese in America." —Richard Dillon

Ng Poon Chew, lecturer, journalist, statesman, and editor of the first Chinese daily newspaper in America, was born on March 14, 1866, in Kwangtung province, China. Chew grew up under the tutelage of a Taoist monk. From his tutor, he gained a taste for education and culture that would serve him well later in the United States. His grandmother fervently hoped that her grandson would someday follow in his tutor's footsteps and enter the priesthood. But the idea of becoming a monk didn't appeal to young Chew; he was more interested in adventure, and he became fascinated with his fellow villagers' stories about the wealth of Gum Shan, or "Golden Mountain," as they called California.

In 1879, while young Chew was still a student, his uncle returned from a voyage to the Golden Mountain, bringing with him eight sacks of Mexican dollars, with a hundred dollars in each sack. The young nephew was duly impressed. Less than two years later, in 1881, Chew himself made the trip to California under the care of a relative. He was fifteen years old. When he arrived, only a year before the passage of the Chinese Exclusion Act, Chew found that the Gold Rush was long past. Instead, like hundreds of other young Chinese boys of the time, he earned his living by working on a ranch. He was hired to work on a ranch in San Jose owned by a Mrs. Travis, a Christian woman. Unlike many other boys, however, young Chew attended public school in San Jose at the same time.

Many of Chew's admirers later praised how "Americanized" the man was. As an adult, his near-perfect English and "faultless and immaculate" dress would always be noted in descriptions of his lectures. This receptiveness to the American way of life was evident in Chew even when he was still a teenager. At a time when many Chinese immigrants were extremely reluctant to replace their old traditions with this new culture, Chew went so far as to cut off his queue, an action that earned him the nickname "Fan Kwei" (foreign devil) Chew.

In 1882 Chew openly gave up Taoism and converted to Christianity, and in 1889 he entered the San Francisco Theological Seminary. Instead of becoming a Taoist priest, as his grandmother had hoped, Chew graduated from the seminary in 1892 and became pastor of the Presbyterian Church of Chinatown.

Chew played a triple role as the church's pastor, organist, and janitor, but despite this heavy work load he found the time to marry. On May 4, 1892, in his first year at the Presbyterian Church of Chinatown, Chew married Chun Fah, or Spring Flower, also of San Francisco. Over the next few years, the couple would have four daughters and one son: Mansie, Effie, Rose, Edward, and Caroline. Each received an excellent education, a rarity for young Chinese-Americans of that era.

After four years at the Presbyterian Church Chew began to feel restricted by the limitations of the Christian ministry, and he began to look for a wider field of service. He realized that the Asian community lacked a strong Chinese newspaper, and with the financial help of a few friends he established a weekly newspaper, the *Wah Mei Sun Bo* (*Chinese-American Morning Paper*), in Los Angeles in 1898.

Chew's weekly survived for more than a year as the first Chinese newspaper to be published outside of San Francisco, despite cynics who predicted that "even if there were a Chinese newspaper, nobody would read it." Its two most successful predecessors, Loo Kum Shu's *Oriental Daily News* and San Francisco's politically powerful *Mon Hing Yat Bo* (the oldest Chinese newspaper in the United States, which later became the *Chinese World*), were also pioneers in Chinese-American journalism, but it was Chew's skills as an editor and his flamboyant personality that earned him the reputation of being the father of Chinese journalism on the Pacific Coast.

Despite Chew's efforts, the Los Angeles of 1898 was not yet developed enough to support a Chinese newspaper. Thus, in 1900, due in part to the requests of a number of rich Chinese merchants, Chew moved north to San Francisco and established the *Chung Sai Yat Bo* (*Chinese Western Daily*). America's first Chinese daily newspaper, it featured Chew as managing editor and boasted a well-known professor of Chinese literature from UC Berkeley, John Fryer, as a member of its editorial staff.

The *Chung Sai Yat Bo* ran continuously for years, stopping its printing only once, during the week following the great earthquake and fire of 1906.

Ng Poon Chew's name and his newspaper were soon well known even beyond California's Chinese communities. In China during this period, freedom of the press was severely limited under the country's monarchical rule, and so both China's educated classes and its revolutionaries also became readers of Chew's newspaper.

As managing editor, Chew began to make a name for himself outside of the Chinese community as well. More and more often he was asked to speak to American groups as well as to Chinese, and he soon became known as an expert on the Chinese immigration and exclusion question. In 1905 he collaborated with Patrick J. Healy on a book entitled *A Statement for Noninclusion*, but almost every copy of the book was destroyed in the 1906 earthquake and fire. In 1908 he wrote a pamphlet called "The Treatment of the Exempt Classes of Chinese in the United States." "The exclusion law," Chew wrote, "has been carried out with such vigor that it has almost become an extermination law. The Chinese population in the United States has been reduced from 150,000 in 1880 to 65,000 at the present time."

Chew used his writings and his lectures to attempt to increase understanding between the Chinese and Caucasians. These efforts were reflected in his service as an adviser to the Chinese consul general during the years between 1906 and the eve of World War I and led to his appointment in 1913 as vice-consul for China in San Francisco.

As Chew's reputation as a speaker grew more and more widespread, he became a leading lecturer on the Chautauqua and Lyceum circuits. (These were popular organizations that fostered adult education through instruction, lectures, and entertainment in the early 1900s.) His "remarkable mastery of the spoken English language, his earnest and direct appeal, and his keen and ever-ready wit," as Dr. Rockwell Hunt wrote in *California's Stately Hall of Fame*, charmed American audiences across the country. Billed as the "Chinese Mark Twain" and as the "Chinese Horace Greeley," Chew soon became the Chautauqua institution's highest-paid lecturer, speaking on subjects ranging anywhere from Chinese "flappers" to America's international relations. Although he often appealed to audiences because of his "Americanized" appearance, he used his appeal to encourage better Chinese-American relations. In one lecture he exclaimed, "The complexion is not the man . . . a Chinese person is a human being, after all, and it has been found that all blood is red."

In 1913 the University of Pittsburgh honored Chew by conferring upon him the degree of doctor of letters. He had truly become one of America's most outstanding Chinese-Americans. His interests and expertise extended to a variety of subjects. He was president of the Chung Sai Yat Bo Publishing Company and was a director of the powerful China Mail Steamship Company. He participated in a number of civic and religious organizations, including the American Academy of Political and Social Science, the American Economic Association, and San Francisco's Commonwealth Club, and he was even a thirty-second-degree Mason.

After Chew's death in 1931, at the age of 65, the *Chinese Digest* remembered him as the man who "has done more than any other single individual of his generation in bringing about better mutual understanding between the Chinese and American people." The "most brilliant Chinese in America" left his mark as a pastor, journalist, lecturer, and diplomat both within and outside of the Chinese-American community.

Dr. Chew had provided his children with the best education possible. Mansie became manager of his newspaper, the *Chung Sai Yat Bo*. Effie became the first Chinese teacher in the Oakland public school system. Rose, born in Los Angeles, graduated from UC Berkeley and also studied at Columbia University. She worked for the International Institute in San Francisco as a Chinese-

Ng Poon Chew, ca. 1920. [Photo from the Chinese Digest.*]*

speaking caseworker and was a consultant on immigration matters from the institute's inception in 1934. Edward was in his third year at UC Berkeley when he enlisted in the U.S. Coast Artillery during World War I. He was the first Chinese to receive a commission in the U.S. Army. After the war he returned to college and completed his civil engineering degree. He was employed by the City of Oakland, where he remained until he retired. Edward passed away in the early 1980s. He and his wife, Jeanette, had two sons. Caroline, the youngest member of Dr. Chew's family, became a well-known dancer.

21   Chew Fong Low

Only a small number of Chinese women were born in the United States before 1870, and little is known of them. Chew Fong Low, a native daughter, is one of the few whose history is known. With no education in either Chinese or English, this remarkable woman raised a large family, managed a huge general merchandise store, and helped improve living conditions in San Francisco Chinatown.

Chew Fong was born in San Francisco in 1869, on Commercial Street. Her father, Chew Yick Foon, had come to America in the first wave of Chinese immigration. He was a prominent businessman and community leader.

When she was only sixteen years old, Chew Fong was married to Jim H. Low, a merchant from Nevada. Jim had been born in China in 1846 in the Toishan district of Kwangtung province, and he had been brought to San Francisco by a male relative in 1849, when he was three years old. He grew up in the city, leaving when he was in his late teens.

For a while Jim drifted from town to town, working when he could. Eventually he found a job with the Central Pacific Railroad, which was building the western end of the first transcontinental railroad. When the rails met up with those of the Union Pacific at Promontory Point, Utah, Jim and the rest of the workers were laid off, and Jim began to make his way back to California. Passing through Nevada, however, he decided that the wild country of the Nevada territory appealed to him, and he used his savings, hoarded over many years, to start a small trading post near Winnemucca. His customers were

hunters, trappers, Paiute Indians from a nearby reservation, and a few outlaws. Jim became a trusted and steady source of supplies for these people. They treated him well, and he began to make a good living.

After a few years Jim decided that he was ready to marry, so he traveled to San Francisco and found a reliable go-between to help him find a suitable wife. Because there were so few Chinese women, he was very lucky to find Chew Fong. Although she was very young, she was from a good family and she was not afraid of hard work.

Chew Fong and Jim Low were married in 1885. As was the custom, they spent a few days feasting and visiting with relatives before leaving for Nevada. Returning to Winnemucca, they opened a general merchandise store, an expanded version of Jim's trading post. Jim would load up a large wagon, hitch up a team of horses, and drive a regular route over a wide territory while Chew Fong took care of the store.

Every two weeks their team of horses would travel the eighty-mile round trip to the railroad station and return loaded with merchandise ordered from San Francisco. Mail was delivered only once a week. Chew Fong and her husband were practically exiles from their friends in San Francisco; they managed to visit their former home only a few times in the years they ran the store.

These were times of widespread harassment of and discrimination against Chinese in the West, but Jim and Chew Fong were never bothered. They were scrupulously honest in their dealings, and the far-flung residents of the area had come to rely on them as their sole source of supply. A posse would have combed the Rocky Mountains if anyone had dared to harm them. The Paiute Indians for miles around always traded at the store, and they called

Jim Low & Co., the general merchandise, hay, and grain store operated by Jim and Chew Fong Low in McDermitt, Nevada, ca. 1890. Low's wagon and team of horses is in the foreground. [Photo courtesy of Charlie Low.]

Chew Fong "Bee Duh," meaning "Auntie," as a token of their regard.

Between 1885 and 1901, Jim and Chew Fong had seven children: John, Fanny, Emma, Frank, James, Henry, and Charlie. (Charlie's story is told in Chapter 49.) As the children grew, each was assigned duties suitable to his or her age and capabilities. There were many chores to be done to keep things running smoothly in this distant outpost, far from the nearest town. As the business grew, hired hands were also brought in to help with the work.

In 1904 they moved the store to larger quarters in McDermitt, Nevada, many miles from Winnemucca. They needed more room for their business as well as for their family, and they continued to prosper.

Jim died in 1909, leaving Chew Fong to carry on with the store and seven children. She worked from early in the morning to late at night, climbing wearily into bed for a few hours sleep at the end of the day. The oldest son,

John, took over the rounds to the outlying ranches and Indian reservations. He and his helpers drove three wagons loaded with merchandise and pulled by a total of fourteen horses.

After a while the other children were old enough to assume some of the burden of managing the store, and Chew Fong's active mind turned to other endeavors. She soon managed to open a store in St. Louis, and later she bought a building in Blytheville, Arkansas, not far from Memphis, in which she opened a store that served workers from the large cotton-growing districts in that vicinity. Thus, by thrift, wise management, and fortunate investments, this Chinese widow accumulated a sizable fortune.

Finally, in 1922, having grown tired of the work and feeling that she had saved enough to move back to China with her family, Chew Fong sold her holdings and returned to San Francisco, where she planned to spend a

Jim Low and Chew Fong Low, ca. 1905. [Photos courtesy of Charlie Low.]

few months before embarking for China. But she found that China was having troubles, with no immediate relief in sight. There were floods and droughts and, worst of all, poor crops, causing famine conditions throughout much of the country. Bandits and warlords terrorized the populace. Chew Fong delayed making the trip, and the family remained in Chinatown.

The living conditions in Chinatown at that time were exceptionally poor, and the family was crowded into what many would call squalid living quarters. Finally Chew Fong decided to do something about it. She met with her children, and they all approved her plan to build—for the first time in Chinatown—a modern apartment building, both for their own comfort and to relieve, in part, the congested living conditions of other Chinese.

After months of careful planning, construction of the

building began in May of 1926 and was completed eight months later. On January 29, 1927, the *San Francisco Chronicle* devoted almost an entire page to an article entitled "High Class Apartment House Exclusively for Chinese Open for Inspection." The subtitle was "Big Building is Monument to Energy, Thrift of S.F. Widow."

The building, 1060 Powell, located at the corner of Powell and Washington streets, still stands today. Built at a cost of a quarter of a million dollars—considered astronomical in those days—the six-story building is made of a steel frame and concrete and contains twenty-five apartments, ranging in size from two rooms to seven rooms. The apartments boasted complete kitchen equipment, breakfast nooks, tiled baths and kitchens, and all the other modern conveniences of the period. The apartments were filled immediately, and from that time on Chew Fong found her hands too full to think again of China.

When the building opened, Chew Fong's youngest son, Charlie, who was overseeing the work and handling the myriad details involved in preparing the building for occupancy, asked the Chinese Six Companies to set the rents for the apartments. The association did so, and these rents remained fixed for about two decades.

When she moved to San Francisco, Chew Fong had sold all of her assets in Nevada and other states, and she had invested the fortune in stocks and bonds, selling only enough to pay for the construction of the apartment building. In 1930, together with many other unfortunate Chinese who had invested their fortunes in stocks and bonds, she lost heavily in the stock market crash. The shock took its toll on her already tired and overworked frame, and her health began to fail.

On May 16, 1936, at the age of sixty-seven, Chew

Fong died at her home at 1060 Powell. She had made innumerable friends in San Francisco, including Mayor "Sunny Jim" Rolph and other prominent figures, many of whom attended her funeral.

22   Thomas Foon Chew

Thomas Foon Chew dared to experiment at a time when "taking a chance" often meant, for the Chinese, taking the only chance you were ever likely to get. His innovative ideas in agriculture and canning earned him the title of the "Asparagus King," and he gained the respect and friendship of literally thousands of people, including many prominent Caucasians as well as Chinese.

Just before the turn of the century, Yen Chew founded the Bayside Cannery in Alviso, a small town near the south end of the San Francisco Bay. It was a small canning business that packed only tomatoes. In 1906 Yen brought his son, Thomas Foon Chew, into the business.

Tom Foon was born in China in 1889 and was brought to San Francisco at an early age. Learning a new language did not come easy to Tom, and when he first arrived he had to be content to study English with children many years younger than himself. He graduated from grammar school at the age of seventeen, and that was the extent of his formal schooling. While he was still in school his family left for Santa Clara county, leaving Tom Foon with relatives. They finally chose Alviso as the site for their new venture—the Bayside Cannery. Tom Foon left for Alviso immediately when his father sent for him.

Tom Foon's innovative ideas for ways to improve the cannery's operations helped the business become the third largest cannery in the United States at the time. Only Del Monte and Libby were larger. When his father passed away and Tom Foon became the sole owner, his business acumen and ability to employ talented people continued to increase the cannery's growth.

One of his inspirations was a process for washing tomato boxes before they were returned to the field for reuse. A conveyor carried the boxes upside down over a wash rack and then flipped them over again for workers to stack. He also had trucks equipped with removable covers and benches so they could perform double duty as both passenger buses and fruit and vegetable haulers. At 5 A.M., with the covers and benches installed, the drivers would leave to pick up workers who lived in the surrounding areas. They would arrive back at the cannery at around 7 A.M. As soon as the workers had gotten out the trucks would be returned to the garage, where hoists were used to remove the covers and lift out the benches. They were then ready to haul field crops. At the end of the day, usually at about 8 or 9 P.M., the drivers would return the trucks to the garage so they could be converted back to buses to take the workers home.

The cannery also depended heavily on water transportation, and Tom purchased a tugboat named *Progress*. The boat was kept so busy that she had two regular captains working two shifts.

In 1929 a new warehouse measuring 118 by 244 feet and thirty cottages for workers were added to the cannery. With the cannery doing so well, Tom bought 180 acres near Yuba City that had never been farmed. A neighbor told Tom that nothing could be grown on that land, but

Thomas Foon Chew in center, between two unidentified men in front of one of his buildings at the Bayside Cannery in Isleton, ca. 1920. His main plant was located in Alviso, near San Jose. [Photo courtesy of Gloria Sun Hom.]

Tom had a knack for recognizing and hiring good men. In 1919 and 1920 he built a canning facility at Isleton and hired a man to work there named William deBack, whose inventive genius proved to be one of Tom's most valuable assets. deBack devised and built the asparagus sorting and processing equipment that helped Tom Foon earn the title of "Asparagus King." He is believed to have been the first person to can green asparagus.

When the asparagus was picked in the field it was stacked in boxes in two rows, with the delicate tips all pointing toward the center of the box. At the cannery the asparagus was dumped onto a conveyor belt, with all of the tips facing in one direction. It would then travel along a series of conveyor belts, each moving a little faster than the preceding belt. This served to spread the asparagus out before it reached the grading slots. The slots were graduated in size so that the smaller-diameter stalks would drop through the first set of slots; farther on, larger slots would enable the next size to drop through, and so forth, until it was sorted into six or seven sizes.

The asparagus then dropped into drums with cradles that lined up the tips so that the bottoms could be cut to length by adjustable knives. It then went into wicker baskets to be blanched in hot water, which toughened the asparagus enough to survive the canning process without breaking the tender tips.

After the asparagus cooled it was put into bins or sinks near the canning operation, where bruises and bad spots were trimmed off. After it was re-sorted, trimmed pieces too small for canning were saved for soup cuts. The asparagus was then put into cans that were square, not round, and sealed. The square shape kept the asparagus from rotating in the cans and thus kept the tips from

he went ahead anyway. Upon securing the property, Tom bought sixty picks, sixty shovels, and some blasting powder. He trucked these supplies and twenty-five Chinese laborers to the site, broke up the ground, blasted the earth loose, and planted trees. He then dug a well to provide water and within a short time came up with the finest peaches in the valley.

Tom also bought several hundred acres near Dos Palos that everyone said would grow nothing; there he successfully grew rice. In addition, he leased thousands of acres of land in the name of Tom Foon Ranch Co. Besides owning business and residential property in San Francisco, he maintained homes in Alviso and Los Gatos.

breaking. The final step was the cooking. The asparagus processed by the Isleton cannery came mostly from 2,000 acres that Foon leased on Sherman Island, near the cannery. By 1920 standards the asparagus equipment was truly fantastic, the first of its kind.

The Bayside canneries packed under several labels. The "Bayside" label was reserved for the better-quality merchandise, with other labels for lesser grades. Bayside also canned for other companies, such as Del Monte, McNeil, and Libby, putting their labels on the cans.

To sell his canned goods, Tom Foon operated, like many other canneries, through a brokerage house. Walter M. Field and Company provided this service for Bayside. Working on a commission basis, the company had canned-food brokers across the country that sold to wholesale houses, chain stores, and overseas customers.

At the peak of Bayside's operation, it is estimated that the canning volume was 600,000 cases or more per year, for gross revenues of around $3 million per year.

By about 1922 Tom Foon began to look around for more help as his older employees began to retire. Fewer young Chinese were available to fill the jobs, so he hired Caucasian help. The first to apply were the Portuguese. Later, Italians, Irish, and a sprinkling of other racial groups were hired. Tom always paid a fair wage by the standards of the day.

Tom Foon always arranged for a celebration at the end of each canning season for all the workers and others who had helped to make the season successful. Dignitaries such as city officials, and even California Governor Rolph, who was a good friend of Tom Foon, attended these affairs at various times.

When Charles Chew, Tom Foon's oldest son, was married in December of 1929, the *San Jose Mercury* carried the story, with the headline "Thomas Foon Chew, Jr. [sic], Son of the Wealthiest Chinese in California, Getting Married." The marriage ceremony lasted three days and was attended by 500 Chinese, including the Chinese consul general and other leading Chinese from throughout the state. On the third day a second banquet, with 500 Caucasian guests, was held at San Francisco's Hang Far Low restaurant.

Tom Foon died of pneumonia aggravated by asthma on February 24, 1931. He was only forty-two years old. A delegation of more than 200 San Francisco Masons attended the funeral service. Five Scottish Rite Masons conducted a ceremony at the casket, Rev. Dr. Daniel Wu of the True Sunshine Chinese Episcopal Church gave a prayer in Chinese, and the president of the Chinese American Citizens Alliance eulogized Tom Foon in English, with Dr. Wu translating into Chinese.

Honorary pallbearers included Caucasians and Chinese of prominence from all walks of life in the state. Among these were the San Jose city manager, the mayor of San Francisco, the president of the California Chamber of Commerce, and officials of nearby communities whom Tom Foon knew well. On May 9 the *San Jose Mercury* reported, "It was the largest funeral ever held in [San Francisco's] famed Chinatown. A service that brought forth 25,000 spectators to see Chinese and Americans alike to pay homage to one of Oriental parentage."

Thomas Foon Chew and his wife had nine children, two of whom died in infancy. The others were Charles, Rose ("Lonnie"), Lillian, Henry, Frances, Ethyl, and Timothy. Their mother, a widow before most of them had graduated from high school, put all seven through college.

PHOTO BY
SUEN'S STUDIO
眾觀映相

PART III

Chinatown
Comes of Age

T
*he years between World War I and World War II were
momentous for everyone in America. The residents of
Chinatown, like everyone else, were affected by the new moving pictures, the automobile, the
Ziegfeld Follies, and the famous song and dance hits; the Depression; and the rumblings of war
from Europe and the Far East. Great changes were taking place in China. The 1911 revolution
had dethroned the last Chinese monarchy and established the Chinese Republic in 1912. By the
early 1920s nearly every Chinese male in America had cut off his queue, and Chinese youngsters
were beginning to get involved in American-style sports and pastimes. Many Chinese adopted the
latest vogues along with every other American, from songs to sins; they drove automobiles,
shopped for the latest gadgets, and learned to speak good English. The serious-minded, such as
those active in the Chinese-American Citizen's Alliance, adopted causes; others formed their own
clubs for various purposes, both high-minded and social; still others became active in American
organizations such as the YMCA, the Boy Scouts, and veterans organizations.*

*There is no way of knowing precisely when it happened, but many Chinese organizations
were maintaining their bookkeeping and other records in English by the end of the 1930s. Some
kept better records than others. For example, I have been able to find much more material on the
Chinatown YMCA than on the YWCA, although the latter was founded only four years after*

First annual track meet arranged and sponsored by the Chinatown YMCA, held at Golden Gate Park in 1920. Chinese from throughout the San Francisco Bay Area participated. Many budding community leaders and business and professional people can be seen here, including Kam Tong, Henry Woo, Jack Chow, D. K. Chang, Theodore C. Lee, Wy Choy, James R. Lee, Park Kwan, Wing Wy, Wong Yee, Alexander Balfour Chinn, Charles Lee, Charles Jung, Dere Shek, Elmer Leong, Loy Kwok, Sooky Ng, Ben Yep, Bing Wong, Tony Jue, and a contingent from the Berkeley Chinese Athletic Club. [Photo by Suen's Studio.]

the former. This is unfortunate, for the founding of the YWCA by a small group of Chinese women in 1916 was regarded as an act of daring in Chinatown at the time. After all, the Chinese Republic was still only a few years old, and some women in Chinatown were still struggling to decide whether or not to stop binding their feet.

The YWCA began its operations in a few rooms at the southeast corner of Stockton and Sacramento Streets, and quickly became a major resource in the community, providing a multitude of services for women that were not available anywhere else at the time. By 1930 it had outgrown its premises. Its members managed to raise over $25,000 to help build a new building at 965 Clay Street, and hired the well-known architect Julia Morgan to design it. Emily Fong, whose story is described in Chapter 41, was one of the founding members and personally raised a large portion of the funds. Like so many of the early American-style endeavors in Chinatown, the YWCA began and prospered with little money and with lots of enthusiasm and hard work on the part of many dedicated volunteers. It continues to serve the community today with a variety of classes and events, but the detailed history of how it evolved over the years has yet to be written.

Despite their successes, their increased confidence, and their hard-won education and practical knowledge, the Chinese still faced severe discrimination. The Exclusion Act was still in effect, and its worst provisions were felt by immigrants arriving at the immigration station on Angel Island, the largest island in San Francisco Bay. Thousands of Chinese were held there for preliminary examination before they could enter the city; many were held for months, and some for a year or more. For the first two years of the immigration station's existence, both men and women were crowded into one building. Separate quarters were eventually provided for the women and children, but they were not a big improvement. The most telling records of this experience are the poems those in confinement scratched surreptitiously on the walls of the barracks; today many of these poems have been collected and translated in the excellent book Island, *published in 1980 by HOC DOI (History of Chinese Detained on Island), and some of the originals can still be seen in the barracks, which have been turned into a museum. The immigration station was just another reminder of the formidable barriers the Chinese still faced as a group even while some of them were learning to play American sports, acquire a good education, and move out of Chinatown into the mainstream of American business and society.*

23   The Chinese-American Citizens Alliance

Originally known as the Native Sons of the Golden State, the Chinese-American Citizen's Alliance (CACA) spearheaded the long struggle to achieve equal rights. It has successfully fought for street lighting in Chinatown, integration of the public schools, a Chinese recreation center, the Ping Yuen housing project, and many other causes; and it is still recognized as the legitimate champion of Chinese-American interests today.

In 1895 a small group of American-born Chinese, tired of being discriminated against by their Caucasian countrymen, decided to form an association to fight the many prejudices they faced in their everyday lives. They met on May 4 and elected the following officers: Chun Dick, president; Sue Lock, vice president; Ng Gum, secretary; Li Tai Wing, treasurer; Leong Sing, marshal; Leong Chung, inside sentinel; and Lan J. Foy, outside sentinel. By May 10, six days later, they had filed an application for incorporation in San Francisco. The name they chose was Native Sons of the Golden State (NSGS). The purposes of the organization were to show the members' pride in being Americans and their patriotism toward the United States, and to seek avenues of advancement into the mainstream of American life.

The early efforts of the group were slow and not always easy. Even some of the elders of the Chinese community scoffed at them, but they struggled along for years. By the turn of the century, American-born Chinese made up a large portion of the total Chinese population of around 14,000. Although many of these were young-

sters, there was still a large base from which to recruit members. When President Chun Dick moved to New York, however, the NSGS began to fall apart for lack of a strong leader.

In 1904 an injection of fresh energy by members Walter U. Lum, Joseph K. Lum, and former secretary Ng Gum revitalized the organization. The group began to gain respect for its role in speaking out against discrimination. Walter U. Lum became president, and he served as Grand President of the CACA in 1912, 1914 to 1917, 1923 to 1929, and 1933 to 1935.

By 1912 Chinese in other areas had heard of the organization and wanted to form chapters. A Los Angeles lodge was founded on May 15, 1912, and an Oakland lodge a month later. The first lodges worked together to establish a mother organization, which they did by forming a Grand Lodge with jurisdiction over local lodges.

Chinese in San Diego and Fresno sought and received authority in 1914 to open lodges in their respective cities. At about the same time, the organization found that many Chinese born to American citizens living outside of California, although they were automatically American citizens, could not join because of the way the charter had been written. The following year, 1915, this problem was remedied with a new charter, and the name of the group was changed to Chinese-American Citizens Alliance.

The purposes and objectives of the organization, as set forth in the charter, were "to form a more perfect body, to inculcate the principles of charity, justice, brotherly love and fidelity among the members, to promote the general welfare and happiness of its members and the Chinese communities, to quicken the spirit of American patriotism, to insure the legal rights of its members and to

purpose

Members of the Grand Lodge of the Chinese-American Citizens Alliance in session in San Francisco Chinatown, some time between 1920 and 1930. Seated in the front row, third from the left, is Walter U. Lum, who helped revitalize the alliance in 1904.

secure equal economical and political opportunities for its members."

One of the group's first attempts to protest discriminatory legislation involved a constitutional amendment introduced to the California legislature in 1913 by State Senator Joseph Caminetti. If passed, the bill would have denied the right to vote to the son of any man not eligible to vote, and would thus have prevented all native-born Chinese from voting. A contingent of NSGS members,

led by President Walter U. Lum and Treasurer Lee Wong, made its first lobbying visit to the legislature and stated its opposition to the bill, helping to defeat it.

Two years later, in 1915, the Department of Labor issued Chinese Regulation Rule #9, which denied American-born Chinese a pre-investigation prior to their departure from the United States. This meant that, upon their return to the country after a visit abroad, Americans of Chinese descent were detained at immigration stations until they could prove that they were citizens. The CACA protested this regulation, and it was rescinded.

The first lodge outside of California was established in Chicago in 1917. Later, lodges were founded in Portland, Oregon; San Antonio and Houston, Texas; Albuquerque, New Mexico; New York; Washington, D.C.; and Tucson and Phoenix, Arizona. In California, additional lodges were established in Salinas, Sunnyvale (now renamed Peninsula), and Sacramento.

On August 10, 1921, the opening of the national headquarters of the CACA was celebrated at its newly constructed building at 1044 Stockton Street. Owned by the Grand Lodge, which oversees all the chapters, the building is also occupied by the San Francisco Lodge. Today it stands as one of the oldest and largest Chinese-American community centers in the United States.

The *Chinese Times*, a Chinese-language daily, was founded in 1924 as the official journal of the CACA. After operating the paper for sixty-four years, the organization determined that publishing it was no longer economically feasible, and it sold the business and property to new, independent buyers in mid-1988.

In the decades since it was founded, the CACA has

continuously fought against all discriminatory legislation. In addition, it has sponsored essay and oratorical contests, scholarship programs, citizenship programs, and other programs of benefit to the community. It has joined in lobbying for community improvements such as street lighting, integration of the public schools, a Chinese recreation center, the Chinese playground, and the Ping Yuen housing project. All these efforts have been successful. During the 1970s and 1980s the CACA actively supported civil rights issues in the Chinese-American community.

The CACA even sponsored a Chinese-American bathing beauty contest. The first was held on July 4, 1948, and the winner was Penny Lee of Oregon. More than 2,000 people attended the popular event. It was held four more times, from 1949 to 1952, and was then discontinued.

In 1973 the organization's bylaws were changed to allow non-Asians to become associate members and to allow women to serve on the board of directors. The first two women named to the San Francisco Lodge were Virginia Gee and Agnes Chan.

Numerous distinguished members of the Chinese community have joined the CACA and participated in its activities. Among them are Municipal Court Judge Samuel E. Yee; the late EOC Commissioner Charles J. Jung; Harry W. Low, Presiding Justice, Court of Appeals; Parking Commissioner Francis H. Louie; EOC Commissioner and Human Rights Commissioner Harvey Wong; Superior Court Judge Lenard Louie; the late William Jack Chow, who was on several commissions; State Board of Education member Agnes Chan; Virginia Gee, Special

Walter U. Lum Place, 1985. Formerly Brenham Place, this street is believed to be the first in California to be named after a Chinese person. The block-long street is situated on the west side of Portsmouth Square in San Francisco Chinatown. Walter U. Lum was a prime force in the Chinese-American Citizens Alliance, the first organization formed for Chinese-Americans.

Assistant to the Chief, Division of Apprenticeship Standards, State Department of Industrial Relations; City Supervisor Thomas Hsieh; and former Community College District President John Yehall Chin.

Today the community continues to look to CACA for leadership in its field. In 1985 the City and County of San Francisco named a street in Chinatown after Walter U. Lum, in recognition of his lifelong efforts on behalf of the civil rights of Chinese-Americans. Walter U. Lum Place replaced Brenham Place, a block-long street bordering the west side of Portsmouth Square. Lum, born in 1882, passed away in 1961.

Above: *The staff of the Chinatown branch of the Bank of America, ca. 1940. The branch had an all-female staff for most of the 1930s and 1940s.* Back row, left to right: *Emma Louie, Beatrice Lee, Daisy K. Wong, Beulah Ah Tye, Rose Lee, Rubye Fung.* Front row: *Annie Quan, Manager Dolly Gee, Florence Tong. Daisy K. Wong was one of the founding members of the Square and Circle club.*

Although Wells Fargo Bank was the first bank to do business with the Chinese, the French-American Bank was the first with a branch in Chinatown. Founded in 1923 with the help of Charles Chang, an employee who had been bringing in Chinese customers for many years, the Chinatown Branch prospered under several names: The French-American Bank soon merged with the Bank of Italy National Trust and Savings, which in turn merged with the Bank of America National Trust and Savings Association in 1930.

Above left: *Graduating class of the Hip Wo Chinese School, June 1928. [Photo by May's Photo Studio.]*

Left: *A classroom at the Hip Wo Chinese School, ca. 1940s. The teacher is demonstrating to her young pupils how to write Chinese words. [Associated Press news photo, courtesy of Hip Wo School.]*

The Sam Wo restaurant, 1988. Sam Wo, a small restaurant at 813 Washington Street, has been in existence for more than seventy-five years. When the city was being rebuilt after the 1906 earthquake and fire, a few laws of inspection were overlooked. As a result, the building that houses Sam Wo was constructed with no side walls and instead relies on the walls of the buildings on either side, saving some important space in the extremely narrow restaurant. Aside from this architectural deficiency, Sam Wo has made a name for itself with its rice gruel, a modest yet delicious dish favored by several generations of customers. The kitchen is just inside the entrance, and customers sit on the second and third floors. [Photo by Nancy Warner.]

Above right: The Young Wo Chinese School basketball team, 1924. Back row, left to right: Harry Mew, Frank Tong, Bew Tong. Middle row: Jack Young, Coach Quon Wong, Willie Jung; front (with ball): William Jack Chow. [Photo courtesy of Bew Tong.]

Right: The immigration station on Angel Island, the largest island in San Francisco Bay. Thousands of Chinese were held here for months and sometimes years while they awaited preliminary examination by the immigration authorities. The large building near the center of the photograph was used for administration and physical examinations; the structure behind it was the women's quarters, the building above it, near the top left corner, was the hospital; and the building at the far right edge of the photograph was the men's quarters. This photograph was taken sometime after 1920. [Photo courtesy of Paul Chow.]

The founding of the Chinatown YMCA was a major milestone for young men in Chinatown at the time, and it has continued to play an important role right up to the present. It was one of the first American organizations that welcomed the Chinese and encouraged them to learn American-style sports, music, and technical skills. It provided a new feeling of freedom and pride for the young Chinese who flocked through its doors to take advantage of the Y's marvelous variety of activities.

At the turn of the century, church missions in Chinatown were searching for a way to bring the predominantly male Chinese community together into a Christian fellowship. They sensed the need for an organization that would serve the increasing number of Chinese immigrants who were caught in the middle between the whites, who persecuted and discriminated against them, and their Chinese neighbors, whose intense provincialism excluded most newcomers. The solution came from a visiting professor from Lingnan University in South China, Jone Wing Quong. At a meeting with local church leaders, Professor Quong raised the possibility of filling this need by creating a local chapter of the Young Men's Christian Association (YMCA). Inspired by Professor Quong, the church leaders applied for and received permission to start a Chinatown chapter. They held an organizational meeting on July 10, 1911, at San Francisco's Oriental Hotel. The next day the new Chinese Young Men's Christian Association became a reality, with the Rev. Chan Lok Shang as its first president.

Local churches took turns playing host to the new

YMCA's public programs during its first year. Lectures on health, education, and religion were the primary focus, but these shared the stage with socials, street meetings, and even a benefit show to raise funds, held in September of 1911. These first programs, like many others in the years to come, were run entirely by volunteers. The work of these volunteers, combined with an encouraging response to their programs, put enough money in the group's coffers to inspire plans to rent permanent headquarters. Soon after Lew Chuk Om was hired as the YMCA's first paid secretary, he arranged to lease the organization's first office and headquarters, at 1028 Stockton Street. The facility was dedicated on May 29, 1912, less than a year after the chapter was founded.

With the new facility, the scope of activities widened. A table game room was added, and Mandarin and Bible classes appeared. Troop 3 became Chinatown's first Boy Scout troop, thanks in part to later support from the YMCA. Looking toward eventual improvements in social status and job opportunities, smartly dressed young men began to flock to the YMCA's new classes in mechanical drawing and English. As activities multiplied, and as the organization gained momentum, larger quarters became necessary. By 1915 the Chinatown YMCA had outgrown its first office and moved two blocks south to a double store at 830 Stockton Street.

Once again, new headquarters prompted new services for the community. Interest in classes continued, and a library and reading room was added with a small but often-used supply of books, magazines, and newspapers in both English and Chinese. Classes were offered in a new, well-equipped woodworking and machine shop. Social activities began to dance to a different beat with the cre-

The old Chinatown YMCA building on Stockton Street, ca. 1912. [Photo courtesy of the Chinatown YMCA.]

ation of the twenty-member Chinese YMCA Orchestra. And the YMCA began to focus more and more on health and sports activities. It became a catalyst in all sports, starting with organized hikes, tumbling, and ball teams. In the decades to come, the Chinatown YMCA's soccer and basketball teams would dominate opponents from both within and outside of Chinatown.

From 1918 until 1922, S. C. Lee served as the executive secretary of the Chinatown YMCA. In a 1936 issue of the *Chinese Digest*, Henry Shue Tom, an activities secretary for the YMCA, wrote that "the unusual ability and personality of S. C. Lee brought the YMCA into the limelight of the entire community." As the YMCA entered the 1920s, it also took the lead in many of the affairs of Chinatown. It began to plan and sponsor parades, including an Easter parade in 1921 that packed the site of the current YMCA at 855 Sacramento Street.

Beginning in the early 1920s, hundreds of students visiting from China were welcomed by the YMCA. Many among the huge influx of students and immigrants needed help in acclimating to a new and different society. The organization responded with counseling and preaching programs for internees detained on Angel Island, while newly arrived students were treated to receptions and tours of nearby university campuses. The early 1920s saw the young, progressive YMCA rapidly becoming one of Chinatown's most important and influential institutions.

During this period the sports teams sponsored by

the YMCA began to make a name for themselves, even outside of Chinatown. The soccer team gained widespread attention as early as 1919, defeating teams from Stanford and a number of University of California campuses. The team's success rested not on size or strength but on its superior speed, agility, and teamwork. YMCA-organized basketball leagues also became popular with young Chinese boys. The YMCA Athletic Carnival and Marathon Race of 1922 attracted young Chinese athletes from all over the San Francisco Bay Area and encouraged boys to try out for their school teams. As community interest in YMCA-sponsored track and field meets grew, the YMCA Marathon became more and more popular, remaining a Chinatown tradition for the next twenty-five years.

The first YMCA camp was organized in the early 1920s, with future board of managers member Chingwah Lee as its director. Young Chinatown residents were given the chance to venture outside the community through camping excursions to Marin and San Mateo counties. Before long, camping became a large part of the YMCA's youth program, and it remains an important facet of the organization. Its summer camp has run continuously since 1933. Today's "Y-kids" learn about camping and outdoors in the rugged terrain of the High Sierra.

The early YMCA also helped guide both "Y-kids" and adults into the American working world. In 1920 the YMCA's new employment service struggled to open up job opportunities for young men outside of Chinatown, although often the only jobs it could find to offer were for houseboys. Still, there were occasional exceptions to this rule. Seasonal harvests in the San Joaquin Delta provided summer work for students and opened the way for others to become farmers.

Soon after its move in 1915 into the double store on Stockton Street, the YMCA's activities had become so popular that it was obvious that an even larger building would be needed. Under S. C. Lee the agency had raised $14,000 to buy a lot at 855 Sacramento Street, funds for building materials and equipment had been secured, and a fund-raising campaign for the new building had been launched. S. C. Lee resigned from the YMCA in 1922 to accept a professorship at the University of Hawaii. His successor was Ling Lew. It was during Lew's administration, in 1924, that the fund-raising goal was achieved. Chinese communities across the country contributed $57,000; a $100,000 contribution from Dr. John R. Mott, president of the International Committee of the YMCA, was the largest single addition to the fund.

November 15, 1924, saw the official ground-breaking ceremony for the new building, led by Robert Dollar of Dollar Steamship Lines, who had contributed $25,000, and the Metropolitan YMCA. Also taking part was Dr. Richard Perkins, YMCA general secretary. Less than a year later, on July 16, 1925, Secretary of the Navy Curtis Wilbur laid the building's cornerstone, with a large crowd of spectators looking on. On February 22, 1926, the Chinatown YMCA's new $225,000 headquarters was officially completed and dedicated, and a full complement of office clerks and secretaries went to work for the organization. At the time, the building was one of Chinatown's largest.

Although I had visited the old YMCA many times as a very young boy, the new building dazzled me with its spaciousness and open-armed welcome to the public. Once again, expanded facilities heralded more activities for the growing YMCA. The new building had a swimming pool,

Some members of the new Chinatown YMCA, 855 Sacramento Street, after a meeting in 1926. [Photo courtesy of the Chinatown YMCA.]

and ever since, the YMCA's swimming classes have been a major community attraction. A new gym became home to the group's basketball leagues and gymnastics classes. For many years the building's facilities served only young men and boys. Women and girls weren't allowed to use the pool until 1933, and a locker room and shower for women weren't added to the building until thirty years after that.

Upstairs, the added space allowed the YMCA to initiate annual father-and-son banquets, to sponsor a businessmen's luncheon club, to offer even more lectures and films on an even wider range of subjects, and to lend a hand with all types of college student activities. The

dormitory rooms offered inexpensive housing to young men from all walks of life, including working men and both American and Chinese students. Tours of industrial plants, universities, and museums were organized. In 1926, for example, more than fifty men met outside the YMCA to tour an aircraft carrier of the Pacific Fleet.

As the 1930s began, Chingwah Lee succeeded S. C. Cheung as the boys' work secretary, Lew Ling resigned as executive secretary, and the YMCA began to do more work with younger children and Hi-Y service clubs. Ties with YMCAs outside of Chinatown developed through sports programs and competitions, and Lee's experience in social work helped give the organization the momentum and range of activities it needed to survive the economic hardships of the early 1930s.

The national depression that played havoc with the nation's economy also had its effect on the YMCA. The organization welcomed the unemployed into its reading room and offered movies four times a week. The movie programs were attended by more than a thousand people each week. Because of decreased income, two secretaries were dropped from the staff in 1931, and volunteer help became an even greater factor in the agency's operations. By 1931 volunteer leaders were staffing the swimming program and hobby clubs, while government recreational leaders provided their skills through the WPA. Volunteer help pulled the YMCA through the depression, and the list of programs offered continued to grow. A harmonica band, a camera club, and a model airplane club were among the new activities that kept the agency going and helped the YMCA remain a source of leadership in the community during hard times.

In 1934 the YMCA balanced its budget for the first time in five years. After maintaining a balanced budget through 1935, the agency bought new office equipment, new lobby furniture, a radio, and other "luxuries" that they had not been able to afford earlier.

As the depression and the 1930s drew to a close, the YMCA's clubs remained active in the community. The Drum and Bugle Corps, for example, performed in a number of citywide festivals from 1937 to 1940, including the China War Relief Rice Bowl Fund Drive parades and the International Exposition of 1939.

World War II brought prosperity back to Chinatown and its YMCA. Shipyards were hiring Chinese for defense work, and young Chinese girls found work in insurance offices. The YMCA sponsored conferences to help Chinese find out about job opportunities. The war was also a time for inter-YMCA socialization, as the Chinatown YMCA welcomed other branches to open houses, neighborhood tours, and often a Chinese lunch or dinner. In return for its hospitality, the Chinatown YMCA received a number of similar invitations from other groups.

During the war the Red Cross, first aid, and civilian defense paved the way for new, coed YMCA groups. The YMCA played its part in the war effort as well; in 1943 the Chinese Hi-Y club joined Eddie Cantor in a twenty-four-hour radio broadcast promoting the sale of war bonds. After the war the YMCA's Young Adult Program gained momentum, fed by an influx of returning veterans.

Its folk dancing and social group, the Ming Swingers, performed at statewide folk dance festivals and were in great demand for local celebrations. In 1947 the agency held a "Hobo Banquet" for its boys, who ate stale bread and drank soup from tin cans to learn about sacrifice and hunger as well as about the YMCA's work overseas. For the older crowd, the organization featured a long list of well-known speakers in the later 1940s.

This period also saw the birth of the Chinatown YMCA's Public Affairs Committee (PAC), dedicated to "participating fully in the affairs of the community." The PAC had its roots in the "Chow Hounds," a group of boys who got together to sample each other's "gourmet" cooking. The group invited friends, talked, and found that the war had left them with an eagerness to help out the community. The Chow Hounds and their buddies organized and formed the PAC to lend a hand in community affairs and to meet other young people, especially girls. The roster in the PAC's early days always included at least thirty members. Among these were future YMCA supporters who were still with the organization thirty years later: Edwin Cheng, Henry S. Louie, and others.

In 1946 the PAC became an official part of the Chinatown YMCA, under Director Henry S. Tom and Young Adult Program Director Homer Eng. Its yearly tuberculosis prevention campaigns featured poster and speaking contests, promoted health education and chest X-ray programs (the first in the community), screened movies on health, and even translated English bulletins. In 1948 the PAC gathered more than 4,000 signatures on a petition for a new recreation center in Chinatown and presented it to the city's Board of Supervisors. This drive led to the building of the Chinese Recreation Center on Mason Street.

Another service group formed during this period and remaining active today is the Alpha Ram Omega (ARO) Men's Service Club. Begun in 1951, the membership consisted of graduates of the former Raven, Atlas, and Mohican Hi-Y clubs who wanted to stay together after graduation. Its members have been group advisers and have donated thousands of hours as volunteers for the YMCA. The club has helped raise campership funds, has held fund-raisers to furnish the organization's conference room, and, in 1957 and 1960, repainted the entire swimming pool and locker room area. Two-thirds of its members graduated from college and found careers in business, engineering, teaching, and a number of other professions, and many served in the armed forces.

The 1950s were a time of change and modernization. New emphasis was placed on leadership training programs. With the assistance of the Metropolitan Administration of the YMCA, high school youth from Chinatown participated in interbranch youth leadership conferences and branch training conferences. At the Model Legislature of 1959, a boy from the Chinatown YMCA, Donald Jin, was elected Youth Governor of California. That same year another boy from Chinatown represented the Pacific Southwest area at the national Hi-Y Council meeting in Colorado, and over the next few years other Chinatown boys were made discussion leaders at regional YMCA conferences.

In addition to leadership training, other programs continued to be successful. The High Sierra camp remained popular and still attracts more than a hundred boys each summer. As part of its Camp Fair, the YMCA held aquacades in its downstairs pool to raise money for its campership fund. The 1950s also saw the YMCA's traditional boys' program become coed. Girls' camping, for example, began in 1957.

In the early 1960s, amid an influx of junior and senior high school students stemming from the postwar baby boom, the YMCA strengthened its emphasis on youth programs. In an attempt to work more with local schools, the agency held a School-YMCA Conference in May of 1961, featuring the principals of Galileo High School and Francisco Junior High as well as representatives of the Chinatown YMCA. Teachers, parents, community leaders, and students attended the conference. The organization also made an effort to reach immigrant youth by hiring more bilingual workers, offering tutoring services and classes, and providing many activities. Fishing off San Francisco's Municipal Pier soon became one of this group's favorite pastimes.

With a steady stream of youth joining the YMCA in the late 1960s, the board decided to try to reach former

YMCA participants, many of whom had become businessmen or community leaders both within and outside of Chinatown. This led to the 1967 Sustaining Membership Round-up, an attempt to regain contact with former "Y-kids," interest them in what the organization was doing, and enlist their support. The campaign raised much-needed funds and broadened the organization's base of support, eventually expanding the membership from 345 to 575.

The 1970s were full of milestones for many of the groups at the Chinatown YMCA. The organization itself celebrated its sixtieth anniversary, and the ARO Men's Club celebrated its twentieth anniversary in December of 1970. Still active, the group continued to sponsor projects for the YMCA's youth program, including the annual Easter Pancake Breakfast and the popular Camp Fair. By 1971 twenty-five years had passed since the Chow Hounds organized the Public Affairs Committee, and some of its members were serving on the Chinatown YMCA's board of directors.

In the 1980s the YMCA continues to provide many of the services it has in the past—summer youth camping, swimming classes, leadership training programs, and athletic programs, to name a few. The YMCA Marathon, begun in 1922 and discontinued in 1948, has reemerged as the Chinatown Run. Immigrant and native-born youth are given the opportunity to interact and learn from one another. In the process, immigrants are helped to assimilate into their new culture, while native-born Chinese learn about their cultural heritage. The building itself has undergone many repairs and upgrades to meet building codes, but it is still underutilized. Despite declining public and private funding, the organization is planning new, expanded facilities, which in turn may bring in some much-needed extra income, according to Alan S. Wong, the executive director.

On September 25, 1987, the Chinatown YMCA celebrated its seventy-fifth anniversary with a banquet at Chinatown's Empress of China Restaurant. The names of many long-time supporters were still visible on the program. As Winfred Tom, president of the Chinatown YMCA's Board of Managers, wrote in the anniversary program, "We are re-dedicating ourselves to providing the YMCA's brand of solid influence and leadership for all our community's young people now and in the future. There is no greater satisfaction than a job well done."

25   Boy Scout Troop 3

The Boy Scout movement was started in Great Britain in 1908 by Lord Baden-Powell. By 1910 it had mushroomed to more than 123,000 members and had been taken up in many foreign countries. In America, the Boy Scout organization was incorporated in 1910 and was chartered by Congress in 1916. Word of the movement had reached San Francisco Chinatown before any local council had been established, and a small group of Chinese boys were the first to form a Boy Scout Troop in the area.

One day in 1914 eight young boys gathered in the play yard of the Chinese Methodist Church. One of them, Chingwah Lee, had obtained a well-thumbed Boy Scout handbook, which the boys studied eagerly. They decided on the spot that they, too, would become members of the Boy Scouts of America.

In addition to Chingwah Lee, the seven other charter members were Lim Wong, Edwar Lee, Tim Wong, Bing Moy, Stephen Moy, Nelson Wong, and King Lee. They invited Lim J. Kwong, an engineering student attending Mt. Tamalpais Military Academy, to be their scoutmaster, and B. Y. Chu, then progressive secretary of the Chinese YMCA, was nominated troop advisor.

Thus was organized Troop 3, the first Boy Scout troop in San Francisco and the first Chinese Boy Scout troop in the United States and probably in the world.

Being without professional guidance, the boys wrote to National Boy Scout Headquarters in New York, stating their predicament. The headquarters notified Field Scout Representative Harry Cross of the Los Angeles Council, the nearest council at the time. Cross made a trip to San Francisco, where he assembled a group of prominent civic leaders to plan a local council. It was not until 1916, however, two years after the formation of Troop 3, that the San Francisco Boy Scout Council was formally organized. (Today, the San Francisco Bay Area Council serves some 45,000 Scouts and volunteer leaders.)

By the time the United States entered World War I, Troop 3 had built itself to the full strength of four patrols, with eight boys in each patrol. Still pleased and proud that they had been invited to serve as Guards of Honor to former President William Howard Taft at the Panama-Pacific International Exposition in 1915, the troop realized that it must expand to support the war effort.

During the war years, under the energetic leadership of Scoutmaster Lauritz Lauritzen, a civil engineer and former Army man, Troop 3 performed many patriotic tasks. Its members won prizes for their sales of Liberty Bonds, participated in parades, prepared bandages, collected aluminum foil and newspapers, served as ushers at patriotic rallies, and distributed influenza masks in districts where health officers hesitated to go. In addition, the troop entertained more than a thousand soldiers and sailors with sightseeing trips through Chinatown.

After World War I the troop introduced camping to Chinatown's underprivileged boys. Each year a number of boys were taken to a two-week camp at Lagunitas. Since the camp was maintained without institutional support and with little adult leadership, the patrol leaders worked hard at various jobs to make the outings possible.

Under the leadership of charter member Chingwah Lee, who became scoutmaster in 1924, Troop 3 expanded rapidly during the 1920s and 1930s, developing into an influential, community-minded organization. Scouts acted as guides in Chinatown for conventions, participated in parades, distributed posters and leaflets for fund-raising campaigns, aided in clean-up movements and old-clothing collections, and performed other civic services.

Athletics gained prominence, with members engaging in track, basketball, and other sports on a large scale in addition to their scouting activities. Today, the troop proudly displays cabinets filled with trophies and medals for athletic and civic achievements.

The formation of Troop 3 did much to help bring about an atmosphere of change in the community. People from different family clans formerly did not mix much in social or business affairs, but how could parents of different clans not become more friendly when their boys marched together, played together, and often shared their tents when camping out?

Many of the scouts earned nicknames. For instance, in the 1920s a reckless boy named Albert Wong earned

Alumni and their wives or girlfriends celebrating the thirty-first anniversary of Boy Scout Troop 3, June 20, 1945. Many of the former troop members were still in the armed forces at the time, making this a small gathering.

the title "Suicide Al" for the way he rode his motorcycle (see Chapter 61). At camp, Henry Leong ("Sang" was his Chinese name) received the moniker of "Nom Wor Sang," or "Buddhist Priest Sang," because he always wore a tiny beanie reminiscent of a Buddhist priest's cap. Ralph Fung ("On" was his Chinese name) was called "Fot Mung On" (Daydreaming On) because of the dreamy-eyed expression he would put on when playing innocent.

Often brothers of the same family belonged to the troop, either at the same time or one following another if there was a big age difference. These included Chingwah, Edwar, Changwah, and King Lee; Thomas, James, and Bill Chinn; Ernest and Albert Sang Loo; Earl, Francis, Harry, and Wilson Louie; Robert and Vincent Poon; George and Bill Jow; Lim, Don, Yuen, and Tze Lee;

George and Kenneth Kwok; Edward, Steven, Frank, John, and James Way Leong; Philip and Silas Chinn; Fred and Charles Hing; Kwong and Allen Lim; Frank and Fred Wong; Lawrence and Martin Joe; and Woodrow, George, and Richard Ong.

During World War II Troop 3 again gave time and service unstintingly to the war effort. This time, however, there was a difference. Many of its former members, some the older brothers of boys in the troop, were serving in the armed forces, earning many decorations—Silver Stars, Bronze Stars, and Purple Hearts. And some gave their all and did not make it home.

On the home front, members of the troop were active participants in all aspects of civil defense; war bond drives, rallies, parades, collection of badly needed defense materials, and night-watch duty during blackouts became second nature to them, and they also served as air raid wardens and members of the state militia.

Following World War II the troop made steady progress in maintaining the traditions and color that have characterized the organization since its founding. When Ronald F. Lee became scoutmaster, the troop again gained strength from within, Lee having been a Troop 3 member who progressed steadily from Tenderfoot to Scribe to Senior Patrol Leader and Star Scout ranking and finally to Alumni Association board member.

Troop 3 alumni can be found in nearly every profession. Of my generation, Chingwah Lee became an authority on Oriental art, lecturer, writer, actor, collector; Edwar Lee devoted a lifetime to the ministry; Major General Dewey K. K. Lowe was commander of the Sacramento Air Logistics Center, McClellan Air Force Base (he recently retired); Lim P. Lee was San Francisco postmaster and political strategist for the late Congressman Philip Burton and is presently a member of the California State Fair Political Practices Commission; brothers Kam and Frank Tong became well-known Hollywood actors; Victor Sen Young, another Hollywood luminary, played Charlie Chan's son and had a part in *The Flower Drum Song*, among other roles; Johnny Kan was a well-known restaurateur; William Jack Chow became a Chinatown lawyer; James Tong became professor of microbiology at the University of Denver; and Edward Leong Way, now retired, became an international authority in the field of controlled substances, particularly alcohol and drugs.

The true spirit of Troop 3 is best indicated by the large number of men who continue to participate in troop activity long after their "graduation" from scouting. In 1934, when a large number of Troop 3 members had passed the age for active scouting, a group of them met and formed the Alumni Association. Their purposes were to promote the welfare and growth of Troop 3, to inculcate the spirit of scouting among the youth of the Chinese community of San Francisco, and to be a service organization to the community. In May of 1958 the Alumni Association incorporated, to put further substance into their efforts and to strengthen the organization as an accessory to scouting in the surrounding areas.

Thus the seeds that were sown more than seventy years ago have come full cycle. Former scouts have seen their children, grandchildren, and great-grandchildren follow in their footsteps to become better citizens through scouting.

26   The Yoke Choy Club

The Yoke Choy Club was founded at a time when young Chinese were reaching out beyond the Chinatown their parents knew, striving to complete not only high school but college as well, and in some cases graduate school. It grew out of the friendship among a small group of young men, and provided the impetus for many more lasting friendships over the years. Athletics were a major focus of the club from the beginning. It also sponsored an orchestra and played an active role in the annual conferences held by the Chinese Students Christian Alliance.

On December 15, 1920, eleven young men gathered at the Chinese Congregational Church at 21 Brenham Place (now Walter U. Lum Place). They had known each other for some years, socializing, attending church, and getting together for any or no reason at all, many times to "shoot the breeze," as they would say. This particular night Joses Lee had called a meeting for a special reason. The other ten were James R. Lee, A. Balfour Chinn, Ton Wong Lee, William M. Chinn, Henry Chinn, Park Kwan, John Wong, James Chew, Cheung S. Lee, and Peter Wong. The meeting was called for the purpose of cementing their friendship by means of membership in a club that Joses Lee proposed that they form.

The proposal met with unanimous approval, and before the night was over they chose the name Yoke Choy Club (in Chinese, *Yoke* means "to disseminate," and *Choy* means "knowledge"). According to Ton Wong Lee, ninety-one-year old patriarch and last surviving member of the charter group, he proposed the name himself. He also reports that the threefold purpose of the club was to promote Christianity, music, and athletics.

The track team of the Yoke Choy Club, winner of the annual Chinatown YMCA track meet held in Golden Gate Park, April, 1922. Front row, left to right: *Ira C. Lee, Wy Choy, William M. Chinn, James R. Lee, A. Balfour Chinn, (unknown), Cheung S. Lee.* Back row: *(unknown), D. K. Chang, (unknown), James R. Chew, (unknown), Henry Chin, and Paul Dunn.*

I joined the Yoke Choy Club in 1926 as the youngest member ever accepted. (Coincidentally, the club had established its original headquarters at the church I was baptized in and attending—the Chinese Congregational Church.) My sponsor was Thomas A. Wong, who was best man at my wedding a few years down the line and later became a medical doctor. The club had some very impressive statistics by that time. A majority of its members were attending colleges and universities, including San Mateo Junior College, UC Berkeley, and Stanford.

Others had moved out of town for their studies, to the University of Southern California, UC Los Angeles, and out of state. A few were businessmen.

The club was founded during a time when athletics were beginning to become popular in Chinatown. Before the 1920s athletic activities were available, but not enough young Chinese had yet been born in America to form very many teams for sports like basketball and volleyball. Then in 1921 the Chinatown YMCA sponsored a track meet at Ewing Field in Golden Gate Park. The Yoke Choy Club walked away with the first prize that year and again in 1922. Chinese clubs came not only from San Francisco, but also from nearby towns such as Oakland, Berkeley, and San Rafael. The winner of the 1922 marathon, Cheung S. Lee, was from Yoke Choy, as were three others out of the first ten runners to complete the race. Gradually some of the Yoke Choy men moved away to attend universities elsewhere, and the club lost in 1923 and 1924, winning again in 1925 in two meets with ten clubs competing. But Cheung S. Lee won all the marathons. In football, against Chinese or Japanese teams, the club won the majority of the games in 1926 and 1927, but failed even to field a team thereafter. The club also fielded strong teams in basketball and tennis, but it was only in tennis that we won all our matches for several years, not only locally, but also against high schools and Chinese clubs in Los Angeles.

Many young Chinese in America were active in the Chinese Students Christian Alliance during the 1920s. Each year, during summer vacation, conferences were held on the East and West Coasts, with irregular conferences in other areas where Chinese were numerous enough to warrant them. The conferences originated in

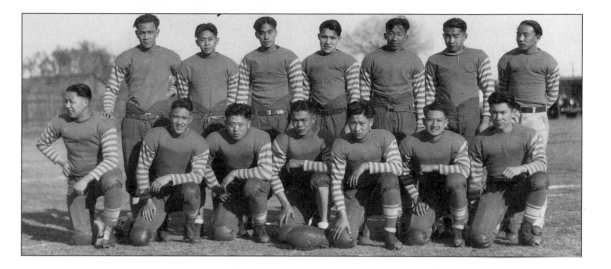

*The Yoke Choy Club football team, 1927–1928.
Front, left to right: Joe Lee, Thomas Wong,
Jacob Yee, Lym King, Joe Chew, Albert Noa,
Ira Lee. Back: Park Kwan, Ed Chong, Thomas
Chinn, Alfred Wong, Ed Suen, Fred Lee,
Peter Lee.*

1902, when many of the young people who attended were not American-born, but had come from China to study at U.S. colleges and universities. This caused a lot of controversy during many of the discussions at the conferences. Students from China wanted to sway sentiment toward China, exhorting conferees to return to China with their degrees to help China become more modern. Chinese-Americans wanted to fight discrimination here and to move as rapidly as possible into the mainstream of America. There were socials, athletics, stunts, and a farewell dance during the several days each conference lasted.

The Yoke Choy Club shone at these conferences, winning medals in athletics and generally winning the silver cup for musical performances. The club stressed musical activities in those days, thus furthering one of its principal purposes. Its members also took Christianity

very seriously at home, and most of them attended one or another of the many churches in Chinatown. The churches were also used sometimes for club activities.

The Chinese Davis Cup team passed through San Francisco several times in the late 1920s, either on their way home or arriving to play matches on the East Coast. They had heard of the Yoke Choy Club, because Joses Lee and others had gone back to China to live and work and had told other athletes about us. As a result, Chinese Davis Cup team member Gordon Lum came to visit, together with W. C. Choy, a teammate. They enjoyed our company as much as we enjoyed theirs, and they were both made honorary members of the club and corresponded with us for years. Another year Davis Cup player Kho Sin Kee came to visit, and I played an exhibition match with him.

Several of the members got together at about that

Members of the Yoke Choy Club celebrating their fiftieth anniversary at the Fairmont Hotel in San Francisco, May 22, 1971. In the front row are the most senior members of the club (left to right): Fay Louie, Thomas W. Chinn, Tommy Yee, Pong "Gor," Joseph Lym King, James R. Chew, Dr. Alexander Balfour Chinn, Yee Wong, James Richard Lee, Wing Wy, Dr. Stanley Louie, Lee Gin-Gin, and Ton Wong Lee.

time to form an orchestra. The Yoke Choy Music-Makers consisted of Walter Louis, the leader; Daniel Yuke at the piano; Wing Wy on traps; Eddie Tom and Al Noa on saxophone; and Myron Chan playing trumpet. After a few months of practice they were playing for social clubs in Chinatown, followed by a few weeks on the radio and their first out-of-town engagement—for the Bayside Cannery annual dance at Alviso, California.

The men's quartet was also frequently on call for church, wedding, and funeral engagements; a Kuomintang convention; the Lions Club Frolic; and over KPO radio. Soloists were also kept busy: Harry Mew spent two years at the New England Conservatory of Music; Wing Wy sang for years with the San Francisco Municipal Chorus; and Thomas A. Wong, one of the most popular singers in San Francisco Chinatown, was an outstanding tenor.

Every spring an anniversary dinner dance at one of the city's hotels, such as the Fairmont, Mark Hopkins, St. Francis, or the Palace, would become one of the most sought-after invitations among the young set. But World War II and the Korean and Vietnam wars took a heavy toll among the active members, and the club gradually became less active.

The Yoke Choy Club still exists today, although it has pretty much reverted to the activities of its original members before they formed the club: socializing, getting together at anniversaries, and shooting the breeze.

Five of the oldest living members of the Yoke Choy Club, 1986: Seated, left to right: Ira C. Lee, Ton Wong Lee, Thomas Leong. Standing: Thomas W. Chinn and Wing Wy. All joined in the 1920s; Ton Wong Lee was one of the eleven founding members.

The twelfth anniversary celebration of the Square and Circle Club, 1936. In the immediate foreground, on the left, is the late Patrick Pichi Sun, vice consul of China and later ambassador to the Philippines, dancing with the author's wife, Daisy "Dillie" Chinn.

27 The Square and Circle Club

When a group of seven young women got together in 1924 to do what they could to help flood victims in China, they never in their wildest dreams imagined that their efforts would evolve into what is believed to be the oldest Chinese women's service organization in the United States. The young women were members of the Chinese Congregational Church (now also known as the United Church of Christ) at 21 Brenham Place (now Walter U. Lum Place). After church services on Sunday they generally met in the social hall to sing, read the voluminous Sunday paper, do the crossword puzzle together, and chat. One Sunday the paper carried an article about the flood and famine in China and the distressed situation of its people. The girls felt that they should do something, no matter how small, to raise funds to help the refugees.

Attending the first meeting of the Square and Circle Club in June of 1924 were Alice P. Fong (Yu), Anne Lee (Leong), Ivy Lee (Mah), Jennie Lee, Bessie Wong (Shum), Daisy K. Wong, and Daisy L. Wong (Chinn). To distinguish between the two Daisy Wongs, the other members gave them nicknames derived from their initials—"Dickie" for Daisy K. and "Dillie" for Daisy L. Ever since, in the club annals and to their friends, they have been known by these nicknames. Jennie Lee passed away during the club's early years. Daisy K. Wong, who will be remembered as one of the club's most ardent, analytical, and dedicated members, passed away on May 9, 1970, while on a trip to Hong Kong. The remaining five members, now in their late seventies and early eighties, have always remained members of the Square and Circle Club. They still attend meetings and serve on committees.

The name Square and Circle Club was selected when the club's first president, Alice Fong, approached her Chinese language tutor, Professor Fung Gee Shau, a distinguished Chinese scholar. He suggested a Chinese couplet that, when translated, means "In deeds be square, in knowledge be all-round." The club's insignia is the ancient round brass Chinese coin (representing the circle) with a cut-out square in the center.

One of the club's initial fund-raising projects was a hope chest raffle in 1926; tickets sold for 25 cents each. The hope chest was filled with all the usual contents: lingerie, towels, linens, and a full-size bedspread embroidered by members at weekly sessions.

In 1926 a columnist for the *Los Angeles Record*, Louise Leung, wrote of the club:

> Whenever there is a flood in China, or an orphan to look after, or the poor to remember—the Square and Circle Club of twenty-four Chinese girls can always be counted on to carry out its motto of Service.
>
> There are other clubs and organizations in Chinatown, lots of them, but this handful of girls has led them all in sterling service to the community and to their country.
>
> Most young girls band together for social purposes chiefly, but not so the Square and Circle members. They have two projects each year in their program of ministering to the needs of their less fortunate countrymen.

In 1933 Dr. Charles R. Shepherd, founder of the Chung Mei Home for Chinese boys, invited the club to offer its services in playing the female parts of an original romantic musical comedy he had written. Entitled "It Happened

SQUARE AND CIRCLE CLUB

FOUNDED JUNE 15, 1924 SAN FRANCISCO

Charter Members *(clockwise from top)*: Alice Fong (Yu), first President; Daisy K. Wong; Anne Lee (Leong); Jennie Lee; Bessie Wong (Shum); Ivy Lee (Mah); Daisy L. Wong (Chinn)

Cover of a booklet containing vignettes of the seven founders of the Square and Circle Club, designed by Lewis Lowe in 1974 for the club's fiftieth anniversary. Clockwise from top: *Alice Fong (Yu), Daisy K. Wong, Anne Lee (Leong), Jennie Lee, Bessie Wong (Shum), Ivy Lee (Mah), Daisy L. Wong (Chinn). Photos were taken at various times between 1930 and 1940. Jennie Lee passed away in the late 1920s.*

Members of the Square and Circle Club of San Francisco celebrating the club's golden anniversary at the Hyatt Union Square Hotel in 1974. The executive board for that year and the five founders are in the center of the front row. Starting with the third person from the left, they are Dorothy Wong, service chairman; Betty Louie, treasurer; Alice Lowe, program chairman; Ivy Mah, founder; Alice Yu, founder and vice-president; Anne Leong, founder; Daisy Chinn, founder and president; Bessie Shum, founder; Rachel Hum, business manager; Rose Lew, secretary; Barbara Quan, custodian; and Frances Chin, financial secretary. [Photo by Pride & Joy, San Francisco.]

in Zandavia," its cast included a king and queen, prince and princess, soldiers, and ladies-in-waiting. The king was played by Wing Wy and the queen by Square and Circle's late, irrepressible Renmi Jue. Thirteen other club members were also featured in the cast. The musical was produced as a fundraiser for Chung Mei. It was performed many times, culminating in a highly successful show at the War Memorial Auditorium in San Francisco's Civic Center.

The club's aims and objectives today remain identical to those set forth when it was formed in 1924. Its work encompasses all facets of community service. The club has provided support for an orphan boy in the Chung Mei Home in El Cerrito for many years; scholarships for San Francisco State University and San Francisco City College students for more than thirty years; camperships to the YMCA and YWCA; sandwiches and cookies for Christmas parties at housing projects; and, with the Chinatown Opti-Mrs. club, food bazaars for Laguna Honda Home for the Aged.

In 1974, fifty years after its founding, the club for the first time designated all proceeds from a fund-raiser to benefit a single organization. On Lok Senior Health Services, established in 1971, had received an initial grant from the San Francisco Foundation in 1972, with matching funds to be raised by On Lok. After two years, less than half of the grant money had been raised. At that point, On Lok approached Square and Circle for assistance. The club's response was to stage a fashion show luncheon at the Hyatt Regency Hotel. The event was a sellout, with more than eight hundred attendees, and the net proceeds gave On Lok far more than the amount necessary to match the funds. Today, On Lok Senior Health Services is a nationally recognized health care service organization and serves as a model for similar groups in other communities. (See Chapter 72 for more information about On Lok's work.)

On the occasion of the club's fiftieth anniversary in 1974, the five remaining founders were interviewed by Mildred Hamilton of the *San Francisco Examiner*. The opening paragraph of her article read, "On the other side of the table sat 250 years of solid community service to the Chinese of San Francisco. And it was a rare, off-their-feet gathering for the surviving five of the seven 1924 founders of the Square and Circle Club."

With the passing years, the Square and Circle Club has been fortunate in recruiting new, young, and supportive members. At times, young members reach a point where family obligations must take precedence over club activities. Generally these members resign and are later reinstated after their families have grown and they have more free time.

The club has met monthly since its founding, except for one year when they met every other month. With a membership now constantly hovering around one hundred, a glance at past and present rosters would reveal schoolteachers, accountants, civil service employees, social workers, a commissioner and docents of the Asian Art Museum, public health nurses, homemakers, pharmacists, insurance agents, and corporate employees, among others. The Square and Circle Club should continue for a long, long time.

28   Chinese Hospital

Chinese Hospital opened its doors in 1925 after a concerted effort on the part of many different organizations in Chinatown to meet the community's urgent need for a new medical facility. Fifty years later, in 1975, another vigorous fund-raising campaign led to a brand new, larger building right next door to the original hospital. Today it is as well-equipped as any hospital of comparable size in the nation, and it continues to receive dedicated support from the large community it serves.

Early Chinese arrivals in California always took care of their own sick and injured. Western medicine was unfamiliar to them, and they had more faith in their own herb doctors with their herbal medicines and poultices. For decades there was no medical facility to serve the Chinese community. In 1900, spearheaded by the Chinese Consolidated Benevolent Association, the community started a small clinic called the Chung Wah Dispensary on Sacramento Street to provide care for the sick and terminally ill. It is believed that the clinic offered both western treatments and traditional Chinese remedies. The dispensary was the sole source of medical care for the critically ill in Chinatown for more than twenty years.

With dispensary resources often stretched to the limit, it soon became apparent that Chinatown needed its own community hospital. Community leaders launched a nationwide fund-raising campaign for the purpose and, after many years, they finally had sufficient funding to proceed. They began making plans by holding conferences with authorities in the fields of medicine and hospital administration. As a result, a modern new hospital called Chinese Hospital was built at 835 Jackson Street, between Stockton and Powell streets. It contained fifty-five beds, including fourteen private rooms. The hospital opened its doors on April 18, 1925.

A Committee of Management undertook the job of overseeing the operation of the hospital. Instead of a board of directors, a group of community organizations served as the directing organization, thus providing representation from a cross section of the community. The fourteen organizations each selected a representative to serve for a specific term.

The initial group of organizations overseeing the hospital consisted of the Chinese Consolidated Benevolent Association, the Ning Yung Benevolent Association, the Kong Chow Benevolent Association, the Sam Yup Benevolent Association, the Shiu Hing Benevolent Association, the Young Wo Benevolent Association, the Hop Wo Benevolent Association, the Chinese Chamber of Commerce, the Chinese Nationalist League in America, the Chinese Free Masons, the Chinese Reform Party, the Chinese-American Citizens Alliance, the Chinese Christian Union, and the Chinatown YMCA.

On the initial staff were four Chinese doctors, all licensed to practice by the state of California: Henry Wong Him, Margaret Chung, James Hinquong Hall, and Joseph Shiang-Min Lee. Julius T. Yee, D.D.S., provided dental care. There were also thirty-two Caucasian doctors on the staff, including ten consulting members. The director of the hospital was Howard H. Johnson, M.D., and the superintendent was Ming S. Jung.

As the years went by the building started to show its age, and plans had to be made to update its facility. A modernization program commenced in 1975, exactly fifty years after the hospital first opened. A Hill-Burton grant provided the seed money to plan a comprehensive health care center. The old building was finally declared unsafe for patient use, and another vigorous fund-raising campaign was necessary to build a brand new hospital next door. The old building was subsequently used for medical offices and the health care center.

Today most of the doctors at the hospital are Chinese, and there is an amazingly low turnover rate of 4 percent per year among the staff. Chinese Hospital has the latest medical equipment and has created its own state-licensed HMO, the first Chinese-sponsored health plan in America, providing twenty-four-hour health care for the large community it serves. It also has an active auxiliary, which sponsors an annual fund-raising campaign.

29   The Chinese Playground

Like so much else in Chinatown, the Chinese Playground grew out of an urgent need that was recognized by community leaders, who fought hard for a long time to overcome the lethargy of City Hall and get it built. For many years it was one of the most heavily used playgrounds in the city. It does not see as much use today, because Chinese use playgrounds all over the city, wherever they happen to live. But the Chinese Playground still fills a need in one of the most densely populated neighborhoods in the country.

The Chinese Playground lies in the heart of Chinatown, on Sacramento Street between Stockton Street and Waverly Place. It was officially named in December of 1927

The Chinese Playground in 1988.

by the City Recreation Commission, and opened during fiscal year 1927–28.

The entire playground covers little more than half an acre. All types of American and Chinese playground games are played on the small site. It occupies three levels and has several retaining walls. On the top level the asphalt courts include a basketball court, a volleyball court, and one doubles tennis court. The middle level is devoted to small children and general play. One section consists mainly of interconnecting wooden structures to climb, crawl through, and run through and around. A small sandbox area occupies one corner. The field house is also located on this level, with a basketball court built over its roof. The bottom level leads out to Waverly Place, and

holds an auditorium with several table tennis tables and a two-step stage.

The playground has been of great value to the community since it opened. In the 1940s it was lighted for night use. According to a 1969 survey of San Francisco's juvenile population, the block bounded by Stockton, Grant, Jackson, and Washington streets was found to have the largest number of juveniles of any single block in the city. This heavily populated section is within a block of the Chinese Playground, which is consequently one of the Recreation Department's most important and busiest units. Chinese schools, churches, the Clay Street YWCA, and the Chinatown YMCA are also located within a radius of two blocks .

The Recreation Department purchased the property for the playground in October of 1925 for $54,112.45. The first director of the playground was Oliver Chang. During its opening year, the total attendance was estimated at 124,332. By 1935–36, the total had increased to more than 155,500. By 1987, attendance figures had dropped to 60,000.

A recreation center at Mason and Washington streets with club rooms and a basketball court was built and occupied in 1952, with early attendance figures averaging about 2,500 per month. In 1987 the figure was around 750 per month.

These figures are altogether misleading unless other factors are considered. For the first half of the twentieth century, Chinese were still more or less confined to Chinatown. From the fifties up to the present time, the figures show that Chinatown's boundaries for recreation and athletic events have expanded to take in much of the rest of the city's public facilities. As the Chinese who now live all over the city and go to public schools and facilities can testify, they do not need to go to Chinatown. They play or socialize wherever they choose. But Chinatown is still teeming with life. New immigrants and refugees are gradually replacing those who have moved away. Another cycle has replaced much of the old.

30   The Cathay Post of the American Legion

The Cathay Post was the first of several veterans' organizations founded in Chinatown. The others are VFW Post 4618, founded in 1945, which has about 200 members; American Veterans of World War II (AMVETS) Post 34, founded in 1961, which has about 125 members; and AMVETS Post 78, founded in 1978, which has about 50 members. The Cathay Post today has a membership of under 100.

The American Legion was founded in 1919 when a group of American delegates from the different divisions of the army got together in Paris to talk about helping their country. That same year, after they returned to the United States, they met again at a convention in St. Louis. American Legion posts were soon springing up across the country, but it was ten years before one was established in San Francisco Chinatown.

Finally, after years of talk but no action, Bert Jacobi, who was employed by the government and was a great friend of the Chinese, consulted M. Spencer Owyang and Lee J. Poo about starting an American Legion post in Chinatown. The following year, 1930, these men were able to get a number of World War I veterans together and, with the assistance of the Chinese-American Citizens Alliance (CACA), met several times in the CACA building. The group quickly grew to thirty, and it was from this nucleus that Cathay Post No. 384 of the American Legion was born. With some help from San Francisco Post No. 1, Cathay Post became one of the more distinctive chapters of the American Legion.

M. Spencer Owyang became the post's first commander, and Lee J. Poo was the first adjutant (secretary). By its second year the post's membership had grown to fifty, a good size in view of the limited number of eligible Chinese veterans in the district. It soon began to attract national attention, as news of the Chinatown post spread all over the country. In its second year Cathay Post Commander Owyang was nominated second vice-commander of the district and was elected by a wide margin.

The Cathay Post was most active in its early years. Hospitalization was one of the first things taken up after the post was organized. Lee J. Poo became service officer and helped place many disabled and sick members in government hospitals. None of this cost the veterans anything; it was one of the benefits the Legion had fought for.

When the American Legion held its 1934 National Convention in Miami, Leland Kimlau attended as Cathay Post's representative. As a result, he became nationally known throughout the Legion. Kimlau had become the second commander of the post in 1932, and he succeeded in bringing the Cathay Post into national prominence.

Since its inception, the Cathay Post has tried to protect the rights of members who were having immigration problems. In 1933 Cathay Post member Charr (his first name is not now known), who was not a U.S. citizen, was faced with the breakup of his family and home through threatened deportation. He had met and married his wife, a Chinese student, in Kansas City. Because she was a foreign student, her marriage opened the door for her deportation, even after the couple's two children were born. Cathay Post officials took the matter up with their representatives in Congress and with Legion officials in Washington. On the eve of her deportation, a wire was received granting Charr's wife an indefinite stay in the United States. Charr later became the first member of Cathay Post to become a naturalized citizen.

The post has also played an active role in community affairs. In 1934, at a time when Chinatown badly needed tourism, the Department Convention was held in San Francisco. With the help of Cathay Post, more than ten thousand people passed through Chinatown during the week of the convention. Most of them had dinner there, and many also attended the Chinese theater.

In the late 1930s the long-awaited Adjusted Compensation Act was finally passed, bringing around $700 to each Chinese veteran. The Cathay Post helped its members file applications for the bonus, which was a big help in the midst of the Depression.

Following V-J Day in 1945, the Cathay Post helped process GI brides and their children under Public Law #346 as non-quota immigrants. This was the first exemption made to the Chinese Exclusion Acts of 1882.

An auxiliary, composed of the mothers, wives, sisters, and daughters of Cathay Post members, became affiliated with the post. Following this, the post took over the sponsorship of Troop 3 of the Boy Scouts of America, the Chinatown Boy Scout troop, and it has remained a sponsor for more than half a century.

31   The Chinese During the Depression

The Great Depression of the 1930s hit Chinatown as hard as it did the rest of the country. For the first time in memory, the family, district, and other associations were unable to help with their members' economic problems. It was unheard of for the Chinese, who prided themselves on their independence and self-respect, to accept charity in hard times. The first Chinese families to apply for welfare were shunned by their neighbors; but within a few years, more than 2,500 Chinese were receiving help from the government.

The first Chinese family applied for unemployment relief in March of 1931. By 1935 the number of San Francisco Chinese receiving assistance from the State Relief Administration had reached approximately 2,300—nearly one-sixth of the Chinese population of San Francisco.

At first, relief took the form of groceries from local Chinese food stores; large families received a basket once a week, and smaller ones received one every two weeks. The amount and type of food was carefully selected to offer nutritional balance. Milk was delivered daily. In October of 1933, to permit families to select their own food, a system of weekly orders or vouchers was attempted.

Beginning in February of 1934, cash relief became the sole form of assistance in San Francisco. A weekly check was sent to each family or individual to cover expenditures for food, rent, utilities, and clothing. The amount depended on the number of persons in the household. In addition, surplus food commodities and clothing were distributed periodically. In San Francisco, the Chinese received the same allowance for food as the white families; in several other counties in California, however, Chinese and other ethnic groups, such as Filipinos and Mexicans, were given a food budget that was 10 to 20 percent lower than that received by whites, with the explanation that these groups had less expensive diets.

Medical care was coordinated at a Central Medical Bureau, to which requests for assistance were referred and where minor ailments were treated. More serious cases were referred to other private or public clinics in the city.

The Chinese social service staff for the San Francisco office of the State Relief Administration numbered eleven workers, seven women and four men. The case aides had at least one contact a month with each case, generally a visit in the home.

A mid-1930s study of the occupational history of the heads of families on relief revealed that the majority of the married men were formerly employed as cooks and businessmen. Among the single men on relief, a more unstable group of workers, most were previously engaged as seasonal workers, laundry workers, and cooks.

After unemployment, the most serious problem for the Chinese relief population was improper housing, a situation complicated by the high rents in Chinatown. An investigation of housing conditions among 119 relief families showed that these families, with 622 individuals, lived in only 268 rooms, an average of 2.2 persons to a room. The problem was actually worse than this statistic suggests, however, because many of the rooms counted were mere cubicles or partitions not large enough to meet United States housing standards. Of the 119 families, only 40 had private kitchens, and only 25 had private bathrooms.

The Moral Effect of Relief

A definite change of attitude toward public support took place among the Chinese population during the Great Depression. The Chinese have always prided themselves on their independence and self-respect. In their eyes, the government did not owe them a living; its role was solely to offer its people protection so that they could labor in peace. The first few families who had to accept relief were looked down upon for accepting charity.

Gradually, however, as the depression worsened and more people sought public assistance, there came the recognition that it was the duty of the public government, the great *wong gah*, to provide for everyone's needs. This concept had previously been foreign to the Chinese mind.

The WPA in Chinatown

The Works Progress Administration (WPA), established in 1935, was created to provide government work for the unemployed. Typical WPA projects included constructing roads, buildings, and bridges. In October of 1935 the first Chinese cases were transferred from the relief rolls to the WPA program in San Francisco. By 1936, of the approximately 500 single Chinese men in San Francisco who had been receiving direct relief from the State Relief Administration, 331 were working on WPA projects; similarly, of the approximately 350 Chinese families on relief, 164 had one member employed in WPA work. With few exceptions, all were working at the lowest occupational level, unskilled labor, at $60 a month for 120 hours of work.

Compared to single workers, WPA workers with large

families were at a major disadvantage. Only one member of each household was eligible for full-time WPA work. Furthermore, WPA workers could no longer obtain the cash, medical services, surplus clothing, and food they had previously received from the State Relief Administration.

The average income of the 164 families having one WPA worker was about $66 per month, including an average outside income of $6.33 per month. The average monthly income of these families while they were on direct relief was about $70 per family. Thus a family with a WPA worker earned about $4 per month less than one on direct relief. Because relief was calculated based on family size, whereas WPA workers received one monthly wage, large families bore the brunt of this drop in income. An eleven-member family received about $48 less per month from the WPA than it had from the State Relief Administration, whereas a two-member family actually received about $15 more per month from a WPA job.

In contrast, the 331 single WPA workers, who earned an average of $60 per month from the WPA program, received an average of only $16.50 per month when they were on relief. Their income thus increased nearly four-fold. The median age of these men was fifty-two years; 28 percent of them were sixty or older.

The redistribution of public money was consequently in inverse proportion to the needs of each Chinese family. Despite these statistics, very few men with large families refused WPA jobs. Some of the work they did was invaluable to the community. For example, in 1939 WPA workers conducted a real property survey of every living unit in Chinatown—a survey that eventually became an important factor in the development of the Ping Yuen low-income housing project (see Chapter 72).

32   "Does My Future Lie in China or America?"

More than fifty years ago, the Ging Hawk Club of New York announced the winners of an essay contest on a very controversial question of the time: "Does My Future Lie in China or America?" The subject was as old as the second thoughts of the earliest Chinese to arrive in the United States. It probably was pondered when the first Chinese pigtail was cut by carousing Caucasian miners; when the first Chinese woman arrived and was received with a mixture of curiosity, disdain, hostility, and friendliness; and when the first nugget of gold was dug from the California hills by a Chinese miner.

Around the turn of the century, when second-generation Chinese-Americans had graduated from college and started looking for employment, they must have wondered whether the years spent acquiring an education had been wasted; and when China finally overthrew the yoke of monarchy in 1912, not a few idealists returned to help build a new China.

The years after World War I held no promise that things would get any better. By the mid-1920s the Chinese population in the United States had fallen to 62,000, its lowest point since the early 1870s, because of the Chinese Exclusion Act that closed the door to Chinese immigrants. With the arrival of the Great Depression of the 1930s, many Chinese gave increasing thought to their desperate situation. It was in this context that the Ging Hawk Club, in 1936, sponsored an essay contest with the theme "Does My Future Lie in China or America?"

Two of the essays—the winner and a runner-up—are reprinted here to record the conflicting thoughts of American-born Chinese of that period. Following the essays are brief descriptions of the subsequent lives of each of the authors.

Does My Future Lie in China or America?

By Robert Dunn Wu, Somerville, Massachusetts

Winning Essay, Ging Hawk Club, New York, 1936

Throughout the early years of the life of any American-born Chinese, he or she is constantly confronted with an important problem, the decision of which will inevitably influence, if not determine his or her future happiness and success. The problem has been well-expressed in the question: "Does My Future Lie in China or America?"

Having been born in America (Roxbury, Mass., 1915), I, too, have been haunted with this problem. Which road should I choose? Which is more advantageous? Which road would lead to more happiness and greater success?

After having given this fundamental problem some thought, I have found that it really resolves itself into four minor problems: First, that of allegiance or patriotism, or race; second, that of service; third, that of employment; and, finally, that of civilization, or culture. Without a consideration of these four significant problems, I believe an answer to the main problem is quite incomplete and inadequate. I propose, therefore, to discuss them as fully as the limited length of this essay will permit.

In determining whether my future is to be in China or America, I have naturally come to ponder the question: To which of these two countries do I owe allegiance? Which country am I obliged to serve?

Ever since I can remember, I have been taught by my parents, by my Chinese friends, and by my teacher in Chinese school, that I must be patriotic to China. They have said: "You should be proud of China's four thousand years of glorious and continuous history, of her four hundred million population, and of her superior culture and civilization. You must be thankful for the traditions and customs you have inherited as a member of the yellow race. What is more, you would not be living if it were not for your ancestors and parents who are Chinese. Most

certainly, then, you are obliged to render service to China, especially in these days of need and stress and humiliation. Don't you realize that the Chinese are mocked at, trodden upon, disrespected, and even spit upon? Haven't you yourself been called degrading names? Have you no face, no sense of shame, no honor? How can you possibly think of staying in America to serve it?"

Now, I do not wish to contradict or oppose these assertions as being unsound. Somehow, however, I feel there is another side to the picture. I owe much pride and gratitude to America for the principles of liberty and equality which it upholds, for the protection its government has given me, and for its schools and institutions in which I have participated. Without them, I certainly would not be what I am now. If Americans have called me names, so have the Chinese who speak of me scornfully as being a "native" (t'oa jee doy) and as knowing nothing of things Chinese.

True, many regard me highly because I am a junior at Harvard; but I can say without ostentation that my American friends also respect me as a student. In fact, they give me more respect because I am Chinese. Whatever I do in school and college in the way of extra-curricular activities or of attaining high grades, I am given much more credit and popularity than an American would receive if he did the same things. Being a Chinese among American friends, then, is a sort of advantage. There are, then, two sides of the picture: I am certainly as much indebted to America as I am to China.

If this is true, then I should serve both equally; but is this possible if I choose a future that lies in America? Certainly, one cannot help China by building a bridge or opening a factory in America; one cannot serve China by curing American patients; one is not aiding China by practicing his principles of government, sociology, or economics in America. It is true, however, that almost every overseas Chinese who has entered college is studying in one of these fields. They all evidently are planning their futures in China; but could we justly condemn them as showing no allegiance to China if they later decided to stay in America to put their studies into practice? I think not, provided they serve China in some other way.

I mean to say that even though one practices his profession in America, he can still serve China by building up a good impression of the Chinese among Americans, by spreading goodwill and clearing up misunderstandings, by interesting the Americans in the Chinese through personal contacts or otherwise, and, if necessary, by contributing generously to the financing of worthy enterprises in China. These are services of inestimable value. These are services which may be even more worthy than the services of those who do their life work in China. It is possible, then, to pay the debt one owes to China and show one's allegiance to Chinese even while living in America.

What of those who would like to find a life-work in America? What are the opportunities for employment? Is it to be contended that a Chinese will be welcomed into American employment as cordially as into positions in China? The facts seem to indicate the opposite. Chinese students have indubitably found it difficult to get employment, to say nothing of getting the more elevated and higher-paying positions.

My brother, a graduate of M.I.T. last year, failed to receive a single favorable reply from different companies to which he sent letters of application for employment. He has returned to China and now has a position with the Nanking government. What shall I say to this? I can say my brother was merely fortunate, as he himself admits in his letter. He was lucky to have a sister who is married to someone connected with the government. In other words, he was given a "pull" up the ladder, a necessary force which most overseas Chinese do not have.

In his last letter, my brother warned me that positions are so few that even men with Ph.D.'s and M.S.'s and M.A.'s are without work. It is evident, then, that employment is hard to get anywhere; in America, perhaps because of the color line; in China because jobs are scarce. The color line, however, does not entirely prevent the American-born Chinese from getting jobs. The chances are small, to be sure, but as in China, there are some opportunities open to certain fortunate people. It cannot be said, therefore, that it is impossible for Chinese-American youths to obtain remunerative positions in either China or America.

If there are possibilities for profitable employment in both countries, then I see no reason why I should not choose a future for myself in America if it happens that I like it better here, or if I happen to be acclimated to the modes of life and social environment here. True, if I receive employment in China, it would almost surely be one of the large coastal cities where there are modern conveniences such as electric lights, running water, quick transportation, and means of sanitary and healthful living. The two civilizations can hardly be said to be conflicting in the material sense, except in minor details. The real harmful conflict is between the two different cultures, the two different outlooks upon life, which, together with the language difficulty, will tend to bring social estrangement to the returning overseas Chinese, whether boy or girl.

If I am to spend my future in China, there must come a time when I shall have to make contacts there. Years of lonesomeness will intervene before I shall be able to speak Mandarin or Cantonese with considerable fluency. Even then, I am afraid my endeavors to make real intimate friendships will fall short of their goals and will merely end in casual acquaintanceships. I have been brought up to live by Christian ideals, by liberal attitudes, and by an optimistic outlook on life.

I think I shall be able to make few close relationships with the young men and women of China, for their background is of utilitarian ideals, conservative attitudes, and of a fatalistic outlook upon life. When these two cultures conflict and clash, the inevitable result is either social estrangement, or a yielding of one culture to the other, a process which is sure to engender much unhappiness, discontent, and despondency.

I have not, perhaps, expressed this point clearly; but I can say that I feel the clash of cultures within me even now, because I live with my father and I contact many Chinese friends who represent the pure Chinese culture. My relatives are also of a different background than myself, and they all advise that I make friends, not for friendship's sake, but with a hope that they will help me get a job sometime. They object openly or become suspicious when I am seen walking with a girl. They pour contempt upon religion, especially upon Christianity, and fail to see the preciousness and value of the individual life. This culture and attitude is contrary to mine, and I fear that I shall be unhappy in the process of yielding to it.

With the conclusion, then, that I owe America as much allegiance as I do China; that it is possible to serve China while living in America; that remunerative employment, though scarce, is not impossible for me to obtain in either China or America; and that I would avoid the unhappiness and social estrangement due to conflicting cultures by staying in America; I think no one could justly accuse me of being unwise if I chose a course of life whose future lies here in America.

Does My Future Lie in China or America?
By Kaye Hong, San Francisco, California
Second-Place Essay

When the conquest of new territory in the United States had stretched to the limits of the Pacific, the old adage of "Go West, Young Man" no longer became applicable to the American youth. Through necessity the modern generation concentrated on the intense development of natural resources and greater industrialization. As the population multiplied, competition for jobs increased, and when the world depression set in the unemployment situation grew acute, resulting in the accentuated distaste for Oriental rivalry in every type of work. As a result the present generation of American-born Chinese absorbed a bitter diet of racial prejudice.

I have learned to acknowledge that the better jobs are not available to me and that the advancement of my career is consequently limited in this fair land. As I express my desire to return to China to create a career, however, I am constantly being reminded that I am American as American can be, that I shall deplore China's lower standard of living, that the chaos of China's government offers me no promise of economic security. In other words I shall be leaping from the proverbial frying pan into the fire, for in the United States I am at least assured a decent livelihood. As proof of this contention they bring to my notice numerous cases of American-born Chinese who have spun the wheel of chance in old Cathay and have returned to the States sadly disillusioned. These arguments have been impressive, but somehow I refuse to be convinced. And, it is for me "Go Further West, Young Man." Yes, across the Pacific and to China.

What then constitutes the lure that beckons me to return, for I'm certainly not a vagabond of impractical hankerings? It is certain that I'm not planning to return just for the pleasure jaunt, for I'm not financially equipped to tour the Orient. Again, I'm not an idealist who responds to the hue and cry of the propagandist, for impassioned slogans, such as "Make the world safe for Democracy," "Your country needs you," etc., leave me coldly unresponsive.

You may condemn me as lacking in patriotism. From one viewpoint, yes. From mine, no, for I am of the belief that I can be of greater service to China by being methodically practical instead of resorting to oratorical displays of vehemence or meaningless pledges of unflinching loyalty. After all, words are cheap.

My patriotism is of a different hue and texture. It was built on the mound of shame. The ridicule heaped upon the Chinese race has long fermented within my soul. I have concluded that we, the younger generation, have nothing to be proud of except the time-worn accomplishments of our ancient ancestors, that we have been living in the shadow of these glories, hoping that these arts and literature of the past will justify our present. Sad, but true, they do not. To live under such illusions is to lead the life of a parasite.

No, I'm not such an egotist to think that my mere presence in China would change its history. In fact, I'm not even aspiring for political prominence as thousands of American-trained graduates have hoped, only to be disappointed to the degree that henceforth they could only find fault with the Nationalist government. I, for one, do not intend cynically to denounce the policies of the Republic. I must confess that the more I learn, the greater I'm aware what a pittance is my knowledge. Numbered among my shortcomings are the intricacies of diplomatic strategy. I'm a layman, and a layman has no business in politics.

You might ask, how are you going to help save China? My policy is not sensational. My deeds will not be heralded in headlines, and my name will not go down in history as a hero of China. I merely intend to become a good citizen of the great Republic. I shall support the Nationalist government, which is now gaining strength with each succeeding day. I shall accept the national policies. I shall place the welfare of the nation above my own. In other words, I shall do my part.

To be more concrete in my theory, I must explain that I believe a nation is as strong as she is economically progressive. In this measure of value, China is relatively destitute. Her industries are unborn, her resources are yet underground, her people are jobless and starving. This must all be changed, for China can never arouse from her lethargy without constructing a stable economic foundation. It is impossible for a nation to rise politically when she stands upon an economic base of quicksand that sucks her down instead of holding her up.

I realize that China cannot be changed from an agrarian populace to that of an industrialized state within a decade, not even a lifetime. It will take many lifetimes. It follows that I, nor any other person, can singly bring about any impressive prog-

ress. It will take hundreds of thousands, millions of young men with vision to build for the future, to start the wheels of industries, to weave a cobweb of railroads and highways across the expanse of all Cathay, to educate everyone in a common language, to send out a fleet of trading vessels, to develop the internal resources, to build a richer life for one and all. Then and only then can the present generation of Chinese really "save their faces." Then and then only will China be truly powerful and respected. It matters not whether capitalism, socialism or communism provides the means of motivation. It only matters that the goal, China's salvation, is accomplished.

I am willing to accept an inconspicuous part in the construction of a new nation. To me and those overseas Chinese with an American background, an American spirit of aggressiveness, an American "go-getter" enthusiasm, China is the land of opportunity. Every vocation is an open field, indeed, every vocation is a "gold mine" for those who have the courage to dare pioneer the industrialization of China.

Perhaps I've been speaking too optimistically in vague generalization. Perhaps I have neglected to emphasize that one must specialize in some distinct field, that one must have a command of the Chinese language, that one must be brave enough to triumph in the hour of adversity. Perhaps I have not made clear that pioneering is no playground for weaklings, especially in the present predicament of having imperialistic Japan as a cut-throat neighbor. China's bed of roses also promises many thorns.

Space will not permit a detailed dissertation on a subject on which volumes can be written. We cannot treat here effectively the various phases of life in America or life in China. It is a greater subject than can be discussed in such restricted space. I can only be dogmatic in my viewpoints and hope that they are coherently comprehensive. And so, it is for me, "Go Further West, Young Man."

Coda: Robert Dunn Wu and Kaye Hong

In 1946 a young chemist named James Jang wrote an article that followed up on the life of his friend Robert Dunn Wu after his graduation from Harvard. Here are some excerpts from that piece:

> I first knew [Robert Dunn Wu] when he came from Boston to San Francisco some six years ago. He was a graduate of Harvard University and at the time was nearing the completion of his doctorate thesis on international law. Having had to work long hours to support himself, Bob's voyage through Harvard was rough to say the least. But in spite of this he managed to take part in many of the student and community activities, among which were Harvard Students' Club, Chinese Students' Christian Association, and the Boston YMCA, serving and chairing many of the committees.
>
> . . . Shortly before Pearl Harbor, Bob went to China. His experiences there were no bed of roses. Starting as a lowly clerk and supplementing his small income by tutoring English, Bob started on his climb up the ladder of his career. After a year of disappointments and frustrations, he joined the Chinese civil service by passing the competitive examination given to thousands of aspirants and winning the coveted position of assistant to one of the assistant secretaries of a government official. His progress during the next several years was slow and obscure.
>
> The next time I saw Bob was in April 1945 when the United Nations were convening in San Francisco. Bob had flown in from Chungking, China, by way of Calcutta and Cairo.
>
> Prior to his departure, Bob had made phenomenal progress, and had become secretary to one of China's top delegates to the United Nations Conference, Dr. Wang

Robert Dunn Wu (far right), winner of the 1936 essay contest with the theme "Does My Future Lie in China or America?" This photograph, taken in 1986, shows him with fellow members of the Chinese and Korean Section, Asian Division, of the Library of Congress. He recently retired. [Photo courtesy of Robert Dunn Wu.]

> Chung Hui, internationally known jurist, former Prime Minister, and the then Secretary General of China's Supreme National Defense Council. Bob, one of the youngest secretaries in the Chinese delegation, took me around and introduced me to his associates and colleagues, and to many of the delegates. With his ability and personality to get along with people, it was apparent to me that Bob has a bright future to look forward to in the Chinese diplomatic corps.

Robert Dunn Wu returned to China for a while following his work with the Chinese United Nations delegation in

Kaye Hong, 1974. [Photo courtesy of Kaye Hong.]

helping to frame the U.N. Constitution. After Red China occupied the Chinese mainland, he came back to the United States and is now living in Maryland. He was a senior reference librarian at the Library of Congress, until he retired.

Kaye Hong remained in the United States rather than returning to China. In recent years he has taken vacation trips to China. He is a retired businessman living in San Francisco.

When the Chinese Digest *made its debut on November 15, 1935, it became the first newspaper published in English for American-born Chinese. Chingwah Lee and myself were the copublishers, and its office was in San Francisco Chinatown.*

Lee and I got acquainted when I joined Boy Scout Troop 3 in 1921; he was one of the founders of the troop. Our friendship continued until he passed away in 1980 (see Chapter 50). We shared a deep concern for and interest in the community. I had spent some time in journalism and the printing trade. When I proposed that we start a newspaper, Lee was receptive, and the Chinese Digest *was born. Newspapers in Chinese had existed as early as the mid-1850s and were published locally during most of the intervening years, but before the* Digest, *none were published in English for Chinese-Americans.*

In 1935, when the *Chinese Digest* began publication, the entire staff was Chinese: myself, Chingwah Lee, William Hoy, Fred George Woo, Clara Chan, Ethel Lum, Robert G. Poon, and George Chow made up the original staff. Although my wife, Daisy, was not an official staff member, she put the final polish on the articles before each issue went to press.

The first editorial to appear in the *Chinese Digest*, which encapsulates our reasons for starting the newspaper, is reproduced on the following page. It should be noted that, beginning around the turn of the century and continuing until after the following piece was written, the Chinese had been more or less compelled to live within Chinatown. As the number of American-born Chinese grew, frustration at this confinement began to build. This editorial appeared at a time when Chinese-Americans

The author at a Linotype machine getting out the Chinese Digest, 1936. [Photo by Digest photographer Wallace H. Fong.]

The staff of the Chinese Digest getting ready to put out another issue of the weekly paper, 1936. Left to right: Daisy Chinn, Thomas W. Chinn, William Hoy, Helen Fong, Chingwah Lee, and Fred George (Chuey) Woo. [Photo by Digest photographer Wallace H. Fong.]

were starting to chafe at the restrictions placed on them by a prejudiced American society, which confined them simply by refusing to sell or rent property to Chinese except in Chinatown.

Why the Digest?

The Chinese Digest is not just a hobby or a business—it is all that with a full-sized battle thrown in. We are fighting on five fronts.

KILLING A CELESTIAL: There are no people in America more misunderstood than the Chinese. From the time of "Sand-lot Kearney" to the present, the Chinese is pictured as a sleepy Celestial enveloped in mists of opium fumes or a halo of Oriental philosophy, but never as a human being. The pulp magazines and Hollywood have served to keep this illusion alive. The "Chinese Digest" is fighting to kill this Celestial bogey and substitute a normal being who drives automobiles, shops for the latest gadgets, and speaks good English.

THE TRUTH IS OUR BATTLE CRY: During the invasion of Manchuria, "Made in Japan" wires were filling the American dailies about "bandits," "misrule," and "Asiatic Monroe Doctrine." The Chinese here know better. They KNOW that the "news" is the result of skillful tampering by such

Chinese Digest *reception on November 1, 1936, for Dr. Hu Shih, the "Father of the Chinese Literary Renaissance." He and Ch'en Tu-haiu began a Chinese literary revolution in 1917 by advocating the use of* peh-hua *(spoken language) as a literary medium in place of the classical* wen-li, *which they considered a dead medium. Chen founded the Chinese Communist Party, and was arrested and imprisoned. Hu Shih went on to earn worldwide honors for his continued advocacy of* peh-hua, *which eventually became accepted. He was honored by over fifty nations around the world for these efforts and for his lifelong dedication to education and literature.* Left to right: *Chih Meng, director of the China Institute in America; Chao-Chin Huang, Chinese consul general; Thomas W. Chinn, editor; Dr. Hu Shih; Patrick P. C. Sun, Chinese vice-consul; and William Hoy, associate editor. [Photo by* Digest *photographer Wallace H. Fong.]*

paid propagandists as "Ratty Rea." Young China wanted to help and contributed its earnings freely. But alas, almost all the "publicity" at that time was printed in Chinese! Furious speeches were made—but almost all in Chinatown! The "Chinese Digest" is prepared to give the truth on the Far East, fearlessly and directly. We believe that the truth is all that China needs—and the world wants.

BRIDGING THE PACIFIC: Without Chinese heritage, Young China here is nothing. With it he is a representative of the oldest civilization on earth. Young China here wants to know more about Chinese art and literature, history and philosophy. They believe they can best enrich American life by contributing these cultural factors here. The old provincial idea about forgetting the best is gone. Enlightened Americanism demands that we keep alive the culture of the old world. The "Chinese Digest" is determined to present the best in the way of classic Chinese art and culture. More than that, the "Chinese Digest" aims to stir up an intense interest in the Chinese language and literature. We believe, with the late B. Laufer, that the learning of Chinese language is easier than the learning of French or German. We enlist your aid to join in the fight to bring scientific teaching methods into the Chinese evening schools.

INTER-TRENCH COMMUNICATION: Chinese in Boston or Portland have natural ties and common interests. Adverse legislation in one is adverse to all. Most of the smaller Chinatowns hardly number more than a hundred souls, and these kinsmen of ours live in isolation and loneliness. They are anxious to know what is going on elsewhere. Conventions of Chinese students or merchants have great sociological consequence, depending on the attendance, often resulting in changes of address or business, or even resulting in marriages. As fast as wire and telephone will permit us we are establishing contacts all over America to serve our readers and make news available to all.

THE WAR ON NEGLECT: Young China Needs Jobs. The progress of any group of people depends primarily on its economic foundation. Give a racially sound people like the Chinese a fair sociological environment and that is all that is needed to get along. At present Chinatowns everywhere are filled to the bursting point with well trained young men and women eager to find a chance to make their way in the world. These young people certainly deserve a chance for they are descendants of pioneers who reached California before ninety percent of the present population of California crossed the plains. They and their forefathers have contributed much to the building of the West. The "Chinese Digest" aims to give publicity to corporations and firms which employ Chinese. By intelligent shopping on the part of our readers we hope to create more openings for our young men and women.

Yes, the "Chinese Digest" is fighting on five fronts. Clubs, lodges, and associations are joining us in the fray. We want to enlist you.

From the very beginning, the *Chinese Digest* was underfinanced and understaffed. Both problems persisted throughout the paper's existence. The staff was not paid; we were all dedicated volunteers, doing the work because we believed in the aims of the paper. The two sources of revenue, subscriptions and advertisements, never reached the levels expected. But Lee provided free office space in his studio, and I set all the type in the Linotype shop I rented, allowing the *Chinese Digest* to continue publication on its limited budget.

At first the *Digest* was published weekly. After a year, however, I could no longer afford to volunteer my time. I was putting in long hours, and I needed to help provide for my three-year-old son. So, starting with the February 1937 issue, I reluctantly relinquished the editorship to William Hoy. The entire paper then had to be typeset and printed by a regular printer and, because of the increased cost, the *Digest* became a monthly publication. It continued as a monthly until April 1939, when Hoy resigned and Chingwah Lee took over. For the balance of 1939—a period of eight months—publication of the *Digest* was suspended.

In January of 1940, Lee formed the China Cultural Society of America and made the *Chinese Digest* its official organ. The society was formed for "those interested in the study, utilization, enjoyment, and propagation of the art, literature, history, drama, and philosophy of China." After the January issue, another issue did not appear until July of 1940, at which time it became a quarterly. A double issue of 40 pages was published for April through September of 1940. This was the last issue of the *Chinese Digest*.

34 Chinese in the Armed Forces

This chapter provides a brief summary of the involvement of the Chinese in the armed forces during World War II, including accounts of two Chinese-American war heroes, Pershing Louie and King Lee. Much of the story remains to be told, however; it is estimated that between 15,000 and 20,000 Chinese served in the armed forces, many of them in combat units, between 1939 and 1945.

In the 1970s the Chinese Historical Society of America decided to find out what it could about the Chinese who served in the U.S. armed forces during the Second World

War. The logical choice to handle the project was a new member of the society, Colonel William F. Strobridge, who, before his retirement, was the historian for the U.S. Army. He and his committee proceeded to publish a notice in the society's *Bulletin* as well as sending news releases to various other publications. In addition, they sought information from Chinese veterans' organizations.

Finally, in the September 1982 issue of the *Bulletin*, the results were published. The original article follows; some extraneous material has been deleted.

Veterans Survey Report

From D-Day on the Normandy beaches to ships in Tokyo Bay, from North Africa to Okinawa, Chinese Americans served in the armed forces of the United States during World War II. The Chinese Historical Society of America's survey of World War II veterans, a service to scholars and community leaders, revealed a rich diversity of wartime assignments for Chinese American men and women. They were on duty with the armed forces all over the world.

Preliminary in nature, but based on responses received from Maryland to Hawaii and Alaska to California, the Society's World War II Veterans Survey indicated that 71% of Chinese American service personnel performed duty with the US Army. An additional 25% served with the Army Air Forces, now a separate component, but then a part of the Army. Air Force veterans flew in the skies above Germany with the 8th and 9th Air Forces and over the Pacific and mainland Asia with the 7th and 14th Air Forces. Sailors, Marines and Coast Guardsmen, serving aboard cruisers, aircraft carriers, destroyers, and naval aircraft, accounted for the remaining 4% of Chinese American veterans. The percentage of Navy, Marines Corps, and Coast Guard veterans is subject to change due to the survey's limited nature.

Somewhat surprisingly, 46% of the veterans surveyed served in the Army's four basic combat arms: Infantry, Armor, Artillery, and Engineers. Chinese Americans occupied front-line positions in Europe with such proud Regular Army units as the 3rd and 4th Infantry Divisions. In the Pacific they were with the hard-campaigning 25th and 32nd Infantry Divisions, and the island-hopping 6th and 77th Infantry Divisions.

A combat-wounds rate of 18% on land, sea, and air for all those Chinese American veterans surveyed belies concepts, fostered by the media, of stumbling, subservient, inarticulate Chinese Americans. The high percentage of men in combat units, on seagoing vessels, and with flight crews, also suggests a need for community support should wartime medical problems reappear as these veterans approach their seventieth birthdays and beyond.

Sometimes pictured as asocial, Chinese Americans instead stepped forward in large numbers to serve their country in World War II, perhaps between 15,000 and 20,000 in total. Some families furnished five and six brothers to the military. Chinese American women also served, in addition to the more traditional Army Nurse Corps, with both Army and Navy uniformed women's branches. Perhaps an indication of the exclusion law's effect, the survey found that 39% of the veterans were foreign born, a figure approaching the foreign-born statistics for the Union Army in the American Civil War. Ten percent of the Chinese veterans had not attained citizenship status when they entered military service.

After the war, 53% of the veterans surveyed elected to use their GI Bill benefits to obtain housing or pursue further education. The high percentage who financed their new homes, plus the fact that most veterans continue to be eligible for various benefits, indicates a potential need for help from genuine community agencies for more aged veterans or their widows.

The Society's survey of World War II veterans points to new fields of endeavor for scholars and community leaders. While the percentages compiled by the survey would probably change with a larger data base, these statistics indicate that military participation in World War II had long-lasting effects on Chinese American life.

The following stories of two Chinese servicemen exemplify the dedication and bravery exhibited by thousands of Chinese who served in the military during World War II.

Pershing Louie

On August 4, 1944, the *Shanghai Evening Post and Mercury*, which at the time was being published out of New York because of the Japanese occupation of portions of China, ran an article about a soldier named Pershing Louie of San Francisco. It read in part as follows:

> Pfc. Pershing Louie, 26, named after Gen. John Pershing, knocked out a German machine gun nest by tossing a dynamite charge over a hedge directly into the German position during the battle for a key hill overlooking St. Lo in Normandy.
>
> According to press dispatches he said, "I ran a few feet and dropped to wait for the blast. It went up very pretty and I ran back to our lines. This morning we found the place blasted, the machine gun wrecked and several Germans were dead."

Louie was born in Fresno and moved to San Francisco with his four brothers and two sisters in 1934. He graduated from George Washington High School and worked

King Lee, 1982. He is the holder of a Silver Star and two Purple Hearts for heroic action in Europe during World War II. His wife, Ngon Ching Wong Lee, and cousin, Edna F. Chinn, (with glasses) are behind him.

at the Mare Island Navy Yard before entering the Army in February of 1942.

King Lee

King Lee, of San Francisco, was drafted on October 22, 1943, and took his basic training at Camp Gruber, Oklahoma, where he earned a sharpshooters medal. Soon thereafter his unit was shipped overseas to the European theater. He was a member of the Blue Devils, 88th Division, 350th Infantry.

It wasn't long before his battalion saw action, and his company of 200 men was trapped and held up for several days near Bologna, Italy. Their losses were tremendous, the company commander had been killed, and they were exhausted and out of food. Finally, on May 11, 1944, Lee volunteered to go out and see what he could do. He wormed his way close to the enemy and the machine gun nest that had pinned his company down. Using rapid fire, he managed to clean out the enemy nest, receiving a leg wound. For this action he was awarded a Silver Star and a Purple Heart.

After recovering from his wound he rejoined his unit and on July 26, 1944, he again distinguished himself with his sharpshooting ability. In the process, however, he was wounded again. This time it cost him his right eye.

He was evacuated, spent time recuperating in the hospital, and received his second Purple Heart. He was finally mustered out on November 15, 1945. In time, he took up his former job as a cook. Lee has a grown family. He recently retired and lives with his wife in San Francisco.

35   Golden Star Radio

It started as a gimmick: The radio show was used to publicize the radio repair and furniture store run by Thomas and May Tong. But before long the store had ceased to exist, and Golden Star Radio was providing their livelihood—as well as playing a vital role in the community's communications network.

"Golden Star is on the air! Quiet, everyone!" This was the cue for every Chinese-speaking family in San Francisco, as well as Stockton, Sacramento, and other areas able to receive the broadcast, to sit down and listen to the daily program. It was a highlight in their lives. You could walk into almost any Chinese business establishment be-

tween 9 and 11 at night and find the Golden Star Chinese Hour turned on; even in restaurant kitchens, a radio would be blaring away while the chef cooked.

The Golden Star Chinese Hour started out on KSAN (KGEI), an early short-wave radio station; it then moved to KLOK before finding a permanent home on KBRG-FM (105.3 FM). There the show aired on weeknights from 9 to 11 P.M. and from 3 to 5 P.M. on Saturdays from its studio at 846 Clay Street. In the forty years that it was on the air, from 1939 to 1979, the program had a tremendous impact on the lives of its listeners, many of whom were illiterate and starved for news. It kept people informed of the progress of many events during those years: the Japanese invasion of China in the 1930s, China War Relief and the Rice Bowl benefits for the hungry and needy, Pearl Harbor and the unfolding of the war, and the events of the McCarthy era. Then there was news of the community.

All the news was faithfully read by announcer May Tong, and hers soon became the best-known voice in Chinatown.

When the show stopped broadcasting in 1979 there was a feeling of deep loss in the community, especially among the elderly and housebound. It had become the longest-running ethnic radio program in the San Francisco Bay Area.

Thomas Tong was the man behind the Chinese Hour during its forty years on the air. He was not, however, the first in his family to devote himself to journalism, politics, and public service. His father, Tong King Chong, was the first Chinese to receive a law degree. He graduated from Kent Law School, a San Francisco night school, in 1912. Two of his classmates were J. O. Tobin, the late president

May Chinn Tong, the "Best-Known Voice in Chinatown," Golden Star Chinese Hour, 1939–1978. [Photo courtesy of Thomas Tong.]

Thomas and May Tong of Golden Star Chinese Hour, ca. 1940. [Photo courtesy of Thomas Tong.]

of the former Hibernia Bank, and former San Francisco Mayor Elmer Robinson.

In the 1890s Tong King Chong was managing editor of the *Mon Hing Yat Bo*, a Chinese weekly published by a group of political reformers in China headed by Kan Yu-wei, the first Chinese to promote democracy in the form of a constitutional monarchy. His solution to China's problems was a modified form of socialism, and he trav-

eled throughout Europe, America, and Asia—wherever there were Chinese—to solicit support. In San Francisco Chinatown, the largest Chinese settlement outside of Asia, his ideas took hold, and the *Mon Hing Yat Bo* was established. It soon became widely read, both in American Chinatowns and in China.

Tong's editorials infuriated the Empress Dowager, and she had Tong's mother and young brother, who lived in China, imprisoned while demanding that Tong return to China to face charges of treason. But Tong stood fast and kept up his hard-hitting editorials. The Dowager, disgraced by the Boxer rebellion in 1900, backed away from executing Tong's family. When the Manchus were defeated and Dr. Sun Yat-sen became president in 1912, he recognized Tong's part in the revolution by making him a member of Parliament and minister without portfolio of the Republic of China. Tong later worked with Oliver Perry Stidger, a San Francisco immigration lawyer and adviser to Sun Yat-sen, helping to draft the constitution for the Republic of China.

Tong King Chong died at the age of forty-seven; his son, Thomas Tong, was only four years old. When Thomas was sixteen and in his first year at Polytechnic High School, his mother became an invalid, and he had to quit school to support her. This was during the Depression, and he had to take whatever jobs came along. For a while he worked as a "lumper" in the produce district, wearing a leather apron and loading potatoes into trucks. At night, he attended the Pacific Radio School.

In time, Thomas married May Chinn, and they opened the Golden Star radio repair and furniture store at 846 Clay Street. Eventually, as a sales ploy to sell his merchandise, he started his radio program. "At that time," he says, "most Chinese homes didn't have refrigerators, and few Chinese spoke English, but they had radios." Thus the Golden Star Chinese Hour was born.

Thomas and May have two sons. The younger one, Ronald, graduated from the University of West Los Angeles Law School in Culver City in 1979 and has a private law practice in Chinatown. Myron, the older son, went to Stanford University, where he received his A.B. in 1956.

In 1962 he received his Ph.D. in bacteriology from UC Berkeley, and in 1966 he earned his M.D. from the UC School of Medicine, San Francisco. After becoming a doctor, Myron entered the navy and served in a medical research unit in Vietnam. He is presently a professor of medicine at the University of Southern California School of Medicine in Los Angeles, as well as chairman of the Liver Cancer Site Team at the USC Center and chief of the Liver Center and director of the Internal Medicine Residency Program at Huntington Memorial Hospital, Pasadena. He has received numerous research grants and has written or been the coauthor of more than a hundred articles and books.

36   The National Chinese Welfare Council

The Chinese in America have experienced discrimination since they first came to this country more than a century ago. They have fought against unfair treatment in the American courts for almost as long. At first, the vehicle the Chinese used for their legal battles was the Chinese Consolidated Benevolent Association (CCBA). Each large Chinatown formed its own CCBA to combat local discriminatory treatment or legislation. Increasingly, however, local CCBAs found themselves needing to band together against statewide or federal actions. The National Chinese Welfare Council grew out of this need.

In March of 1957, more than a century after the first Chinese arrived in the United States, CCBAs from across the United States sent delegates to a national conference of

Chinese communities in Washington, D.C.; 124 delegates from thirty-five cities attended. As a result of this meeting, the National Chinese Welfare Council (NCWC) was formed to represent the interests and welfare of all persons of Chinese descent. From the West Coast, where the largest concentration of Chinese lived, the following persons were selected as delegates: Chang Chun Lam, Hoo Shuck, John Yehall Chin, James Loo, Earl Louie, Clarence Poon, Joseph Quan, S.K. Wong, Shee Gang Lee, Pok Kai Yee, Robert Young Sing Lee, and Jackie Wong Sing.

By 1963 the organization had refined itself into nine districts: Hawaii, the West Coast, the central states, the East Coast, the South, Los Angeles, the North, Washington, D.C., and the New England states. Eighty-five delegates met that year.

NCWC activities included public relations work with senators and congressmen, conferences with the Immigration and State Departments in Washington, obtaining recognition from the U.S. Information Association (USIA) for publication throughout the Far East, and joining with seventy-two other organizations to form American immigration and citizenship conferences.

On August 20, 1964, the House Judiciary Committee on Immigration and Nationality invited the NCWC to testify regarding a proposed amendment to the immigration law. The organization sent attorney Jackie Wong Sing of San Francisco. The following is excerpted from his testimony as it appeared in the House Congressional Record (the amendment was subsequently passed):

In the 1850s, the Chinese were welcomed in the West for the development of farms, mines and the construction of railroads. When the economic depression hit California in 1870, the Chinese were singled out for exclusion and these laws prevailed until 1943 when a quota was first established and the Chinese were allowed the privilege of being naturalized. No doubt the first groups of migratory Chinese were NOT the educated and intellectual type according to our standards, but they were industrious, honest, law-abiding and peaceful. This picture has since been changed after the repeal of the exclusion laws. Several Congressional Acts . . . have made possible the migration of Chinese scholars, scientists, engineers and other skilled persons outside of the quota restrictions. These immigrants, together with the descendants of the first immigrants, have helped create a reservoir of manpower and material and spiritual wealth beneficial to the welfare of the United States. In every field, the Chinese have distinguished themselves and have made valuable contributions toward America's security, growth, progress and prosperity.

. . . In considering the proposed amendments to present immigration law, the primary purpose of H.R. 7700 would provide for a gradual elimination of the National Origins Quota System and also erase the Asia-Pacific Triangle. Passage of this law will, once and for all, and forever, remove all traces of national and racial discrimination in our laws to all minority racial groups, NOT just the Chinese.

On July 15, 1965, the Senate Judiciary Committee on Immigration and Nationality again invited the NCWC to present the views of the Chinese. Jackie Wong Sing was again the spokesperson.

Since the mid-1960s, the NCWC's activities have been reduced to occasional appearances before various committees in Washington, D.C.

PART IV

Breaking Through the Barriers

*M*ost of the people described in this part of the book were born between 1880 and the 1920s, although a few, such as the Louie tennis sisters (Chapter 69), were born much later. They all made lives for themselves in mainstream America as well as in Chinatown, despite the barriers imposed by decades of discrimination. Some, such as William Wai Fong (Chapter 54), had to carry their struggle to the courts; others, through luck, or education, or a good idea, or plain determination, have emerged from the cocoon of Chinatown to work with their peers in a multitude of occupations.

I have begun with the story of my own life, not only because it is familiar, but also because my experiences as a young man growing up in the Chinatown of the 1920s and 1930s were similar to those of other young Chinese-Americans of that era. Many of us still felt strong ties to China as well as to America. My father moved to San Francisco from North Bend, Oregon, primarily to ensure that his children would not lose touch with their Chinese heritage. Chinese language schools were and still are important institutions in Chinatown, spawning friendships that last many years. This emphasis on Chinese language and culture was partly a product of our heritage, and partly simple necessity: the Chinese knew they had to rely on each other in their struggle to survive in America.

I regret that I have not been able to include more people's stories. Chapter 38 consists of several brief descriptions of people I know whose lives, for one reason or another, deserve recognition in a book like this. But there are many others, both working people and professionals of one kind or another, whose steady, quiet achievements over the years are no less worthy of note, and whom

---

Company F, 17th regiment of the California State Militia, 1942. The company was assigned to protect Chinatown during World War II in the event of an invasion. In this photo state militia officials congratulate Chinese community leaders for the fine review of the Chinese company.

I have been unable even to mention due to space limitations. I hope that the stories that are included will give some sense of the variety of talents and personalities that have emerged from Chinatown in my lifetime. The great progress that Chinese-Americans have made over the last half century or so is not due solely to the many "firsts" that have been achieved. Those who came afterward had no fewer difficulties to overcome; for every outstanding success story, there are hundreds of others whose lives and work, though outwardly less spectacular, have been just as important to the Chinese as a group as they have slowly but surely made their own way in America.

I didn't know whether to be happy or sad when our family moved from North Bend, Oregon, to San Francisco. We had to grow up in a hurry or get trampled by the people around us. It took us a long time to realize that Chinatown was a small community like any small town. In both North Bend and Chinatown, people might not socialize together, but everyone knew all about everyone else.

I was born on July 28, 1909, in North Bend, Oregon. My parents named me Tom Chinn; I later changed my name from Tom to Thomas Wayne. Father was head cook in a lumber camp, and we saw him only once every few weeks. Mother, who had been in the United States for only a short time and spoke little English, thus had the job of raising us. I was the third of seven children. Susie and Marian were my elder sisters, and after me came Edna, James, William, and Mae. Two older children, Sam Soo Hoo (his "paper" name, for immigration purposes) and Toy Woon, were born in China to Father's first wife, Lee Suey Ho, who passed away when the children were very young, as described in Chapter 19.

We were one of only two Chinese families in North Bend; the other family ran a grocery store on the other side of town, and we saw them only once a month or less. Thus our dealings were primarily with non-Chinese. All of the children we played with were Caucasians, and we all went to the same school, a little red schoolhouse a few blocks above our street, up a little hill. We got along with the other children fairly well, all things considered. We children always spoke English, except around our parents, and we learned only enough Chinese to carry on basic conversations at home.

We were a close-knit family, looking to Mother for comfort and protection. She saw us through the many childhood diseases and crises bravely and without help. Once a month or so, Father would be able to come home for a couple of days. Sometimes he would bring us delicious apple jelly that he had learned to make from the peels left over from making apple pies. Mother had learned to make jelly too, as well as pies, cakes, and bread. In the summer we would go to nearby wild blackberry patches and fill our pails with the large, ripe berries so Mother could make pies. All in all, those were the happiest childhood days I can remember.

In 1919, when I was ten, Father decided that we should move to San Francisco. He and Mother feared that we children would lose touch with our Chinese heritage, and they wanted us to be able to read and speak Chinese and to learn as much about our culture as possible. We older children had been studying Chinese after school with an elderly Chinese man who with his wife rented a shack behind our house, but it was not enough. With no Chinese community in the town, our parents felt we were becoming too isolated from the culture of the motherland.

After Father had settled his affairs in Oregon by appointing a real estate man to handle our property, we left North Bend for San Francisco—the mecca in the United States for Chinese seeking rapport with their countrymen.

Arriving in San Francisco and entering Chinatown was frightening. After the open spaces of Oregon, Chinatown seemed very confined. The buildings were jammed right up against one another. I couldn't wait to get to our

Sam Soo Hoo, the author's half-brother, 1917. He was killed in 1918 in one of the last actions of World War I.

The widow and two adopted sons of Sam Soo Hoo in China, 1922. Sam's remains were shipped back to his Toishan village in 1921, with an escort of honor from the U.S. government.

new home. Imagine my deep disappointment when we finally arrived at 24 Spofford Alley! It was in a narrow alley and was nothing but a small storefront with a long back room. It was also a shock to learn that we weren't welcome outside of Chinatown and that people didn't leave Chinatown unless they had a good reason. To a boy like me, having lived all my life in an atmosphere where all our friends were Caucasian boys and girls, our new home presented a problem of vexing proportions.

The front portion of the store became our living room, and Father partitioned the back section into three smaller "rooms," all of which opened onto a long hallway that ran from the front all the way to the back. He and Mother had a tiny room in the rear, the girls had the middle portion, and we three boys had the room just behind the storefront. The wooden partitions were about 7 feet high, and the doorways were only curtained off; there were no doors between rooms. Off the back end of the hallway was the enclosed toilet, and next to it was the sink. Alongside that was a tiny stove consisting of three gas burners sitting atop a long, tin-covered bench, and next to it was a chopping board. That was our kitchen. An old galvanized tub became our bathtub and hung upon the wall when not in use.

Spofford Alley had originally been called "New Spanish Alley" in Chinese because it had been the site of a number of gambling houses frequented primarily by Spanish or Mexican people. (Another such alley, originally called

"Old Spanish Alley," is now Ross Alley.) Those establishments had been burned out long before we moved there, however. There were several interesting places in our alley. The headquarters of an organization called the Freemasons was there (not connected in any way with the American Free and Accepted Masons), and it is still in the same location today. It began as a cross between a secret society and a protective society for members who needed defense from other, more troublesome, groups, and also worked to oust the monarchy in China.

My sister Mae remembers noticing a little store called Tong Kee across the street from where we lived. They didn't sell anything, but the place was frequented by beautiful women dressed in fancy clothes and wearing lots of perfume. They lived directly above the store and would throw down a key from the second floor when a man rang the bell. Many years later she realized that it was a house of prostitution.

At night, we and the other residents of Chinatown practically barricaded ourselves in our homes. This was because from before the turn of the century until well into 1925, petty crime abounded in Chinatown—robberies, burglaries, and tong wars. The storefront that we lived in had a double door, and the upper half was made of glass. One door was generally boarded up, but the door where we went in and out had a curtained window. Decades before our arrival, the residents of Chinatown had set up a system of protecting the glass in their windows and doors at night by fastening an inch-thick board over the windows. We would slip the board between two galvanized inverted U-shaped metal pieces at the top and then screw it into place at the bottom. We boarded the windows and doors in this manner every night at dusk

The Chinn family shortly after arriving in San Francisco, 1919. Left to right: *William, Lee Shee (mother), Thomas, James, Marian, Chinn Wing (father), Mae, and Edna (behind Mae).*

and uncovered them the following morning. (Recently, in 1988, I checked and found the brackets still there, sixty-eight years later.)

When school began later that year, we started classes at the Oriental School, on Washington Street between Stockton and Powell, the only school we were allowed to attend. The students were all Chinese, and the teachers all Caucasian. The classes were much larger than the ones we had attended in Oregon, but we adapted easily. In 1924 the name would be changed to Commodore Stockton School, its name to this day.

In addition to public school, my brothers and I soon began attending the Chung Wah Chinese School on weekday afternoons from 5:00 until 8:00 and on Saturday mornings from 9:00 until 12:00. There we were taught

24 Spofford Alley, the author's home upon arriving in San Francisco from Oregon in 1919. For many years the family placed specially made boards over the windows at night to keep them from being broken by burglars or members of feuding tongs. The brackets that held the boards in place were still there when this photograph was taken in 1988, even though the windows had not been boarded at night since the mid-1920s. [Photo by Nancy Warner.]

to read and write in Chinese. I found it hard to adjust to both English and Chinese classes daily, however, and always received low grades in the latter.

We children had a lonely time of it for the first couple of years that we lived in San Francisco. We learned to our dismay that the spoken language in Chinatown was about 85 percent Chinese, interspersed with a smattering of imperfect English. To make matters worse, Chinatown had nearly a dozen Cantonese dialects, as well as its own slang. For example, one man asking another to have a cup of coffee with him would say, "Let's go for a cup of coffee" in Chinese, but when he reached the last word, "coffee," he would say "kah-feah," using a word that was neither Chinese nor English, but slang based on the En-

glish sound. Even when we could understand their Chinese, we were lost when it came to the local slang.

Because we could not converse in Chinese easily, we were not comfortable trying to talk with the other children, nor they with us. They didn't really accept us. Even our thoughts and vision differed from theirs; ours extended beyond the borders of Chinatown. We were generally excluded from their circle, and they would tease us and play pranks on us. We and other newly transplanted Chinese-Americans were given the name *hor gee doy mo no* ("American-born boy have no brains"), and it stung.

It would not have been so bad if there had been other children to play with. But because we were required to attend the Oriental School, which had been built especially for the Chinese, and because we were restricted to Chinatown, there was no chance of finding more compatible friends. Over time, of course, we learned many of the idioms of Chinatown, but we were never comfortable speaking Chinese, except for the little we used to talk with our parents.

Among our saving graces during this period were the churches built in Chinatown to convert the Chinese to the Christian faith, supported by American missionaries and their mission boards. Coming into Chinatown in the mid-1800s, most of the churches began to hold classes in English, taught primarily by people who had been missionaries in China and who therefore could speak some Chinese. At the beginning of the class they would have a Bible lesson. These classes gave the Chinese a chance to learn some English, while the churches were able to give a Christian sermon to their captive audience.

After a while I discovered the Chinese YMCA, a small place at 830 Stockton Street. By now it was 1921, and I was old enough to get around on my own. I started to spend most of my free time at the Y. There was a billiard table, and people could learn to play instruments and join a band. They also taught English and held exercise classes. I became very involved in the athletics they sponsored.

That same year I turned twelve and thus became eligible to join Boy Scout Troop 3, the first all-Chinese Boy Scout troop in American history. My involvement with Scouting and the training I received as a boy would have a lifelong influence on me. Also of deep significance was that becoming a Boy Scout led me to meet Chingwah Lee, a man who would become my mentor and lifetime friend. In 1921 he was attending the University of California and was assistant scoutmaster of the troop. He had been instrumental in the founding of the first Chinese Boy Scout troop in 1914, having come across a used Boy Scout manual. The scoutmaster of our troop was American and, needless to say, Scout activities were all conducted in English, which suited me just fine.

Between the Chinese Y and Scouting, almost all of my spare time was taken up. What little time I had left over was devoted to one other activity: reading. In the early 1920s I discovered our neighborhood's modern public library. I practically lived at the North Beach Library (later renamed the Chinatown Library) at 1135 Powell Street. The librarians all knew me well, particularly the head librarian, a stout, elderly Italian woman. She took an early interest in me and helped me out by choosing and laying aside books for me. I loved adventure stories and read all I could about knights in shining armor, King Arthur, Rome and the Coliseum, and the intrigues and battles fought in Europe. I came to know early European history fairly well. My mother used to have to get out of bed at 1:00 or 1:30 A.M. to tell me, "Lie down, close that book, and shut off the light—you'll wear out your eyes!"

By 1922, my father had decided that the Chung Wah Chinese School was not the place for me to learn Chinese. I was not learning easily. The classes were the same size as those in public school, which meant twenty-eight or thirty students to a classroom. He decided to enroll me in a private class with a clansman, Chin Dook Jow, who had been a teacher in China before emigrating to San Francisco. He had ten to twelve pupils, and Father was sure this would provide the personal attention I needed. After several months he had some doubts, but he insisted that I keep at it.

From the early 1920s until late 1922, Father worked as a cook for the Southern Pacific Railroad maintenance crews. The job involved cooking aboard an old railroad car; the kitchen was at one end, and a dozen or more chairs were clustered around a couple of tables at the other end. The crew bunked in a second car. Sometimes, depending on the job, a locomotive would move the cars to a work site, but more often the cars would remain on a siding while the crew used hand cars, with a handle that they pumped up and down, to reach a piece of track needing repair.

I accompanied him on a short trip once, to give him a hand, but Mother would not let me go after that, fearing that it would interfere with my studies.

Finally, in 1923, Father's health forced him to give up this strenuous work. We children found out later that he had suffered a mild heart attack. Relegated to Chinatown once more, he decided to start a small restaurant on Clay Street, just below Kearny. By this time, he reasoned, he could expect some part-time help from his older children.

He had only a small number of customers, barely enough to cover the overhead, but for a while he was as happy as could be.

By 1923 my sisters had begun to meet girls who were visiting San Francisco Chinatown from the smaller Chinese communities in the surrounding rural areas. These girls and their families would come in to Chinatown on weekends to buy goods or attend the Chinese opera. Like us, these children came from small towns where they went to school with Caucasian boys and girls, and their English was better than their Chinese. My sisters welcomed them with open arms. When they were old enough, these girlfriends would be allowed to come to San Francisco by themselves, and they would stay with my sisters in their little room for days and even weeks at a time. And another place or two could always be set at dinnertime when these friends dropped in unexpectedly.

By this time I had become the man of the family whenever Father was not home. Years later my youngest sister, Mae, would tease me about how I used to borrow some of Mother's *pow fa*, or hair "oil," to slick back my "sheikish patent leather hair," as she called it. *Pow fa* is made of shavings from a tree that grows in China. When placed in water, the shavings give off a thick, clear liquid that is odorless and colorless. Mother would brush or comb this into her hair to keep it in place and give it a beautiful sheen.

During all this time I rarely left Chinatown unless I had good reason to do so. I was afraid to leave, as were most of the people I knew, adults and children alike. Chinese boys who left Chinatown were often beat up; this happened to some of my friends.

Soon, however, I was to travel far from Chinatown.

In 1924, Father decided to send me, the oldest boy, to China for a Chinese education. Plans were quickly made. I was to go with a first cousin named Chin Ying Fay. He was many years older than I and had been born and raised in China, so he was familiar with his homeland and our little village. He watched over me and provided guidance on the trip.

We were booked on one of the early "President" ships. We traveled steerage—in the bowels of the ship, sleeping in lined-up hammocks—and were allowed to come up for fresh air occasionally. It was an adventure. There were several youngsters aged twelve to twenty, and a group of older people of fifty to sixty-five or so. Long tables and raised planks for seating were set up in one section of our quarters, and three times a day we were fed. All we would have was rice, brought to us in large wooden or tin buckets, and a couple of vegetable dishes and occasionally bits of meat. There was plenty of tea. Men played *pai gow* (dominoes) or sometimes regular card games. Others played Chinese checkers or smoked and read Chinese books.

I was to discover later that as early as 1912, when China became a republic, a trend had commenced among families of means to send a boy—generally the oldest—back to China for an education. The Chinese were seldom able to find jobs outside of Chinatown. Even the well educated with degrees from universities were reduced to taking jobs as waiters, dishwashers, or janitors, or they worked as clerks for Chinatown stores, getting paid only a few dollars a week. Many felt that the new Republic of China might offer them better opportunities, provided they could read, write, and speak Chinese.

The ship arrived in Hong Kong, and we left immediately for our village. This meant crossing the border and getting on a train in China. Several hours later we arrived in a fairly new town called Kong Yick Fou. There we boarded a Sunning Railroad train, which took us to Toishan City. The journey took us almost a day.

While I was living in my father's village and going to school, I met a couple of old men, village elders, who spoke a little English. These men had spent many years in the United States, doing farm work and helping to build the Central Pacific Railroad, and had then returned to China to retire. They loved to relive their experiences in America with whoever would listen, and they found in me an eager audience. It allayed my homesickness to hear a few American phrases and talk of home. Their stories were what originally sparked my interest in Chinese-American history. Some of the things they told me were so fascinating that I thought they should be recorded. I was just a youngster, however, and soon other events would push these ideas from my mind. I had been in China for only a few months when I learned that Father had passed away. He had been ill and unable to work for some time. I left immediately for the United States.

When I got back I had to go to work to help support the family, and thus I wasn't able to go back to school. Father's long illness had drained the family's financial resources. I took any work I could get. For a few weeks I picked fruit in the San Joaquin Valley. Then I became an insurance agent in Chinatown for the American National Life Insurance Company, a company based in Texas. After two months I was fired; they found out that I was only sixteen years old. The office that hired me hadn't looked at my application very carefully, so my age wasn't discovered until the form reached the home office.

Although that job was short-lived, it led me to another job that I would hold for seven years. The district supervisor who had hired me to be an insurance agent told me of an opening with the California Inspection Rating Bureau, an organization formed by insurance companies to inspect California business facilities with certain hazards or risks in their type of work and to offer lower premiums when such businesses were operating safely. I became a file clerk for the San Francisco office, located in the downtown financial district, at 216 Pine Street, and I worked there from 1926 to 1933.

This job might not sound like much, but I was the first Chinese-American ever to get a job in an insurance-related office in this area. Although my work was always described as outstanding, I was never promoted. There simply weren't any openings for anything better for me. I was very happy with the job, however, because I was getting wages that were much higher than anything I could hope for in Chinatown. I started at $75 per month, and this was gradually increased to $100. Once I had a job and could afford tuition, I began taking evening courses in business administration, advertising, and journalism at Healds Business College and through UC Extension.

This was one of the happiest periods of my life; for the first time, I was able to come out of Chinatown and mingle with people other than the Chinese. My fellow workers were very congenial, and they were always asking me about Chinese customs and so forth. We were able to spend time talking as we worked, which made the atmosphere quite pleasant. A young man I met working in the same building was especially friendly, and in 1932 came with his girlfriend, Muriel, to visit us in Chinatown. His name was Bert Stewart, and we hit it off very well. He later became president of the National Automobile Club.

Mother had to find full-time work too. She began working at a basket factory, making decorative clay fruit and attaching it to the woven bamboo baskets, which were then sprayed and painted. The other children also earned money to help with expenses by shelling cooked shrimp at home for a shrimp company. Mother pitched in when she could. The shrimp company had a regular route through Chinatown, and they would bring a huge basket containing about 50 pounds of the shrimp. We would shell the shrimp, putting the meat in one pile and the shells in another. Four or five of us would do this at a time, and we would sometimes make twenty-five or thirty-five cents a day. Our entire home would smell of shellfish after one of these shrimp-shelling sessions.

Times were hard, and everyone, especially Mother, made sacrifices in order to pay our expenses. We did have a telephone and an old phonograph with a few records, including "It's a Long Way to Tipperary" and "Song of India." Sometimes, for a treat, the younger children would pull their little red wagon to a wholesale bakery on Broadway near Sansome Street that sold broken cookies in big bags for 25 cents. People would have to get there early in the morning, before they were sold out. For dinner, Mother usually made rice and a dish with some cut-up pork and a lot of vegetables—whatever was available at a low price. All told, the ingredients for a typical dinner for the seven of us would cost twenty-five to thirty-five cents.

When my sister Edna finished beauty school, she set up a folding screen in a corner of the store and opened a little beauty shop, which she ran for about a year. She gave haircuts, marcels (waves crimped into place with a heated curling iron), and paper curls. Somehow, with all of us contributing in any way we could, we scraped together enough to live on.

For many years I had been deeply involved in athletics. I went out for every sport that the Chinese community offered—track, basketball, football, tennis, and so on. I was the Chinatown handball champion and won medals in track and field, and much later, in 1936, I became the national Chinese singles tennis champion. The only type of sport I wasn't involved in was swimming and water sports, for the simple reason that when I was young there was no pool in Chinatown, and Chinese were not welcome at any of the pools outside of Chinatown. There were also no sporting goods stores in Chinatown. Any time we needed athletic equipment we would have to go to a store downtown, where we were not always welcome. One day I got the idea of starting my own sporting goods store, in the storefront that served as our living room at the front of our home.

In 1929 I opened for business on evenings and weekends, after my regular job as a file clerk. To my knowledge, this was the first Chinese-run sporting goods store in the country. I had someone come in to teach me how to string tennis rackets, and the salesmen I bought from showed me all the things I needed to know about the various other types of athletic equipment. I knew all of the sports-minded young people in Chinatown and was able to get a certain amount of business from them. The sales volume wasn't great, but the store was panning out.

Before I was sent to China to attend school, my division of Boy Scout Troop 3 (there were three divisions; I was patrol leader of one and became assistant scoutmaster in 1927) started to meet at the Chinese Congregational

Church every Friday night, and I began attending the church. When I returned to the United States after my father's death I resumed my involvement in the church, and on Easter Sunday, 1925, I was baptized. Among the group baptized at the same time was Daisy Lorraine Wong. I began teaching Sunday school, and Daisy (Dillie) and I became part of a group composed mainly of boys belonging to the Yoke Choy Club and girls belonging to the Square and Circle Club. (These clubs are described in Chapters 26 and 27.)

None of us dated as couples; we went around as a group, with everyone paying their own way. It was not until four years later, in 1929, that I asked Dillie for a date. We became engaged that July, and the following year, on June 8, 1930, we were married.

In 1931, after a year and a half of running the store from Spofford Alley, I decided I needed a larger store on a regular street rather than in an alley. I found a suitable one at 876 Sacramento Street, right around the corner from the Chinese playground, and Dillie and I moved out of our small apartment at 752 Stockton and into the store's back room. Tahmie's Sport Shop, as I called it, was soon open for business. I still continued my work at the California Inspection Rating Bureau, and Dillie kept her job as a teletypist with Western Union.

In 1932 our son, Walter, came along. Dillie took some time off after he was born, but then she went back to work to help make ends meet, while my mother took care of Walter.

A few months after our son's birth, the manager of the San Francisco headquarters of the Wilson Western Sporting Goods Company, one of my suppliers, asked me what I thought the market was like for sporting goods in

Friday morning Bible Class, 1929. For nearly a decade, classes were held for Chinese business people from 7:30 A.M. to 8:15 A.M. every Friday at the present Cameron House. Attendance varied from a dozen to as many as twenty-five.

China. I told him that it was a rather poor country but that I thought it was becoming more sports-oriented. He then asked if I would consider becoming their representative in China and opening up that market. His idea gave me a lot of food for thought. They didn't offer me any pay, just the sales territory, but it seemed like a golden opportunity.

So in March of 1933 I resigned from my job, sold the sporting goods store, and left for China. Dillie and Walter moved into an apartment on Brooklyn Place, across from the sport shop. My plan was to become established, find a place to live, and then send for my family. The day I set foot on Chinese soil, however, newspapers were reporting that America was considering going off

A Chinese Student Conference at Stanford University, 1928. These conferences were popular in the early part of the century. They were generally held during summer vacation and offered opportunities for students from colleges and universities all across the country to gather and discuss academic, economic, political, cultural, and social problems. As the Chinese became more assimilated into the mainstream of American society, attendance at these conferences declined, and they are no longer held. On this page, the author is third from the right in the front row. Thomas A. Wong, on his left, was the best man at his wedding. The author's wife, Dillie, is just behind the author. [Photo by May's Photo Studio.]

西美中國 Chinese Student Alliance, W. S. 26th Conference, Stanford University, 1928

the gold standard because of the Depression. This caused all international trading to be frozen because the currency would be in such a state of flux. I ended up spending only a few months in China, unable to drum up any business. I was very disappointed.

During my travels in China this time, I had occasion once again to ride the Sunning Railroad, the same one I had ridden on to get to my father's village in 1924. This time, however, I learned the railroad's history. It seems that a man named Chin Yee Hee (or Chin Gee Hee) had, as a boy, left China for California and worked his way from San Francisco northward, stopping wherever he found work. He eventually went to work for James J. Hill when Hill took over the affairs of the Great Northern Railroad. Chin Yee Hee remained with Hill for many years and gradually became familiar with just about every task involved in the construction and operation of an American railway.

Eventually Chin felt he had no more to learn. He had managed to lay aside enough to be called a rich man in China, and around the turn of the century he decided to return to his native land and, in Sunning City, his birthplace, build a railroad. In 1900 he left the employ of Jim Hill and started to raise money for his venture among his Chinese compatriots in the United States. He then returned to China and raised the rest of the money he needed there.

Shortly thereafter he gathered a group of Chinese civil engineers, graduates of UC Berkeley and Stanford University, according to an article that appeared in the *San Francisco Examiner* on October 25, 1908, and built the Sunning Railroad. It was financed and built entirely by Chinese, with no outside help, and it was a big success.

Hearing this story revived my interest in Chinese-American history, and I resolved to do what I could to record these stories some day.

As things turned out, the Sunning Railroad survived for less than fifty years. In 1932 Japan started its aggressive expansion, moving its armies into China and causing much destruction and death. Following VJ Day in 1945, it was discovered that the Sunning Railroad had disappeared entirely. It had been dismantled to prevent the invading Japanese armies from using it in the late 1930s. It was never rebuilt.

Years later, a friend who knew of my interest in the railroad gave me an album of photographs showing all of the stations and commemorating the opening of the line. He had received the photographs because his grandfather was one of the overseas Chinese stockholders in the railroad. When I found out that the people in the area through which the railroad had run wanted to build a memorial in honor of Chin Yee Hee but that they weren't able to locate any photographs, I had a complete set made and sent to them. They were overjoyed, and the photo set is now prominently displayed. Years later I heard from Chin Yee Hee's grandson, Woon C. Chan. He now lives in Monterey Park in Southern California, where he owns a restaurant.

When I got back to the United States after my business in China didn't pan out, things were very bad. It was during the heart of the Depression, and I couldn't find a decent job. Finally I decided that I would have to create my own job, and I went to school. McClymonds High School in Oakland had a printing department with all the necessary equipment. They printed their own school paper and papers for some of the other high schools.

They were taking in a few nonstudents who wanted to learn the printing trade, and I was lucky enough to be accepted as one of them. I spent close to a year and a half there, learning to set type on the Linotype machine and make up type into forms for printing, and I also took some journalism classes to supplement the knowledge I had previously acquired.

In mid-1935, after I left the school, I approached Chingwah Lee, my friend since my Boy Scout days, to see if he would finance me in a joint venture to publish the first English-language newspaper for Chinese-Americans. He was just getting ready to leave for Hollywood, where he had a big part in the movie *The Good Earth*, featuring Paul Muni. He agreed to the plan, and every week he sent a portion of his pay to me to help put out the *Chinese Digest*, as we called our weekly newspaper.

I operated the *Chinese Digest* for a little over a year without making any money and without accepting any salary. It was a financial strain on my family; we had to depend on my wife's paycheck and what few dollars we had saved. So after a year I reluctantly had to resign and leave the job to Chingwah, who said he would take it over and see what he could do with it. His film was almost completed by this time, and he was returning to San Francisco. (The *Chinese Digest* is discussed at greater length in Chapter 33.)

I was then able to get credit to start a small Linotype composition firm called Chinn Linotype Composition. My plan was to provide trade (wholesale) typesetting to printers, publishers, and advertising agencies. The publishers and advertising agencies never did materialize, because my plant was too small for them, but I was able to make a living out of it.

The cashier's cage of the Sun Wah Kue restaurant at 848 Washington Street, January 1987. The cage has been in use since the restaurant opened in 1929. Sun Wah Kue is a favorite place for many of the community's businessmen and women to meet and hash out business deals. More than half a century ago, the author became editor/copublisher of the Chinese Digest *here, over a waffle and a cup of coffee.*

Although Pearl Harbor was not yet on the horizon, the Japanese had been causing "incidents" in China since the early 1930s. By the late 1930s Japan had committed many acts of aggression and landed troops in various parts of China, and open conflict had commenced.

The Chinese in America had been sending money to China as well as sending medical supplies and food to help the Chinese civilian population. As matters got worse, the Chinese community in San Francisco united in a big effort to support China. They boycotted Japanese goods;

picketed boats loading scrap iron for Japan; and organized fundraisers like the Rice Bowl Parties, for which all of the Chinese clubs and associations created an organization called the "Federation of Chinese Clubs" to pool their efforts in putting on shows and dances, etc. In 1937–38 I was made treasurer of the Federation, at the same time that Bessie Kai Kee (Mrs. Henry) Woo was president. The Chinese Six Companies created an English-language press bureau and put me in charge of it. Among other young journalists I met at that time were Stanton Delaplane and Herb Caen of the *San Francisco Chronicle*. But my business started to suffer, and I reluctantly relinquished my volunteer work.

When the United States entered World War II after Pearl Harbor I was given 3A draft status, meaning that I wouldn't be called immediately because I had a family. After a few months, however, I was told that everybody who could possibly do so had to get into defense work or face being drafted. The profits from my typesetting business weren't that great, so I closed it down and sold everything. I took a job at Western Pipe and Steel Co. of California in South San Francisco, thinking to myself, "So the sons and daughters of Chinatown have finally made it; they're working outside of Chinatown!" Almost anyone could get a job in the shipyards during this time. Work went on around the clock, and many Chinese-American women were working alongside the men. I was a shipfitter with I.D. badge number 4867. I couldn't get used to the work, however, and after several weeks I left to take a job at the Army Quartermaster Market Center. This was a fairly new department of the quartermaster general's office.

The idea of the Army Quartermaster Market Center (QMMC) was to establish depots around the country where fresh food could be purchased at peak season and stored in refrigerated warehouses. Fresh fruits and vegetables, dairy products, and meat could all be stored in strategic locations, depending on the requirements of troops stationed at various overseas sites. In addition, large quantities of fresh food were needed for shipment to our forces located in our area. Sometimes we also purchased for the navy.

I started out mainly as just another office worker, and a few months later I was promoted. I kept on getting promoted until I was given the title of Chief of Storage and Distribution. I was in charge of cold-storage warehouses from the Oregon border as far south as Fresno. All of the fresh vegetables, dairy products, and meat and poultry being shipped in and out of these warehouses were my responsibility. At times, in order to catch seasonal goods such as fresh vegetables, as many as 200 or 300 railroad cars would be shuttling in and out of our leased and government warehouses.

I remember one early incident especially well. One of our potato vendors in Stockton claimed they had not received payment for a carload of potatoes shipped to a Southern California naval installation. Months of correspondence produced only a denial by the navy of having received any such shipment. As our office was the contracting QMMC, the vendor was quite insistent that we investigate. This was done with the navy by phone and telex. They still said no shipment had been received. Finally our office sent me to make a final attempt to show the vendor we were making every effort to be helpful. On my arrival, I was able to unravel the problem. I telexed my office that I had secured confirmed acknowledgment of delivery from the navy, and recommended that the vendor be paid at once. Shortly thereafter I received a letter from the vendor, thanking me for locating the $10,000 carload of potatoes. I still have the letter, a memento of one of my most cherished "good deeds" as a Boy Scout.

In 1941 the civil defense and air raid wardens organizations came into being. After the attack on Pearl Harbor on December 7, 1941, the movement gained urgency. At the time, we were living on the outskirts of Chinatown, at 1239 Washington Street near Taylor. One day someone called to ask me to attend an important meeting at a financial district office. I didn't know the man, a Mr. Frizzell, but he said that a friend had recommended me to be a company air raid warden in charge of the Chinatown district. He asked me if I knew Chinatown well and whether I could organize local air raid wardens to handle the district. I answered that I did and could, and he assigned me the job on the spot.

John Kan (who later became the owner of Kan's Restaurant) became my assistant, and I had no trouble recruiting volunteer wardens, the only trouble being that many were working odd hours and split shifts. After December 7, however, everyone realized the potential danger and pitched in to do the job.

The situation involved a great deal of responsibility, as property and lives were potentially at stake. For the first time in such a vital citywide activity, Chinatown's people and Caucasians living in the area designated as Chinatown worked together as a cohesive force. The Fairmont Hotel, one of San Francisco's largest, happened to be just inside our area. During our early air raid practice drills, when every light in the city was supposed to be blacked out so that it could not be seen from the outside,

there would always be those who forgot to comply and left lights burning. This was often the case with rooms in the hotel, and our wardens would rush into the building and, with hotel personnel, attempt to locate the source of the light. Eventually, perhaps because we had to list the violators after each practice, the big office buildings, as well as the hotels, decided to get exemptions from our local wardens, as long as they provided their own air raid warning system and policed themselves.

In 1942 I reached the point where I could no longer spend the daytime hours that the job of air raid warden entailed, and I reluctantly resigned. My respite was brief, however. A couple of weeks later, John Kan approached me about joining the California State Militia (CSM). Our duties, he promised, would not involve nearly as much time as those of an air raid warden. His persistence overcame my objections, and we met with Captain (soon to be Major) Maurice H. Auerbach. I became commander of Chinatown Company F of the California State Militia, and John Kan was second in command.

I soon found that a good number of my former air raid wardens, through no urging on my part, had joined the militia. Among them were Walter Lee, who became the sergeant major; Thomas F. Leong; Earl Sun Louie; Lawrence Lew; William J. Wong; George Ong; Roy Au Kwok; and many others. We trained at the State Armory at 14th and Mission streets, and in time John and I received our commissions, John as second lieutenant and I as first lieutenant. We assembled our company and, with a drum corps leading the procession and Inspector John Manion of the Chinatown police squad to clear the way, marched from Pine Street to Pacific to declare our readiness to defend our part of town.

Company A, air raid wardens of San Francisco, 1942. The company was responsible for the Chinatown area: Pacific to Pine and Kearny to Mason streets.

The author is third left from the center. Police Inspector Jack Manion of the Chinatown squad is the third person to his left. [Photo by May's Photo Studio.]

After about a year I had to resign from this position too. My job with the QMMC was too demanding, and in June of 1942 Dillie and I had moved from San Francisco to our dream home in San Mateo, a town on the peninsula south of the city. I was satisfied, however, that in each position I had laid the groundwork for others to continue.

After the war ended, of course, our office did not disappear suddenly; it gradually wound down, and during those years of 1946 to 1949 there was still a great deal of activity at the QMMC. But I was feeling the pinch because a lot of discharged officers were scrambling for civilian jobs. It was made very obvious to me that a friend of my commanding officer was after my job. I finally decided that after seven years of working for the government it was time to get back into my trade, so in 1949 I resigned from the QMMC. I started another typesetting

business, called California Typesetting Company, on Kearny Street near California. By this time I had saved enough money to start a larger plant than the one I had owned before.

With more equipment, I had promises of work from outside of Chinatown, from non-Chinese businesses, but it never materialized. I got a little work from some of the smaller shops, but not enough to compensate for the

larger plant. In 1956, after six years, I had to close down. I was totally wiped out financially.

I then went to work for some of my former competitors, who were glad to get an experienced operator. I worked for quite a while as an operator, proofreader, and makeup man. Finally, in 1971, my boss, the owner of Gollan Typography, Inc., one of the largest typesetting plants in San Francisco, decided to sell out and retire. His

Shortly after Pearl Harbor the state activated the California State Militia, which was supposed to help local authorities maintain law and order in the event of a direct attack. Here, Captain (later Major) Maurice Auerbach (left) is in conversation with the author, company commander (center), and John Kan, deputy (right). The company was responsible for the Chinatown area.

father had started the business in 1915, and he had eight or nine Linotype machines plus all of the other necessary equipment. It was a large plant and the asking price was a few hundred thousand dollars, but that was a bargain.

The foreman of the plant, Robert C. Stevenson, and I were very good friends, and he wanted to take over the business, but he didn't have the money. Nor could I

afford to buy the plant myself. But I was able to get a loan from friends, and I helped my friend the foreman so that he could buy in and become a junior partner. I still needed a little more money for operating capital, however, so I turned to my son, Walter, who by that time was a full journeyman typesetter, and he agreed to invest in the business and became a silent junior partner as well. I held a majority interest.

Robert and I operated from 1971 until 1980, when we decided that, because of the increasing computerization of the typesetting industry, the plant would soon be obsolete. So, with Walter's concurrence, we sold out. The plant was dismantled and shipped overseas to a business in a less-developed nation that was accustomed to setting type by hand and thought that the Linotype machine was the answer to its problems. They were happy, and we did fairly well on the deal. After that, I retired.

One of my main goals since the 1930s has been to record and preserve the history of the Chinese in the United States and to draw attention to the contributions they have made. I started the *Chinese Digest* in 1935 with that aim in mind, and I began accumulating material on the subject at about the same time. After World War II, I began giving occasional talks on Chinese-American history to various groups. In 1962, still wanting somehow to promote the preservation of Chinese-American history, I invited four friends to join me in starting a Chinese historical society. They were Chingwah Lee, H. K. Wong, Dr. Thomas Wu, and C. H. Kwock.

The first formal meeting of the Chinese Historical Society of America took place on January 5, 1963. Thirty-one people came to the meeting, which was held at my house. They were both Chinese and Caucasians; all were deeply interested in Chinese-American history. One of those attending was Gladys Hansen, a librarian I had known for many years who later became (and still is) the Archivist of the City and County of San Francisco. She had encouraged me to organize the society when I spoke to her about it, and it was partly due to her urging that I finally decided to do it.

That meeting was the beginning of my involvement with the Chinese Historical Society, whose activities are described in more detail in Chapter 71. I was elected as the first president and was reelected to that office each of the next three years. During the first year of the society's existence I started a small newsletter for our membership, which by 1966 had become the *Chinese Historical Society Bulletin*, a monthly publication that is still in existence. I served as the editor for fourteen years, until 1980, when I retired and turned the job of editor over to Annie Soo. For the entire fourteen years that I was editor and had my own typesetting plant, I donated all the typesetting, and my friends Lawton and Alfred Kennedy, as well as Henry Louie and Woody Moy (Eastwind), donated the printing.

Soon after we started the society we found that we were inundated with requests from teachers, schools, professors, and others who needed information about Chinese-American history. After responding piecemeal to individual requests for several years, we decided to hold a seminar that would provide educators across the country with the materials they needed to teach Chinese-American history. The seminar was held in 1969 at the Chinese-American Citizen's Alliance auditorium, and it was attended by nearly 400 people. I edited a syllabus for the event, with Him Mark Lai and Philip Choy as associate editors, entitled *A History of the Chinese in California: A Syllabus*, which is now in its sixth printing. Today the society is still selling almost as many copies each year as it sold in the very beginning.

In 1969, the same year that we sponsored the seminar for educators, I presented a paper at the World Conference on Records in Salt Lake City entitled "Genealogical Sources of Chinese Immigrants to the United States." Although I was very busy, I saw the invitation to speak as a chance to get wider recognition for our historical society. I was one of 8,000 delegates to the conference; they came from forty-six nations, including the Soviet Union.

In 1972, when the country began planning the American Revolution Bicentennial celebration in 1976, I was invited by the president's Bicentennial Administration to represent the Chinese Historical Society and the Chinese on the National Advisory Committee on Racial, Ethnic, and Native American Participation. As I traveled back and forth to Washington to attend the various committee meetings, I got the idea of doing something locally to commemorate the Chinese presence in America. I proposed that the Chinese Historical Society sponsor a national conference called "The Life, Influence, and Role of the Chinese in the United States: 1776-1960." The conference was approved and was held at the University of San Francisco on July 10 through 12, 1975, a year before the Bicentennial, so that the proceedings could be published and made available for the celebration in 1976. I was chairman of the conference, the first national conference on Chinese-American studies.

San Francisco was also celebrating its bicentennial in 1976, and in 1975 I was invited to become a member of the History Committee of the San Francisco Twin Bicentennial, chaired by C. Albert Shumate, M.D.

Far left: *The author's sister Susie, 1898–1986; this photograph was taken in 1982. [Photo courtesy of Greta Dy Foon Lee.]*

Left: *The author's brothers and sisters, Christmas of 1988.* Left to right: *James, William, the author, Mae, Edna, and Marian (in front of Edna). [Photo by Lorri Ng.]*

Over the years a number of distinctions and honors have come my way, all unsolicited and for which I am exceedingly grateful. In 1971 the California Historical Society gave me an Award of Merit; in 1976 I received Awards of Merit from the Conference of California Historical Societies and the American Association for State and Local History. The Chinese Historical Society of America and the Chinese Culture Foundation awarded me a Scroll of Honor in 1980 in conjunction with the Second National Conference on Chinese-American Studies. I received a second Award of Merit from the Conference of California Historical Societies in 1982, and in 1987 the City of San Francisco, through the committee in charge of celebrating its birthday, awarded me the Laura Bride Powers Memorial Award at the city's 211th birthday celebration at the Presidio. The award is "for contribution to the cultural and historical renown of San Francisco."

I have also served on the board of trustees of the California Historical Society, on the board of directors of the Chinatown Neighborhood (Geen Mun) Center, and as foreman of the 1983–84 Civil Grand Jury of the City and County of San Francisco.

To bring my little family into focus, our only child, Walter Wayne, was born November 5, 1932. He married his high school sweetheart, Frances Lynn Quock, in 1953. Frances' father is Fat Quock, whose family owned the Hong Sang Poultry Market in Chinatown for decades. Our grandchildren are Deborah Elaine (Debi), who married Philip Shealy; Louis Wayne, who married Deborah Louise Wong (Debbie); and Sherryl Ann, who married Jeffrey Frediani. Our great-grandchildren are Christopher Wayne Chinn, three years old; Erika Nicole Shealy, one and a half years old; and Alyssa Kay, born to Sherr and Jeff just as this book nears completion. Louis and Debbie are expecting their second child soon.

Most of the people mentioned in this chapter have been my friends for years. Their stories, although told only briefly here, deserve to be heard, either because of their achievements or because of their importance to the Chinese-American community.

Seid Bok Sing and Seid Gin Jow

Seid Bok Sing and Seid Gin Jow (better known as John A. Seid) are names that did not ring a bell with me at first. Both were much older than I was, and it was only when I went through Jane Seid's album that their contributions to the Chinese community began to register. Bok Sing was the father of John A. Seid, who was Jane's father.

The Seid family is from the Sunwui district of China. John was born here in 1897 and attended Sacred Heart High School, where he played fullback on the football team in 1914 and 1915.

Both men served in many capacities in various associations and helped out with benefits in Chinatown. John was an active participant in the Chinese exhibit at the 1915 Panama Pacific International Exposition. Father and son served together on the Committee of Management of the Chinese Hospital when it opened in April 1925. They were well known on both the West Coast and the East Coast. On one occasion, around the turn of the century, Seid Bok Sing made a hurried trip to New York City, where a tong war was ready to break loose. He walked into the headquarters of each faction, where last-ditch preparations for action were underway, and brusquely told them, "There will be *no* fighting!" And there was none.

Left: *Seid Bok Sing, a community leader actively involved in many Chinatown endeavors, ca. 1920.* Right: *Gin Gow Seid, better known to his American friends as John A. Seid, ca. 1920. [Photos courtesy of Jane M. Seid.]*

Chin Lain

In an 1876 directory of businesses in San Francisco Chinatown, included in this book as Appendix C, there is a listing for Hang Fer (sic) Low & Co. Hang Far Low, a famous Chinese restaurant originally located at 713 Dupont Avenue (now Grant Avenue), was probably established some years prior to 1875. The original restaurant building was destroyed in the 1906 earthquake and fire; when it was rebuilt on the same block of Grant Avenue, it became the most sumptuous Chinese restaurant in the West. The restaurant later changed management and is

On hand to bid Clara Chan bon voyage on her boat trip to China in 1936 were (left to right) sister Frances; parents Mr. and Mrs. Chin Lain; Clara; and brother Myron. Behind are sisters-in-law Mrs. B. K. Chan and Mrs. Myron Chan. Brother Albert (B. K.) Chan could not make it.

now known as the Four Seas Restaurant. It is in the process of being sold again as this book nears completion.

In the period shortly after the turn of the century, the controlling partner of Hang Far Low was a man by the name of Chin Lain. He was a leading elder of the Chinese community and was well known among the Chinese in America. He was the head of such powerful organizations as the Chin Family Association, the Suey Sing Tong, the China Mail Steamship Company, the Ning Yung Benevolent Association, the Ning Kui Kung Wui (a working men's business association), and others. Chin Lain was known for his loyalty and support to his friends and associates, and one of his strongest traits was his willingness to support community enterprises.

At the same time, Chin Lain was also the controlling partner in the Mandarin Theater and the *Chinese World* newspaper, with interests in numerous other commercial enterprises. His office, at the rear area of the restaurant,

was no bigger than a large closet and was furnished with a simple desk and chair. A man of fine physique and stamina, at the age of sixty-seven he single-handedly overcame three robbers who tried to waylay him on his way home, sending two of the attackers to the hospital.

In 1938 Chin Lain's wife, Ann, passed away. A couple of months later, Chin Lain himself passed on. He had requested a simple funeral, asking that friends donate money instead to China's refugee fund. (Japan had invaded China the previous year.) Because of the great respect the members of the community had for him, Chin Lain's funeral, on July 24, 1938, was the best-attended in memory. The walking procession, at two abreast, stretched for more than four blocks. This was followed by 222 automobiles, interspersed with several bands and a Chinese orchestra, followed by a troupe of actors in symbolic roles.

Chin Lain's son Myron passed away in 1951, and Albert died in 1972, but his daughters, Clara and Frances, and daughters-in-law, Eva and Pearl, still live in the San Francisco Bay Area. For many years Myron and I were members of the Yoke Choy Club, playing on the football and tennis teams in the late 1920s and early 1930s.

Walter Lee and the Chew Chong Tai Store

Located at 905 Grant Avenue, next door to the Fat Ming stationery store, is the old Chew Chong Tai store, dating back to at least the turn of the century and perhaps earlier. The owner, Lee Lop Sang, started the business as a general merchandise store, but without foodstuffs. He originally sold antiques, but lacking a good English vocabulary, he decided to change the business to a variety store.

Lee carried classical books (in Chinese) as well as scrolls for calligraphy and Chinese brushes, inks, and inkwells. Anything that a Chinese scholar would want for his study was available at the Chew Chong Tai store. He sold old knickknacks as well. Lee was a pillar of the community, always ready to help, and he was an elder in the large Lee family association. He passed away many years ago, but his son, Walter, continues to operate the store.

Walter and I met and became friends in the early 1940s. After America declared war on December 8, 1941, the day after Japan's attack on Pearl Harbor, and the California State Militia was activated, Walter, Johnny Kan (later of Kan's Restaurant), and I volunteered. We were assigned to recruit men from Chinatown to serve in a community company. We did, and Company F, 17th California Infantry, came into being. We were under the command of Major Maurice H. Auerbach. I was company commander, John Kan was assistant commander, and Walter was top sergeant. Walter was the man with years of ROTC experience, and he actually trained the company. John and I handled the administrative end of the duties.

Today, with John Kan gone, Walter and I and a few other members of Company F, such as George Ong and Thomas Leong, see each other occasionally in Chinatown and reminisce about our days of active inaction.

The Wong Brothers

George, Frank, and Fred Wong are friends from the 1920s. George is the closest to my age. He boxed professionally up and down the West Coast for a few years, and he taught me the basic skills of boxing—in case, he said, I

Three of the author's early boyhood friends: brothers George, Fred, and Frank Wong, ca. 1970. [Photo courtesy of Fred Wong.]

needed to defend myself. He later moved to Los Angeles, where he worked as a deputy sheriff until he retired.

Frank and Fred were in Boy Scout Troop 3 when I was an assistant scoutmaster. Both boys were members of the troop's champion basketball team of the 1930 to 1935 era. Frank owned a grocery store for many years. He passed away shortly after he retired. Fred worked for the U.S. Postal Service; he is now retired and devotes his time to golf and traveling with his wife, Mabel.

Edward Leong Way

Edward Leong Way comes from a family of seven children, of whom he is the eldest. Their dedicated mother saw to it that the children were all well educated. The boys also found time to be a part of Boy Scout Troop 3 and devoted much time to a wide range of community service. All of the boys, as well as the youngest sister, attended UC Berkeley.

Edward became a pharmaceutical chemist, receiving his B.S. in 1938, his M.S. in 1940, and his Ph.D. in 1942. He went right from graduation to the Merck Company, a pharmaceutical manufacturing firm. His rise from this first job was meteoric, and today he is internationally known in his field.

In 1949, after several years with Merck, Edward left to take a position as assistant professor of pharmacology at the University of California, San Francisco. He became a full professor in 1957 and served as chairman of his department from 1973 to 1977. During this period he took several leaves from the university for special assignments, including USPHS Special Research Fellow at the University of Berne from 1955 to 1956 and Visiting Professor of Pharmacology and China Medical Board Research Fellow at the University of Hong Kong from 1962 to 1963.

In the ten years before his retirement in 1987, Edward held twenty-nine special appointments and positions. He was on the Narcotic Addiction and Drug Abuse Review Committee, National Institute of Mental Health, Department of Health, Education and Welfare, and served as chairman of that committee for several years. He received many awards during his career and was the author or editor of approximately four hundred books and articles.

Edward married Madeline Li on August 11, 1944. They have two children, Eric and Linette, and two grandsons.

Professor Edward Leong Way and his wife, Madeline, in 1962. The plaque they are holding reads "American Pharmaceutical Association Foundation Research Achievement Award."

Reverend Dr. Tso Tin Taam

The Reverend Tso Tin Taam was a friend of mine for more than half a century. He was the eminent and popular minister of the Chinese Methodist Church in San Francisco for thirty-one years. An articulate speaker in both English and Chinese, he was also a student of Chinese culture. His personality shone through everything he did, and his conversation was always interesting and, quite often, humorous.

I first met Rev. Taam when he came to the Chinese Congregational Church, where our pastor was Reverend Bing Yee Leong. It seemed that "T. T." had met Rev. Leong and his family while he was attending school in Chicago, where Rev. Leong was pastor at a Chinese church. T. T. fell in love with Martha, one of Rev. Leong's daughters, and they became engaged. Rev. Leong moved to the San Francisco church with his family shortly thereafter, and T. T. followed upon his graduation. Martha and T. T. were married in San Francisco on June 20, 1929. He continued his studies at the Pacific School of Religion, where he received his M.A. in 1934, his B.D. in 1935, and his D.D. in 1955.

T. T. was the pastor of the Chinese Congregational Church in Berkeley, California, from 1932 to 1935. Over the years he served as a pastor in Los Angeles and Canton, China, finally returning to San Francisco in 1938 to take up duties as pastor of the Chinese Methodist Church, where he remained for nearly thirty-one years. When he retired in 1968, the community gave a farewell tribute to honor him as a man who not only had spent many years with the Chinese Methodist Church but, more importantly, had also given unstintingly of his time and energy to the entire Chinese community. He had also found time to become a prison chaplain for the city and state.

When T. T. retired, he had served as principal of the Chinese Christian Union Academy (the Hip Wo Chinese language school), president of the Sam Yup Benevolent Association, president of the Chinese Six Companies, chairman of the Direct China Relief Corporation, third president of the Chinese National Christian Conference,

Children leaving for home after attending Hip Wo School from 5 P.M. to 8 P.M. Reverend T. T. Taam is on the right. Classes were held in classrooms rented from the Chinese Methodist Church. This picture was taken in the 1940s. [Photo courtesy of Hip Wo School.]

and president of the San Francisco Chinese Christian Union. He was also chairman of Mayor George Christopher's Advisory Committee and served on Mayor John Shelley's EOC Executive Committee and the Chinatown Cultural Development Committee (Gateway to Chinatown). He was a Mason; a 32nd Degree Scottish Rite Mason; an Islam Temple Shriner; and a member of the

Chinese-American Citizens Alliance, the Ling Nam University Alumni Association, the Alpha Lambda National Fraternity, and the Pui Ching Alumni Association. On the occasion of T. T.'s eightieth birthday, a perpetual scholarship in his name was established at the Pacific School of Religion.

T. T. Taam passed away on February 16, 1984, leaving behind his wife, Martha; two sons, Martin and Calvin; and six grandchildren.

Helen Wong Lum

Helen Wong Lum, 1986 winner of the U.S. Tennis Association Women's Age Division 55 Championship, the U.S. National Indoor Tennis Championship, and the U.S. National Hardcourt Championship.

Helen Wong was her name when I first met her in the 1940s, and she was a serious-minded young woman with great natural athletic ability. Helen started playing tennis at the age of eleven. By the time she entered Star of the Sea High School she was a budding basketball star, playing for the St. Mary's Chinese Mission parish in the Catholic Youth Organization (CYO) league. The St. Mary's team was the league champion in 1947 and 1949 and was runner-up in 1948. As a member of the 1948 All-Star team, Helen established a CYO record by scoring 32 points in one game. In 1949, while attending the Examiner Basketball School, she scored 32 consecutive free throws and made 49 of 51 shots, a record never topped.

It was in tennis, however, that Helen excelled. She was a Chinese national champion but played only occasionally after winning that title. When she was forty years old and ready to play in seniors tournaments, her doctor informed her that she had lupus, an incurable and sometimes fatal disease. Helen stopped playing tennis and was inactive for more than a decade. She finally went to see

another doctor, who informed her that the disease was in permanent remission.

Thus, at the age of fifty, after being away from the game for ten years, Helen started playing in tournaments sponsored by the Northern California Tennis Association. She won every tournament in her age division, including the Northern California Senior Sectional, the Women Players of Northern California Senior Tournament, the Bank of San Francisco Senior Tournament, the 86th Annual California State Senior Championships, the Senior Grand Prix Play-Offs, and the State Center Senior Championships.

In 1986 Helen won a national title by defeating the top-seeded player, Nancy Neeld of Albuquerque, to win the U.S. Tennis Association Women's Age Division 55 Championship. The USTA ranked her number two in the nation for Women's 55 Singles. She went on to win the National Indoor Championship and the National Hardcourt Championship.

On May 24, 1988, Helen Wong Lum was inducted

into the San Francisco Prep Hall of Fame (a hall of fame for achievements in sports among those who attended San Francisco high schools). She was the only woman among the group of fifteen so honored.

Mae Wong and Leland Dea

Mae Wong and Leland Dea were both born in the Hoiping district of Kwangtung province, China, and came to San Francisco during World War II, when they were in their early twenties. Their limited elementary English education ended when both had to go to work. Up to this time, neither one knew of the existence of the other.

Luckily, Mae's cousin had friends visiting from Hoiping. Mae was invited to a gathering. So was Leland. They met, and after a period of getting acquainted, they were married in 1950. Mae had been working for Ti Sun Hardware and Furniture Co., at 1123 Grant Avenue, since 1942. Leland was working at his grandfather's store, Ginn Wall Hardware Co. After their marriage, both of them started saving every penny they could toward the day when they could have their own business.

Their children soon started to arrive. In order of birth, their names are Diana, Terry, Cynthia, Laurie, Donna, and Darryl. By 1968, when the owners decided to retire, Mae and Leland had saved enough to purchase Ti Sun. From then on, the Ti Sun became the children's rendezvous after school. They grew up helping with and learning about the business. Eventually, one after another, they married, and so far have presented their parents with eight grandchildren. Ti Sun Co. moved to 614 Jackson Street in 1986.

I've known the family—or rather Mae and Leland—almost from the beginning. This close-knit family is typical of Chinese families in which the parents are from China. Like earlier immigrant families, Mae and Leland embraced the work ethic and willingly made great sacrifices to bring up and educate their children.

Thomas Toa Fong

Thomas Toa Fong was born in 1913 in the village of Gow Bay Hong, Shing Hong Lea, in the Hoiping District of Kwangtung. He came to San Francisco in June of 1929. After a month at the immigration detention station at Angel Island he landed in the city, where he attended English evening classes for immigrants at the Baptist Church at 1 Waverly Place. There he developed a close relationship with his teacher, Henry Shue Tom, which would last a lifetime. Henry Tom later became the executive director of the Chinatown YMCA.

Tommy, as he became known, started out as a domestic, helping an uncle in a private residence in the Richmond district of San Francisco. He attended Francisco Junior High School and then Lowell High while working at various odd jobs, finally becoming a general helper at the Haas Candy Co. He was paid $12 a week when he started; in the early 1930s, his wages were cut to $9, then $8, until the Depression put Haas out of business in 1932.

Tommy continued his schooling and worked at whatever jobs he could find. He was working in Burlingame as a houseboy when Japan invaded China in 1932. In San Francisco, the Chinese Six Companies had rallied the Chinese community to send food, medicine, and financial

Eva and Thomas T. Fong in 1983.
[Photo courtesy of Thomas T. Fong.]

assistance to their beleaguered country. The Six Companies also issued a call for volunteers to learn flying and go back to China to help the small Chinese air force. Tommy responded enthusiastically. He got his license, but by the time he qualified the Japanese were making deep inroads into Chinese territory, and he was not among those who had left for China when the program was discontinued.

In 1934 Tommy opened a tiny bakery shop in Chinatown's Ross Alley, after an uncle had taught him how to make Chinese *beong* cakes. He also took on a $30-a-month second job in addition to baking, but the pace was too much for him. He was sick for three months, lost the bakery shop, and had to start all over again.

In 1936 he met and married Eva Joe, from Courtland, California, in the San Joaquin Valley. The Depression had brought her to San Francisco to work. By then Tommy was working for the Art Co., selling clothes and other merchandise and working on commission. He bought a Chevrolet to get around. In 1937 he opened a jewelry store—"Sammy's," on Sacramento Street, later on Washington, and finally on Grant Avenue as "Tommy's." He had to close the store in 1940 when another Japanese invasion of China disrupted his sources of supply.

After that he left San Francisco and bought 400 acres of farmland in the Imperial Valley in Southern California, where he grew rice, barley, sugar beets, and flax. Tommy and Eva had their first child, Tommy, in 1942. Ronald was born in 1944; that same year, Tommy speculated successfully on Mexicali garlic, bought a couple of thousand acres for garlic growing, and became an exporter, shipping carloads of his crop to Italy and Manila and, after World War II, to many European nations and also to South America. He was the only garlic broker in Northern California during this part of the 1940s.

In 1948 he returned to San Francisco and opened "Tommy's" jewelry store again, this time at the southwest corner of Grant Avenue and Pacific, where he remained for the next twenty years. In 1956 their last child, Louise, was born.

In addition to running his jewelry store, Tommy invested in a partnership that built the Royal Pacific Inn at 661 Broadway. He was also involved in the development of the 800-car Portsmouth Square Garage, built underneath Portsmouth Square in the heart of Chinatown.

Not long after this, Tommy bought a dilapidated building in the Fisherman's Wharf area. After investigating several plans for the building, Tommy hit on the idea of turning it into a wax museum and surrounding the museum with specialty shops. It became a big tourist attraction, and Tommy decided to close his jewelry shops. In 1985 he bought the Movieland Wax Museum in Buena Park, Southern California.

Gloria Sun Hom with her husband Peter and children (left to right) Jennifer, Leslie, and Patty, ca. 1986.

Today Tommy Jr. is in the computer field, Ronald is general manager of both museums, and Louise is involved in commercial art and film work. Tommy Fong is semiretired, although he still goes to his office, upstairs from the San Francisco museum, every day. Each Friday he and Eva shop for food, pack their car, and depart for Sonoma, where he maintains a lodge where family and friends come often to enjoy his hospitality. He has donated generously to the Chinese community over the years.

The Sun Sisters

From 1935 to 1937, when I was editor of the weekly *Chinese Digest*, Chinese Vice Consul Patrick P. Sun wrote for us as a "China expert." He went on to become China's ambassador to the Philippines. While in San Francisco, Sun met and married Rose ("Lonnie") Chew, daughter of Thomas Foon Chew, the founder of the Bayside Cannery (see Chapter 22). Two of Sun's daughters helped me with

this book: Gloria Sun Hom, who provided me with material on her grandfather, and Sylvia Sun Minnick, as one of my advisors. Both sisters have published their own books about Chinese-American history. Gloria is the head of the Department of Political Science at Mission Community College in Santa Clara, and served until recently on the California State Board of Education.

39   Joe Shoong

Joe Shoong, the founder of the National Dollar Stores, was one of the first Chinese-American millionaires. His formula for success was simple: to provide the same quality merchandise and services at the same low prices that he would appreciate if shopping for himself. He also established the Shoong Foundation (now the Milton Shoong Foundation), which has provided support for a broad range of community projects over the years.

Joe Shoong's roots go back to the Chungshan district of Kwangtung province in South China. In 1903 he opened a small dry goods store called the China Toggery in Vallejo, a few miles north of San Francisco. Shortly after the 1906 earthquake and fire, his success with his Vallejo store led him to open a second store in San Francisco.

Those first two stores were the beginning of the National Dollar Stores chain. He kept expanding, one store at a time, until he had a total of sixty stores spread across seven western states and Hawaii. In less than two decades, Joe Shoong became one of the first Chinese-American millionaires.

He next embarked on a second career in real estate.

Left: *Joe Shoong, one of the first Chinese-American millionaires, ca. 1930. He operated a chain of National Dollar Stores on the West Coast, with clothing factories based in San Francisco Chinatown. He also established the first Chinese foundation to help meet the needs of the Chinese community. [Photo courtesy of Chinatown YMCA.]* Right: *Milton Shoong, Chairman of the Board, Milton Shoong Foundation, ca. 1975. [Photo courtesy of the Milton Shoong Foundation.]*

And because he himself had been denied a formal education, education became one of his top priorities. In 1926 he founded the Joe Shoong School for underprivileged children in his native Chungshan District in China. He provided the school's entire budget until the Communists took control of mainland China in 1949.

In the meantime he was grooming his son, Milton, to take over the reins of his considerable estate. After attending UC Berkeley, Milton became interested and deeply involved in aviation. During World War II he was invited to serve as a technical advisor to the Chinese Air Force, and he participated in the Chinese war effort by training Chinese pilots in a large-scale flight preparedness program conducted in Washington, D.C., under the auspices of the U.S. government. Following the war, Milton founded his own airline, Executive Flights, Inc., operating out of the Oakland International Airport and providing air charter services throughout the United States, Canada, and Mexico.

When Joe Shoong passed away in 1961, Milton became president and chairman of the board of National Dollar Stores, Inc. After making sure that the business would continue to prosper, Milton turned to the task of expanding and improving the potential of the Shoong Foundation, which his father had established in 1941. San Francisco Chinatown had been one of the earliest beneficiaries of the foundation: nine private Chinese schools, Chinese Hospital, Chinese churches, the Chinatown YMCA, and many other groups received assistance. Another major project was the Chinese Community Center in Oakland. The foundation donated the land and matched the building funds provided by the Chinese community to create the cultural center. Ever since its opening, from 300 to 400 children have attended the center's school every day in the late afternoon and early evening, after a full day at public school.

Under Milton Shoong's leadership, the Shoong Foundation was instrumental in helping to establish the Chinese Historical Society of America (see Chapter 71). It provided the society with a headquarters in the form of a fifteen-year, no-rent lease in a distinctive building in San Francisco's Chinatown, along with a $25,000 grant for traditional decoration of the building's exterior and a complete restoration of the interior.

The Shoong Foundation has also provided a 250-seat "little theater" for the Storyland Children's Zoo in San

Francisco; a Chinese Tree Tea House and Garden for Children's Fairyland in Oakland; and an entire building for the Chinese Hospital in San Francisco, enabling the hospital to derive financial support from rental revenues. The list goes on and on. Here is a sampling of some of the other recipients of Shoong Foundation grants:

> Amateur Athletic Association
> American Cancer Society
> Boy Scouts of America
> Cerebral Palsy Center
> Chinese churches
> Chinese Community Center
> Chinese Historical Society of America
> Chinese Hospital
> City of Hope
> Easter Seal Society
> The Guardsman
> Holy Names College
> Joe Shoong Chinese School at Locke, California
> Salvation Army
> San Francisco Special Olympics for Mentally Retarded
>   Children
> United Bay Area Crusade
> YMCA

The Shoong Foundation is believed to be the first Chinese nonprofit foundation organized for the specific purpose of providing assistance to those in need. The present board of directors consists of Milton Shoong, president and chairman of the board; Charles Pius; F. Gerard Fitzpatrick; Theodore K. Lee, D.D.S.; Peter G. Mantegani; Paul B. Godkin; Howard J. Garrigan; and Dwight Wright. Fred Hom is secretary of the foundation.

40   Faith Leong Owyang, D.D.S.

The first Chinese woman to graduate from an American medical school received her diploma in January of 1904. Faith Sai So Leong was the only woman in her class of forty. She set up her dental practice in San Francisco Chinatown soon after. Just ten years earlier she had arrived from Canton, China, unable to speak a word of English.

Sai So Leong came to San Francisco in 1894, at the age of thirteen. Her parents had entrusted her to the care of a cousin for the journey, hoping that she could be educated and brought up in America. Like many other Chinese parents who encouraged their children to emigrate, they expected that she would find better opportunities in her adopted country and would eventually send them money to help them in their old age.

A young lady teaching English in Chinatown, Agnes Nickerson, took Sai So under her wing and brought her to her home. Agnes's mother, Mrs. E. J. Nickerson, adopted Sai So, and she and Agnes helped her all they could. The first four years were particularly hard for Sai So. It was not only a matter of learning English; this thirteen-year-old child also had to make the transition from Chinese to American culture and living habits. Mrs. Nickerson took her to Grace Church, where Sai So was baptized and given the baptismal name of Faith. But at home she was called Sai So, since Mrs. Nickerson did not want to separate her in any way from her own people. Mrs. Nickerson was also in constant touch with Sai So's parents in Canton to keep them informed of her progress.

Faith Sai So Leong with her adoptive mother, Mrs. E. J. Nickerson, in San Francisco, ca. 1890. [Photo courtesy of Edwin Owyang, M.D.]

Sai So had always been very dexterous with her hands, and had evinced an interest in anything mechanical. One day Nickerson's husband dropped his set of false teeth. Sai So screamed, wildly frightened. She said she expected his head would fall off next. The intricacy of the dentures fascinated her, and she ended up choosing dentistry as her profession.

She worked hard at her studies and succeeded in enrolling at the College of Physicians and Surgeons in San Francisco. The students and teachers at the college were friendly and supportive, and she found little difficulty with any of her classes, with the exception of dissecting. The Chinese have an aversion to dead bodies, and the first time Sai So entered the dissecting room she nearly fainted. But she got over it. She was a hard worker and a popular student, making good grades.

On August 12, 1905, Faith Sai So Leong graduated and received her diploma in the Alhambra Theater, where the graduating class gave her a rousing round of applause. Out of her class of forty graduates, all men except for her, she ranked among the highest. She passed the State Board examination and opened her dental office soon after at 847 Dupont Street (now Grant Avenue). Business was so-so at first. The American newspapers had written about her graduation, and one writer, Ruth Berg, commented that "she has chosen a work which few of her western sisters have dared to attempt. Out of the whole (Chinese) nation numbering over four hundred million inhabitants, Dr. Faith Sai So Leong is the only woman who has ever studied and practiced dentistry. In fact, she is the only Chinese woman in the world who has chosen this line as a profession." The publicity eventually helped, and her practice was growing rapidly when the earthquake and fire destroyed most of San Francisco on April 18, 1906. Her office and laboratory were totally destroyed.

It took a while, but on July 23, 1906, she found quarters at Eighth and Harrison streets in Oakland, where she reestablished herself. In a short time her practice was flourishing again. Her greatest loss from the fire, she considered, was the loss of her college diploma, and though a duplicate was soon secured, it was not quite the same.

Now there was a steady stream of patients to and from her office: men, women, and children, wealthy merchants and community leaders—all to be examined and taken care of by "a slight slender girl enveloped in a long white apron, deftly manipulating the bright instruments and tinkering among her laboratory paraphernalia while one of her countrymen occupies her big dentist chair," as one visitor described her.

After three years she decided to take a vacation. On July 22, 1909, she closed her office and boarded a ship for

The Chinese Dentist Club of San Francisco, ca. 1909. Dr. Faith Owyang was treasurer of the club. [Photo courtesy of Edwin Owyang, M.D.]

China. Within two months she met Nam Owyang and they fell in love. They were married on September 19, 1909, at the Methodist Episcopal Mission in Hong Kong. They did not return to San Francisco until August 5, 1910. By the following month she had once again opened her practice, this time at 1108 Stockton Street. She also joined the Chinese Methodist Episcopal Church.

Faith's first son, Edwin Owyang, was born on November 5, 1913, and another son, Eric, was born January 2, 1919. Faith was a popular dentist, and the family lived a happy life, with both boys eventually completing their studies at universities. Edwin became a physician, and Eric a pharmacist.

One day in May of 1929, Faith was walking along the sidewalk on Grant Avenue when she was suddenly struck by a car that was out of control. She was taken to Harbor Emergency Hospital suffering from multiple fractures and internal injuries, and she passed away on May 10, 1929, at the age of forty-eight.

41 Emily Lee Fong

Emily Lee Fong passed away on May 21, 1988, at the age of ninety. We were both members of the Chinese Congregational Church, and we had known each other since the 1920s. One of her younger sisters, Jennie Lee, helped found the Square and Circle Club, the oldest Chinese women's service club in America (see Chapter 27). Emily herself served her community as well as her city, state, and country in many volunteer capacities over the years.

Emily Lee Fong was honored in 1982 as an "Outstanding Chinese-American Mother" by the Chinese Women of America. She explained her many good works by saying, "Someone had to do it, and I had some time." Her obituary in the *San Francisco Chronicle* of June 3, 1988, read as follows:

> Mrs. Fong and her mother came to San Francisco from Canton in 1899, when she was two years old, to join her father. One of her first memories was of the San Francisco earthquake and fire in 1906, when the family camped in

Golden Gate Park before moving briefly to Oakland to live with relatives.

After the family returned to San Francisco to live, she helped care for eight younger brothers and sisters in living quarters above a cigar factory that her father and uncles operated and in which she worked.

She was a 1916 graduate of Girls High School but her education ended there when her father decreed she could not attend college because she was needed at home.

She became a charter member of the Chinatown YWCA in 1916 and in 1930 Emily with two other women drove from the Pacific northwest to Southern California and raised $25,000 to help build the new Chinatown YWCA at 965 Clay Street. In World War I she helped organize a YWCA Red Cross Auxiliary, and also taught Chinese women to roll bandages, and assemble first-aid supplies and earned a driver's license in order to chauffeur for the Red Cross.

In 1919 she married Bing Sun Fong, a student from Lingnan University in Canton who was studying at Stanford University. Their residence became a fraternity for all Lingnan students studying locally or traveling through to other universities across America.

When the Sino-Japanese War erupted in 1937, she helped her husband rally more than a hundred Chinese associations and organizations throughout the United States to China's cause, and raised money for China War Relief.

During World War II, with two of her sons in the Army, Emily joined the American Women's Voluntary Service, sold war bonds in Chinatown and drove soldiers to Letterman Army Hospital (now Letterman Army Medical Center).

Emily was chair of the Chinatown YWCA board from 1934 to 1944. After her husband died in 1947, Governor Earl Warren appointed her a notary public. She was also a life dean of the Chinese Congregational Church and the church's first woman moderator. In 1986 the Metropolitan YWCA recognized Emily and her daughter, Florinda (who also served as chair of the Chinatown YWCA), as the "Mother-Daughter Generation of Leadership" for their community service.

On the day she died, May 21, 1988 she was honored in absentia by the United Church of Christ in Northern California, which includes the Chinese Congregational Church, at its conference in Asilomar as one of five Outstanding Lay Women of the Church. She is survived by her daughter, Florinda Huang of San Francisco; three sons, the Reverend Matthew Fong and Wilmer Fong of San Francisco and Dr. Albert Fong of Novato; eight grandchildren; and five great-grandchildren.

Her children followed her example in their commitment to community service. Matthew started his career in Hong Kong by serving as secretary for the Hong Kong YMCA from 1949 to 1971, with time out to attend the Yale Divinity School. He graduated in 1956 and came to San Francisco to be ordained at his mother's church, the Chinese Congregational Church, before returning to the Hong Kong YMCA to complete his term of service. In 1971 he returned to San Francisco to work as a social worker for North East Medical Services, a medical center near Chinatown, and went on to become Executive Director of the Oakland Chinese Community Council and Executive Director of the Chinatown YMCA, a position he held from 1974 to 1978. He then became senior minister at the Chinese Congregational Church, where he served from 1978 until he retired in November of 1987. He still continues to work as principal of the Hip

Wo Chinese school, which is sponsored by the church. He lives in San Francisco with his wife, Yee Ling.

Wilmer worked with the Chinatown YMCA for fifteen years before leaving to became a teacher in the San Francisco Unified School District. Albert is a medical doctor in Novato with his own practice. Florinda served the Chinatown/North Beach YWCA for years as a director and in many different volunteer capacities.

42   Frank Yick

Frank Yick became known in the Oriental restaurant trade throughout the West and later as far away as Tahiti. The gas range he designed is still manufactured by the company he founded, which is now run by his eldest son, Bob.

Frank H. Yick was born in 1889 on Pacific Street, in San Francisco, near the spot where he later had his metal-fabricating shop at 772 Pacific Street. As a boy he started working for his father as an apprentice cigar-maker in Chinatown. He was in his mid-twenties when he decided that he would take up the sheet metal business. He learned the trade and began to experiment. Around 1920, after visiting a few restaurant kitchens, he decided that he could make a much more efficient range for cooking. Up to this time almost all Chinese restaurants, as well as businesses that fed their employees at work, cooked on brick stoves fueled by wood or coal.

Frank spent a lot of time visualizing his new range and planning the type of shop and machinery he wanted. Finally he set up a small fabricating shop, Frank H. Yick

Frank Yick and wife Jung Shee, daughter Mabel, and son Robert, ca. 1910. [Photo courtesy of Arthur Yick.]

& Co., and from his drawings made the first models of the range he felt would revolutionize the cooking world. His first models were made of iron, which had limitations from the standpoint of molding a range for a specific work area or of keeping it rust-free. Later, when it became

Two views of the Frank H. Yick & Co. shop on Pacific Street (now Avenue), ca. 1950. Top: Frank is smoking a cigar near center. Bottom: Opposite end of shop. Frank is on extreme right. [Photos by Bill Hutton, courtesy of Arthur Yick.]

available, he began working entirely with stainless steel, which allowed him more flexibility in fitting customers' specifications.

The range Frank designed is still used in many restaurants today. Directly over the range where the stainless steel wok (Chinese frying pan) sits is a water spigot. Underneath the wok is a gas burner with three rings, one inside the other, which can completely surround the bottom portion of the wok with a uniform high heat that cooks food much faster than any other method. The smallest model range has one or two gas burners, each putting out as much heat as a home furnace. When the food is cooked and removed, the chef turns off the gas, turns on the water spigot, and sweeps away the remains of the last dish with a short-handled brush. This residue is brushed out along a shallow gutter along the range that leads into a garbage chute. Now the wok is ready to cook the next dish.

Frank's idea did not catch on immediately. He may even have had to cajole the first small restaurant to try out his new range. Business was slow at first, but once stainless steel became available, he was on his way. Soon orders were coming from far and near. Eventually he was shipping his Chinese-style gas ranges to Hong Kong, South America, Alaska, and the South Pacific. The new range became a favorite with literally thousands of Chinese and other restaurants in San Francisco alone, and with the many Chinese businesses that used to feed their employees at work.

When the elegant Empress of China restaurant opened in 1965, Frank put in a range 75 feet long, with water-cooled stainless steel counters and dozens of cooking surfaces and wells into which woks could fit. All are based on the Chinese principle of rapid cooking. "By having intense heat flow up around the round bottom of the wok, almost any dish can be cooked in two minutes," according to Arthur Yick, one of Frank Yick's four sons. "This means that meats and vegetables can be cooked thoroughly without having the flavor and color stewed out of them."

Almost all of the Yick gas ranges are custom made to match the varying need of the customers. And not all, by any means, are used for Chinese cooking. The Hunters Point Naval Shipyard has a range that takes a 4-foot-diameter wok; California farmers who employ Mexican field hands use the ranges for cooking beans and other Mexican food in large quantities; and Japanese and Polynesian-style restaurants around the world use them routinely. Frank Yick's company also manufactures gas-fired ovens that roast whole pigs in less than half the time taken by conventional ovens and can be adapted for smoking meats or warming food.

When Frank Yick passed away on September 24, 1970, at the age of 81, his eldest son Bob became president, and brothers Leroy, Arthur, and Albert became partners. A few years ago the latter three brothers retired, and Bob became sole owner. He changed the name of the firm to Robert Yick Company Inc., and moved the shop to larger quarters at 261 Bayshore Blvd. in San Francisco.

When Frank Yick passed away, he was a very wealthy man. Aside from his four sons he had a daughter, Mabel Yick Yee, who lives in San Francisco. Over his lifetime he made many contributions to his community. One of his charitable works was his large donation toward the purchase of the land at 720 Washington street for the Buddha's Universal Church. In addition, Frank provided

One of the gas ranges sold by the Robert Yick Company. [Photo courtesy of Joseph Yick.]

all the trucks and mechanical devices needed while the church was being built, as well as sending over his employees occasionally for specialty work. (The church was built entirely by volunteers; see Chapter 70.)

43   C. C. Wing

The story of C. C. Wing, one of Chinatown's pioneers in the world of San Francisco attorneys and businessmen, began more than a hundred years ago in China, with a teenager named Jack Wah Chan.

In 1848 Jack Wah Chan decided to leave Sunwui, his small village outside of Canton, to seek his fortune in the gold fields of California. Arriving in the gold country, Jack saw other avenues to success besides prospecting, and he opened the San Loong Company, a small general store in Napa. Over the next four decades the store prospered, first by supplying and grubstaking gold-hungry forty-niners, and then by selling to the farmers, ranchers, and vintners who later settled in and around Napa.

As Jack's store grew, so did his family. As the years passed he became the father of five boys and two girls. Chan Chung Wing, born on March 25, 1890, in a small room above the store, was the second of Jack's sons.

When "C. C.," as Chan Chung came to be called, was only three years old, Jack took his family back to Canton, where they lived for the next six years. During this time, C. C. helped his father collect rent from farmers in nearby villages. On one of these trips, just before the Chinese New Year, C. C. and his father were attacked by a band of robbers brandishing long swords. Not satisfied with the money that C. C.'s father had with him, the robbers burned C. C.'s face with incense and threatened to kill the boy if his father didn't come up with more. Fearing for his son's life, Jack was forced to bring the robbers into their village and give them all the money he had at home.

Sailing back home to San Francisco was an adventure. In the 1890s, it took more than thirty days to make the trip from China to California. Near Shanghai the Chan family's ship caught fire, and its passengers were forced to spend hours in lifeboats while the ship's crew fought the blaze. C. C. and his family were lucky—the fire was eventually put out without any serious damage or injuries.

When his family returned to Napa in 1899, nine-year-old C. C. had to start school in the first grade because of his poor English. Nevertheless, despite being the only Chinese boy with a queue in Napa Grammar School, in one year he had learned the language well enough to skip from the first grade to the fourth.

As a teenager, C. C. helped his family pay its bills by working at a series of strenuous, low-paying jobs. In one such job, at the Napa Hotel, a typical day involved waking up at five in the morning to start the fire in the hotel's wood stove and then going to school, only to return to the hotel at lunchtime and after school to wash dishes. For this C. C. was paid $15 a week.

Over the next couple of years, C. C. discovered his talent for selling. He sold everything door-to-door: stocks, loan certificates, family portraits, greeting cards, and even mail-order men's suits. Eventually he had saved enough money to buy a diamond ring that he saw in the window of a jewelry store in Oakland. The store's owner was at first suspicious of a young Chinese teenager who had $300 to spend, but when C. C. explained that he had earned his money selling door-to-door, the jeweler immediately gave him a trayful of diamond rings to sell. C. C. sold them quickly at a number of local gambling houses, making enough of a profit that the jeweler trusted him with $50,000 worth of diamonds to sell on consignment. Again he made a large profit, this time traveling back and forth between Chico and Sacramento selling the diamonds to Chinese laborers, farmers, and storekeepers. Selling would play an important role throughout C. C.'s life.

In 1908 C. C. was sent to San Francisco to attend high school, and he received his diploma from Lowell High in 1912. His father wanted him to become an engineer, so C. C. applied to UC Berkeley and was finally accepted not long after he started working for the Bank of Italy (which later became the Bank of America). He was able to bring Chinese accounts into the bank, and his salary paid for his tuition and fees.

Being an engineer wasn't the career that C. C. had in mind for himself, however, so he left Berkeley and began taking night classes at the St. Ignatius School of Law (now a part of the University of San Francisco). He graduated magna cum laude in 1918. A year later he passed the California bar exam with one of the highest scores ever recorded—96 percent—and became the first Chinese-American to practice law in California's courts.

As San Francisco's only Chinese lawyer, C. C. faced much discrimination and prejudice. In a 1982 interview he remembered, "My law work was very good. But they told me I could not make a living practicing law on account of my race, because the Chinese would not employ me as a lawyer, and naturally the Americans would not employ a Chinese lawyer." Despite critics who said that he would starve to death, C. C. prospered, handling everything from auto accidents to criminal cases to income tax returns.

Faced with discrimination in many courts, and often dealing with judges who refused to recognize him, C. C. lost most of his local court cases but won many on appeal. During the early years of C. C.'s law career a number of unemployed Chinese men were being harassed by San Francisco policemen, who hit them with clubs and warned them to leave town. On behalf of these unemployed men, C. C. filed thirty lawsuits against the city's police department and helped end the harassment without any of the suits coming to trial.

C. C. also faced discrimination when, in 1922, he decided to buy a home in San Francisco's Sunset District.

Sixteenth Annual
Dinner Dance
C.C. Wing Agency
March 23, 1956
Forbidden City

The C. C. Wing Insurance Agency has held an annual dinner dance at various San Francisco locations since 1940. This photograph shows the dinner dance held in 1956 at the Forbidden City Nightclub. C. C. Wing is just to the right of the microphone at the long table in the far back. Nowadays only big spaces like the Fairmont Hotel's Grand Ballroom can handle the large number of guests. [Photo by Gabriel Moulin Studios, San Francisco.]

At the time there were no Chinese living in the area, and his neighbors weren't anxious to welcome them into the neighborhood. A local Catholic priest went so far as to offer C. C. $2,500 to sell his house and move out of the district. C. C., himself a Catholic, was shocked, but he refused to move, even when neighbors harassed him and threw their garbage onto his lawn and into his garden.

In his leisure time C. C. was an active golfer and bowler. In 1928, he, Charlie Low, and Dr. James H. Hall founded the Chinese Golf Club, which is one of the largest sports organizations in the community today. His daughter Linda is currently social director of the club, sixty years after her father helped found it.

C. C. practiced law for nearly twenty years, but his first love was still selling. As a lawyer, he helped Chinatown residents with a number of services besides legal advice, including banking, loans, investments, and income taxes. This experience eventually led to his appointment as the first Chinese-American head counsel for the foreign exchange department of the Chinese branch of the Bank of Italy. His sales talent also led to another first: Despite common stereotypes of Chinese-Americans at the time, in 1937 C. C. was able to persuade Occidental Life Insurance to grant him the first exclusive agency in Chinatown.

The C. C. Wing Agency rapidly became one of Occidental's most successful branches. By the 1940s most life insurance companies no longer had to convince people of the need for insurance; but C. C. and his agents had to sell the need and the insurance itself to a community that was unfamiliar with the product. In 1943, after only seven years, the agency could already boast Occidental's top female agent (Julia Wong), one of the company's all-around top agents (Albert K. C. Chow), and one of the best records of any Occidental agency in the country. And in the midst of this intense selling, the C. C. Wing Agency had a shining record in community affairs. As Occidental's company magazine put it in 1944, "man for man and woman for woman, it probably puts as much time, effort and thought into helping the United States and United Nations war effort as any organization of its kind in the country." Still later, C. C. established the C. C. Wing Endowed Scholarship at the University of California at Berkeley, one of his many philanthropies.

In 1982, at the age of ninety-two, C. C. visited Hong Kong and his ancestral village of Sunwui in the People's Republic of China.

Over the years C. C. and his wife, Margaret, had five children: Linda, Winnie, Wing Jr., Timmy, and Chuckie. When C. C.'s firstborn turned out to be a girl instead of a boy (as is traditionally hoped for by most Chinese families), he transferred his ambitions to her. Linda, as the oldest, became C. C.'s confidante, and it was to her that he turned when he needed action. Since his death in 1983, Linda has headed the C. C. Wing Agency. Today the agency, whose office is close to San Francisco's famous Transamerica Pyramid, employs more than sixty Chinese-American agents across California.

Linda is a graduate of UC Berkeley and combines running the insurance agency with her own law practice, which she operates out of the same office. She is a single mother of an eighteen-year-old son, serves on the board of managers of the Chinatown YMCA, is active in the UC Berkeley Chinese Alumni Association, and is an all-around athlete, her favorite sports being tennis and skiing. She received her law degree in 1978, exactly sixty years after her father received his, also from the University of California. Today she is firmly continuing the tradition her father began so many decades ago.

Hugh Kwong Liang grew up in Chinatown, but he traveled to more places and did more things than possibly any other Chinese-American of his generation. I first met him in the late 1970s. We often got together during his regular visits to San Francisco, where he liked to spend part of every summer—to give him a chance, he said, to visit his old friends and to get away from the sweltering heat in Washington, D.C.

Over time, we found that we had a lot in common. As a very young man, he had attended the Chinese Congregational Church at 21 Brenham Place—the same church I joined some dozen years later—and had sung in the choir. We both knew many of the same members of the congregation. I eventually discovered that when Hugh had first embarked on his singing career, in 1912, his quartet had taken along a young lad of sixteen named Harry Haw as an understudy. Harry would later have his own show, called "Honorable Wu's Showboat Revue," a revue that included Harry's kid sister, Florence (see Chapter 47). Harry's oldest sister, Annie, was my wife Daisy's mother.

While Hugh and Harry were performing their paths crossed regularly, and they would often get together after their shows. When the movies became popular, however, vaudeville shows like theirs gradually disappeared, and Hugh lost touch with his former fellow performers. After reading of Hugh's early friendship with Harry and Florence Haw, I decided to spring a surprise on him. So, in 1983, I brought Hugh and Florence together for the first time in more than half a century. They greeted each other with enthusiasm and spent the visit happily reliving old times. When Hugh left for Washington a few days later, both were looking forward to another reunion the following year. But it was not to be; he passed away before the reunion could take place.

Hugh Liang's father, Liang Kai Hay, arrived in San Francisco in 1871. One day he played a game of Chinese lottery and won $10 on a bet of 50 cents. On a hunch, he bet the $10 and played the same numbers again. It was his lucky day. His $10 broke the lottery bank, and he won $10,000, a fortune in those days.

With his winnings, Liang Kai Hay leased a building at 823 Washington Street from a real estate firm called Landry C. Babin, whose family owned several buildings in Chinatown. The Liang family occupied the top floor and subleased parts of the building to other Chinese families. In the basement, Liang started a small grocery store. Because he was regarded as a lucky man and was thus respected and looked up to, the little grocery store was soon doing very well. He married a young girl of the Loo clan, who gave birth to Hugh, their firstborn child, on February 7, 1891. In time, three more sons and a daughter were born.

Times were bad for the Chinese, however. The family was persecuted at every turn. The children would come home frightened by bullies, their bodies bruised and scratched and their clothing torn. Their mother tolerated this as long as she could, but one day early in 1900 she told Liang that she couldn't take it any longer. She wanted to return to China, where she knew she would receive a warm welcome in her family's village. She took all the children with her except for Hugh. She left him behind, she said, so that he could look after his father.

When Hugh was old enough to form friendships with his fellow elementary schoolmates, three of them were particularly close to Hugh. These three boys were Christians whose parents had decided to remain in America and had cut off the long queues that betokened ties to the

Chinese Manchu monarchy. Only Hugh's father, who wavered between Christianity and Buddhism, required that his son keep his queue.

The four friends roamed Chinatown until they knew every nook and cranny it offered. Their itch to explore then led them to venture into the surrounding areas. Although most times they came back unscathed, white boys caught them a couple of times and beat them up. Hugh, the smallest, was the easiest to catch—they just grabbed his queue! Hugh's friends would then have to rush back to free him, and all four would suffer the painful penalty. Finally, after one of these beatings, Tom Gunn, the leader of Hugh's four-man "gang," had the other two hold Hugh down while he cut off Hugh's queue, thus lessening the chances of capture. When Hugh's father found out, he was furious and banned Hugh from the house. He had to live with other Liang cousins for ten days until they could pacify his father.

Later, as a young man, Tom Gunn, the boy who cut off Hugh's queue, became interested in airplanes. He managed to induce the famous Wright brothers to teach him to fly and soon became so proficient that he was certified by the Aero Club of America, recognized by the Federation Aeronautique Internationale as the governing authority for the United States. He was given license number 131, meaning that he was the 131st person to receive a flying credential in America. It was dated June 19, 1912, when Gunn was just twenty-one years old.

Gunn made a name for himself as both a pilot and a stunt flyer, and the Chinese authorities soon heard of his expertise. In 1915 he was invited to Kwangtung, China, to demonstrate flying. He built a special plane and brought it with him, thrilling thousands of people with his spectacular stunts. In 1917, after convincing the authorities that airplanes were here to stay, he was commissioned to return to America to buy some. He did, and returned a few months later with several planes, along with pilots and mechanics. Among the pilots was his great friend Arthur Lym, also of San Francisco. Together, they taught many young Chinese to fly. Gunn's health was failing, however, and he died in Shanghai in 1924 at the age of thirty-six. Arthur Lym remained in China, where he became a general and later commanded the Nationalist Chinese Air Force in World War II. His daughter, Mrs. Renee Lym Robertson, now lives in San Francisco.

Hugh was still in elementary school when his father became sick and developed pneumonia, from which he died on August 4, 1905, at the age of fifty-two. His body was returned to China for burial in his native village of Shek Gong in the Yanping district of Kwangtung. Suddenly Hugh was left alone, with no close family other than the Liang clan. His father's helper at his small grocery store, a distant cousin named Lung Tin, became responsible for both Hugh and the store.

On April 18, 1906, San Francisco was devastated by the famous earthquake and fire. Hugh Liang's experiences during that catastrophe are best told in his own words, taken from his unpublished memoirs:

Chinese superstition has it that there is a big Earth Dragon which controls the earth. . . .Once in a while, he wakes up and moves his body. Whichever part of his body moves, that's the part of the the earth [that] shakes. So on April 18th, 1906, the Earth Dragon must have gotten the itch or something and shook his body vehemently. And by so doing, he surely shook the hell out of San Francisco. When the Earth Dragon shakes, it [is] called *Dey Loong Jun*. . . .

I was living in the back room of my father's store at 823 Washington Street with my guardian, Lung Tin, whom my father entrusted with the store after his death. About 6 o'clock on the morning of April 18th, 1906, I was fast asleep. Suddenly, I was rocking from side to side in my bed. The debris from the cracked ceiling was pouring down on me. I thought I was in a boat about to drown with water all over me. Cousin Lung Tin rushed to my bedside and shook me, yelling, "Get up! Get up! *Dey Loong Jun! Dey Loong Jun!*"

I quickly jumped out of bed, put some clothes on and rushed to the front door and looked out. I saw the whole front of the building across the street crumbled and the people screaming and struggling to get out of bed. Luckily, our building stood the shooks and did not crumble. But slight tremors from the quake [could] still be felt. Cousin Lung Tin told me to hurry and gather up my belongings, in case we must leave the building. Father had an old Chinese trunk made of strong oak wood with a Chinese key. I put everything father left me in that trunk and then went outside to see what was going on. Washington Street was not paved, but the cobblestone street was cracked open at many spots by the quake.

In the meantime, it seemed that the whole population of Chinatown was out on the streets, chattering and wondering what to expect next. Rumors were coming to Chinatown that fires had started at many locations around the city. . . .

It was also rumored that the quake had broken the city water mains and there was no water to put out the fires. . . . In desperation, they decided to dynamite buildings to create lanes so that the fire could not leap over. But the wind was so strong, the flames leaped over anyway. . . .

During the early hours, Chinatown seemed fairly safe. There was that big playground [Portsmouth Square] at Brenham Place above Kearny Street, with Washington Street and Clay Street on each side. There were no buildings, only trees. It seemed unlikely that the flames could leap over the big playground to Chinatown. Besides, people had gone to the famous

Kwong Chow Temple and consulted the revered Kwan Kung (Warrior God), and Kwan Kung assured us that Chinatown was safe and no one would have to leave. So the merchants and everybody stood firm and hoped for the best. However it wasn't too long [before] the fire was approaching Chinatown on all sides. It was coming up from Montgomery and Kearny Streets toward the playground on Brenham Place. The wind was so strong, [the fire] just swept past the trees and everything . . . right into Chinatown. Now the panic was on!

Merchants hastily packed as much as they could of their most valuable merchandise on horse-drawn trucks trying to get out of the city. The trucks cost $100 per load and not many were available. What was left in all the stores . . . burned up later.

Some trucks were also there to take passengers at $50 per person. Cousin Lung Tin decided to pay the $50 and go on one of those trucks. But he told me he was sorry he could not take me along, as he did not have any more money.

Before he left, Cousin Lung Tin tried to console me with his meaningless advice. He said he was sure I could survive the ordeal as I was young and an American citizen and spoke the language and therefore should not be afraid of the future. So he hopped on the truck and went his way. I have never heard from Lung Tin to this day.

That was surely cruel and heartless on Lung Tin's part. I was sure he had money, as he took every cent from father's store when we left. As the truck pulled away with Lung Tin, it was the first time I broke down and cried. . . . What was to become of me, now that I was left penniless and all alone in this mess?

But there was nothing I could do but take courage to carry on and follow the crowd of refugees up over the hills away from Chinatown to face the Fate awaiting us. I dragged my father's big trunk from block to block up toward Nob Hill as the fire kept crowding towards us.

As I looked down the hill and saw the whole Chinatown burning, including the building on Washington Street where I was born and spent my childhood, a feeling of true sadness and awe came over me. To think, even the sacred Kwong Chow Temple with the revered Kwan Kung (Warrior God) were burned to ashes. Nothing was left of old Chinatown, it seemed.

However, in the midst of that great disaster, there was one incident which could be termed a modern miracle. . . . St. Marys Church at Dupont and California Streets somehow withstood the earthquake and fire and remained erect to the end. . . .

Now the fire kept coming closer. I could hear the continued dynamiting of buildings from distant parts of the city. There was no food or water, even though I did not feel a bit hungry. Then what was I to do? Oh yes, carry on and on! So I turned away from my dear old Chinatown for the last time and joined the slow march with the other refugees.

Presently, City officials directing the refugee march approached us and told us to proceed toward the open grounds at the Presidio Army Post. So we did as directed and dragged ourselves slowly toward the Presidio.

Upon our arrival at the Presidio about 6 P.M., soldiers rushed to help us. First, they distributed canvas tents to us and showed us how to put them up. Each tent [had to] contain more than one person. I met up with a boy named Jimmy Ho, who was sixteen and all alone like myself, and asked him to share a tent with me. He did not have any baggage, so my father's trunk was the only thing we had in our tent. During this time, the city continued to burn. The fire was so intense and the wind so strong, that the sparks came flying in from the flames and landed all over the top of our tent. Luckily, water was now available. We had to spray water on the canvas top of our tent at intervals, to prevent it from catching fire.

Suddenly . . . I heard a woman crying for help a few yards from us. Ho and I rushed over to her tent. We found a young Chinese woman in her early twenties, who had just given birth to a baby. Several Chinese ladies were already there to help her. Her husband was running around frantically looking for a doctor. Then we noticed her tent was very hot from the sparks, so we sprayed the tent for her and returned to our tent.

Now, to my bitter surprise, my father's trunk had disappeared. Evidently some heartless persons [had stolen it]. So that for me was the last straw. Now . . . I really felt hopeless and downhearted. My friend, Jimmy Ho, felt so sorry for me and perhaps for himself too, that he broke down and sobbed. Jimmy said he had relatives among the refugees, and that he would like to set out to find them. . . . I agreed with him that he should by all means try to locate his relatives, and wished him success. So Jimmy Ho reluctantly bid me farewell and went on his way.

It was now getting dark and the fire was still raging and edging closer. I had the feeling that even the Presidio was not safe. I then made up my mind that eventually I must face death. . . . Strange as it may seem, I was not afraid any longer. The horrors of the day and my personal sufferings throughout the ordeal may have deadened my nerves. But I was thinking, even though my thoughts were wild and morbid. I was willing to accept the cruel Fate of death. But how to die was the question. My alternatives: (1) I will not be burned to death! (2) I may starve to death, which cannot be helped. (3) Death by drowning seemed the easiest. So I chose No. 3. . . .

I was told there was a body of water some distance away. So, while the other refugees remained in their tents, praying and hoping that the fire . . . [would not come] to the Presidio, I set out to look for the water front. . . .If the fire should come close to me, I [planned to] jump into the water and drown. It was that simple! So I walked and walked in total darkness, not knowing where I was going. Then suddenly something caught my attention. I thought I saw a light flashing at intervals from an object on the distant horizon. As I approached closer to it, it looked like a boat. My heart was at once gladdened. . . . As I got closer, I also saw two army trucks. Soldiers were unloading things to put on the boat. I crept quietly toward the boat. And while the men were busy at the trucks, I quickly sneaked on the boat, and hid under a table.

Very soon, I felt the boat start to move. I was really scared.

I must have regained my nerves, for I was shaking all over, wondering what they were going to do to me when I was found.

Soon, I heard footsteps come near and the light was turned on. Then I knew I was in the kitchen, as the men were talking about food. Suddenly, one man yelled out, "Look!" He reached under the table and pulled me out. They immediately called for the captain. There were only about six or eight men on that boat. They all came around and seemed surprised. The captain acted very stern and started to question me. I told the whole story of the earthquake and fire and the terrible ordeal I had been through. To my surprise, the captain and the men were all very sympathetic . . . I then had my first food in over twenty-four hours. They gave me some meat and vegetables and coffee and told me to help clean up things in the kitchen, which I gladly did. The next morning, April 19th, we arrived at the town of Napa. No words can adequately describe my feelings that morning, when I realized I was at last out of the nightmare in San Francisco. . . .

Before I left the boat, the men took up a collection in coins and gave it to me with their best wishes. I shall never forget their kindness. [I awakened to the fact that] these men were the real Americans. They were so nice and considerate. It was a far cry from the . . . prejudice and harsh discrimination I had previously known.

In the period of recovery that followed the earthquake and fire, Hugh had reason to be thankful that his father had been a respected leader of the Liang clan association and for the reservoir of friendships he had developed over the years, which made it possible for him to continue his education. His clansmen and friends in Oakland, Napa, Vallejo, Sacramento, San Jose, and elsewhere generously provided small stipends to enable Hugh to stay in school.

From the time that he started grade school Hugh had always made friends easily. In his early days at school, he found a lifelong friend in Chan Chun Wing, more popularly known as C. C. Wing (see Chapter 43). While attending Sacramento High School, he made several other good friends: Julius Yee, Herbert Chan, and Albert Chan. Julius Yee was a sprinter on the track team, and Herbert Chan was a halfback on the football team. Julius and Hugh graduated in 1910, becoming the first two Chinese to graduate from Sacramento High School. Albert Chan, after completing his studies there, returned to San Francisco to help his father, Chin Lain, in one of the family businesses, the Hang Far Low Restaurant. Julius Yee went on to become a successful dentist in San Francisco. Herbert Chan took up pharmacology and opened his own pharmacy in San Francisco Chinatown.

Upon his graduation from high school Hugh, having struggled through three different schools in four years, always on the brink of financial disaster, wanted to attend college. He finally managed to enroll at UC Berkeley at the age of nineteen. He had realized early that he was not an athlete, being only 5 feet 3 inches tall and weighing 105 pounds, yet he wanted to do something. He finally enrolled in the ROTC. Although he made very good progress, he was denied promotion because of his race. His commander told him to resign and said that he would be given full credit for the two-year course. After giving the matter deep thought, Hugh felt he had no alternative but to resign. When his friends learned of this, word found its way into the Chinese newspapers, causing an uproar in the Chinese community. Sometimes, however, good comes from bad. Hugh was asked by the Chinese Six Companies in San Francisco to teach the students in its Chinese school how to drill and march, to build up the spirit of the otherwise lackadaisical students. When a stipend was offered Hugh gladly accepted, as he was always short of money.

Hugh came to San Francisco from Berkeley every week to train the students, and the boys all seemed to enjoy the break from their studies. He also found time to look into a new organization recently brought over from England—the Boy Scouts. In 1912 Hugh managed to get a copy of the Boy Scout handbook and started teaching a few of the boys things he learned from it. He was not able to enroll the boys in the Scouts, however, because of the enrollment fees and because there was no local recruitment office, so he abandoned the effort after a short time. (This may have been the same handbook that Chingwah Lee obtained in 1914, as described in Chapter 25.)

In the meantime, the headmaster of the Columbia Park Boys School, Mr. Evans, heard about the Chinese boys' drill and came over from North Beach to watch them practice. He complimented Hugh and then asked if his boys could come over to see them and get acquainted. Hugh enthusiastically consented, and on a Saturday afternoon the American boys arrived in a large bus. When they got out of the bus, Hugh's students cried out in surprise: All of the boys had band instruments! The Columbia Park boys lined up and started serenading their peers with "America" and other tunes. After a few numbers, Evans asked the Chinese boys to join them in a march, and so, with the band playing, Hugh's boys fell into line with their wooden guns, to the applause of a large crowd that gathered to watch them marching to and fro along Stockton Street. The gathering was the inspiration for the New Cathay Boys Band, later renamed the Cathay Club Boys Band (see Chapter 12).

Later, Hugh realized that he had just witnessed the first organized social interaction between American and Chinese youths. Never before had young Chinese and American groups even mingled to talk, let alone develop friendships and exchange ideas with each other.

Hugh did not stay with the band, nor was he to finish his studies at UC Berkeley. He was distracted one day by a newspaper ad announcing a Chinese vaudeville act appearing at the Odeon Cafe on Market Street. The performers were Don Tin Yaw and Chan Suey Ying, a singing and comedy team from Chicago. They were the first Chinese to appear on a western stage, and Hugh and his friends were curious to see the act. They were unable to get into the restaurant, however. The management said that customers would not stand for Chinese being served in the same restaurant with them, in spite of the fact that the entertainers were Chinese!

Soon, however, another unexpected turn allowed Hugh to satisfy his curiosity about the act. The owner of the Odeon, Tony Lubelski, was not able to fill his restaurant consistently because a new craze had hit the country: the male quartet. His customers were going elsewhere, to restaurants that featured these quartets. Lubelski soon decided that his duo needed to expand into a quartet, and he sent his performers into Chinatown to find two more singers.

Eventually they found Hugh Liang and his good friend Henry Lee singing in the choir of the Chinese Congregational Church. They brought the two back to Lubelski, who took them over to the café piano to test their voices. Liking what he heard, he then asked the four to try singing as a quartet. Lubelski was ecstatic; their voices blended perfectly! With little ceremony, he signed all four to a one-year contract at the attractive rate of $35 per person per week, with all expenses paid. Thus the first

Chinese male quartet in the world was born, late in 1911. They called themselves the Chung Wah Quartet. Henry Lee was first tenor, Don Tin Yaw the lead singer and second tenor, Chan Suey Ying the baritone, and Hugh Liang the bass. After a period of practice, they developed a repertoire of songs and elementary dance numbers.

When they were ready to begin performing, they found to their surprise that Lubelski had formed a company to produce a musical play called "The Night Follies of San Francisco," consisting of two big acts. The first took place on the Barbary Coast; the scenes of the second act were in Chinatown. The cast totaled thirty-five, all Caucasians, including singers, comedians, specialty acts, and a chorus of eight young women directed by a Scottish lady named Mrs. Sterling. The featured number was the finale, in which the girls danced the Scottish Highland Fling. Hugh's quartet was to join in the latter stages of the finale.

The show opened at the Savoy Theater in San Francisco on March 3, 1912. The girls did a Chinese dance number in costume, and the quartet did their vaudeville routine, both acts receiving spontaneous applause. Then came the finale. First the girls came out and danced a chorus of the Highland Fling. Then the quartet joined them, dressed in kilts. The audience took one look at them and began to roar with laughter. Don Tin Yaw sang "I Love a Lassie," the song made famous by Sir Harry Lauder, and received a big hand.

The girls then went into another chorus of the Highland Fling, and the quartet tried to dance with them. Don, Chan, and Hugh kept pace with the girls, but poor Henry Lee had to struggle to keep up and became confused. He was mad at himself, and the audience sensed it. The madder Lee got, the louder the audience laughed.

Suddenly, somehow, Lee's kilt got loose and started to fall off. He got hold of his kilt and started to run off stage, and the other three were forced to follow. The audience, still laughing, stood up and applauded for minutes, forcing the quartet to come out for bows. But Lee wouldn't join them because he felt so ridiculous. Finally, they had to push him out to take a bow by himself. The next day one of the newspapers' critics wrote that "The dawn of a Chinese comedian has arrived," and said that the quartet was the best feature of the show.

The Follies played in towns throughout California for the next six weeks, until April of 1912, but then Lubelski decided to close the company because of the overhead; he wasn't making any money. He kept the quartet, however. And because the Highland Fling had been such a big hit, he renamed the quartet the Chung Wah Comedy Four. They were billed as "the world's only Chinese exponents of harmony and fun." They played in San Francisco theaters such as the Portola, Princess, and Wigwam and received an invitation from owner Koo Tai Chong to perform at the Ye Liberty theater in Honolulu, Hawaii. They accepted and performed to capacity audiences for two weeks, from June 17 to July 1, 1912. During their stay they were received in the local Chinese community as honored guests.

Upon their return from Hawaii they were met by Lubelski, who asked the four boys if they would like to go to New York so that they could try their luck on Broadway. After some hesitation, the four consented and made preparations to depart. In the midst of their packing, they were suddenly set upon by a distraught young Harry Haw. Harry was a friend of Hugh's and had followed the progress of the quartet since its beginnings. Now he was about to lose them. He begged them to take him along as an understudy, in case one of the quartet got sick. His father would pay all of his expenses, he said, so it would not cost anything. Lubelski consented, and Harry was allowed to accompany them.

On July 22, 1912, the five of them and Lubelski left San Francisco for New York with a stop in Chicago. The layover was for the benefit of the two original members of the quartet, Don Tin Yaw and Chan Suey Ying. Their home was in Chicago, and both of their families were at the station to greet them: Don's mother and his sister Minnie, and Chan's mother and his brother George. Both of their fathers had passed on. They spent six days in Chicago and saw many shows and vaudeville acts.

When they left Chicago for New York on August 1, 1912, they were accompanied by Minnie, Don's seventeen-year-old sister. Harry had convinced her to form a dancing team with him. Upon their arrival in New York the two went their own way, and the quartet lost its understudy. Shortly after they were settled in New York the tenor, Jimmy Chan, became ill with a cold that turned into pneumonia; he was sent back to his family in Chicago, where he died eight days later.

Hugh Liang had, with the assent of the other three boys, acted as spokesman for the quartet, so Lubelski sent him on a talent hunt to find a replacement for Chan. He soon found James Ah Chung of Boston, who had been singing locally for parties and banquets. Lubelski was pleased with Ah Chung's voice, and he hired him to complete the quartet.

It was time for a new contract for the performers, and Lubelski agreed to pay each member $60 per week plus transportation when they worked and to take care of expenses during layoffs. The quartet began practicing their routines while Lubelski made the rounds of the booking agencies, carrying a briefcase full of material about the new act he was bringing to Broadway. He had reckoned wrong, however, about his ability to sell the act without an audition. All of the agencies insisted upon seeing the quartet perform first, which Lubelski refused to do. He kept going to the agency offices, but after his first visit no one paid him any attention.

Finally, however, a minor miracle occurred. Lubelski was called into the inner sanctum of a small booking agency, where he met a man by the name of Mike Shea. Shea told Lubelski that he had a couple of top vaudeville theaters in Buffalo, New York, and Toronto, Canada. He would give the act a one-week trial in Buffalo, "and that," he told him, "should earn you enough money to return to California with your Chinese act." Lubelski humbly took the offer.

On August 17, 1912, the quartet left for Buffalo for their "make or break" engagement at Shea's theater. They opened on August 19 and were the biggest hit among the eight acts in the show. When they returned to New York, they met with a different reception than before. This time they were led right into the private office of the manager of United Booking Offices, and they had to hire an agent, Max E. Hayes, to handle bookings for their act. It was the big break for the Chung Wah Four (the name they finally chose), the only Chinese male quartet in vaudeville. They performed in the big time for twelve seasons, from 1912 to 1924.

In 1924 Hugh's mother became ill with heart trouble, and he took a leave from the quartet and left for Hong Kong from Vancouver in June of that year. He enjoyed a reunion with his mother in Canton, and then visited Shanghai for a while before coming back to America. Upon his return he went to Minneapolis to visit a close friend and associate, Walter C. James. James convinced Hugh that vaudeville was on the wane. The moving picture business and the advent of talking movies was sure to put most of the vaudeville acts out of business, James said. Hugh decided to stay with James and join him in a flourishing restaurant business. He contacted the Chung Wah Four and found that they were doing well, and they parted on good terms. Thus ended Hugh Liang's career on the stage.

In the next few years, until 1931, Hugh operated successful restaurants in Minneapolis and in Canada. In 1932, with banks closing and unemployment lines growing longer, Hugh went broke. He returned to New York to take any job he could find and became the maitre d' at a Chinese restaurant.

In 1937 the Major Bowes Amateur Hour was one of the darlings of the radio world. The show was broadcast over the NBC radio network, and amateurs from all over the country were auditioning to appear on the program. Out of hundreds of competitors, Hugh was chosen as the featured soloist. For the next eighteen months it was his voice that introduced the Major Bowes Amateur Hour, singing "Old Man River."

Once again Hugh gained the attention of friends, who persuaded him to become the manager of The Casino Royal in Washington, D.C., a restaurant serving Chinese and American food and with a stage show that featured the best entertainers. The restaurant was finally sold in 1953, but the new owners wanted Hugh to stay on as manager. He did, remaining in the position until 1968, when he retired at the age of seventy-seven. After retiring,

Hugh Liang at the Baldwin Hotel in 1982, at age ninety-one, during a visit to San Francisco. He is holding a photo of himself taken during his regular appearance on the Major Bowes' Amateur Hour radio show in the 1930s. Liang sang the song that opened each show.

he devoted himself to enjoying life and traveling with friends.

Hugh never married. He had enjoyed his stage career, during which he appeared on the same program with many of the top stars of the period, such as Sophie Tucker; the Mills Brothers; Mae West; Harry Houdini; Olie Olsen of Olsen and Johnson, of the musical comedy "Hellzapoppin"; Mary Marble; Fred Allen and his wife, Spain; and Eddy Foy and the Seven Little Foys. A few other Chinese had also been successful on the stage. Prince Lai Mon Kim was a good lyric tenor who sang popular songs of the period. His real name was William Kim Lai, and he was from Portland, Oregon. Then there was George Wong Louis of San Luis Obispo, a fine steel guitarist who used the stage name of Prince Wong; and Haw Chung and Rosie Moy, a ballroom dancing duo.

Hugh Kwong Liang passed away in May of 1984 in Washington, D.C.

Chin Mon Wah and Andrew Young

Chin Mon Wah, the father, was an entrepreneur in the restaurant business and a prominent leader in Chinatown. Andrew, the son, became a sports car enthusiast and yacht salesman.

Like many other Chinese, Andrew Young's grandfather arrived in San Francisco in the 1860s to seek his fortune. He went to the gold fields, but he didn't make the big strike that would leave him rich. He then worked on the Central Pacific Railroad for a while. Andrew does not know much about his grandfather's odyssey, only that he returned to China, not as poor as before, but not as rich as he had envisioned. The money he brought back enabled him to send Andrew's father, Chin Mon Wah, to California in another attempt to strike it rich.

Chin Mon Wah was only fifteen years old when his father put him aboard a ship in Hong Kong. He arrived in San Francisco in 1910, but he did not stay there long. He set out almost immediately for Boston, where he worked from 1911 to 1914, wisely investing his earnings for a good return. But Chin didn't care for Boston's harsh weather; it was either too hot or too cold. So, in the winter of 1914, he returned to San Francisco, to live in a more temperate climate. He found the city bustling with activity as it prepared for the 1915 Panama Pacific International Exposition, scheduled to open the following year. There was much to be done, and anyone who wanted to could find some sort of work.

Chin had other ideas, however. He wanted to put his money to work for him, instead of slaving away in some

The Chin Mon Wah family, 1931. Left to right: *Laura, Ng Shee (mother), Andrew in Ng Shee's arms, Comfort, Nancy (behind Comfort), Chin Mon Wah (father), and Edward. [Photo courtesy of Andrew Young.]*

shop or restaurant. He found many businesses in need of money, as well as opportunities for investing in real estate, for becoming a partner in different enterprises, and, at times, for making outright loans to people he knew would repay him with liberal interest. His fingers were in many deals, and gradually he became wealthy.

In 1938 Chin and his lifetime partner, Chin Kwok Yen (no relation), made a large investment in opening a nightclub called the Lion's Den, at 950 Grant Avenue. Things went well; in 1943 they bought the building, and in 1947 they opened the Kuo Wah Restaurant on the main floor.

Chin made a return trip to China, where he married

a young woman, Ng Shee. They had a baby girl, whom Chin named Nancy. When Nancy was six months old, Chin left for San Francisco again. Because of immigration laws, it wasn't until Nancy was ten years old that he was able to bring his wife and daughter to San Francisco. Over the years the family grew, and Laura, Edward, Comfort, Andrew, and, finally, Florence, arrived.

Chin Mon Wah became a prominent man in Chinatown. In addition to the numerous offices he held in various local organizations, he was national president of the Chin Family Association. He also established scholarships for students at UC Berkeley.

Chin's son Andrew Young took over his father's business and also ran the Kuo Wah Restaurant for years before he grew tired of the repetitious routine. He then leased out the restaurant, which over the years saw several changes of ownership. It is currently operated under the name Grand Palace and is owned by Mrs. Florence Fang, wife of John Fang, the publisher of *Asian Week*, an English-language weekly for Asians.

In 1950 Andrew joined a group of friends to found the San Francisco Chinatown Sports Car Club. The founders were H. K. Wong, president; Paul Louie, vice president; Harding Leong, secretary; and Andrew Young, treasurer. The club used the Santa Clara fairgrounds as the center of its sports car activities. It had dozens of national champions in its associate membership roster over the twenty years the club was active.

Andrew owned several sports cars, but his favorite was a 1953 MG-TD Mark II, which he raced in the amateur class. Honey, H. K. Wong's wife, raced in the women's amateur class, and an associate member, Doug O'Brien, was the club's representative in the experienced class.

Andrew Young in his MG, 1954. A member of the San Francisco Chinese Sports Car Club, Andrew raced his car in the 1954 Cancer Drive Benefit at Pebble Beach, as well as in benefits for other charity causes. [Photo courtesy of Andrew Young.]

In one race, Andrew was assigned the number 143 for his car; this would be the number called as he crossed the finish line. When Andrew whizzed by the finish line, however, the judges couldn't find his number. Andrew had to point out the large numbers "143" written on the car in Chinese!

Andrew married Nellie Low in 1953. They have three children: Andrew Carston, Andrea Leigh, and Allison Lynne. Andrew's mother, Ng Shee, passed away in 1958. His father, Chin Wah, passed away in 1972, and was sorely missed by the community as well as his family.

By 1969 Andrew had found a new interest. He became the representative of Hong Kong and Taiwan yacht builders. Operating out of his office above the Grand Palace Restaurant, he has been selling small boats and yachts to enthusiasts ever since.

46 Dr. James Hinquong Hall

The life of Dr. James Hinquong Hall was filled with milestones, both for Chinatown in general and Chinese-Americans in medicine in particular. He is remembered as a community leader as well as one of the first western-trained doctors to practice medicine in San Francisco Chinatown.

On July 11, 1895, in a small village in the province of Kwangtung, Quan Shee Hall and her American-born husband, Sam, became the parents of a boy whom they named Hinquong. Soon after the turn of the century Quan Shee, Sam, and Hinquong emigrated to San Francisco. Hinquong, then twelve, was given an American name, James. Although he knew no English, he soon entered Chinatown's Oriental School (later renamed Commodore Stockton School).

When James was still a young, spirited boy, who wanted nothing more from life than to learn the trombone, his father began making plans for his son's future. Sam, who would later be described in a magazine article as having the "manners of a genial old Oxford don," had noticed that most young Chinese coming to the West Coast were starting small businesses or going into law and that practically no Chinese were studying medicine. He and a friend, an American doctor named Henry Warren, agreed that this would be a good field for his son. And so, while he was still in elementary school, James was on his way to becoming a doctor.

After graduating from the Oriental School, James went on to the city's Polytechnic High, alma mater to a

Sam and Quan Shee Hall, parents of James, Elizabeth, and Flora Hall, ca. 1907. [Photos courtesy of Elizabeth Hall.]

number of Chinatown's community leaders. He and his family lived in a small flat at 19 Stone Street, a tiny alley below Powell, off Washington Street. In 1911, when he was still in high school, the Cathay Club Boys Band was organized, and from the very beginning James was part of the nucleus of the band. By the time he was ready to graduate, he had begun to show the leadership qualities that would make him an important member of the community.

Upon his graduation from "Poly," James was accepted to Stanford University. He was no longer the little boy from Kwangtung who couldn't speak any English. At Stanford he was a well-dressed and handsome undergrad. He joined Stanford's all-Chinese fraternity, Eta Delta Sigma, early in his college career, and before long he became a member of the small Stanford Chinese Student Club as well as an intramural tennis player.

Academically, James made a wise choice and became a chemistry major, a strong pre-med field that would also allow him to follow some other career if he was unable to afford the long years of medical school.

Although it wasn't easy, James and his family managed to pay his way through both undergraduate and medical school. Sam had opened a small curio shop, but it had not prospered, and he was forced to become a cook for wealthy American families to support his family. During the school year James earned money waiting on tables, and he spent his summers picking fruit in country orchards. A few scholarships also came his way, helping to ease the financial burden. He graduated with a B.A. in chemistry in 1919 and received his M.D. three years later, in 1922. Even after graduating, James retained lifelong ties with Stanford, serving as a trustee of the Stanford Chinese Students' Clubhouse and as a member of the Stanford Alumni Association's Half-Century Club.

After a grueling internship at San Francisco County Hospital, James received a Rockefeller Foundation grant to study eye diseases at Peking Union Medical College in China. The grant finally provided some financial security for James, so before leaving for Peking he married his high school sweetheart, Gloria Kim-Lau, the American-born daughter of a local dentist, and the two left for China together.

James had lived in China until he was eleven, but it was Gloria's first visit to the motherland. "[It was] my own country, I knew that," she said later in a magazine interview, "but so strange to me it didn't seem possible." It was strange in some ways for James, as well. He had

James Hall when he arrived in San Francisco as a twelve-year-old boy from China, 1907. [Photo courtesy of Elizabeth Hall.]

lived just outside of Canton as a boy, and the hospital where he was to do his research was in North China. The customs and traditions were different, and the people spoke the Mandarin language, not the Halls' familiar Cantonese. Fortunately the hospital, which was affiliated with the Rockefeller Foundation, conducted its affairs in English. Thus at the hospital, at least, the Halls were able to speak English.

Returning to San Francisco Chinatown in 1923, James embarked upon what would be a forty-year career

James Hall and Gloria Kim-Lau, his high school sweetheart, at his graduation from Stanford, 1922. [Photo courtesy of Elizabeth Hall.]

in medicine, becoming one of the first Chinese-Americans to practice western medicine in the United States. He began with a general practice in Chinatown, offering medical help at reasonable fees (or, according to his wife, for no charge if his patient was short of funds). He gradually built up his practice and soon became quite successful.

In 1925 James became one of the founders of Chinatown's Chinese Hospital, located at 835 Jackson Street, across from his old office. James was one of the hospital's top surgeons, and in 1930 he became its chief of staff. He headed the small but growing hospital for fifteen years, until 1945.

In addition to his skill as a doctor, James had a good mind for business. He was one of the few investors who sold out before the stock market crash of 1929.

In 1933 James and Gloria moved to a seven-acre estate in Los Altos, along with their son, Melvin, and James's parents, Sam and Quan Shee. Two houses already existed on the site, and the elder Halls lived in one while Dr. and Mrs. Hall and Melvin had the other. Inside, the house was filled with what the *Ladies' Home Journal* described in 1942 as a "Chinese Renaissance" in interior decorating. Behind the house, on a landscaped mountain, was a modern swimming pool.

Growing up with his grandparents as well as with his parents, Melvin soon became adept in Cantonese, although when he was with his parents the three generally spoke English. It was often Melvin who translated his grandmother's Cantonese into English for the Los Altos store clerks and shopkeepers.

By the time the Halls made the move to Los Altos, James was more than a successful surgeon: he was a community leader. In 1937 he became a director of the Bank of Canton, which had helped finance the construction of the Chinese Hospital. Much later, from 1969 to 1970, he served as chairman of the bank's executive committee and chairman of the board. He was also a director of the Chinese-American Citizens' Alliance and later became its president, and he served as medical examiner for a local draft board in the 1940s. All of these duties he fulfilled while supervising the staff of the Chinese Hospital and supporting his parents and family.

Melvin, following in his father's footsteps, attended Stanford. He made Phi Beta Kappa in his senior year and graduated with honors. He received his medical degree in 1959. After internships at the Santa Clara and San Mateo Hospitals and residencies at Santa Clara Hospital and the Veterans' Administration Hospital in Palo Alto, he began practicing as an ear, nose, and throat specialist in Watsonville and at the Santa Cruz Ear, Nose, and Throat Clinic.

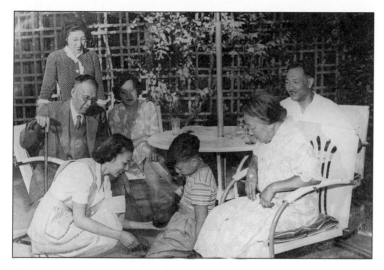

The Hall family relaxing at their home in Los Altos, 1942. This photograph was taken by Martin Kunkacsi of the Milwaukee Journal *and was used in an article about the Halls in the December 1942 issue of the* Ladies Home Journal. *Left to right:* Elizabeth (standing), Sam (James's father), Gloria (James's wife), Flora playing with dog, Melvin, Quan Shee (James's mother), and James. *[Photo courtesy of the Hall family.]*

He died of a heart attack in 1973, just after performing life-saving surgery on a young boy. He was thirty-eight years old.

Melvin and his wife, Lucille Chan, formerly of Redwood City, had two children, Kathryn and Michael.

In the early 1960s, after a long and distinguished career, James retired. He passed away in his sleep on October 6, 1974, at the age of 79. His father had died in 1953. After James's death, his mother lived with his sister Elizabeth until her death in 1977 at the age of 100.

Harry Haw was my wife Dillie's uncle. In 1912 he became an understudy to the Chung Wah Quartet—the first Chinese quartet to make it all the way to Broadway in New York. Harry never got to sing with the quartet, but he was taken along to New York. From there, he started out on his own. He and a Chinese girl started a dancing team that performed in cabarets and nightclubs. Finally he hit on the idea of putting on a whole act. Presto! Meet the Honorable Wu and his Chinese Showboat Revue! His show, which had a cast of sixteen, appeared on the big eastern circuits: Loews, Fanchon and Marco, Pantages, Orpheum, and others. He brought it to the West Coast only once, in 1930, playing in Los Angeles and San Francisco.

Harry Haw, born in San Francisco Chinatown in 1897, was the only boy in a family of four children. His three sisters were Annie, Frances, and Florence. Their parents, Haw Soon and Jair Shou, were the owners of a Chinese art goods store call Fung Tai, located on the southwest corner of Dupont (now Grant Avenue) and Jackson. The 1906 earthquake and fire forced the store to close, but Harry's father was able to start it up again that same year. Jair Shou passed away shortly thereafter. Haw Soon continued the business while the children were growing up, but he died in about 1916, and the store was closed.

Harry was not a very robust or athletic young man; he tended to be more interested in reading and in things musical and dramatic. He was also mature for his age, interested in young people older than himself rather than in his peers. So it was not surprising that he developed a friendship with a boy several years older than he was. Hugh Liang was about fifteen years old, and Harry was ten going

The Haw sisters and brother, ca. 1924. Front: *Florence and Annie.* Back: *Frances and Harry. [Photo courtesy of Florence Haw Jung.]*

on eleven. Perhaps because Hugh was also a small person physically, and perhaps because he was a bit lonely, he tolerated Harry and at times even enjoyed his company.

Harry studied hard but was not a good student. He preferred to read other material than textbooks. Liang, who had no family in America (his father had passed away when he was fourteen and his mother, four brothers, and sister were in China), was trying hard to get an education and at the same time earn enough to live on. Although there were many periods when the two wouldn't see each other for weeks or months, whenever they met, it was always as old friends.

One day, when Harry was nearly sixteen years old, he ran into Hugh Liang again. Both were older and had more in common, and Hugh excitedly told Harry that he and a friend who had been singing together in the choir of the Chinese Congregational Church had been contacted by a Chinese singing duo from Chicago. These two singers were being urged by the owner of a restaurant where they were performing to find two more singers to form a quartet, barbershop quartets being all the rage at the time. There was talk that if they proved successful in San Francisco, they might be sent east to try out for the big time, maybe even Broadway!

Harry begged to be allowed to watch their practices, and so Hugh got permission from the others for Harry to come, as long as he kept quiet and remained inconspicuous. Harry agreed and watched the four young men meld into a unit that eventually met the qualifications of the restaurant owner, Mr. Tony Lubelski. Lubelski signed the quartet to a one-year contract, paying each member $35 per week. Harry was included in the exuberant celebration that took place that night.

The quartet received good reviews, and Lubelski decided to take them back east, to New York, to see if they could make good there. Harry was disconsolate. He would lose his friend, and to make things worse, he would lose the glamor of being associated with the popular quartet. Then a thought struck him: What if one of the four got sick and couldn't perform? Harry decided to ask Hugh Liang if he could come along as a substitute. But Hugh felt that he couldn't ask Lubelski to pay for an extra person's expenses, and he also doubted that Harry's father would allow him to leave home so young. Harry talked Hugh into accompanying him to sound out his father, to get his permission and his help with expenses. Harry argued long and hard, saying that this was like schooling. He'd be learning a trade, he said. His argument carried weight, and Haw Soon agreed to pay for Harry's expenses if Lubelski was willing to take him along. This posed no problem, as long as it didn't cost Lubelski anything, and everything was set for their departure. On July 22, 1912, the quartet left San Francisco with Lubelski. Tagging along and acting just as important was sixteen-year-old Harry Haw.

When the train pulled into Chicago four and a half days later, the families of the two Chicago boys, Don Tin Yaw and Chan Suey Ying, were waiting to greet them. They stayed in Chicago for six days, during which time Harry struck up a friendship with Don's seventeen-year-old sister, Minnie. When they resumed their trip on August 1, 1912, they had an extra passenger. Minnie had received her mother's and brother Don's consent to form a dancing team with Harry to try to put together an act suitable for a theater spot. Don had been angry when she first asked him, since neither he nor their mother could

afford to pay her expenses. But Harry offered to help out, and Lubelski agreed as long as it did not interfere with his plans, and so the matter was settled.

When they arrived in New York, Harry and the quartet went their separate ways. The quartet, which called itself the Chung Wah Four, met with success and performed together for twelve seasons (see Chapter 44). Harry and Minnie began taking dancing lessons. They soon met a man who said he was a promoter of young talent for the stage and would like to be their manager. He told them that the latest dance craze was the "Texas Tommy" and said that if they could learn it and work up a good routine, he would find them work.

When Harry and Minnie were ready with their act, the man had them audition for Mr. Churchill for the show at his famous Churchill's Restaurant on Broadway. Churchill liked their act, and they also made a big hit with the patrons. They performed in the show for twenty weeks, and the first Chinese dance team in the country was born.

This initial success did not continue, however. It appears that, over the next few years, Harry tried several partners with minimum success. There was just enough work to encourage him to keep trying.

It might be said that until 1919 or so Harry was just in training, learning the ropes of show business. He began to notice that shows were getting bigger and small acts were starting to disappear. Harry decided that in order to succeed he had to have a special appeal, something that had never been done before. He took some time off to formulate a plan.

In about 1922 or 1923 a mysterious personage from the Orient appeared on stage. For the first time in America, a Chinese company staged a show that combined East

"Honorable Wu's Showboat Revue," 1925. The show played the American stage from 1924 until 1933, mostly on the East Coast. [Photo by Mitchell of New York, courtesy of Florence Haw Jung.]

and West: Young Chinese men and women in silk and golden splendor, under the direction of "Honorable Wu" (Harry Haw), put on a splendid show that dazzled the audience with the richness of its costumes and scenery. This was not the traditional staid and formal Chinese opera. There were Flora Dora songs and dances, a Black Bottom number for which the dancers wore silk blouses and shorts, and Honorable Wu himself portraying Al Jolson or Eddie Cantor or Frisco Joe with a big black cigar. The show took off, and for most of the 1920s Honorable Wu and his Chinese Showboat Revue made the rounds in the big time. It was on the Loews, Fanchon and Marco, Pantages, Orpheum, and other circuits, playing most of the time on the East Coast.

Harry brought his show to the West Coast in August of 1930. The following review appeared in the *Los Angeles News:*

> In form a miniature revue, "Chinese Nights," featuring the Honorable Wu and his all-Chinese cast from the land of the lotus blossom, is delicately handled. The Honorable Wu has a soft and musical voice as well as a capably executed fantasy. Faint odor of temple incense, stirring jangle of native instruments, and contrasted with modern jazz. . . . You will never forget the enchantment of it all, for after all the individual numbers are forgotten, the beauty of the costumes and settings will linger lovingly in the memory.
>
> The Honorable Wu is in himself a sensation. Imagine a Celestial who can impersonate George Arliss and in the next breath imitate Eddie Cantor, Al Jolson and Frisco.

Vaudeville was rapidly giving way to talking moving pictures, however, and it all but disappeared with the onset of the Great Depression of the 1930s. Harry disbanded the revue when his contracts were not renewed and moved on to Hollywood. There he had only minimal success, with bit parts in a few pictures, including *The Stowaway,* which starred Shirley Temple.

Harry gave his last performance in 1945, while volunteering his services, along with many other former stage and screen stars, in a big World War II War Bond drive. As he finished his act, he tripped and fell off the high stage of the Hollywood Bowl, suffering severe injuries from which he died a short time later. He was forty-eight years old.

48   Howard Seeto

Fate played a good hand for Howard Seeto. Arriving in San Francisco with no trade or education he could use in America, he got his chance when Henry Ford employed him and a hundred other Chinese boys to help the Ford Motor Co. bring American know-how to China. Things didn't work out quite the way Henry Ford had planned; but Howard and the others learned a valuable trade at a time when the automotive industry was growing by leaps and bounds.

Howard Seeto arrived in San Francisco from China in 1916. For the next several years he was just another young man working at odd jobs without any prospect of advancing himself. He couldn't spend more than a couple of hours each evening learning English, and he knew of no other way to improve his qualifications.

Late in 1921 Howard learned that a Professor Joseph Bailie was looking for bright young men to enter a training program with the Ford Motor Co. in Michigan. The program was designed to teach Chinese men to repair automobiles, trucks, and other motor vehicles. Howard immediately went to the Chinatown YMCA to inquire.

It seemed that Joseph Bailie was the son of an Irish tenant farmer, born in Ireland on July 11, 1860. He graduated from the Royal University of Ireland in 1888 and entered the Union Theological Seminary in New York. After being ordained as a Presbyterian minister, he was sent as a foreign missionary to Soochow, China, and was eventually appointed to the teaching staff of the Imperial University of China in Peking. Here Professor Bailie remained, teaching and volunteering in any way he could

A group of Henry Ford's students in Michigan to be trained in Ford automobile plants, 1923. The young men in this group, like many others, rented a house during their five-year training period. Front row, left to right: *Hom Chuey, Wong Wing You, Victor Chew, Gee Choo.* Back row: *Jow Sing, Wong Ng Hong, Howard Seeto, and Hom Chong. [Photo courtesy of Howard Seeto.]*

to better the plight of the common people of China. He began to promote the idea that a Bureau of Industrial Missions should be created by the university to teach industrial skills. He wanted students to learn a trade so they in turn could help the common people improve their standard of living.

But the wheels of progress sometimes turn slowly, and Bailie was unable to advance the idea further. He came back to America on a sabbatical and started describing his idea here. Somehow or other—probably because he had already spent over thirty years in China and was considered a practical and hard-working man—he began to get the ear of important people. Eventually, after sev-

eral meetings with some of the staff at the Ford Motor Co., Bailie got to meet Henry Ford. It was a meeting of two kindred minds, both out to better the world.

The upshot was that Henry Ford hired Joseph Bailie to go out and recruit a hundred young Chinese men. They would come to the Ford Motor Co. training school in Michigan. In the mornings they would spend time improving their English, as well as learning some of the technical terminology for motors, machinery, and parts. In the afternoons teams would be assigned to different parts of the plant and taught how all the Ford products were manufactured, assembled, tested, and repaired. For a period of several years they were expected to live near the plant and to find their own rental housing, food, and upkeep. For this each man would be paid sixty dollars a month. This was a princely sum in those days, and it turned out that most of the boys were able to save a good portion of it.

Howard Seeto became one of the students. He reports that they first sorted themselves according to which part of China they came from. Howard and seven others from his district got together and rented a house big enough to provide space for them all. They took turns shopping for food, cooking, washing up, and doing household chores, and after the first month or so, by pooling their expenses, they found they could each save quite a bit of money.

The Ford staff explained that Henry Ford had visions of going to China to set up big hydraulic plants, highways, and all of the things that were making America great. When everything was set, the necessary permission from China had been obtained, and the students had been fully trained, they would be expected to act as the nucleus of the huge force necessary to accomplish these objectives.

In the meantime, Professor Bailie had traveled around the country and recruited most of the hundred students. Soon the news had reached the colleges and universities as well as Chinatowns, and applications were coming in faster than he could handle them. But the news he was getting from China was bad. It was not a good time to begin such an ambitious project. China was still pretty much in the hands of warlords, each fighting to maintain his own territory. There were famines and floods. And China had become a republic less than a decade previously, and was not yet doing any long-range planning.

Finally, with no improvement in sight, in 1927 the Ford Motor Co. began closing down the training school for the China project. Howard Seeto completed his five-year term that year. Professor Bailie went back to China to continue his missionary work. He passed away in 1935.

Howard returned to San Francisco, and most of the other students returned to their homes. Howard remembers one friend, Tom Gin Chong, who did go to China and settled in 1928 in Shanghai, where he held a supervisory job with the Shanghai Motor Bus Co. When Japan swept into China during World War II, Tom returned to America, and is now operating a restaurant in New York.

Howard opened an auto repair shop in the late 1920s near the Asia Garden Restaurant at 772 Pacific Street. Business was good, so he also opened the Powell Garage on Powell between Washington and Jackson in 1932. Eventually he disposed of his Pacific Street garage and purchased the property on Powell. In 1941 he married Kay Woo, a former elementary school principal from Hoiping district in China. They have three sons. Victor is a civil engineer (UC Berkeley 1966). He volunteered in the Peace Corps and came back to San Francisco State University to earn his M.A. in social work with Asians Inc. Dewey attended UC Berkeley for a while, then transferred to MIT to earn his B.A. in economics (1968). He went on to earn his Ph.D. from Columbia University, taught at Rutgers for awhile, and then returned to San Francisco. He has been an economist with Pacific Gas & Electric since 1978. Warren earned his B.A. (1973) and M.A. (1974) in architecture from UC Berkeley, and studied city planning at MIT. He has been a loan officer with the California State Housing Financing Agency since 1975.

While Howard has been retired for many years, he has been a community volunteer since he returned to San Francisco in the 1920s, and is still active in the Chinatown YMCA.

49 Charlie Low

The story of Charlie Low's mother, Chew Fong Low, is told in Chapter 21. She raised a large family in Nevada before moving to San Francisco, where, with Charlie's help, she built Chinatown's first modern apartment building. I got to know Charlie around the time the apartment building opened; we were both members of the Yoke Choy Club (described in Chapter 26). We also played football together, although Charlie soon dropped off the team when his other activities claimed priority. He became well known in San Francisco as an entrepreneur, nightclub owner, and polo player.

Charlie Low was born on June 9, 1901, in Winnemucca, Nevada, where his parents owned a general merchandise store. In 1904 the family moved to McDermitt, Nevada, to a larger store and roomier living quarters.

When Charlie was old enough, he would climb aboard the wagon his father drove and make the rounds to the ranches and Indian villages in the surrounding territory. As he grew older he was taken under the wing of the outpost's ranch hands, and he soon became an expert rider. He won many a bet riding half-wild horses, a talent he was to exploit in later life when he became a four-goal polo player, riding with some of the country's leading proponents of the sport.

Jim Low passed away in 1909, leaving his seven children and widow to carry on. Through much hard work, they managed to keep the store going and to continue to prosper. As he grew into his late teens, Charlie had a brief fling at being a dress designer in St. Louis, Missouri, but he closed the business when the craze for Chinese fashion died down. He then joined two of his brothers to open another dress shop in Atlanta. However, in 1922, when their mother decided to retire and move to San Francisco, with the intention of eventually leaving for China, the brothers closed shop and moved along with the rest of the family.

In San Francisco they had to be satisfied with living in Chinatown, but they did not like it. The buildings were crowded and run down. Their mother's thoughts of leaving soon for China grew dimmer as they heard nothing but bad news about conditions there. Finally, realizing that the situation in China might take years to resolve itself, Chew Fong Low decided to build the first modern apartment building in Chinatown. Her sons and daughters reported that many of the younger generation wanted more room, more comfort, and, above all, a more modern, sanitary, and respectable place to live.

Charlie, then in his mid-twenties, became the central liaison between his mother and the builder. When work started on the building in May of 1926, Charlie became the person responsible for making decisions and giving orders. Eight months later, the army of builders completed the job. The building opened to much public fanfare and was filled with tenants immediately.

Charlie spent the next decade becoming one of the first Chinese-Americans in a number of occupations, any one of which would have satisfied a less ambitious person. He established a stock brokerage, an insurance agency, a real estate firm, an employment service, and a legal advice office. The stock brokerage is a good example of his entrepreneurial talents: He was playing the stock and bond market actively when he approached a brokerage house—Russell Colvin and Company in the San Francisco financial district—with the proposition that it open an office in Chinatown and put him in charge. The firm agreed, and his office soon opened at 756 Sacramento Street. It did well until the 1929 stock market crash caused the closing of many brokerage houses, including the one Charlie represented. He ran the other businesses until 1936, when Prohibition was repealed. Then he opened the first bar in Chinatown, at 702 Grant Avenue, and named it the Chinese Village.

During this period, in 1930, Charlie married Minnie Louie, from Fresno. Their life together was short, however. Minnie died of meningitis in 1931, after only a year of married life.

After running the Chinese Village for two years, Charlie decided that San Francisco needed a Chinese nightclub, with dancing and a floor show. In 1938 he leased the premises at 363 Sutter Street, a short block and a half from the "entrance" to Chinatown at Bush Street and Grant Avenue. He spent a small fortune transforming the interior into a luxurious Chinese pleasure palace, and on December 22, 1938, the Forbidden City nightclub opened to the public. Success was not immediate, but the club was soon thriving, and over the years hardly a day went by without a visit to the Forbidden City by stars from stage and screen, public figures, and even heads of state.

Charlie had to work diligently to find the right people to perform in his shows. He had trouble finding talented Chinese women to perform, because in the Chinatown of that period traditional parents were reluctant to have their daughters on stage. It was when he made his second wife, Li Tei Ming, the star of his show that the club's popularity soared to new heights. Li Tei Ming also badgered a reluctant Charlie into having a floor show featuring Chinese women only. Charlie finally consented, and gave her the job of finding the performers. This she did, but in the beginning they were not all from San Francisco Chinatown. The Forbidden City became so popular that Charlie had to enlarge the club. Noel Toy became his next big star, followed by Jessie Tai Sing. And early on Charlie became a millionaire. After his divorce from Li Tei Ming he married twice more, both times to star performers at his club. His third wife was Betty Wong of New York. After that marriage ended, he married Ivy Tam of Hong Kong.

In spite of his financial success, Charlie did not forget Chinatown. The club put on many benefits over the years, for causes such as the purchase of an ambulance for the Chinese Hospital and, during the World War II years, for the Red Cross. In addition, he gave generously to many other worthy causes. The club closed in 1961 after twenty-three years.

A souvenir from the Forbidden City nightclub, 1948. The club photographer, after taking a photograph of a nightclub visitor, would enclose it in a folder like this one.

Charlie always found time to relax and enjoy his success, even in the club's heyday. He bought a luxurious 72-acre ranch in the hills of Pleasanton, which he named "Forbidden Acres," and hardly a month went by without large groups of friends dropping in to enjoy his hospitality. He built a large chicken coop, an enclosure for tame deer, a pheasant and peacock area, and two big barns, one to house his polo ponies and another for his Arabian show and race horses and his sulkies and gear. There was also a large swimming pool as well as promenade areas.

Charlie was the first president of the Chinese Optimist

ticed in Golden Gate Park. After twelve years he retired from this time-consuming sport. His constant activity eventually sapped his energy, and he gradually slowed his pace.

In 1988 he was still hale and hearty at age eighty-seven, living a life of ease and privacy in the building at 1060 Powell Street that the family built in 1927. He keeps a very low profile these days, except, as he chuckles, with old friends like me. He is happy and content to live out his days alone with his memories.

50　　　　　Chingwah Lee

Starting in 1921, when I joined Boy Scout Troop 3, Chingwah Lee was an essential part of my life. He was unequalled in his knowledge, capability, and common sense, and he did much to help bring Chinatown out of the Chinese village mentality and into modern America. He spent twenty years as a scoutmaster; instigated many popular activities, such as the Daily Vacation Bible School and the first Chinese-American high school paper, the Tri-Termly Toots; *and was always ready to go out of his way to help any person in need of counseling—all with the best of grace, without expecting any reward. He was my mentor for many years. As we grew older and became good friends, we shared various interests and projects, including the* Chinese Digest *and, much later, the Chinese Historical Society of America. I especially remember his willingness to teach my wife and me and some of our friends the fundamentals of Oriental art; he met with the eight of us every week for over a year. Chingwah was one of my dearest friends, and I miss him a lot.*

Charlie Low with three of his horses, 1942. He was probably the first Chinese to play polo regularly and was president of the San Francisco Polo Association for more than a decade. [Photo courtesy of Charles Low.]

Club, and he, with Chan Chun Wing and Dr. James Hall, founded the Chinese Golf Club. He was a four-goal polo player, playing with Will Tevis, William Gilmore, and other well-known polo stars. He was also elected president of the San Francisco Polo Association when it prac-

Chingwah Lee was born on February 28, 1901, in San Francisco. His father, Dr. Kam Chuen Lee, was from the Chungshan Yuan region of Canton, Kwangtung province. His mother, Yoke Lum, was raised in Shanghai. Her father had been a Cantonese shipbuilder and had traveled frequently between Shanghai and Canton. Yoke Lum, his favorite child, accompanied her father to Shanghai when she was old enough to travel and was raised there until she was sixteen. Presumably, the fathers met and the two sides arranged the marriage.

Chingwah's parents arrived in San Francisco shortly before Chingwah's older brother, Changwah, was born. Chingwah followed soon after. His father was an herbalist and was also associated with a firm called Sun Gum Wah, located at 736 Washington Street, which imported firecrackers and other items from China. He was more interested in importing and selling Chinese antiques, such as porcelain, bronzes, and paintings, however, and he soon became involved in this activity.

After Changwah and Chingwah, three more brothers and three sisters were born to the family. In order, they were Edwar, King, Agnes, Horace, Cora, Marion, and Elmer. With so many siblings, Chingwah did not want to ask his parents for financial help for college, so, as early as sixth grade, he began to work as a houseboy for American families. He would live with the family and do domestic work in the mornings, before school, and then help with dinner after school, learning to cook in the process.

In 1914, when he was thirteen years old, Chingwah found a used copy of the Boy Scout handbook. He and a group of seven other boys began to dream of having their own Boy Scout troop, and so they bravely wrote to the Boy Scout headquarters in New York. Lord Baden-Powell had started the Boy Scout movement in England only six years previously, and scouting in America was just getting under way.

Their request was turned over to Mr. Harry Cross in Los Angeles, the nearest Boy Scout representative. After receiving their letter, he traveled to San Francisco and organized the San Francisco Boy Scout Council. Before the San Francisco council began, however, Boy Scout Troop 3, the first all-Chinese Boy Scout troop in the United States and perhaps in the world, came into being. Chingwah recalled the troop's activities in a 1973 conversation/interview with me:

> We were also lucky to have a very interested man by the name of Westerborough or something similar. He was of Germanic descent and he was a great outdoorsman. He told us from the very beginning that the joy of scouting does not lie in having uniforms, does not lie in having drills, but in going out into the woods. So our troop was among the earliest to have hikes and overnight trips and summer camping. We used to arrange camps up and down Marin County. They are all communities now. But in those days they were just whistlestops for a small railroad. That would be Corte Madera, Larkspur, and Inverness. None of us was over sixteen or seventeen, but we managed to have two-week camps in that region.
>
> I remember how thrilled we were when we learned to swim in Lagunitas Creek. The water was freezing cold, but we were so anxious to swim, we dived into it anyhow.
>
> There were a lot of comic things and almost tragic things that took place in our camp. One time we were all gathered around the campfire singing songs as usual. One boy who was not of scouting age, but who we had invited to come along simply because his brother was joining our camp, picked up a new bullet left on the ground by deer

hunters. There were a lot of deer in Marin County at that time. Unthinkingly, he threw this bullet into the campfire, and pretty soon we heard "Poomp!" And when we looked around we saw two holes in our tents. We were all sitting around the campfire, and the marvel is that the bullet didn't hit any of the boys. Ever since that day, we made very certain that no one carried any firearms to camp, not even a BB gun.

A supporter of all students, Chingwah was the instigator of an English-language paper for the Chinese High School Students' Club. The purpose of the club was to allow Chinese students from different high schools to meet one another at dances and other get-togethers and to give them a chance to discuss common issues and problems. Called the *Tri-Termly Toots*, because it was published three times per semester, the paper was a mimeographed affair put together by Chingwah and Dillie (Daisy L.) Wong (whom I would later marry). Among other things, Dillie put together the first crossword puzzle to appear in a Chinese paper.

Prior to this time, as Chingwah pointed out in our interview, Chinatown was essentially a bachelor community, with about 200 Chinese men for every Chinese woman. In order to avoid being mistaken for the prostitutes that were inevitably drawn to the predominantly male community, Chinese housewives would wear nothing but black. But by the mid-1920s, the high-school-age Chinese girls were beginning to close the gap in numbers, and the Chinese High School Students' Club was popular with students of both sexes. Because Chinese men traditionally do not socialize much with Chinese women, the club represented a break with the old ways as Chinese high school students began to adopt American attitudes.

After graduating from high school, Chingwah entered UC Berkeley. He majored in anthropology and also explored psychology, animal behavior, and agriculture. "I'm one of those untameables," he said when asked about his education. "When I'm supposed to learn one subject, my interest suddenly turns to another." Throughout his life, his inquiring mind would lead him from topic to topic in this way. As a result, the breadth of his knowledge was truly impressive.

While he attended college, Chingwah also helped out with the programs at the Chinatown YMCA, which had just moved to a new building. Here are his recollections of that experience:

When the YMCA was in the old location at 830 Stockton Street, it was a very loose organization. We used to hold meetings, not just scout meetings, but we also had gymnastics classes and story-telling classes. Then, after they raised a quarter of a million dollars and built this palatial place at 855 Sacramento Street, the new secretaries were not used to mingling with kids. So they had this beautiful place and nobody would go there. They were beginning to worry, and finally they decided to call on me for help.

I was not too anxious to help because I was going to college. I had very little time and I said no. But they said, "You've got to do something to help us. How would a boys' secretary salary do?" I said, "How much?" When they said, "Two hundred dollars a month," that was a different story. For one who's going to college, to get that much changed the whole picture.

I started a Thursday night story-telling session. That would be in the boys' lobby, a beautifully clean lobby but we would gather around there and we would tell stories, usually a story with a good moral built around it. And then we would tease them by saying, "Next Thursday we are going to tell about the lone giant in a tiny village who managed to combat evil." It would create quite a lot of excitement. In fact, the boys looked forward to these gatherings. In that way we upped the attendance at the Y. Prior to that it was just like a funeral parlor. Nobody went there.

While he was in college, Chingwah also came up with the idea to have Troop 3 provide a free guide service to tourists wanting to visit Chinatown:

I remember there was a convention and they were quite disturbed because the only commercial firm that took people through Chinatown was run by taxicab drivers, and they knew nothing about the background of the Chinese. They would invent weird stories about Chinese doing impossible things—having a war every Saturday night and so on. So we were determined to combat these sightseeing companies. There were at least half a dozen so-called professional guides. They would get a badge from City Hall with the word "Guide" on it and then they would charge the tourists two dollars each and show them nothing, just take them around. By furnishing free service, we managed to replace these commercial guides.

The Pacific Sightseeing Company, for example, had a few sightseeing buses, and that tour was so unsatisfactory that there were frequent demands for refunds. So finally the bus company came to us and asked if we would furnish guides to them, and we managed to train many high school students to give a well-presented tour of Chinatown, and we made arrangements with the temples so that we could go there. Especially we went to the Kong Chow Temple while it was on Pine Street near Kearny. And we went to the Tin How Temple, which is on Waverly Place. Occasionally, when these two temples were overflowing with our tourists, we even managed to squeeze in a very remote one known as How Wong Temple off an alley. But we managed to show the tourists the real temples. And we explained the background of the Chinese religions.

When he left college, Chingwah, following in his father's footsteps, began dealing in Chinese art and antiques. At first he arranged small-scale exhibits in different places, such as a small shop under the old Shanghai Low Restaurant on Grant Avenue. Eventually, in 1934, in the midst of the Depression, he rented a storefront at 9 Cameron Alley (now called Old Chinatown Lane, a name change that Chingwah was instrumental in bringing about) for $60 per month and started the Chingwah Lee Studio. He renovated the shop at his own expense. "When I moved into that place," Chingwah recalled,

it had not been used for years. Someone had died there, I think, and nobody wanted to move into such a place. The plastered ceiling had mostly dropped down to the floor, and all you saw was the huge amount of debris in the place. And it was infested with rats, of course. The walls had bowed out like a curve because of the sagging of the building. We had to saw off part of the tongue-and-groove walls so we could straighten them up again. Then these walls were so well worn that we put plasterboard and plywood boards over them to renovate the whole thing.

After he had been in business for a year or so Chingwah's expertise became known to the Hollywood movie industry, and he began to serve as a technical consultant for movies that needed to have Chinese art objects in certain scenes. At about the same time Irving Thalberg decided to produce a film version of *The Good Earth*, Pearl Buck's epic novel about China. He wanted at least half of the cast to be Chinese, to give it an authentic look. Chingwah was

The Daily Vacation Bible School, 1921. This summer school for the Christian children of Chinatown was founded chiefly through the efforts of Chingwah Lee, in cooperation with the Christian churches of Chinatown. The school, staffed by many local volunteers, met every weekday during summer vacation. Many of these children are still in the community. Chingwah Lee is the tall person on the left, in front of the doorjamb. Classes were held in the Chinese Christian Society building (in the background), the only building large enough to hold all of the children. [Photo by Suen's Photo Studio.]

recruited to help round up Chinese actors and actresses for the film:

A few of us—Mr. Porche, Mr. Segal, Mr. Paul Muni, and I—went clear up to Seattle, Washington, and worked our way down to San Diego trying to find acting talent. We thought it would be simple, because when you put an ad in the paper in English, Americans would flock there by the hundreds. But when you put an ad in the Chinese paper, nobody would respond because no one was that crazy about acting.

So we had to go among the different communities and ask if anyone was interested in movies, and a few of the boys responded, of course. Then we ran into difficulties. If they looked the part, they did not speak English. If they spoke English, they would not know how to act. So despite our strongest efforts, we rounded up only about six candidates that we thought were good enough to test for their acting ability.

But we did get several very important people. One was a local friend by the name of William Law—Law Sui Yut—he looked the part and he spoke English. He was a great success. The most surprising thing was when Mary Wong was given a screen test. They wanted a young bride and so wanted a girl that had all the freshness of youth. We thought we couldn't get a girl who filled that bill, but since Mary Wong was the prettiest girl in Chinatown at that time, we suggested she take the screen test, and to our surprise she won out over many others as the young bride. Bear in mind that at that time she was already a mother, if not a grandmother. But yet she was so youthful looking that she got the part.

We still needed talent, however, and so Paul Muni suggested that I take a screen test. I did, and I was lucky to land a very important part in that picture. That movie is still looked up to as one of the best at the time on the Chinese. It was chosen by the Guggenheim Foundation for its historic series. That means that 100 to 200 years from now you will see *The Good Earth* because it will have been re-copied onto fresh film.

Just as Chingwah's role in *The Good Earth* was getting under way, I convinced him to enter into a joint venture with me. I wanted to start an English-language newspaper for the Chinese community, and he agreed to be a partner and to invest in the project. And so we started the *Chinese Digest*, a sixteen-page newsmagazine that came out once a week. It was the first professional effort to bring to the burgeoning numbers of Chinese-Americans a newspaper in English about their peers in America. There were no fewer than four Chinese-language dailies in Chinatown, but not even a monthly or weekly English-language paper.

To keep costs down, we used Chingwah's office at 9 Cameron Alley as the *Digest* office. Later I would sometimes wonder if Chingwah ever felt a little anxious about our using his place. He had started collecting antiques by then, and he had beautiful objects in glass cases and on shelves all over the place. He was in Hollywood for weeks at a stretch, and I held the key to his office!

At least one of the editorials that Chingwah wrote for the *Chinese Digest* brought about an improvement in the community. There was a great need for a women's hotel in Chinatown to provide a place to stay for visitors from out of town. Chingwah's editorial pointing out this problem prompted the directors of the Methodist Church Home Mission to open the Gum Moon Residence for Ladies just above the church.

The staff of the *Chinese Digest* had to think about

closing down the publication by 1940. Military needs for manpower were increasing, and both staff and subscribers were being called up. Finally Chingwah enlisted as well, even though technically he was too old to join the army. He was able to get in because of his linguistic abilities; a friend of his, Leland Kimlau, recommended him, and he became an army interpreter. He was the oldest man in his company. The *Digest* did stop publication in 1940.

Chingwah served in the army for nearly a year. He was stationed at the Presidio at Monterey. After he was discharged, he returned to his art and antiques business. He had decided that he wanted to leave a museum for Chinatown, and with that idea in mind he began to invest as much money as he could in Chinese art objects. Through his studio, Chingwah was also responsible for introducing Asian art to many people from all over the world. They would write him letters telling him that they had become collectors of Asian art after visiting him in his studio. His contacts ranged from heiresses and duchesses to people of average wealth who were simply interested in Asian art.

Chingwah continued to work for Hollywood occasionally, both as an actor and as a consultant on Chinese and Asian art. In addition he continued to give tours for such companies as Gray Line, Cook's Tours, and American Express.

In 1962 I approached Chingwah about another possible joint venture—I wanted to start a Chinese historical society. Again he responded enthusiastically and, together with H. K. Wong, C. H. Kwock, and Dr. Thomas Wu, we founded the Chinese Historical Society of America. At the time none of us could have predicted the success our society would have or the recognition it would receive. As

of this writing, it has members across the United States as well as in Canada, England, Germany, the Netherlands, and the Far East. It also has a small museum, with no admission charge, that receives thousands of visitors each year from around the globe as well as from all parts of the United States. There are many plans for future growth, among them a building fund for a new home. Unfortunately, Chingwah will not see the attainment of that goal. He passed away on January 2, 1980.

51   Albert and Jack Chow

Albert Chow came from a small town, but he was a natural entrepreneur. He quickly made himself indispensable in San Francisco as the Chinese interpreter for a law firm, which almost immediately appointed him the firm's representative in the Chinese community. When his brother Jack followed Albert to San Francisco, it was to complete his high school education at Commerce High School. Jack went on to law school and became a respected community leader.

The Chow brothers, Albert and William Jack, were originally from Fresno. Albert, born in Fresno in 1902, was the first to come to San Francisco, arriving in the 1920s. He was a bright young man, able to make the most of his opportunities. After making the transition from "country boy" to "city boy," Albert found that his superior command of the English language was a big asset, and he soon became an interpreter for the Chinese family associations. Within a few years he was assisting Caucasian firms and individuals in their dealings with the Chinese community.

President Harry Truman in Chinatown with two of his good friends, brothers Jack Chow, attorney (center), and Albert Chow, a past president of the Chinese Consolidated Benevolent Association, ca. 1945. [Photo courtesy of William Jack Chow.]

Before long he caught the eye of the law firm of White and White, which hired him to act as an intermediary in all the firm's dealings with the Chinese.

Albert's brother, William Jack Chow, became just plain "Jack" when he arrived in San Francisco to start his high school education at Commerce High. He was born in Fresno in 1909 and came to the city a few years after his brother. Upon graduating from high school he continued his education in the Bay Area, attending St. Mary's College and Hastings Law College. After passing the bar, Jack became the first Chinese deputy district attorney in the United States. Later, while practicing immigration law in the offices of Chow and Sing, he was active in

many other capacities, both in and out of Chinatown; he served as commissioner of the San Francisco Parking Authority, chairman of the S.F. Housing Authority, and president of the city's Civil Service Commission.

Jack helped to build the Democratic party in Chinatown and served on the staff at several Democratic national conventions. He and Albert were personal friends of President Harry S Truman. Jack was a strong advocate of civil rights for the Chinese.

Under Albert's guidance in his early years in Chinatown, Jack grew to know the community well. He served as president of the Chinese Six Companies, of the Chinese Chamber of Commerce, of various Chinese district associations, of the Chinatown Optimist Club, and of the Chinese Sportsmen's Club. He was a founder and first president of the Asian American Bar Association, and he also served on the Grand Executive Board of the Chinese-American Citizen's Alliance. In addition, he was involved in a number of civic organizations. He was honored many times, including being named the City of Hope Man of the Year. It was with such connections that he helped bring about a better understanding of the need for cross-cultural and ethnic relations.

Both Albert and Jack were staunch Democrats, with strong ties to the White House. The story is often told of how President Harry Truman, during a motorcade in his first campaign for president, saw Albert Chow on Grant Avenue, stopped the motorcade, and shook hands with him in recognition of their early friendship. In his law office are prominently displayed pictures of Chow with Presidents Truman, Kennedy, Carter, and even Nixon.

Albert passed away in 1957, leaving his wife Florence and several children and grandchildren. Jack passed away on April 11, 1988, leaving his wife of fifty-one years, Anne; a son, Dr. Edward A. Chow; a daughter, Sylvia Eng; and several grandchildren.

52   Dr. Collin H. Dong

The Dong clan owes a great deal to Dong Tien Shong, the patriarch of this large family. The Dongs have made their mark in both San Francisco and Watsonville, where Collin Dong grew up. Their collective professional competence and dedication to their community are astonishing.

Collin H. Dong spent the first eighteen years of his life in Pajaro, a small agricultural community near Watsonville in the Pajaro Valley, between Santa Cruz and Monterey, before moving to San Francisco. In a 1971 talk before the Pajaro Valley Historical Association, he gave the following account of his family background and of his boyhood in Pajaro's Chinatown:

The saga of the Dong family began in 1873 in the city of Hong Kong. Dong Tien Shong, which translated means Dong Heavenly Star, an ambitious lad of 19, had just finished his apprenticeship as a goldsmith. He had heard glowing tales about the golden hills of California. He bought passage on one of the clipper ships to San Francisco, hoping to pick up enough gold to return home to continue with his profession. The clipper ship on which he traveled had a capacity of 75 people, but the exploiters had filled the ship with 150 passengers.

In the overcrowded ship without enough food, air, and water, young Dong became ill the very first day of the voyage, and continued to be violently seasick for the next 40 days. He often told us about his agonizing and terrifying sea voyage. He recalled that when he left China he was measured at 5 feet 9 inches tall, and 150 pounds, and that when he arrived in San Francisco and went through customs, he was only 5 feet 7 inches tall, and 120 pounds.

Stepping off the ship, Dong Tien Shong expected some sort of a welcome from his relatives. But instead he stepped into an atmosphere thick with the first anti-Chinese feeling in San Francisco. The economic boom of the Pacific Coast had come to an end. Railroads had been completed, five million acres of swamp land had been reclaimed, and the industries that were needed on the West Coast had been developed. The mines had been closed and the period of quick money had ended. Thousands of people were out of work. Some of the white immigrants were the strong and adventurous types who had no intention of working for wages. Their failure to make a fortune in the West and their consequent bitterness created an anti-railroad, anti-corporation, anti-capital, and especially an anti-Chinese sentiment.

As the number of Chinese immigrants grew, the animosity toward them also grew. Soon every ship of Chinese immigrants landing on the San Francisco wharves could depend on a welcome of rocks and bricks from the howling and screaming hoodlums.

After staying about a month with San Francisco relatives to recuperate from his long and arduous trip, young Dong was advised to go to the Salinas Valley to look for work because there the anti-Chinese feelings were almost nonexistent. Taking his relatives' advice, he boarded a stagecoach to Gonzales, where he found work with a Spanish family. After four years of labor serving as a cook, houseboy, and handyman, he learned to speak Spanish fluently and almost forgot his Chinese.

From his $20 a month salary, he managed to save $800. He then quit his job and started a small general merchandise store of his own. This was the only one of its kind in Gonzales and catered exclusively to Chinese agricultural workers. He stocked his store with everything from clothes and shoes to picks and shovels. From San Francisco he brought in imported Chinese foodstuffs, vegetables, and other foreign items. For the next five years, his store flourished, and he started another one in Salinas. In the meantime he had sent to China for his younger brother to manage one of his stores.

In 1893 there was an economic boom around Pajaro Valley. A new Chinatown was being built. One of the organizers persuaded merchant Dong to sell his interest in Gonzales and Salinas and invest in this new Pajaro venture. He took over two of the new buildings, #3 and #4 Chinatown Street. On the second floor of the #3 building, he opened the first Chinese restaurant in Pajaro. On the ground floor Dong started another store similar to his prosperous Salinas and Gonzales operations. During the next seven years he was not only a successful restaurateur and mercantile operator, but he had also invested in farming, which brought him rich returns.

Because he was still a bachelor, all of his cousins were pressuring him to return to China to acquire a bride and carry on the family line. Remembering that horrendous and terrifying experience he had coming over on the clipper ship from Hong Kong, Dong found many excuses to delay his trip to China. Two years previously his young brother had returned to China to establish his family, but he had died of an intestinal disease before he had any children. Now it was Dong Tien Shong's responsibility and obligation to marry and to carry on his blood line. Since he had repeatedly refused to return to China for this purpose, his relatives sent word throughout California that there was a wealthy and influential merchant in Pajaro Valley who was looking for a bride.

. . . Ninety-five percent of the Chinese immigrants were sojourners whose wives were in China, and therefore there were very few families with daughters of marriageable age in America. Fortunately for Dong, a go-between or matchmaker from Marysville brought him a picture of a very beautiful 16-year-old Chinese girl. Being satisfied with the picture of the proposed bride, he sent a picture of himself back to the young lady for her approval.

Many years later, Mother told us that several members of her family had tried to discourage the marriage because of Dong's advanced age of forty-four years. They feared that she would become a young widow soon, but Dong outlived all of his critics.

Finally, when the preliminary amenities were settled, both families went through the typical betrothal and marriage ceremony, which the Chinese have carried on for centuries. The first step was an investigation of the family tree, to make sure that for the past three generations there had been no insanity, no contagious or hereditary disease.

. . . The second step in the formalities was a period of exchange of gifts, consisting mainly of special cakes, wine, barbecued pig, and other comestibles. These exchanges helped to improve the relationship between the two families.

The climactic day was on October 10, 1899, the wedding day between Dong Tien Shong and Jue Yuk Gee (Jue Jade Pearl). A horse and carriage decorated with Chinese banners brought the bride from Watsonville Junction to #3 Chinatown Street. She wore a beautiful red gown embroidered with dragons. Her lovely features were covered with a heavy red veil.

The bride's arrival in Chinatown was heralded by the firing of hundreds of strings of firecrackers, and it started a carnival celebration that lasted for three days and nights. Two Chinese orchestras and several opera singers were brought in from San Francisco to entertain the guests. It was the largest and most festive wedding held outside of San Francisco. The old-timers of Pajaro who attended the festivities were so impressed that they were still talking about it when we were teenagers.

In retrospect one can see that there is no element of love in a typical Chinese marriage arranged by a matchmaker. But all things considered, the degree of happiness that often reigns in the family is very surprising. The old system is to marry first and make love afterwards. We may condemn and laugh at this

Chinese view of marriage, but in all the years of my parents' marital relationship, I never heard them quarrel.

On January 15, 1901, the hopes and prayers of all their relatives and friends were answered—the first male child was born to this union. There was great rejoicing, and another huge community celebration was held one month after the baby's birth.

From 1901 to 1918, eleven little Dong children were born to this couple. Two of them died in infancy, and the other nine—six girls and three boys—were all brought up in this little bit of China in Pajaro Valley. I was the second child, born to the family on May 19, 1903, and I spent the next 18 years of my life in the Pajaro Chinatown, with very little contact with Caucasian families except for a few hours that I spent in the American schools.

In the early part of this century, the permanent population of this little village [Pajaro] was about 1,000 to 1,500 people, with a transient agricultural population during the season swelling it to about 2,000 or 3,000. The Pajaro Chinatown was built and owned by the Porter family. It consisted of a main street with approximately twenty wooden buildings on each side. The structures were built in the conventional Western style, similar to those we all see in the Western movies on television. The ground floor of each building was used for business, and the second floor was used for living quarters. However, there was one structure at the end of the street called the Chinese joss house, the architecture of which was different. It was graphed with some Chinese ornamentation, with carved pillar decorations, and topped with the traditional curved Chinese roof.

Directly across the street from the joss house was a Methodist mission. It was headed by Mr. Dollenmeyer, the minister, and Miss Reis, the Sunday School teacher. The purpose of this mission was to teach English at night to the Chinese who were interested in learning the language and to conduct a Sunday School to acquaint the children and young adults with Christianity. They made no attempt to try to convert the older members of the community, because that would have been a hopeless task.

The remaining buildings of Chinatown were occupied by the following businesses: six mercantile stores, two poultry and meat markets, one restaurant, several fan tan and gambling houses for the relaxation of workers on their days off, two barber shops, and one herbalist, with his dozens of drawers of different medicinal herbs. The herbalist also acted as the physician for the community.

Next to the joss house was a small volunteer fire department. The businesses in this Chinatown catered exclusively to the Chinese of the surrounding areas. Their stock and merchandise was geared to the needs of the Chinese immigrants, and occasionally a few Caucasians would venture into Chinatown to purchase Chinese tea or eat in the restaurant.

The social structure of the Pajaro Chinatown was a prototype of all other Chinatowns. The most important social unit in the Chinese society was the family, not the individual, not the village, and not the state. It was a patriarchal society with the father ruling over his family, its property, and even the marriage of his children. Obedience and filial piety were ingrained in childhood, resulting in respect for the elders. The immigrants from China to Pajaro Valley brought along these attitudes and philosophies, which definitely influenced their behavior here in America. For many years, the Chinese people would not bring their disputes or quarrels into the American courts.

The joss house, at the end of the street, had a large hall for the gathering of elders of the clans for settling of dissent and discord. They formed a council that imposed a variety of punishments ranging from a reprimand to removal from the clan's roll. This naturally involved a loss of face for the offender. Another very good reason for not bringing their problems and quarrels out to the American society was that the Chinese did not wish to spoil their image of being a peaceful and honest people.

The religious beliefs of the heathen Chinese, as they were referred to, have fascinated Americans for over a century. The joss house did not equate with your churches. There were no

The Dong Tien Shong family in 1921. Standing, left to right: *Ella, Alice, Eugene, Collin, Hubert, Hattie, and Lily.* In front: *Father Dong Tien Shong, mother Jue Yuk Gee, Marian, Emma. [Photo courtesy of Hattie Dong Kwong.]*

routine services or meetings held in this temple. The temple was used only in periods of need and for offerings during certain times of the year.

The Chinese really were not a very religious group; nor did they believe in any one religion. This was not surprising in a people who had always respected the beliefs of others and had found no inconsistencies in accepting parts of the beliefs of several religions. It is a phenomenon typical of the Far East. No one in China would find incongruity in the same family using the ritual of one religion for a marriage ceremony, that of another for celebrating a birth, and that of a third religion for marking a funeral. Long before St. Paul said, "Prove all things,

hold fast that which is good," Eastern philosophy advocated it, and the Orientals practiced it.

The typical Chinese immigrant is a religious and ethical eclectic, drawing the essence of his beliefs from Confucianism, Taoism, Buddhism, and Christianity. In our home there were prominent places for two golden idols; one in the living room and one in the kitchen. During certain holidays we were taught to go through the ceremonial practices of the Chinese eclectic religion. Bowing before these images, burning incense, lighting red candles, we thanked them for all they had done for the family and the house during the past year. The prayer would end with the burning of paper money, pieces of rice paper with symbols of money drawn on them.

Then on Sunday the religious eclecticism of the Orientals manifested itself, for there were no objections from Father when Mother dressed all of us in our best clothes to attend Sunday school to be inculcated with the enlightening principles of Christianity.

The social life in this Chinese community was practically nil except for two holidays, Chinese New Year and Ching Ming, the memorial day for the dead. The celebration of Chinese New Year is a seven-day affair. Chinese people for miles around converged on the Pajaro Chinatown. This was the annual vacation for the workers. They came to renew old acquaintances and friendships, to visit relatives, and to participate in burning fireworks for good luck. They came to contribute money for the poor by giving to the collectors during the lion and dragon ceremonial dances. They enjoyed listening to the Chinese orchestras with the cymbals and drums playing the Chinese songs, which brought back fond memories of their younger days in China. The colorful banners and lanterns along the streets and the seasonal delicacies of the banquets were a great treat for the hardworking Chinese immigrants.

To us youngsters these were the happiest days of our lives. Mother would dress us in colorful costumes, and along with Father, who was dressed in his best Chinese silken gown, we went from door to door to pay respects to the store owners and to every household in the Chinese community. The adults of the whole community had prepared little red packages containing 25-cent pieces, called *li shee*, to give to the children. It is an old legend that the giver of *li shee* on New Year's Day will have a lucky year. After a day's collection of these red packages, our pockets were usually quite full. In our early teens, I remember, my older brother, Gene, and I would open a few of these packages and race across the bridge to Trevethan's tamale parlor. There we would gorge ourselves with two or three beef tamales.

Ching Ming, the spring festival, was also called the sweeping of the tombs. This was the time for commemorating the dead. Horses and buggies, bicycles, and other modes of transportation carried most of the community to Whiskey Hill, where the Chinese cemetery was situated. The purpose of the trip was to pay respects to the dead by renewing the markers on the graves, planting greens and flowers, and making the area clean and beautiful.

The ceremony at the grave site included lighting red candles, burning incense, burning idol paper money, and shooting firecrackers to eliminate the demons and specters that may have been around. A small amount of wine was poured in front of the grave site, and a feast for the dead and the guardian of the cemetery was spread out on the ground. When the dead had partaken, the living, who were waiting near, consumed the good food. There were also many other holidays on the Chinese calendar, but they were not celebrated by these hardworking sojourners whose only purpose in life was to save enough money to return to China.

As for the subject of food, chop suey and chow mein have been advertised so much that many Americans think that these are the only foods aside from rice that the Chinese people eat. Actually, neither of these dishes are to be found in China; they are American-style Chinese food. The early settlers in these Chinatowns had different routines of eating than the American families. The typical American breakfast is at seven, with lun-

cheon at noon and dinner at six. But the Chinese immigrants did not adopt American habits of eating, nor American cuisine. The usual routine was breakfast at nine, dinner at four, and a light snack before retiring.

Their menu was a very simple one. It consisted of salted fish, a fresh vegetable dish somewhat like chop suey, Chinese sausages, salted pork, eggs, and, of course, rice. However, during celebrations and holidays, especially on Chinese New Year, the limitations were lifted. Banquets of every conceivable exotic dish were prepared. It would not be an overstatement to maintain that the Chinese are the best and most experienced cooks in the world. Chinese dishes can be reckoned in the thousands. Holiday banquets usually consist of bird's nest soup or shark's fin soup, followed with lobster Cantonese, Peking duck, sweet and sour barbecued pork, and many other exotic dishes.

Another fascinating observation about the Chinese immigrants is that in spite of their decades of American cultural influence, their food and eating habits up to the present day have changed very little. The only concession that they make in the various Chinatowns is coffee and donuts for breakfast. Luncheon and dinner and snacks are still mostly Chinese food.

. . . It has been postulated that the Chinese have the greatest respect for education and therefore they would sacrifice anything to have their children educated. This did not apply to the sojourners who came to America from the villages of China. Although these people theoretically valued education, their feelings for China were such that they could not fully accept American schooling.

In the Pajaro Chinatown there were two or three other Chinese families that had children. Perhaps three or four of these children graduated from grammar school, but they were then immediately sent to China for a Chinese education, which they think is superior to yours. The dream of the sojourner was that his son would take over his established business in America and remit money to China when the sojourner retired there.

Fortunately for us, our father was an exception. Thinking

back, it seems to me that his whole life was dedicated to one purpose, that of encouraging all of us, boys and girls alike, to have a complete and thorough education—high school, college, and graduate school. For that period of the century, this concept was an exceptional and rare one, whether the parent was Chinese or Caucasian.

Father maintained his courage and determination to carry on his ideals throughout the cycles of boom and depression that struck our country and economy from time to time. During one cycle of depression when business was poor and the family income meager, there was despair and pessimism among the children. Several times my brother Gene and I wanted to quit school, go to work, and help support the family. But when Father was confronted with any problem, especially with one presented by his foolish children, he would quote his sagacious and profound philosophy: "Heaven brought us here, and Heaven will take care of us!" After discussing the pros and cons with us, he would always persuade us to go on with our schooling, and for that I am eternally thankful to him.

. . . On March 20, 1933, a catastrophic fire enveloped and destroyed the Pajaro Chinatown. Some of the inhabitants had already moved away, others had returned to China, and many of them had moved across the bridge to the New Chinatown at the south end of Main Street. Only about 100 old-timers remained there.

In spite of a severe cold, Father rushed down to help his old friends. He brought blankets, food, and clothing and made coffee for the homeless. He continued without sleep long into the night to arrange for the comfort of his helpless and bewildered friends. He exhausted himself seeking shelter for them. The next day he was stricken with pneumonia. And nine days later, on March 31, 1933, at the age of 78, a wonderful man passed away. I am sure he went to Heaven.

It was in 1893 that Dong Tien Shong participated in the birth of the new Pajaro Chinatown, and in 1933, exactly 40 years later, he stood helpless and dejected watching his old home being consumed in an agonizing and fiery death. This no doubt contributed to his demise.

After graduating from high school, Collin left Pajaro to attend UC Berkeley. He graduated from Stanford University School of Medicine in 1931 and set up practice on Grant Avenue in San Francisco Chinatown.

In 1938 Collin was seriously beset by rheumatoid arthritis, an affliction he attributes to the American diet he had adopted. He began experimenting with a simpler diet, going back to the seafood, vegetables, and rice he and his family had lived on in Pajaro. To his relief, his symptoms all but vanished. Encouraged by his success, Collin began recommending this simple diet to patients suffering from arthritis. He found that the majority of people who tried the diet experienced reduced pain and regained some of the mobility they had lost.

In the mid-1970s, after treating arthritic patients for a number of years, Collin, together with Jane Banks, a former patient, wrote *The Arthritic's Cookbook* and *New Hope for the Arthritic*. Both became best sellers, and today the "Dr. Dong Diet" is famous. Although Collin has often faced criticism from the medical establishment, which asserts that there is no connection between diet and arthritis, two recent controlled studies support his theories, and the testimonials of thousands of patients who have been helped by his diet inspire him to continue his work.

Collin's three children are named Eileen, Colleen, and Galen. He and his wife, Mildred (Valpey), have been married for forty-five years. In addition to his medical career, Collin has built two modern high-rises in San Francisco. The first, built in 1957 on Telegraph Hill, is an apartment building based on the architectural principles of Frank Lloyd Wright. The second, Mandarin Tower, a seventeen-story office and apartment building in Chinatown, was built in 1970. Collin has his office in this building, where he continues to practice, long after his Stanford classmates have retired. In his office hangs the original sign, lettered in both English and Chinese, that once hung outside his first practice on Grant Avenue.

In 1983, for Collin's eightieth birthday, his children held a dinner in his honor at the Stanford Court Hotel in San Francisco. The menu was planned by Collin and followed his dietary principles.

Collin's relationship with his two brothers and five sisters has been close and loving. Eugene, his older brother, attended the UC School of Pharmacy in San Francisco, graduating in 1927. He entered UC School of Medicine in 1936 and, following his internship, returned to Salinas where he practiced medicine until he passed away.

Ella, who followed Collin, attended UC Berkeley, where she majored in education. After graduating, she married Quong L. Lee, her brother Collin's roommate at Stanford. Alice was raised by her maternal grandmother in Marysville. She attended a school of cosmetology in San Francisco and for a time owned and operated the Lilac Beauty Parlor. Later, after studying at Armstrong Business College, she worked in Collin's medical office as receptionist and bookkeeper.

Hubert attended UC San Francisco Medical School and interned in Los Angeles. He currently has a busy practice in San Francisco.

Harriet (Hattie) became well known in San Francisco Chinatown because of her community involvement. She was one of the leading Chinese women tennis players, and it was to her and her first husband, Hayne Hall, that I sold my sporting goods store in 1933. They operated it for several years before selling it to another local couple, Davisson and Josephine Lee.

In 1935 Hattie helped to organize the Chinese Tennis Club, which is still active today. She was also instrumental in founding the Chinese Badminton Club and the Chinese Theatre Guild of the Chinese YWCA.

After her divorce from Hayne Hall, Hattie married K. L. Kwong, president of the Bank of Canton and formerly the consul general for Manila and San Francisco. After her husband's death, she became interested in golf and bridge. She started the first duplicate bridge game in Chinatown, and the club has produced thirty life masters since it was organized in 1960.

Lily was the quiet child of the family, and after graduating from the Pajaro and Watsonville schools she worked as secretary for the superintendent of schools. After seven years she left to marry William Lee, the owner of a San Mateo wholesale floral business, which they developed into a million-dollar operation.

Emma graduated from UC San Francisco Medical School, where she specialized in ophthalmology. She married Harry Chong, M.D., and they opened a practice in Salinas.

Marian graduated from Watsonville High School and later received her D.D.S. from the College of Physicians and Surgeons. She practiced dentistry in San Francisco for a time before marrying Lyman A. Lowe, D.D.S. They moved to Salinas and practiced together there for several years, when Marian retired to raise her family.

53   Alice Fong Yu

Alice Fong Yu was the first Chinese public school teacher in San Francisco, and she worked in the city's school system for forty-four years. As one of the founders of the Square and Circle Club, she devoted a great deal of her spare time to volunteer projects. In 1976 the San Francisco Examiner *named her one of the Most Distinguished Ten of the Bay Area, recognizing "those special people who care about this city, who care about people less forunate than they, and who do something about it."*

Alice Fong Yu's father, Fong Chow (intimately known as Suey Chung), arrived in the town of Washington, in Nevada County, California, in the late 1890s. He ran a general merchandise store there, supplying food to the Chinese miners, and he also ran a gold mine that he leased. He married Alice's mother, Lonnie Tom, sometime in 1900 or 1901. Their first child, Theodore, was born in 1903. Alice, the second child, was born on March 5, 1905. Five other children were born while the family lived in Washington: Minnie, Taft, Helen, Albert, and Marian.

Fong Chow had been running the mine for a number of years, gradually making improvements to it, when he lost the lease; the owners decided to take back the mine and work it themselves. He then decided to move his family to Vallejo, where he opened a grocery store. Three more children, Leslie, Martha, and Lorraine, were born after the move.

It was in Vallejo that Alice began attending Sunday School. At first the church sent someone into the Vallejo Chinatown to teach the children, but after a while they went to regular classes at the Presbyterian Church and joined its congregation. It was unusual at that time for Chinese to be invited to join a white congregation; most churches set up missions in the local Chinatown and kept their activities separate. She recalls, "The Christian people were the first ones to let us join their groups. We joined their Sunday school and attended their Christian Endeavor Conferences. When they held conferences in the country, they would take us children along and we would have to stand together and sing 'Jesus loves me, this I know . . .' and things like that that to show what their outreach program had done."

In 1923 Alice graduated from high school and moved to San Francisco to attend San Francisco Teachers College. At first the head of the school, Frederick Burke, would not accept her at the college. "Nobody is going to hire you when you graduate," he told her, "so why study to be a teacher?" At that, Alice says, "I flared up, because I'd faced so much discrimination. I said, 'I'm not going to stay here; I'm going to China to help my people.' Then he agreed to accept me."

Alice did not have to return to China to find work as a teacher, however. In 1926, right after she graduated, she was hired to teach in the Commodore Stockton school, which the Chinese children in San Francisco were required to attend. She was the first Chinese public school teacher in San Francisco. The new principal of Commodore Stockton had requested a teacher who could speak Chinese, because there was no one in the school who could communicate with the parents; the teachers were even having trouble understanding the English spoken by the children. She would teach there for the next thirty-one years, until 1957. Although well qualified, she was never promoted.

Soon after arriving in San Francisco, Alice began attending the Congregational Church in Chinatown and became involved in its activities. She taught Sunday School, sang in the choir, and organized a young people's forum. Eventually she became the church's representative to a young people's group formed by all the churches of Chinatown. Another church activity involved helping to organize a Lake Tahoe Western Conference for young Chinese Christians from the West Coast, still an annual event in the late 1980s.

Alice and a group of six young women got in the habit of staying after church on Sunday and reading the paper together and chatting. Their conversation often turned to ways in which they could serve the community and get more women to participate in public service. One of their influences was the women's suffrage movement, which had made headlines a few years earlier. These discussions led to the formation of the Square and Circle Club, now the largest active Chinese women's service organization in the United States and the one that has met continuously for the longest period of time. "So much community service had to be done, and nobody was doing it," Alice says. "We felt that we could bring women together and use our talents, our energy, and be more loving and caring in doing things for the community."

Alice had continued her Chinese education by studying with a private language teacher, and it was he who came up with the name Square and Circle, after the Chinese saying "In deeds be square, in knowledge be all-round."

The Square and Circle Club set to work helping young women who came to San Francisco from the countryside to find jobs. They also helped expand the work being done by the Chinatown YWCA and later assisted them in starting a rooming house for women. A few of the rooms were reserved for visitors from out of town, and Alice became the YWCA's first house mother. She also ran a Friday breakfast club—a men's and women's discussion group—at the YWCA and helped start a Bible class for Sunday School teachers.

In its early years the club also took part in the Chinese New Year's parade. Alice recalls, "I remember we made our own float, and if we didn't have a float, my sister Minnie and I, the only ones who could ride a horse, rode in the parade; we were the only Chinese women riding horses. And we were the only Chinese women's group to put in a float."

The first large fund-raiser put on by the Square and Circle Club raised money for flood relief after a huge flood devastated the area around Canton, China. It was a great success because most of the Chinese in San Francisco had emigrated from that area. Since then the club has held a fund-raiser annually, raising money for many worthy causes. For more details on the Square and Circle Club, see Chapter 27.

Alice also became a participant in almost all of Chinatown's activities. At Commodore Stockton she helped the principal to identify needy families and get help for them, and she also helped to organize a clothes closet, where mothers could get clothes for their children, as well as a sewing group where mothers could sew their children's clothes.

With her sister Minnie, who was the first Chinese public health nurse in the state, Alice gave talks to public service organizations that were taking care of poor Chinese families. She also served on the committee running

Mei Lan Yuen, a foster home for babies whose families couldn't care for them; she later became the president of the committee.

Alice's experience in helping stage benefits for the Square and Circle Club served her well when World War II came along and she was recruited to put on shows, called Rice Bowl parties, to raise money for the Chinese War Relief Association, which was supporting the Chinese army against the Japanese. "We used St. Mary's auditorium to put on shows, the largest auditorium at that time," she says. "Ticket lines were so crowded that the lines formed around the block on Washington Street. After each show, we had to let the audience out the back door. As soon as we let one group out, new people were pushing in already—just one show after another." In addition to San Francisco, they gave performances in Grass Valley, Vallejo, and San Mateo.

Alice represented the Square and Circle Club at the War Relief Association's meetings. It was through her work for this organization that she met her future husband, Jon Yu, a writer and journalist who wrote editorials for the *Young China* newspaper. Jon served as secretary and wrote news releases for the association. They were married in Tucson, Arizona, in December of 1940. Their first child, Alon ("Al" for Alice, "on" for Jon), was born the following December.

Their second child, Joal, suffered from cerebral palsy, caused by a difficult delivery. Alice went to UC Berkeley to learn about how to care for children with this problem, and she began taking classes in speech therapy to help the child with his speech. She received certification as a speech therapist in 1957. "Right after I got these additional credentials," she recalls, "I was sent to teach speech therapy right away, teaching throughout San Francisco, from kindergarten to high school. I was sent to different schools, on a different route every day, five days a week. And that was my special assignment up to my retirement."

In 1966 Alice and Jon made a trip to Asia, to travel and to visit Jon's mother and brothers, whom he had not seen for nearly thirty years. While they were in Kuala Lumpur, Malaysia, Jon suddenly became ill. He was taken to a hospital, where he passed away on October 7.

Alice retired in 1970, after working for the San Francisco School District for forty-four years.

54   William Wai Fong

I've known William Wai Fong since we were boys. I would often go to his father's lantern shop to watch a big lantern take shape as his deft hands turned thin bamboo strips into a skeleton; he would then sheathe it with silk cloth and finish by painting a design and words such as "Prosperity" or "Long Life" onto the cloth.

William's grandfather came to San Francisco in a sailing ship in the 1850s and, upon landing, headed for the gold country, much as thousands of others did in the heyday of the California gold rush. He was only moderately successful in his endeavor but still managed to return to China after a few years. He traveled again to the United States in the 1870s, accompanied by his wife, Hom Shee, aboard the first steamship to make the Pacific run to China. He made intermittent trips to the gold country to try his luck and again met with moderate success by working the tailings of abandoned mines.

During this time his wife was kept busy in San Francisco. Over the next several years, she gave birth to four sons. The family grew up, and in time the oldest boy, Kong Mun Knep, took over a lantern-making shop when its owner decided to return to China. Each of the other three brothers also worked for a time at the lantern shop, which was located on the 800 block of Dupont Street (now Grant Avenue), near the site of the Empress of China Restaurant today. The shop was on the second floor of a wooden building, and strips of bamboo, bolts of colored silk, waxed paper, and tassels littered the place as each lantern was hand-shaped into one of the many designs ordered by customers. They also made and sold kites.

Business went very well until the morning of April 18, 1906, when the earthquake and fire hit San Francisco. The building housing their business was destroyed. The brothers moved to Oakland and, in Oakland's small Chinatown, started up the lantern business again. Business was slow to pick up, however. By 1912 the oldest brother had died, and the second brother continued to operate the shop. Brother number three left to live in Sacramento. Finally, in 1914, William's father, the youngest of the brothers, took over the shop when the second brother decided to retire and move to China.

William's father and mother moved the lantern shop back to San Francisco and set up shop at 915 Stockton Street. After his father passed away, William and his mother operated the business. But the lantern business was slowly dying, because faster ships to and from China were bringing large selections of merchandise to compete for the same business. Finally, in 1940, William decided to close the last Chinese lantern shop in America, and he began to ponder what to do next.

One day he had an inspiration. The number of babies being born in Chinatown was growing steadily. Why not start a milk distribution business? He applied for and got a license from the State Department of Agriculture to handle the distribution of milk, and he contracted with the Spreckels-Russell Dairy Company for his supply. He soon had a number of business contacts, such as restaurants, grocery stores, and other milk consumers, and began delivering milk to them. Then his problems began.

The first hint of trouble arrived when Golden State and Borden's Milk Company, who had almost a milk monopoly in Chinatown, decided they did not want to share their business with a new upstart. They united with the AFL Milk Wagon Drivers Union to stop William. First, the city health department refused to issue a delivery permit to Fong Brothers, the firm name used by William, the principal owner; his brothers Fong Locke and Fong Wing; and another partner, Roger Lee. Without a city delivery permit, Fong Brothers theoretically couldn't operate. The union played along by barring the firm from joining the union.

William decided he wouldn't stand for such treatment, however. He made up his mind that he would carry on the new business as far as he could, and he went ahead and operated anyway. Two weeks went by, and then he was suddenly arrested and warned by the court to desist. He doggedly continued. Arrested again, he was issued an injunction and warned that he would be fined if he did not stop delivering milk. After William's third arrest, he was fined $25 for delivering milk without a permit. He wanted to refuse to pay the fine, but his lawyer, Robert L.

William Wai Fong in 1987.

Levy, finally persuaded him to pay it, telling him that otherwise it might jeopardize any appeal he made later.

Fong Brothers finally got some help from Sam Young, president of the Chinese Workers Mutual Aid Association. Young decided to bring William's case before the Citizens' Anti-Discrimination Committee, which had been set up in cooperation with the U.S. War Production Board. The committee was headed by Mrs. Robert McWilliams. Fong Brothers had printed a leaflet about their situation in which they denounced their unfair treatment, saying that each time they appeared in court, Steve Gilligan, business agent of the Milk Wagon Drivers Union, a Teamsters' affiliate, and city health department officials were always present. After a protracted legal struggle, Fong Brothers finally won its battle and was never bothered again.

On June 3, 1949, several years after Fong Brothers' rough beginnings, the *Chinese Press* wrote the following story about the company, headlined "Fong Brothers Deliver Milk to 500 Chinatown Families":

Do you know your neighbor, the milkman? In San Francisco's Chinatown most folks do, because the only Chinese milk distributor here, and a pioneer in this field, is Bill Fong, a longtime San Franciscan.

His staff, including the deliverymen, are well-known neighborhood "kids," all former GI's now back home and raising families on—milk.

Fong, who established Fong Bros., 935 Stockton Street, distributor for Spreckels-Russell Dairy, in 1941, has seen his business grow from a $30,000 gross to $200,000, a healthy sign in a healthful business which now serves 500 Chinese families and 60 Chinese restaurants.

Fong's staff is composed of: Jonathan K. Yee, 24, 1546 Powell Street, driver and supervisor for retail route home delivery. Yee, in the service 2 years, was wounded in the Battle of the Bulge, and holds a Purple Heart. He is a member of Cathay Post 384, American Legion. He is married to the former Jean Jow and they have a daughter.

Roger Lee, 25, 1941 Washington Street, solicitor and collector, has been with Fong since 1941. His wife is the former Grace Fong. Frank Lee, 22, who has worked close to a year as delivery man, served in the European theater during the war.

Maurice Choy, Jr., 21, 1547 Clay Street, is delivery man. Choy also is married and father of a young son. He is the son of Maurice Choy, Sr., of the Bank of Canton here.

Fong's socially active daughter, Vivian, is his bookkeeper. "From the beginning of this business in 1941 as a one-man enterprise to its present enlarged service," said the owner, "Spreckels-Russell Dairy has cooperated to maintain better quality, better service both wholesale and retail." He stated that Spreckels-Russell ice cream has won the California State Fair gold medal for eight consecutive years. Latest improvement, said Fong, is the newest homogenizing machine in the market.

A special feature appreciated by busy Chinatown customers is daily delivery on the milk routes, Sundays included. Each day sees the milkman on his way from Drumm Street east and west to Van Ness Avenue and from Pine Street north to Bay, for this small Chinatown business has, since 1941, grown to city-wide delivery—and serves the rest of San Francisco county and San Mateo county as well.

If you ask Chinatown's milkman, he'll tell you he's not surprised at this increased milk demand, for since the war Chinatown's had its biggest baby boom—and of course the best must be had for King Baby.

In 1988, forty-eight years after its formation, Fong Brothers Milk Distributors was still operating without a delivery permit as a distributor of milk. William annually gets only a grocery store permit that allows him to deliver milk.

55   Elizabeth Ling-So Hall and Flora Hall Chong

While her brother, James, was becoming a successful physician (as described in Chapter 46), Elizabeth Ling-So Hall was making inroads for Chinese-Americans in San Francisco's school system.

Unlike their brother James, Elizabeth and Flora Hall were born in San Francisco after their parents moved to the United States. Elizabeth, the older of the two sisters, went to a Methodist-Episcopal kindergarten class held in Chinatown, before the family moved to San Mateo for four years. In San Mateo she and Flora attended San Mateo's Central Grammar School, where they learned both to speak and to read English well, which was uncommon among bilingual children of that period.

When the family moved back to San Francisco, they did not return to Chinatown. Instead they lived in Pacific Heights. The Halls were one of the first Chinese families to live outside of Chinatown; by then the passage of time had softened some of the harsh anti-Chinese attitudes, and discrimination had lessened.

Elizabeth and Flora were given special permission to go to Pacific Heights School rather than to Commodore Stockton School in Chinatown, which James had attended years earlier. James helped persuade the school officials to allow his sisters to attend the neighborhood school; the girls' excellent English was one of the deciding factors in the decision. They were the first Chinese students in the school.

Later, Elizabeth and Flora went on to Polytechnic High, their brother's alma mater. "At Poly," Elizabeth recalled in a 1977 *San Francisco Examiner* article, "I had wonderful teachers who encouraged me to take up education. I won a scholarship to Cal [UC Berkeley] and I was on my way."

After two years at UC Berkeley Elizabeth transferred to San Francisco State College, where she earned a B.A. and a teaching credential. At State she helped found Sigma Omicron Pi, the college's first Chinese sorority, and she served as its first president. Flora, who attended San Francisco State for a year before transferring to UC Berkeley, joined the Berkeley chapter of Sigma Omicron Pi. It was at Berkeley that she met Arthur Chong. They graduated in the class of 1936, and were married in 1941.

After receiving her teaching credential, Elizabeth was ready to teach, but found that she couldn't get a job. The

Flora Hall Chong (left) and Elizabeth Ling-So Hall in 1988.

San Francisco school district already had three Chinese teachers, and they thought that was enough. "We'll call you when we need you," they told her. Elizabeth taught English in Chinatown for a while and then went back to San Francisco State to earn her master's degree, during which time she also served as head teacher at Frederick Burke Nursery School, the college's student training school. She then taught at Midtown Nursery School, a private school, and gained valuable experience in child growth and development. It wasn't until 1941, ten years after she received her teaching credential, that the district called her back.

Her first assignment was at Chinatown's Commodore Stockton Elementary School, the former Oriental School. It was in 1950, during her twelve-year stint there as a first-through-sixth-grade teacher, that Superintendent of Schools Herbert Clish finally ordered the "Oriental School" inscription removed from the cornerstone of the school. Looking back, Elizabeth felt fortunate to have been able to teach all the grades from first to sixth while she was at Commodore Stockton.

In 1953 Elizabeth was appointed assistant principal of Sarah Cooper and John Hancock elementary schools. Four years later, in 1957, she was promoted to principal. With this appointment, she became the first Chinese-American principal in the San Francisco public school system. Her phone still ringing off the hook with congratulations, she remarked on what she thought becoming a principal would be like in an interview with radio station KCBS: "As a teacher I had a classroom and direct contact with my children, their growth and development. Now I will be an administrator, facing the same problems but in a more general way and with a larger group. It will be a challenging experience."

Elizabeth later transferred to Spring Valley Elementary School, where she was principal for ten years. She then retired, having spent forty-two years in education, as she said, "making friends and working with children, parents, and teachers to bring out the best in them."

After her retirement in the early 1970s, Elizabeth spent time looking after her mother, Quan Shee Hall, who died in 1977 at the age of 100.

Flora and Arthur have two children, Robert Arthur, a dentist, and Richard Jay, an optometrist. Robert has three sons. The entire Hall family gets together annually at Christmas and, in keeping with tradition, they celebrate Chinese New Year by gathering for a visit with the present family matriarch, Elizabeth.

56   John Kan

John Kan was an innovator in the restaurant trade. In addition to concocting new flavors of ice cream and starting the first Chinese food delivery service, he attracted national attention with his meticulous approach to cooking, his descriptive menus, and the pleasant atmosphere at his restaurant.

John Kan was born in 1907 in Portland, Oregon, the youngest of four children. His parents moved the family to San Francisco when John was four years old. In San Francisco his father started an art goods store, while his mother ran a small restaurant in conjunction with his father's business. It was his interest in his mother's cooking and especially her recipes that drew John into experimenting with new dishes. As he grew older he sought out flavorful and exotic foods, a quest that eventually led him to travel to the Orient in search of secret recipes.

None of his experiments excited Chinatown as much as when young John started making ice cream for Philip Fong at his Fong Fong fountain and lunch counter, an innovation among Chinatown businesses at the time. John concocted the first lichee ice cream and also made kumquat-ginger ice cream. He then opened another new type of business—a "food-to-go" establishment named Chinese Kitchen at the corner of Mason and Pacific. Choices ranged from simple won-ton to complete meals, and customers could pick up the food or have it delivered piping hot to any location in the city.

After World War II John opened a new, expanded enterprise, Kan's Restaurant. His kitchen was enclosed in glass, so that his customers could observe the sanitary and meticulous cooking of their food. He developed a dictionary type of menu, with descriptive phrases for each dish, thus educating his American customers about Chinese food. He is also credited with being the first to place a giant-size lazy susan in the center of each dining table, thus putting each dish within the reach of every diner and avoiding the necessity of passing the dishes around.

John's concern for meticulous service, immaculate surroundings, and beautiful, interesting decorations and his personal interest in each patron's satisfaction earned for Kan's Chinese Restaurant numerous national awards, among them many Holiday Magazine awards.

John made and kept friends easily, and he attracted wide attention. A stream of Hollywood stars began coming to Kan's. Danny Kaye became a fixture, even going into the kitchen to concoct some of his favorite dishes himself, much to the delight of the kitchen crew.

John and his wife, Helen, were always ready to offer service and support to the Chinese community, and one has only to visit the Gum Shan Room in Kan's Chinese Restaurant to know how proud he was of his Chinese heritage. In 1963 he commissioned Jake Lee, a well-known Chinese artist, to paint twelve scenes depicting the Chinese pioneers of America. These large paintings cover the walls of the room and instantly transport one into the life of the Chinese in the nineteenth century.

John passed away on December 7, 1972, and Helen died in 1975. Before she passed on, Helen sold Kan's Chinese Restaurant to their close friend Guy Wong. Guy and John had ties going back to Chung Shan, China, where their ancestral villages were in close proximity. Guy has been able to continue John's legacy since 1975, retaining the customers and friendships John made over the years as well as developing his own following.

H. K. Wong

I met Henry Kwock Wong while I was editor of the Chinese Digest *in 1935. He spent a great deal of time as a young man promoting activities to better the lives of both young and old in Chinatown. An ardent sportsman, he became the manager of local basketball and tennis teams, was a founder of the Chinese Sports Car Club, and took the lead in many community projects and organizations.*

Henry Kwock Wong, better known as "H. K.," was born in San Francisco in April of 1907, the year after the earthquake and fire. His parents were Kim Lun and Tai Gee Wong. He was the oldest son in a family of twelve children, and his formal education ended at seventh grade so he could help support the family.

H. K. worked at any job he could find, and that prepared him for the variety of challenges that later faced him. He was also a great lover of sports, although his participation was mainly behind the scenes. In 1935 his proposal to start a Chinese Tennis Club met with instant approval among his peers, and the club with that name celebrated its golden anniversary in 1985. The Chinese National Tennis Championships were initiated by the club and are still held today. In 1942 he was Executive Secretary of the Chinese Consolidated Benevolent Association, better known as the Chinese Six Companies.

H. K. got to meet many of Chinatown's business people in connection with the job he held with the Bank of Canton, and in 1941 he became a partner in the Ti Sun Hardware and Furniture Co. He sold his interest twenty-nine years later because of his many other activities. In the 1950s alone he was public relations man for the Sports Car Club of America and a founder of the Chinese Sports Car Club in 1955–56.

In early 1957, noting the increasing traffic congestion in Chinatown, he was the first to turn observation into action. He urged a coalition of local leaders to back a plan to build Portsmouth Square Garage, which has become, since it was opened in 1962, a crucial factor in alleviating local traffic.

H. K. was the founder of the "Miss Chinatown USA" pageant in 1958, which is annually a big part of the Chinese New Year activities; and because his son Wesley belonged to Boy Scout Troop 3, he became an advisor for the Scout-O-Rama and other activities in 1959. He was also technical director for Universal Studios' *Flower Drum Song* in 1961; a founding member of the Chinese Historical Society of America in 1963; a founding director of the Empress of China restaurant in 1965 as well as its PR man and president; and a director of the Gas Appliance Society of Northern California, PG&E, from 1966 to 1968.

In June of 1968 a group of Chinatown leaders formed a committee to seek out the facts about, and seek solutions for, the many interrelated problems the community was facing. Sixty-seven dedicated men and women on the original committee, representing the entire community's thinking, set out to formulate the guidelines for a task force of more than 300 persons who worked as members of committees or subcommittees or as advisers. Three cochairs were chosen to head the project: Lim P. Lee, Albert C. Lim, and H. K. Wong. Alessandro Baccari was chosen as project coordinator.

The project started on June 12, 1968, and was completed on April 21, 1969. The findings and recommendations covered 834 pages, and were published as the *San Francisco Chinese Community Citizens' Survey & Fact Finding Committee Report*. Only a few typewritten copies were prepared and submitted to Mayor Joseph Alioto's office for the benefit of city officials and for scrutiny by the press and other interested parties. However, an abridged edition of the report came out under the same name on August 15, 1969, composed of 227 printed pages.

The report illuminated many areas of concern, and paved the way for various social service agencies such as On Lok, NEMS, Self-Help, Geen Mun, and others to get grants and community development funds, while other community agencies were able to increase their funding. Lim P. Lee, Albert C. Lim, and H. K. Wong were indefatigable as cochairs, working as hard as all the other volunteers. This project, so useful and helpful in generating financial and moral support for the community, never received the publicity it deserved, but it was one of the highlights of H. K.'s memories.

H. K. remained active from the 1970s until 1985. He was in charge of public relations for the People's Republic of China Exhibit—Archaeological Finds held at the Asian Art Museum in 1975; a director of the Camino California Bank, Palo Alto; director of the Oral History Program of the Chinese Historical Society of America, 1980–1985; Advisor, North Beach Museum, Eureka Federal Savings & Loan Association, 1981; Advisor, Pacific Heritage Museum, Bank of Canton of California, 1981; PR man for the Chinese Community Cable Car Restoration, 1981; and a director of the San Francisco Convention and Visitors Bureau, 1978–1984.

For these and many other contributions, H. K. Wong received the national Jefferson Award from the American

H. K. Wong presenting one of his paintings of bamboo to President Jimmy Carter, 1979. [Photo by Kem Lee Studio, courtesy of Mrs. H. K. Wong.]

Sir John Yehall Chin and Lady Sybil Chin, 1981. Pope John Paul II made Chin Knight of the Holy Sepulchre for his dedication in public service. [Photo courtesy of John Yehall Chin.]

John Yehall Chin learned English at St. Mary's Chinese Catholic Mission at 902 Stockton Street. He became a devout Catholic, and from then on served the church and the school in many capacities. Throughout his life his goals have been uncomplicated: service to his church and community and devotion to his wife, Sybil, and his family.

John Yehall Chin was born on March 2, 1908, in Toishan, China. He came to the United States on a clipper ship that took nineteen days to get from from Hong Kong to the Golden Gate, and he was quarantined on Angel Island for a month before he joined his father in San Francisco.

He attended school at St. Mary's until the eighth grade, at which time his father told him he'd have to support himself if he wanted to complete his education. So he got a job as a cook with Eugene Fritz, the owner of a big apartment building on Market Street, and was able to earn enough to attend Healds College in San Francisco. He graduated from Healds in 1932, and was then asked to return to St. Mary's as a teacher in the language school. After serving in the army during World War II, he again returned to St. Mary's as an administrator, a post he held for many years.

St. Mary's was very active in the San Francisco Chinatown community. The St. Mary's Drum Corps became a familiar sight at parades and other events in San Francisco, and played a prominent role in the grand opening of the Bay Bridge in 1936, the Golden Gate Bridge in 1937, and the World's Fair in 1939. That year the corps

Institute for Public Service in 1978. He was listed in the 1981–1982 *Who's Who in California*, and in 1987 he was listed as one of "101 Memorable San Franciscans" in the San Francisco Examiner Centennial Issue (1887–1987). In addition, he was a journalist for the *Chinese Digest, Chinese World, East West,* and *Asian Week,* and journalist/editor for the *Chinatown News,* Vancouver, B.C., and *Jade* magazine, Los Angeles. He also edited the book *San Francisco Chinatown on Parade* for the Chinese Chamber of Commerce.

In 1957 he married Honey Quan. They had one son, Wesley, and a daughter-in-law, Rebecca. H. K. passed away on January 13, 1985.

toured a number of cities, including Los Angeles during the Moon Festival.

In 1942 John Yehall Chin was elected president of the Chinese Comsolidated Benevolent Association, known popularly as the Chinese Six Companies. He was elected again in 1954, and served a total of five terms in this position. He became what is known as a *shunan*, an influential leader in the Six Companies. Among many other contributions, he played a major role in settling a dispute between the association and the teachers at the language school it sponsors.

In 1964 he was appointed to the first Human Rights Commission in Washington, D.C. A few years later, in 1967, he was asked to help resolve a labor dispute in Chinatown involving the garment industry. Most garment factories were well known for underpaying their workers. It was a complex situation; the manufacturers were not paying enough money to the subjobbers, who said they couldn't afford to raise wages. The dispute was finally settled after everyone was persuaded to give a little.

In 1972 he ran as a candidate for the community college board. Thirty-four candidates were running for seven seats in the June election. It was a difficult campaign, and there were many prominent people running against him, but he received the most votes of the five that were elected. He was then elected president by the other board members.

Daisy Wong Chinn's life could be likened to a kaleidoscope— it seems that more than one person must have been involved in so many different activities. I will only add that she has been my wife for fifty-nine years. She tells her own story here.

I was born Daisy Lorraine Wong on November 8, 1908, at 60 Wentworth Place in the heart of San Francisco Chinatown. I was the eldest of seven children (two of whom died in infancy and early childhood during the flu epidemic of 1917).

My parents, both of whom were also born in San Francisco, were Walter Fie Wong and Annie Haw. My father was a remarkable person. Although he had only a few years of formal schooling, he became a self-taught, well-educated man. His handwriting in English was as beautiful as his calligraphy in Chinese. His musical talent included playing all the Chinese instruments available to him at the time—the Chinese flute; the mandolin; the *erh-hu*, which is a two-stringed instrument played with a bow; and the butterfly harp, a multistringed instrument played with two delicate, slender, flexible bamboo wands. Often at night he would accompany Mother on the butterfly harp as she sang Chinese opera. Through English correspondence courses he became adept at playing the banjo, the accordion, and the zither. Yet he often said to me that he couldn't understand how I could play the piano, reading five or six notes at a glance.

When I was about three years old we moved to Stockton, California, where we stayed for several years while

Father found work where he could. Then the family moved to Hanford, California, near Fresno, where Father became an interpreter for a Chinese herbalist named Y. T. Sue, whose office was in China Alley. (It was customary for herbalists with American patients to have English-speaking interpreters assist in their practice.)

Father moved us back to San Francisco when I was in the third grade. During his three years as an interpreter he had absorbed enough knowledge to become an herbalist himself, and he hung out his shingle in a two-story house at 1852 Buchanan Street, between Bush and Sutter streets. His office was on the first floor, and he brewed herbs for his patients in the kitchen in the back. Our living quarters were on the second floor. Later he worked as a clerk at the pharmaceutical firm of Boericke & Runyon in downtown San Francisco.

After we returned to San Francisco I attended the Oriental School on Washington Street. The students there were all Chinese; it was the only public school Chinese students could attend in those days. We were required to speak only English at school, for which I am grateful because it allowed me to expand my knowledge and grasp of this second language. We spoke Chinese exclusively at home.

My eighth-grade teacher was a wonderful woman named Agnes O'Neill. She really drilled English, spelling, and grammar into us, and she always sat me in the front of the first row. At this time, the very first essay contest among grammar school students was sponsored by the Community Chest (forerunner to United Way). Miss O'Neill had the entire class write essays under the title "Suppose Nobody Cared?" She selected mine to be entered in the contest, and I came out winner of all the entries in the San Francisco school system. My first "publicity" photograph was taken by a news photographer for the *San Francisco Call* on January 23, 1923.

In the early 1920s, when I was still attending grammar school, I and some of my friends earned pocket money by working as waitresses at Aladdin Studio, located on Sutter Street. (The child labor laws had not yet been enacted). The restaurant was run by two Jewish sisters, Harriet and Minnie Mooser. Most of us worked only on Saturdays, at lunch or tea time, earning 35 cents an hour. They provided our lunch and colorful aprons, which we took home each Saturday and laundered.

One of my dearest and oldest friends, Daisy K. Wong, worked as the pantry girl. I can still see her putting three little dabs of meringue on each of the lemon tarts that were favorites with the host of theatrical people who were close friends of the Mooser sisters. Among the celebrities who visited the restaurant were Harry Houdini, the world-renowned magician and escape artist; Vivian and Rosetta Duncan, famed entertainers in the "Topsy and Eva" musical; and Sophie Tucker, the popular singer and stage personality of that era.

A few lucky girls also worked the dinner shift, and they were paid 50 cents an hour. The tips were very good, especially at dinnertime. I remember particularly a chum and classmate of mine, Hattie Chan, who always managed to save $5 a week to deposit in a savings account. At the time, Bank of Italy (the forerunner of the Bank of America) was very community-minded about encouraging students to save. Each week a bank representative came to the school and collected whatever savings we wished to deposit.

Grammar school children could also earn money for

school expenses by doing housework and odd jobs found through the YWCA. Occasionally, inexperience and a lack of familiarity with American life would cause one of us to make a blunder. One time I worked as a housegirl after school for a nice couple on Green Street. I cleaned and did a little cooking. My employer told me that I could eat anything I wanted. One day a can of artichoke hearts really intrigued me. I had no idea what they tasted like or that a young girl could not possibly finish a whole can all by herself. After opening and tasting them, I realized all this and felt so guilty that I wrapped the balance in newspaper, put them in the garbage, and left a note in my employer's mailbox saying how very sorry I was and that I felt I could no longer continue working for her. In another instance, Lillian Chan, my close friend and later maid of honor, worked for a couple on Nineteenth Avenue. The husband was an avid golfer and had beautiful woolen socks. His wife asked Lillian to wash them, so she soaked them in hot water. The rest is history!

The YWCA jobs were intermittent. For instance, we would sometimes be hired by a socialite to receive the hats and coats from the guests at a gathering at her home. We would be thrilled to be inside one of these handsome mansions, not to mention the 50 cents an hour we were each paid. We naturally wore Chinese dresses.

One time a movie about China was being shown in one of the downtown theaters. Before the movie came on there was a prologue, in which I took part. Dressed in Chinese clothes, Ivy Lee and I sat in a box seat and served tea to each other while the spotlight shone on us. Then the spotlight moved to the center of the stage, where Tse Wing Quong stood in front of the curtain and sang a great baritone solo. He later became a well-known artist whose paintings now hang in the United States as well as in Paris and other European cities. His signature was simply "Wing." His favorite subjects were older people, and he remarked to us once, "Do you realize it takes many decades of life to produce those wrinkles?" He was so intrigued with Tom's mother, who was then in her nineties, that he wanted to paint all of her wrinkles, especially her hands. His gift to us was one of these paintings, which now hangs in our living room.

In June of 1923 I graduated from grammar school, and for four years I attended Girls High School, a respected institution at Geary and Webster streets. I majored in math, receiving straight A grades in all of my math courses. My goal was to be a math teacher.

When I was about fourteen years old I started going to the Chinese Congregational Church on Brenham Place (now Walter U. Lum Place). In time I began teaching Sunday School, playing the piano for young people's evening services, and accompanying several very good male soloists at different functions. The people I usually accompanied were Harry Mew and Dr. Thomas A. Wong, who was also our best man in 1930. My cousin Minnie Fong (now Mrs. Ira C. Lee) had inspired me to take piano lessons by playing a stirring military march for me. I signed up with the Christensen School of Music, where they taught the chord system for popular music. After every payday at the Aladdin Studio, I would purchase one piece of sheet music from Sherman, Clay, and Company.

At the same time I used to pal around with a second cousin, Alice P. Fong, who was a few years older than me. (She would later become the first Chinese-American teacher in the San Francisco school system, as described in Chapter 53.) When she and several other girls wanted to start a club to stage a benefit for victims of the Hong Kong flood and famine in 1924, I was one of the seven young women who founded the Square and Circle Club, believed to be the largest and oldest continuous Chinese women's service club in the United States (see Chapter 27). For the Club's Golden Anniversary in 1974, I was elected president.

I also helped out at a vacation Bible school that served the many Chinese children who had no other activities during summer vacation. Chingwah Lee organized the sessions for a number of years. I was still in high school, but Mr. Lee asked me to be on the staff, so I gave Bible lessons to the younger children and taught the girls handicrafts such as making hand-hemmed handkerchiefs, which were very popular in those days.

In 1925 the Chinese Students Christian Alliance Western Conferences were held on the Stanford University campus. The alliance was composed of students from many western states. Other alliance conferences were held in the Midwest and on the East Coast, generally with several hundred attending at each location. Stanford was very generous in allowing us to use their classrooms for orations and debates; their dormitories; Stanford Union for our meals; their sports facilities for our track meet and tennis tournament; and their auditorium for our farewell dance. It was my honor to be selected Queen of the Conference in 1925. My cousin Minnie Fong won the women's tennis singles title, and together we won the doubles title that year.

After graduating from high school in 1927 I entered UC Berkeley, where I had two more years of math courses. I was one of a rare breed because there were only six Chinese girls—Ella Dong, Elizabeth Hall, Renmi Jue, Stella Lee, Daisy K. Wong, and myself—on the entire campus. There were plenty of Chinese boys, however!

One of my other courses was in the Mandarin language, which was gradually replacing my native Cantonese in China. For this course I received a D grade! I was admittedly neither surprised nor disappointed, since I simply would not speak in class. I felt that, as a Chinese person, I would be expected to give a perfect presentation—which I couldn't, so I didn't try.

During my college days, I helped pay my tuition by working at the National Dollar Store dress factory located at 728 Washington Street (now the Golden Phoenix Restaurant). Its Chinese name was Chung Hing, and the factory was light and airy. Older women worked side by side with younger women and students. Each person had her own sewing machine, and we were paid by the piece or garment. The dresses we worked on were cut and sewn at the factory to be sold in the National Dollar retail stores.

One day when I returned to work from class, I found a big bundle next to my machine. When I asked the foreman—a very stern man named Joe Sun, the father of San Francisco's Lawrence Joe, M.D.—what was wrong, he said that the gathering at the waistline of the dresses was not evenly distributed. I could see in my mind's eye the disappearance of that week's school expenses, and I sat down and cried. Soon Mr. Joe came over, took the bundle of dresses, and said, "Never mind. We'll let them pass this time." To this day I still remember his kindness.

During the years that I attended the Congregational Church, we seldom went on individual dates. As a rule, the girls, mostly Square and Circle members, and the boys, including Thomas W. Chinn, my future husband, did things as a group. Events included riding the ferryboat to Muir Woods (the boys would bring along their ukeleles and a great songfest would dominate the trip—such simple pleasures!); hiking to the top of Mt. Tamalpais; a seventeen-mile hike to Stinson Beach; a hay ride down the peninsula to see the new Moffett Naval Air Hangar at Sunnyvale (then considered the "utmost"); dances at the International Institute; and outings to athletic events, musical programs, and dances. Sunday afternoons were usually spent at the church social hall, with the whole group doing the large crossword puzzle in the Sunday paper.

In the late 1920s and early 1930s, denim factories were very prevalent in Chinatown. These ranged from large factories that manufactured denim pants from beginning to end, doing their own cutting and sewing, to the smaller factories that did everything but the cutting of the cloth from patterns. At the latter, the cut-out pieces would be delivered to the factory for sewing in big bundles of generally five dozen. The first workers would usually try to select a medium size, since the larger sizes required more stitching and the smaller sizes were more difficult to handle.

Later my parents had one of these smaller factories. It was named Leon Sewing Factory and was located at 724 Kearny Street. They had about fifteen employees. A hired cook prepared lunch and dinner for the workers. The fifteenth of every month, which we called "Joe Jit," was an occasion for a specially prepared gourmet dinner.

Until about 1930, very few Chinese were hired by American corporations. If any were hired, it was generally because the company planned to open a Chinese or Chinatown branch. This was the case when I was hired by Western Union in 1930. I happened to find out about the opening one day when I was at my hairdresser's on Jackson Street near Powell. Her name was Violet, and she was one of the earliest Chinese hair stylists. The phone rang, and it was Mr. Ming S. Jung telling Violet that he had been hired by Western Union to be manager of the Chinatown branch planned for 667 Grant Avenue (now the location of Bargain Bazaar). The company wanted to hire Chinese girls to be trained at their teletype school in San Jose for three months before employment. I applied and was one of the three hired.

The classes in San Jose ran five days a week, eight hours a day. Each class had about ten students, and the day was divided into three topics: spelling and geography; teletype routine, which involved the use and many applications of the newly invented communication device; and the "story of the teletype machine," in which we learned about the maintenance of the machine and how the entire complicated mechanism worked, from the moment a person touched a key—which ratchet tripped which wire, the springs, electrical impulses, and so forth—until the letter was printed out on tape. The last subject intimidated many of the women students because of the mechanics involved. However, it was "duck soup" for me, perhaps because of my math background.

While we were at the school, we stayed at a hotel at company expense. We paid for our own meals, and we could take the train back to San Francisco on weekends. About twenty-six people at a time attended the school, and they came from all of the western states, so we had a chance to meet a diverse range of would-be employees. At graduation time I was elected class president. The faculty gave us a luncheon at the Commercial Club in San Jose on March 29, 1930, and I composed some appropriate words to the tune of "When the Moon Comes Over the Mountain," which we sang as we said farewell. In a letter to Mr. Cook, then the president of Western Union Telegraph Company, the school principal stated, "Daisy Wong has won the highest grades of any student who has thus far enrolled, although her scholarship and nationality stirred competition which brought two other students in as her close seconds."

Thomas W. Chinn and I were baptized on the same Easter Sunday in 1925. Although we knew each other at church, it was four years before he asked me for a date. We were engaged on July 20, 1929, and married on June 8, 1930. Our only child, Walter, was born on November 5, 1932. Walter married Frances Quock, and we have three grandchildren and three great-grandchildren.

Our wedding combined Chinese and western traditions. It took place at Hang Far Low, 731 Grant Avenue, the oldest Chinese restaurant in the United States. In the 1930s it was fashionable for young Chinese couples to have their wedding ceremony at a Chinese restaurant, followed by a banquet. An altar would be set up with floral decorations and candelabras, and an upright piano would be rented for the occasion. The traditional ceremony included a minister, a flower girl, bridesmaids, and groomsmen, and there would be a short wedding march. At our wedding there was also a Chinese musical trio consisting of a trumpet, cymbals, and an *erh-hu*.

Since the banquet hall was located on the third floor, the trio was stationed at the top of the stairs, before the entrance to the banquet room. Whenever any guests came up the stairs, the trio would break into a cadence of welcome. There would be a long blast from the group: The trumpet went "dee-dah, dee-dah," and the cymbals responded with one loud "cha-pong." The timid little *erh-hu* sort of provided the link between everything. It was very festive and definitely ear-splitting!

Limousines were hired for the event to pick up the guests from their homes. Whenever strict protocol was followed, a banquet never started until everyone was there (or the hosts knew the reason for a guest's absence).

In those days, "go-betweens"—persons who acted as arrangers between the bride's family and the groom's, to smooth conditions for the marriage—were still sometimes used, although we did not follow this custom. My paternal grandmother, a strong and well-built person, occasionally was asked to be one. One of the go-between's tasks on the day of the wedding was to escort the bride out of her childhood home. This was accomplished by having the bride climb on the back of the go-between and literally be carried piggyback out of the house to a waiting limousine. My grandmother took me along with her one time to Oakland, and I had an opportunity to watch her perform this rite.

One of the most memorable events of our lives occurred on March 3, 1983. To our eternal surprise, my husband and I received an invitation from President Ronald Reagan to attend a state dinner honoring Queen Elizabeth II of England and Prince Philip, Duke of Edinburgh, in the Hearst Court of the M.H. de Young Museum in Golden Gate Park. The reason we were chosen is still a mystery to us. Regardless, we felt highly honored to be included in this select group. Of the 256 persons at the dinner, only 156 were nonofficial people.

On the day of the dinner, the White House social

secretary alerted us by phone that for security reasons only one entrance to Golden Gate Park, at Tenth and Fulton streets, would be open. When we arrived at the park entrance we were checked in by security people. As we entered the handsomely redecorated Adrian Court of the Asian Art Museum, our invitation was again scrutinized by an elegantly gowned hostess. She then walked us over to a uniformed presidential aide, who announced our names over the microphone to the guests assembling for the reception. The press and other media people were lined up behind a rope barrier to our right.

To our delight, during the social hour the guests were very cordial, introducing themselves to one another. We were all on common ground. Evangelist Billy Graham was the first to introduce himself to us. Mrs. Graham, the daughter of missionaries, said that she had been raised in China for the first seventeen years of her life. Then I spied 49er quarterback Joe Montana leaning against one of the columns, although Tom said he looked too small to be a football hero. We went over to introduce ourselves, and Montana and his wife were most cordial. Later, Shirley Temple Black came around in a delicate, light-orange-hued chiffon gown with a floating back panel. After a short conversation she asked, "Have you seen my husband? He's probably looking for me, but I'm so short, I doubt he can see me!"

We also met Dr. William Rial, president of the American Medical Association; Associate Justice of the Supreme Court of California Frank K. Richardson; Philip Caldwell, chairman of the Ford Motor Company; Mrs. Laurence Lane, Jr., whose husband is publisher of *Sunset* magazine and a former ambassador; and Mrs. Yvon d'Argence, wife of the former chief curator of the Asian Art Museum. When we were asked to queue up to be introduced, we happened to line up right behind television anchorman Ted Koppel, whose wife said they were happy to be in California again to see their former Stanford classmates. Where else could an average citizen have the opportunity to meet so many celebrities in the course of an hour?

We were excited to learn that we were to be individually accorded the honor of being introduced by the chief of protocol to President Reagan, Queen Elizabeth II, Nancy Reagan, and Prince Philip (in that order). By the time I got to Mrs. Reagan, I was so exhilarated, I said, "This is just like a dream!" Prince Philip, hearing this, gave me a great big smile and extended his hand.

We then discovered that at state dinners, spouses are not seated together. When a presidential aide led us to our tables, it was a wonderful surprise to find ourselves seated close to the head table. I was in the middle of the first row of round tables, directly facing Nancy Reagan, and Tom was in the second row center, facing the queen. We were so close that we could see Her Majesty's diamond tiara, necklace, and rings shimmering and dancing as she talked. I could see the large mobile pearls inside each diamond circlet in her tiara move with her.

I was seated next to Ian White, then director of the M. H. de Young Memorial Museum. When I asked him how security was at the park, he said, "Mrs. Chinn, there are more policemen here than there are trees in Golden Gate Park."

To complete our happiness, we later received from the White House a color photograph of the two couples taken aboard HMS *Britannia*, anchored at Pier 50 in San Francisco Bay.

60   Albert C. Lim

Albert Lim is one of those persons who is forever involved in community service, always volunteering for that crucial role that will make a project possible when no one else is willing. This chapter sketches only a few of the events in his life; but I should also mention that we've known each other for over sixty years, and that for more than twenty of those years he was my doubles partner in tennis. I never had to cover his side of the court—he always covered it like a blanket!

Mow Fung Company, at 733 Washington Street, is a nationally known Chinese vegetable store. It was established some time between 1912 and 1914 by Lim Dick Young, who came to the United States from Tai Land village in the Toishan region of South China in about 1910. He left his wife and family behind in China. Mow Fung Company started as a small store but soon was shipping all types of Chinese vegetables to customers throughout California, and by the 1920s it was reaching beyond the confines of the state. The store has generally been one of Chinatown's largest suppliers of winter melons, a favorite year-round Chinese vegetable.

In 1918 Lim Dick Young brought his oldest son, Lim Guey Him, to San Francisco to help in the store. Guey Him soon returned to China to get married, and in 1920 he returned to San Francisco with his youngest brother, Albert, age eleven. Albert attended the Oriental School and the Morning Bell Chinese School. Considered a prestigious Chinese-language school at the time, Morning Bell was located on Hangah Alley, off Sacramento Street near Stockton Street. Later, Lim Wei, the other brother, also arrived to help with the store. Being young adults, neither of Albert's brothers attended public school. Albert was the only one to receive an American education.

Their mother stayed behind in China, and she did not come to the United States until 1960. By that time it had been nearly forty years since she had seen her first-born son, Guey Him. The only sister, Ngan Suey Lim Lui, now in her nineties, never emigrated to the United States. She lives with her family in Hong Kong.

Business was good at Mow Fung, and the elder Lim soon decided that it would be better for Albert and Lim Wei to get a more rounded Chinese education by learning the Mandarin language also. So in 1922 the two brothers and a cousin left for Tientsin, China, and entered Nankai Boys School, where they studied for six years.

Returning to San Francisco in 1928, Albert attended Heald Business College for three years. In the latter part of 1931 he left for Shanghai to manage a hat factory. This time he spent seven years in China, until he was forced to return to the United States in 1938 after the Japanese occupation of Shanghai. From 1942 to 1946 he taught Mandarin at UC Berkeley. Subsequently he was manager of the *Chinese Nationalist Daily* in San Francisco and was also a sales representative for United Airlines from 1952 to 1954.

In 1955, when his brother decided to retire, Albert returned to the family business and managed Mow Fung Company until his own retirement in 1984. Business flourished during this period. The company shipped vegetables by air freight to customers across the country. In the last few years, however, many customers have dropped out, either to grow their own vegetables or to patronize new growers in their own locale. This has allowed Albert to devote more time to community affairs.

Albert was always a believer in community service. Among his many activities, he was president of the Lim Family Association during the latter part of the 1950s, president of Ning Yung (a group of people representing several different clans, all from the same district and speaking the same local dialect), president of the Chinese Six Companies during 1960, and a director of the Chinese Chamber of Commerce for close to twenty years, beginning in 1958. He also served as vice president of the Chinese Chamber of Commerce in 1971.

During these years he was often asked to speak before community groups. Because his experience embraced a larger part of China than did that of most of his contemporaries, Albert was considered an expert on China, especially since he knew many of China's leaders, several having been schoolmates of his in North China. During this period China was still the homeland of most of Chinatown's elders, and news and interpretations of events in China still commanded large audiences.

One of the most colorful movies with a Chinese theme to be produced in Hollywood was *Flower Drum Song*, starring Nancy Kwan. Albert, along with the late publicist H. K. Wong, served as technical advisor for the film, which was produced at Universal Studios in 1963. The film's premiere at the Golden Gate Theater in San Francisco received a tremendous turnout.

In 1960, 1964, and 1971 Albert was comaster of ceremonies for the Miss Chinatown USA pageant. Organizers for the first fashion show of pageant contestants in 1966 were confronted with many difficulties. To fill Louie's of Grant Avenue Restaurant with 300 persons was "a chore," according to a member of the early committees. Today, the fashion show is one of the main fund-raising events during Chinese New Year. The proceeds are used for the work of the Chinese Chamber of Commerce. Held for many years at the Empress of China Restaurant, the show has outgrown that establishment's capacity of 800 and is presently held at the Meridien Hotel.

Despite his busy involvement with community affairs, Albert and his wife, Eva (née Tom), whom he married in 1931, always opened their home in Berkeley when the Miss China contestants came to participate in the Miss International contest in Long Beach or the Miss Universe contest in Miami. Since the Taiwan government did not have a budget for the Miss Chinas and their chaperones, they would be invited to stay with the Lims in the interim between the contest's end and their departure for home.

The first Miss China, Janet Lin, came in 1960 to enter the Miss International competition. She spoke neither English nor Cantonese, and so the Lims on many occasions had to be her interpreters in Mandarin. (During this period only a very small percentage of the Chinese in San Francisco spoke Mandarin.) The Chinese Tea Forum, of which Albert was a founder, provided a luncheon meeting every year to allow the current Miss China to meet the public. The club was formed to provide a forum for the exchange of ideas about contemporary problems among citizens who are more comfortable speaking and writing in Chinese than in English.

In 1970, after a flight from San Francisco to Taiwan for their vacation, Albert and Eva were welcomed at the airport by a dazzling array of ten beauties, all former Miss Chinas. This was their way of thanking the Lims for housing them and making them feel welcome during their stay in the San Francisco Bay area.

Albert E. Wong

When we were Boy Scouts together in Chinatown, Albert Wong was always the point man for getting things done. Like many others from Chinatown, he moved around a lot from one job to another. However, his experiences as a pilot in the Far East were unique.

Albert E. Wong was born in China on January 10, 1910, in the Sunwui district of Kwangtung province. His grandfather had arrived in the United States in 1870, while his father, Wong Sue, came here in 1890. Eventually Wong Sue went to Watsonville, about a hundred miles south of San Francisco, where he started an apple-drying plant. He returned to China after many years and married a woman from a neighboring village named Young Shee. Albert was born the following year, after his father had returned to Watsonville. It was then that Albert's father decided that he would move his little family and settle in the United States.

When Young Shee and Albert arrived in 1916 they were met by Wong Sue and tarried only briefly in San Francisco before leaving for Watsonville. Albert's brother, Frank, was born in Watsonville. Frank became an aeronautical engineer, now retired and living in Oakland.

Wong Sue suffered a stroke in 1918 and was taken back to San Francisco to be cared for at the old Tung Wah dispensary, the forerunner to the present Chinese Hospital. He passed away in 1921.

Meanwhile Albert was enrolled in elementary school in Watsonville. After he graduated, Albert opted for learning a trade rather than attending high school. He enrolled at Heald Automobile Engineering school at Sutter and Larkin streets in San Francisco and spent several years there, learning the skills required to repair automobiles and motorcycles. It was about then that he received the nickname "Suicide Al." He would sometimes take a motorcycle out "for testing," zoom up the California Street hill at high speed, and shoot several feet into the air at the top next to the Fairmont Hotel before touching down.

Soon after completing his course at Heald, he decided he would like to take up flying. In 1931 he started taking lessons at the Oakland Airport, and after he became proficient and passed the tests he received his license. He immediately left for China with his mother and brother Frank. His mother and Frank were returning to the ancestral home; but Albert was in search of adventure. The Sino-Japanese war was imminent, and he wanted to enlist and become a pursuit pilot in the air force. But he had no connections to make that possible. He ended up becoming an air mail pilot for several years. He flew for the Southwest Aviation Corp., a feeder airline for China National Aviation. Gradually he was also learning much about Chinese culture and language that he had not known while living in America.

When the war started in 1937 his flying days ended, and he became a mechanics instructor in the Chinese Nationalist Army. He was given the rank of captain, and he and his staff taught newcomers for two years. Then he was assigned to a tank corps in Hunan province, where he spent his time overseeing the maintenance of tanks. He went through several campaigns in the armored corps. Eventually his knowledge of the English language stood him in good stead. He was assigned to British Intelligence, near the border between Hong Kong and the mainland, for a year and a half.

Then Pearl Harbor was bombed, and Albert was assigned to the Flying Tigers as a liaison officer. The Flying Tigers were a group of Chinese and American flyers from the United States who went to China as volunteers to help repel the Japanese in the late 1930s. After Pearl Harbor they were placed under the command of U.S. General Claire Chennault, and with reinforcements became a part of the Fourteenth Air Force. Albert served with them until the war ended in 1945. While he was still with the Flying Tigers, he met a refugee named Mabel Ho from British Guiana. They were married in 1942 in Waichow, China.

When the war ended Albert and Mabel returned to San Francisco and then retired in Oakland. They have five children: Lawrence, Marian, and Brian, who all work for the Pacific Bell; and twins Timothy, an electronics engineer with Hewlett-Packard, and Thomas, a television technician with Lockheed Space.

62   Kee Joon

Kee Joon was one of the first pioneers to bring the best in Chinese culinary arts—both in the kitchen and in the dining room—to restaurants in America. His Empress of China Restaurant has won many national awards since it opened in 1966.

Kee Joon's father, Yee Yuen, had a restaurant named Hang Far Low in Santa Barbara around the turn of the century, and it was there that Kee Joon began his career in the restaurant business. He started in the kitchen as a busboy and dishwasher, and gradually became fascinated as people came into the kitchen to congratulate his father for a wonderful dinner, exclaiming over this dish or that. Joon became a more earnest and observant worker, and before long was helping his father in many different capacities, learning from him the secrets of gourmet cooking and the art of running a restaurant successfully.

When the family finally sold the business and moved to San Francisco, Joon was shipped off to China to acquire a Chinese education. He spent several years studying there, including many evenings visiting well-known dining places, getting to know the chefs, and compiling an enviable store of recipes and special dishes for all occasions. When Joon came back to San Francisco he continued to immerse himself in the many facets of operating a successful Chinese restaurant by western standards. By the late 1950s he was ready to start on his own.

San Francisco's famed Hang Far Low Restaurant (not connected in any way with the Santa Barbara restaurant of the same name), in business since the 1860s, finally closed in the late 1950s. A new group took over the premises, entirely refurbished it, and opened the new Four Seas restaurant in early 1960. Joon and his group opened the Imperial Palace, with Joon as general manager, just a couple of weeks later. It was an instant success. Joon catered to a special clientele that included American gourmets seeking an upscale Chinese restaurant meeting all their criteria for a spotless, well-operated dining room. Joon had cannily worked toward meeting this standard. In 1966 he and his investment group opened the Empress of China, another phenomenally successful restaurant.

The Empress featured two floors of dining: a two-

Kee Joon, 1987. [Photo courtesy of Kee Joon.]

room dining area and a more intimate, smaller Emperor's Room seating twenty-five, all on the top floor of the new Chong Investments six-story building at 838 Grant Avenue. Directly under this is the Empress of China Ballroom, a combined dancing and banquet room seating over 600 persons and featuring a stage and fashion-show runway. In 1974, not content with this, Joon embarked on another elaborate restaurant in Burlingame named Kee Joon, facing San Francisco Bay. This venture was also a big success. The Hearst family and many other well-known people were regular customers for years.

In 1988 Joon retired and sold this restaurant, wanting to enjoy a life of leisure. This was fine for a time, but his restlessness started up again, and he finally took on consulting assignments, the latest as dining consultant to the new Fairmont Hotel in San Jose. But Joon is saving a good part of his retirement time for his family: his wife Edna, daughter Barbara and son-in-law Jack C. Yee, daughter Jackie and son-in-law Dan Marr, and many grandchildren.

63   Lim P. Lee

Lim P. Lee and I have known each other ever since we both joined the Boy Scouts, and we have also shared many of the more mature (and more mundane) activities of adulthood. His record of service to his community and his country is an impressive one, and he still enjoys writing—an interest we have shared ever since we both got involved in the Chinese Digest *in the 1930s.*

Lim P. Lee was born in Hong Kong, and he and his parents came to San Francisco when he was eight months old. As he often joked with friends later in life, "If my parents had only been a little more patient, I'd have been a native San Franciscan." Lim attended local public schools and then graduated from the University of the Pacific in 1934. He did graduate work at the University of Southern California from 1934 to 1936, and received a Juris Doctor degree from Lincoln University School of Law, San Francisco, in 1954.

Lim enlisted in the U.S. Army in 1943 and graduated from the Military Intelligence Service Language School at Fort Snelling, Minnesota. He served with the Counter Intelligence Corps in the Philippine Islands and Hokkaido, Japan.

While he was in Japan, Lim was involved in an incident that never reached the public. When MacArthur's troops took over Japan, a small contingent was sent to Hokkaido, an island about the size of Maine. Arriving there, they found that the island contained coal mines, steel mills, and large factories, which were operated by captured slave labor: Chinese prisoners of war, including many from the Nationalist Chinese army, and former

Chinese guerrillas, all working under Japanese overseers and guards. The number of prisoners was in the thousands. When the prisoners finally realized that the U.S. Army had arrived, they rioted and started beating up their Japanese captors. The small U.S. Army contingent couldn't control the riot with their limited force.

Lim was the only Japanese and Chinese interpreter who arrived with the U.S. force. When no solution seemed possible, Lim was asked if he could think of a way to stop the riot. He came up with a plan that was immediately put into effect. At Lim's suggestion, the commanding officer ordered all Chinese Nationalist officers to a special gathering. There the commanding officer said that he was representing his commander-in-chief, General MacArthur. As such, he was swearing in all of the Chinese Nationalist Army officers at their original military rank, but assigned to the U.S. Army temporarily. Then he ordered these officers back to their stations in the factories and mines to restore order until they were relieved. They did as they were told and were able to help the troops from the 77th Infantry Division bring the riot under control. Lim was pleased that he had helped contain an ugly situation. He was honorably discharged as sergeant in 1946.

Lim had a long and honorable record in San Francisco city government. From 1939 to 1963 he worked in the Public Welfare Office and the Juvenile Court (except for the period of his Army service, from 1943 to 1946). He then accepted the position of Field Representative for Congressman Phillip Burton in 1963, and performed in that capacity until 1966.

One day in early January, 1966, San Francisco Postmaster John F. Fixa telephoned Congressman Burton about his intention to retire. Burton called Lim and asked him to come to the old Del Webb Hotel at Eighth and Market streets immediately to discuss an urgent matter. When he arrived, Burton said, "You are to be the next postmaster of San Francisco."

When Lim recovered from the shock, he asked, "Why me?" Burton replied that if he did not make an immediate recommendation to President Lyndon B. Johnson, he would be swamped with applications for the job, since the position was a political plum. Lim asked for time to call his wife, Catherine, to discuss the matter. When he hung up he told Burton, "I'm your man."

Lim went to Washington for four days of interviews with various people from Postmaster General Lawrence O'Brien on down. Then the Postal Inspection Service made their background check. Finally, on January 21, 1966, Raymond Holmquist, regional director of the Post Office Department in San Francisco, told him that the postmaster general had appointed him acting postmaster pending civil service qualifications and U.S. Senate confirmation. In July of 1967 Lim was formally appointed postmaster of San Francisco by President Johnson. He served for fourteen and a half years under presidents Johnson, Nixon, Ford, and Carter.

Lim P. Lee became a member and then chairman of the Board of Veterans Affairs for the state of California. He was active in the Veterans of Foreign Wars, Chinatown Post 4618, and is former Vice Chairman of the National Legislative Committee; Post Commander of American Legion Cathay Post 384; former Legislative Liaison Committeeman, California American Legion; Legislative Director, Golden Gate Post 34, American Veterans of World War II, Korea, and Vietnam (AMVETS);

and executive member of several civic organizations. He has received numerous awards, including the Distinguished Alumni Award in 1980 for Public Service by the University of the Pacific. He was on the five-member Fair Political Practices Commission of California, appointed by Secretary of State March Fong Eu, from 1985 to 1988.

Lim P. Lee and his wife, Catherine, were married in 1941, and have four children: Rosalind Lee Chooey, Dorinda Ng, Lynette Lee, and a son, Chesley. Their sons-in-law are Calvin Chooey, Albert Ng, and Lester Lee. They have six grandchildren.

64　　　　Ling-Gee Chan Tom

My family and Ling-Gee Chan's family were the only Chinese families in North Bend, Oregon, so we were good friends as youngsters. She came to San Francisco with her sister Foo-Gee to work as operators at the China 5 Exchange (described in Chapter 7), where they were both employed for more than forty years.

Ling-Gee Chan's father, who was born in China, was named Jing-hing Chan. He was an honest and industrious family man whose main ambition was to inculcate Chinese language and culture in his children. Ling-Gee's mother, May Lee, was born in San Francisco's Chinatown in 1898 or 1899. When May was seven or eight years old the earthquake and fire of 1906 destroyed most of San Francisco. In the excitement and confusion some members of the Lee family became separated from each other. May was found, wandering alone and lost, by Frank Yick

(a man who later in life became the millionaire owner of the Frank H. Yick Co.; see Chapter 42). After trying without success to locate her parents, Frank Yick adopted May, and thereafter she became known as May Lee Yick. She was not to meet her real parents again until some twenty years later.

After May Lee and Jung-hing Chan met and married, they left for the town of North Bend, in Coos County, Oregon. All six of their children were born there: Shee Loy, Won Loy, Ling-Gee, Foo-Gee, Quong Loy, and Sun Loy. Occasionally May would come back to San Francisco with some of the older children to visit Frank Yick and the rest of his large family. On one of those visits she made the acquaintance of a young lady who lived next door. Her name was Florence Loo, sister of Kern Yee Loo, whose father Loo Kum-shu had founded the Chinese Telephone Exchange. Florence also worked at the phone exchange, and she and May grew to be close friends. One day while they were watching May's two young daughters playing nearby, Florence said to May: "Soon, when your two daughters grow older, I'm going to see that they work in the telephone exchange!" May was pleased and laughed, taking it as a jest.

By 1929 the Crash had come and gone, leaving the country devastated and starting the Great Depression in its wake. Television had not yet been invented, and the radio was still a new toy enjoyed by few. To while away the time the Chan children played records on their phonograph, humming and beating time to the music. The older ones were part of the high school band, and all soon took up music. A music teacher named Mrs. Leighton Platt recognized their talents and became their devoted teacher. By 1931 they had started the "Chan

Orchestra." For the next four years they were to be remembered by townspeople from far and near for their musical abilities. They were on radio station KOOS, playing for half an hour each Wednesday. They played in Portland, Oregon. Each of the young people could play at least two instruments and could tap dance and sing as well.

A Chinese salesman from San Francisco, Tang Sin Shek, who was making a trip around the Pacific Northwest selling Chinese herbs and tea, came into town one day looking for a Chinese restaurant. When he asked the Chans, they explained that there wasn't one in North Bend, but invited him to stay and have dinner with the family. Naturally, the children played for their guest. He was impressed, and invited them to come to San Francisco to perform in a benefit for the Chinese Hospital. This was in 1935; the group came and their performance was a great hit. They also performed for the St. Mary's Catholic Chinese Center and again played to a capacity audience.

That same year they had another visitor in North Bend. Florence Loo, by now the chief telephone operator of the Chinese Telephone Exchange, came to urge the parents to allow their two daughters, Ling-Gee and Foo-Gee, to come to San Francisco and work as telephone operators. The jest had become a serious offer, but the parents still hesitated. Florence told them there was one position available immediately, and a second one available soon. She pointed out that such openings did not come up very often, and that she could fill them easily, but that she would rather have Ling-Gee and Foo-Gee working for her. The big advantage the Chan sisters had was their thorough familiarity with the English language—something most Chinatown women had not been able to acquire.

Ling-Gee Chan Tom, switchboard operator for the Chinatown Telephone Exchange, 1944. [Photo courtesy of Ling-Gee Tom]

The question was put to the girls. They were excited and wanted to go, so the parents consented. They entered the telephone service in 1935, and did not retire until 1981. Switchboard operators became obsolete in 1949, when the telephone network changed over to the dial system. The sisters were then transferred to the Pacific Telephone and Telegraph Co., and worked there until they retired.

Over the years the Chinese exchange (known locally as the China 5 Exchange), with its unique office and its coterie of operators, attracted visitors from around the world. Both girls were often picked for special duty. They made movies and shorts for Paramount Pictures and Twentieth Century Fox. In 1936 they participated in the Chinatown Rice Bowl to raise funds for the refugees in famine-stricken China. In 1939 they worked at the World's Fair at Treasure Island, posing for numerous pictures, magazines, books, and newspapers.

In 1945, when President Truman opened the United Nations Conference in San Francisco, Foo-Gee was chosen to work as a bilingual operator at the Veterans Memorial Building. Ling-Gee went to work at the Opera House in Secretary-General Dag Hammersjold's office. His secretary was late arriving from New York, and he needed someone immediately. After his secretary arrived, she asked Ling-Gee to stay on to help her. There she met many famous people, among them General Dwight D. Eisenhower, Nikita Khrushchev, Andrei Gromyko, H. M. Molotov, and many others. Soon afterwards she was loaned to the U.S. delegation, housed at the Fairmont Hotel, where she was saw a constant stream of U.S. delegates: John Foster Dulles, Henry Cabot Lodge, Douglas MacArthur, Harold Stassen, and many others.

In 1949 Ling-Gee was chosen to participate in Eddie Cantor's program "Take It Or Leave It." You chose your own topic, and if you answered every question correctly you won $64.00. Ling-Gee picked the category of Hollywood stars. Eddie Cantor asked the questions. He said: "Ling-Gee, I am going to give you the name of some stars; would you give the names of their spouses, wife or husband . . . like George Burns/Gracie Allen?" Ling-Gee was an avid reader of movie magazines, and she knew the names of the spouses of every movie star. Eddie Cantor said, "Ling-Gee, my gosh, do you have a memory!" And she replied, "My gosh, I have to . . . in my work I have to

know the name and number of every one of our 2,200 telephone subscribers!" She won $64.00. Then Cantor asked her if she'd like to go for the $64,000 question. Ling said yes, she'd try. He asked, "Who wrote Casey at the Bat?" Since she didn't know anything about baseball (she knew football), she wasn't able to provide the answer.

As far as anyone can ascertain, the Chinese telephone operators were among the first, if not the first, Chinese members of a regular union to walk a picket line. As early as 1943, union organizers had attempted to persuade the phone operators to join the union. The telephone company manager told the organizers that the operators were satisfied with the way things were, and turned them away. The union was persistent, however, and the next time the operators were permitted to sign a petition to indicate whether or not they wished to join the union. Since joining the union meant an increase in salary, the women operators unanimously decided to join. But joining the union also meant joining in union efforts to fight for better conditions and pay. In 1947 there was a nationwide strike of telephone operators, and the Chinese operators were out on the street carrying banners and marching around their telephone office. The businessmen in Chinatown were naturally furious, and called them all kinds of names.

Among the hardest-hit businesses were the lottery establishments. When the strike took place, the runners for the lottery games were not able to phone in their lottery transactions to Oakland, where their headquarters were located. Runners were like agents. They solicited lottery business, collected the money, and marked the tickets chosen by the buyers. It was also the job of the runners to phone in their take to the headquarters in

Oakland twice daily. The telephone exchange hired retired employees who crossed the picket line to handle the switchboard and avoid paralyzing business in Chinatown.

In 1960 Ling-Gee married Edward L. Tom of San Francisco. He passed away in 1977. After Ling-Gee's retirement in 1981, she found time heavy on her hands. All this came to an end when her many friends in the telephone company found out about her dilemma. One day she received a phone call. The phone company had started a museum, and had a lot of old memorabilia in the form of phone books, phone equipment, and photos, among other things. They wanted to know if Ling-Gee could help organize and run the museum. Ling-Gee said "yes!" to everything, and today she is still active in the museum.

Ling-Gee is very proud of her brother, Won Loy Chan, who lives with his wife, formerly Ruby Joe, in San Mateo. Won Loy attended Stanford and graduated in the class of 1936, the only Chinese that year. Along with his degree in economics he also took ROTC and received a commission in the U.S. Army Field Artillery Reserve in June of 1936. He entered law school at Stanford in the fall of 1937, but when his brother Shee Loy passed away suddenly he took a leave of absence to help his parents with the family business.

Following Pearl Harbor he received orders calling him to active duty in the Office of the Assistant Chief of Staff for Intelligence (G-2), Fourth U.S. Army. He became a Japanese intelligence specialist, and it wasn't long before his co-workers dubbed him "Charlie Chan"— a name he proudly accepted.

Serving faithfully as a lieutenant interrogating prisoners of war, he advanced and became a colonel in General Joseph W. (Vinegar Joe) Stillwell's staff. He took part in Stillwell's Second and Third Burma campaigns, including the bloody battle for Myitkyina in June, July, and August of 1944. He made numerous hazardous reconnaisance flights behind Japanese lines in single-engine light aircraft. In 1945 he was transferred to the War Department General Staff, Military Intelligence Division. He later served in the Office of Naval Intelligence and the Central Intelligence Group. He retired in 1968 and wrote a book called *Burma: The Untold Story* (Novato, Calif.: Presidio Press), a personal memoir of combat intelligence.

65   Paul H. Louie

Paul Louie was a financial and business genius. Even as a young man he was both well-to-do and willing to serve his community, though he did not go out of his way to publicize his contributions. He played an important role in the fight to get city approval for the construction of the Portsmouth Square Garage in the heart of Chinatown—a vital necessity today for the merchants who rely on tourists and customers from other parts of the city.

Paul Louie, one of San Francisco Chinatown's more influential civic leaders, was born on December 2, 1924, in Toishan County, Kung Yick City, Kwangtung Province, China. His family emigrated to San Francisco when Paul was four. He had five brothers and sisters—Henry, Agnes, Helen, Stanford, and Rose—as well as a stepbrother, Lawrence, and stepsister, Betty.

Paul's father, Louie Gar Yee, was a merchant who came to San Francisco by way of Australia. Once he arrived in San Francisco, he sent for his family to join him. He was a partner in San Francisco's Fung Cheung grocery store at Jackson Street and Grant Avenue. Later he became managing partner of Kwong Hang Importing/Exporting Company, also in San Francisco.

In his youth Paul attended Chinese school, became president of the student body at Francisco Junior High School, and graduated from Polytechnic High School. He attended UC Berkeley, majoring in psychology and minoring in speech, and received his bachelor of arts degree in 1947. He entered Hastings Law School but left before graduating to join the family's import/export business during a period when an embargo was placed on imports from China.

In 1949 Paul married Hazel Wong from Los Angeles. They had one son and five daughters: Joanne, Leland, Janet, Adrienne, Celia, and Clarissa.

Paul's civic involvement began early in his business career. He joined the Chinese Chamber of Commerce and soon became the first chairman of its Chinese New Year Parade. Later, in the early 1960s, believing strongly that more parking was needed if Chinatown was to prosper and grow, Paul was instrumental in the fight to get city approval for the building of Portsmouth Square Garage in the heart of Chinatown. He acquired the necessary financing for the project and became its founding president and member of the board of directors, a position he held until his death in 1983.

Over the years Paul became a prominent businessman, although he had never had any formal business education. He was an idea person, with the initiative needed to bring his ideas to fruition. In 1959 he and investors outside of Chinatown organized Civic Federal Savings and Loan. He was a founding director of the bank and later became its president. After it merged with Southern California Savings and Loan, he became a director. In another venture, he gathered investors and built the Royal Pacific Motel on Broadway near Grant Avenue.

Paul felt strongly that Chinatown needed to have its own bank, so in 1961 he organized the Bank of Trade, one of the first new independent banks in California in many years. He became president and chairman of the board at thirty-seven.

In the late 1960s he purchased a large lot in San Francisco's Marina district and with a partner developed a 231-unit apartment complex. It was called Marina Cove and was sold in 1987. In 1974 Paul and Kee Joon organized and built the Kee Joon Restaurant in Burlingame. He became its chairman of the board and served in this role until his death.

Paul was also a founding director of the Pacific Bank, a trustee of Golden Gate University of San Francisco, a regent of Cogswell College of San Francisco, and the first chairman of the City of Belmont Finance Committee, among other distinctions.

Despite all of his commitments, Paul was a good father and family man. He enjoyed taking his children to zoos, museums, and football games, and on school breaks they would travel to Yosemite, Lake Tahoe, and other vacation spots.

He died of a heart attack on June 5, 1983, at the age of fifty-eight.

Hazel Wong Louie

Hazel Wong lived in Los Angeles until she met and married Paul Louie. Her stories of her early years there are fascinating, whether she's describing how she learned to cuss or how she put herself through college.

Hazel Wong was born on February 8, 1926, in Los Angeles. She was the youngest of the five children of Don Sue and Yee Shee Wong, the others being Andy, Anna, Ruth, and Wayne.

Hazel remembers her father, Don Sue, as being "fearless and adventurous." He was born in 1889 in China, in the Toishan district of Kwangtung province. Like many before him, he came to California to earn money to support his wife and son in China, arriving in the early part of this century. He was able to bring his family over in 1920.

Don Sue worked in a produce market in Los Angeles for a while and learned English at a mission there. He then bought a 40-acre farm in Indio, California, but lost it during the Depression when he could not pay the taxes. When they lived on the farm, Hazel remembers standing outside the doorways of the homes of the Mexican farmworkers and peering in, curious about their way of life. Some evenings, she says, "my father would take me to visit the 'clubroom' located in the back of a store, where his single male cronies would relax over a game of chance. They loved having me sit there watching them gamble. That's where I learned Chinese profanity."

About their life during the Depression, Hazel recalls,

Like everyone, we were poor during the Depression. To generate income, my mother and I would leave every morning at 5 or 5:30 A.M. to de-stem strawberries at a neighbor's garage (he was a broker or in-between person) before I attended elementary school. Later we would sort walnut meat from shells in our home. The shells we burned as fuel for heat. There was no home furnace. Water was heated only to wash clothes and for bathing. My clothes were hand-me-downs, and when they got too short, my mother added a hem to lengthen them, usually in a different fabric. My first store-bought garment was required by my junior high graduation (McKinley Junior High); it was a navy blue skirt. Our toys were minimal: jacks, marbles, empty thread spools, and jump ropes.

We never felt deprived or unhappy, however. I have fond memories of a happy childhood and fun wherever I went.

Returning to Los Angeles after losing the farm, Don Sue opened a grocery store in the city's black ghetto, where Hazel learned a new set of profanity. "By the age of twelve," she says, "I was very proficient in cussing."

Their new neighborhood was a tough one. The store was robbed several times. One night, during yet another robbery, Don Sue grabbed his gun and chased the intruders, firing repeatedly. Hazel and her sister Ruth hid in the back room of the store, positive that their father had become a murderer. It turned out that he had been firing over their heads. He was never troubled again.

Don Sue soon found a local "clubroom," in the back of a restaurant, and he enjoyed relaxing with his friends over a game of mah-jongg. One day, after he had excused himself to go to the bathroom, the place was raided and his friends were taken to jail. But Don Sue was safe,

Paul and Hazel Louie, ca. 1960.
[Photo courtesy of Hazel Louie.]

When I went the first time, I took the streetcar on Central Avenue to Pershing Square, where I transferred to the Westwood bus. It took 1 1/2 to 2 hours. No one assisted me. I registered and declared my major. I thought it would be challenging to take the hardest major and took mathematics. It was a challenge, all right.

Each morning, my mother would walk me to catch the streetcar on Central Avenue. It was scary at that time. I hid in the doorway of a storefront until the streetcar came at 5:15 A.M. My mother suggested I live on campus after a year of this. I was accepted in the Y Co-op at UCLA and lived there until I graduated in January 1949. The house mother thought I was quiet and would be a stabilizing influence, so she placed me in the Yellow Room. We had parties every night, inviting others to join us in midnight meals and placing mattresses on the roof when it got too warm. It was good, clean fun.

Hazel put herself through school by working as a long-distance telephone operator, twenty hours per week when school was in session and full time on holidays and during the summer. After she graduated in 1949, Pacific Telephone promoted her and transferred her to area headquarters in Los Angeles. In September of that year she married Paul Louie and moved to 1118 Broadway in San Francisco. The telephone company promised to find her a job in their office in San Francisco. While she waited for the job to come through she worked at the Lawrence Radiation Laboratory in Berkeley on a secret project called the Livermore Project, which was working on the hydrogen bomb.

Pacific Telephone soon found Hazel a management position at its company headquarters at 140 New Montgomery Street in San Francisco. She worked on the bud-

having chosen an opportune time to answer nature's call. Although Don Sue saw nothing wrong with a friendly game of mah-jongg for himself, he was very upset with his children when he found them playing poker for pennies, and he sternly told them that it was not allowed.

Hazel attended Jefferson High School in Los Angeles, where she was a student body officer and president of the Chinese Club. She graduated with honors in 1944. Because of World War II more job opportunities were opening up for minorities, and Hazel's father urged her to get a job instead of attending college. But Hazel was bent on getting a college education, and she applied to and was accepted at UCLA. She recalls, get and on special studies and analyses, and later, when the company began computerizing its data, she worked to develop sample sizes with a given degree of accuracy. The Louies moved to Belmont in 1952. In 1956, after thirteen years, Hazel left her job to raise a family.

Over the next nine years, Hazel and Paul had six children: Joanne, Leland, Janet, Adrienne, Celia, and Clarissa. "There were eleven years of daily diaper-washing," she recalls. "Paul helped me when he could, but this was the time when he was most productive in his job."

Although she was no longer working for pay, Hazel was far from idle. In addition to raising the children she became involved in numerous school-related activities, including Girl Scouts and the PTA. She has twice received the PTA's highest award.

She also became involved in politics. While working for Senator John F. Kennedy's presidential campaign in 1960, she got the idea of putting political messages in fortune cookies. She hand-stuffed hundreds of cookies with the message "Let's Back Jack" for a speech given by the senator at San Francisco's Cow Palace, in which he proposed the creation of a Peace Corps. She later had fortune cookies made for a tea at the Fairmont Hotel in San Francisco, given by Rose Kennedy to raise funds for Robert Kennedy's presidential campaign.

Hazel also loves to travel. As soon as the last child was out of diapers, Paul and Hazel made a trip to Europe, leaving the children with various friends and relatives. There have been many trips since then, including ones to China, Hong Kong, New England, Washington, and the Grand Canyon. Her other interests include antiques and tennis.

As for the children, Joanne studied urban planning and public administration at San Francisco State University and works as an assistant city planner in Daly City, California. Leland has a degree in economics from UCLA and is currently cash management director for Union Federal Bank in Los Angeles. Janet also has a degree in economics from UCLA and is currently a securities trader with Union Bank in Los Angeles. Adrienne graduated from Sacramento State University, where she majored in physical education. She currently works for Digital Equipment in Santa Clara, California, doing accounts payable. Celia graduated from UC Berkeley with a degree in architecture. She works for a firm of consulting and research engineers in Emeryville, California. Clarissa recently graduated from UC Davis with a degree in managerial economics and is working for a law firm in Burlingame, California.

67   The Honorable Harry W. Low

Harry W. Low's name has been mentioned often as a candidate for California's Supreme Court. If he has not actually been appointed, it should not be seen as his fault, but the fault of his political party—he is a registered Democrat in a state with a Republican governor. Politics aside, Harry Low's friends can vouch for his honesty and fairness in all matters, and also believe that he has yet to reach his full potential.

Harry Low's grandfather, Leen Gong, arrived in San Francisco from Canton, China, in 1885. He worked in different laundries for fifteen years, until he had saved up

Honorable Harry W. Low, Presiding Justice of the California Court of Appeals, First District, Division Five, in 1986. [Photo by Romaine of San Francisco.]

enough money to buy his own laundry in the town of Riverbank in Stanislaus County, California. Business was good enough that Gong was able to send money to China for his daughter, Ying, and her husband, Tong Low, to come to California. They arrived and, after working for a while, were able to purchase their own laundry in Oakdale, a small community east of Modesto. The seller was another Gong family, cousins of Leen Gong; their youngest daughter, March, had been born in the building that housed both their laundry and their home. This was the building in which Harry Low was born, on March 12, 1931. Forty-four years later, in 1975, Judge Low had the pleasure of swearing in his Oakdale cousin, March Fong Eu, as California's new secretary of state.

The Lows were the only Chinese in Oakdale, a town of 2,000. As a young lad Harry spent many summers on the Stanislaus River playing with the barefoot "roughnecks" of the valley community. Everyone seemed to have a bicycle, and riding throughout the town was a major activity.

When World War II broke out every able body was put to work, helping on the farms and working in stores and at various other jobs. At the age of ten Harry held many odd jobs—paperboy, gardener, janitor for a small Oakdale law office, turkey feeder and picker, and fruit harvester. By age twelve he was working in a butcher shop and grocery store, and he continued this work through college and even law school. He still has a retired membership card for the butcher's union, which he sometimes carried to labor conventions when he was a commissioner on the Worker's Compensation Board.

At Oakdale High School Harry was active in student government and was president of his junior and senior classes. He participated in a two-week American Legion Boys' State in Sacramento, where he was elected mayor of his "dormitory-city." The winner of an oratorical contest and scholastic awards, Harry liked extracurricular student activities as much as he did his academic studies, and he soon decided that he was interested in law and perhaps public service.

When Harry graduated from high school in 1948 the family expected that he would join his father in their grocery business, which had succeeded their initial laundry venture. But Harry had his own ideas, the first of which involved getting a higher education. He enrolled in Modesto Junior College, becoming the first in his family to attend college. Two years later, in 1950, he was able to transfer to UC Berkeley on a scholarship. He received his degree in political science and business administration in 1952. While at Cal he met his future wife, Mayling, who graduated in 1953 and worked as a hospital dietitian. They were married in 1952, just before Low entered Boalt Law School.

Ironically, when Harry announced that he had decided to go into law, his family thought it was a crazy idea. There were only about thirty Asian lawyers in the whole San Francisco Bay Area, and many of the major law firms didn't begin to hire Asians until at least 1975. He persisted, however, and received a law degree from Boalt Hall at UC Berkeley, where he taught legal research and writing after graduation. His students included Ed Meese III, Cruz Reynoso, and Robert Puglia.

In 1956, only a year after graduating from law school, Harry became a deputy attorney general in the California Department of Justice. He specialized in tax work, doing collections and prosecutions, defending suits for tax refunds, arguing criminal appeals, and writing legal opinions for Attorneys General Pat Brown and Stanley Mosk.

Ten years later, in 1966, Governor Pat Brown made Harry a commissioner on the Worker's Compensation Appeals Board. The governor later appointed him to the municipal court, on which he served from 1966 to 1974, and he was presiding judge of that court in 1972 and 1973. He was elected to the superior court in 1974, on which he served from 1974 to 1982. He also served as supervising judge of the juvenile court in 1981 and 1982. In 1982 he was appointed to the California Court of Appeal. His current title is Presiding Justice, Court of Appeal, First District, Division Five.

Harry has dedicated much of his time to participating in state, city, and community affairs. His activities number in the dozens. He was president of the California Judges Association from 1978 to 1979 and chairman of the Board of Visitors of the U.S. Military Academy at West Point from 1980 to 1981. He has also served on numerous judicial committees, held teaching posts, and was editor of the *California Courts Commentary*, a publication of the California Judges Association, from 1973 to 1976.

Despite his busy schedule, he still finds time to tend his garden, play tennis, and spend time with family and friends. He has three children. His son Larry is a partner with a local law firm and specializes in corporate securities law. Larry and his wife, Doreen, have one daughter, Rachel. His daughter Kathy is a certified public accountant; she works as the director of franchise service and is director of sales for a well-known fast food corporation. His son Allan is an associate with another law firm and is a litigation attorney.

Concurrent with all this, Harry has kept up a steady schedule of court activities, serves on the Board of the National Center for State Courts, and is a member of the American Bar Association's Appellate Courts Committee and the Commission on Minorities. Regarding the latter, he notes that it was not until the 1950s that the American Bar Association revoked its written policy of excluding blacks and other minorities from membership. "It's just in the past two decades that major progress has taken place," Harry says, but he points out that major law firms are still slow to promote minorities to partnership positions.

68 Sinclair Louie and the China Bazaar

Bazaars are known worldwide as markets where goods of every description are sold. They have been operating in San Francisco Chinatown since shortly after the gold rush, when the Chinese sought other means of making money. They carry everything from trinkets to exotic jewelry and furniture, in all price ranges.

Bazaars to some were only a first step toward specializing in art goods of high quality. One of the earliest antique collectors and art appraisers in San Francisco was Tong Bong of Sing Fat Co., which began operating in 1866, according to its letterhead. The same letterhead listed a wide variety of merchandise: cloisonne, bronzes, porcelain, carved ivory, ebony furniture, jade, lacquerware, screens, silk gowns, fancy goods, antiques, and curios.

Since that early period, bazaars have flourished and faded with the financial ups and downs of the times. Two major events played a part in the fortunes of bazaar operators in Chinatown in this century. In 1906 the earthquake and fire wiped out the entire community's buildings. Then, during World War II, no merchandise was available from the Far East, again causing many businesses to close their doors. Unlike many other entrepreneurs in the bazaar business, Sinclair Louie and his father Louie Fong Hock managed to keep their store going through thick and thin.

While it would not be fair to say that Sinclair Louie made his fortune through his own efforts alone, it was really his business acumen that made it all come together. His father started the original China Bazaar, but things really started to hum when Sinclair took over the business—and they are still humming.

China Bazaar's Sinclair Louie family. Left to right: *May and Sinclair Louie, daughters Eva Louie Lee and Betty Louie Chin in 1988. [Photo by Hanson Photography.]*

On December 4, 1939, Louie Fong Hock opened the China Bazaar on Grant Avenue despite the rumblings of war from the Far East. He managed to make a living out of it until the attack on Pearl Harbor two years later. Then things started to get tight. Goods of any sort from abroad were impossible to import. Only the fact that he carried a large inventory in anticipation of the coming war helped him out for a while. Somehow he managed to hang on, hoping for the future.

In the meantime his son, Sinclair, was growing up and learning to help out in the store. When Sinclair, who had thoughts of becoming a medical doctor, wanted to go to UC Berkeley, his father demurred, telling him he needed his help with the store. Sinclair obeyed. Then he had to join the army, serving as an assistant gunner in General George Patton's tank units in Europe for the duration. After the war ended in 1945, Sinclair started in again at China Bazaar. Soon he began making trips to the Far East to reestablish relations with the manufacturers who had formerly supplied their business. Shortly thereafter, Louie Fong Hock began to suggest that maybe it was time he saw some grandchildren. Sinclair had the same thing in mind, but said he couldn't find the right girl.

He happened to mention this to one of his schoolmates, James Fung. Both had attended the Nom Kue Chinese language school. James replied that he had an aunt living in Hong Kong who had a couple of beautiful daughters. But how could Sinclair get to meet them? James concocted a plan: he would buy a box of fountain pens and have Sinclair deliver them personally. So on his next trip to Hong Kong, in 1947, Sinclair delivered the pens. After a whirlwind courtship, May said "yes," and Sinclair and May Chan were married in Hong Kong on October 18, 1947.

After Sinclair brought his bride back to San Francisco, the beaming father held a banquet and then sat back to await the arrival of his expected grandchildren. There were three: Betty, Eva, and Robert.

In 1949, when his father opted for semiretirement, Sinclair and May began to make plans to add additional stores. China Bazaar was to be the flagship of their commercial empire. They worked long hours and plotted out each new addition as carefully as they raised their children. One by one, over the following years, they opened additional stores: Bargain Bazaar, Canton Bazaar, Ginza (in the Japan Trade Center), Jade Empire, Empress Fine Arts, and Far East Flea Market. Altogether they have over 200 employees in their seven stores. They have participated in or contributed liberally to many community activities in Chinatown over the years.

Today Sinclair is chairman of the board; his wife May is president; their daughter Betty Louie Chin is chief executive officer; and their daughter Eva Louie Lee is sales manager. Their son, Robert, passed away in 1977.

China Bazaar has indeed become the flagship of the largest bazaar business in San Francisco Chinatown. Many believe it is the largest Chinese bazaar business in America.

69   The Louie Tennis Family

When Chinatown got its first tennis court in 1927, the community was a bit amused. A tennis court in Chinatown? Who could afford to buy a racquet? But over the years the court, lopsided as it was, became a mecca for generations of Chinese tennis players. As the years rolled on and racial tensions lessened, many Chinese learned the sport and played on most of the city's public courts.

The four Louie sisters have won more than thirty championship tennis titles. Mareen, the youngest girl of the family, is better known by friends and sports writers as "Peanut." Her remarakable talent has repeatedly sent many higher-ranked senior players to the sidelines.

The father of the well-known Louie sisters is Ron Louie, Sr., a Northern Shaolin Kungfu Sifu who has his studio in San Francisco. While his girls were still young he was responsible for transporting them to tennis tournaments all over the continent. Their mother, Alice, came to San Francisco from Seattle, where her family and sister, Amy Yee, live. Amy became a top tennis star in the Northwest, and her children, Joyce, Linda, Gordon, and Gary, also took up tennis and were highly ranked in their youthful years, with both girls winning college tennis scholarships.

Alice would play with Amy occasionally, "just to rally," but left for San Francisco to raise her own family. There are four girls and one boy: Marcie, Marna, Marisa, Mareen, and Ronnie. As soon as they were old enough to hold a tennis racquet Alice would take them out to the Lafayette and Golden Gate Park public courts and teach them the rudiments of the game. She ended up taking them to the courts every day and rallying with them for hours. It was Alice's dedication that turned each child into a top tennis player. Except for a few lessons from Dennis Van der Meer, the well-known tennis pro, her children have developed and learned from each other the strokes, strategy, and timing that have brought them success in nearly every tournament they've entered.

Marcie, the oldest of five children, held thirteen United States Tennis Association junior championships, beating Chris Evert in the 14s and 18s in 1970, before turning professional when she reached the age of eighteen. In 1975 she was ranked number five in the United States. That year she beat Margaret Court in the Family Circle Magazine Cup tournament in Florida and was in the Virginia Slims Championship Playoffs for three years in a row, from 1974 to 1976. She also ranked number ten

Mareen "Peanut" Louie has ranked for years among the top fifty professional tennis players in the world. [Photo copyright © Michael Baz, reproduced with permission of Mrs. Alice Louie.]

for a while, then number fourteen in the world among tennis-playing women. Marna has won three junior national titles. She is now a park and recreation director at Golden Gate Park and a teaching pro at Watergate in

Emeryville. Marisa has won the Women's Open Championship of San Francisco, and is now a teaching professional at the San Francisco Tennis Club. Ronnie, the only boy in the family, has also been a nationally ranked player, was number one man on the USF varsity squad, and is also a teaching pro at Watergate in Emeryville and at Tanglewood in Hayward.

Mareen "Peanut" Louie, the youngest girl and most famous member of the family, had already won fourteen national titles by the age of sixteen, and her tennis future was assured in January 1980 with a first-round victory in the Avon Futures over top-seeded Ann Kiyomura. The other girls have now settled down and play only occasionally, but in 1988 Peanut was still playing as a pro at Wimbledon and various other tournaments, and she still ranked among the world's top fifty players. She recently married Timothy A. Harper, publisher and editor of a women's tennis year book.

Two of the famous Louie tennis family of San Francisco: Mareen "Peanut" Louie (left) and Marcie. [Photo by The China Post, *New York, reproduced with permission of Mrs. Alice Louie.]*

PART V

Contemporary Chinatown

*C*hinatown today is much different than it was at the turn of the century; but certain details repeat themselves in the cycles of change. For example, twenty years ago the business altars described in Part I of this book seemed to have disappeared. Nowadays, with the new influx of immigrants from the Far East, they are common again. As the saying goes, the more things change, the more they stay the same. The latest immigrants, however, can benefit from numerous nonprofit organizations that will help them learn English and advance themselves. These organizations in turn grew out of efforts on the part of earlier immigrants and their descendants to break through the barriers imposed by discrimination and to bridge the gap between Chinese and American culture.

Part V describes just a few of the nonprofit groups and other organizations that are important to contemporary Chinatown. Many of the recent arrivals know little of the hardships their predecessors had to overcome. As recently as the 1950s, for example, there were many areas in San Francisco where Chinese could not buy a home. From the 1960s to the present, however, discrimination has been on the wane. Today the Chinese have entered or are free to enter almost any trade or profession.

Large numbers of Chinese are employed in Silicon Valley (known as the Santa Clara Valley before it became a mecca for computer technology) on the San Francisco Peninsula. Many own their own businesses and are leaders in the computer field. For example, Grace and Bernard Tse were cofounders of Wyse Technology in 1981; today Wyse has 3,500 employees and produces more computer terminals than any other company in the world except IBM. Everex, a company founded

---

A street scene in San Francisco Chinatown, ca. 1986. [Photo courtesy of Chinatown Neighborhood Improvement Resource Center.]

by Steve Hui in 1984, had grown to 1,050 employees by 1987, with sales of over $200 million and a plant in Hong Kong. Other Chinese-owned firms in Silicon Valley include Qume Corp. (David Lee), Solectron Corp. (Winston Chen), KOMAG (Tu Chen), Sigma Design (Thinh Tran), and Mini Micro Supply (Dr. Wu Lieh Ho).

Chinese are also moving into the higher echelons of the financial world. The same is true in education, science, and medicine. Advances have been made in the political arena as well. In 1988 Thomas Hsieh became the first Chinese supervisor to be elected to office in San Francisco. Boards of education and the schools themselves are laced with competent Chinese professionals. And Dennis Wu, an accountant, was recently elected president of the San Francisco Commonwealth Club, the first nonwhite president in the club's eighty-five-year history.

Chinese-Americans today have won a place for themselves in American society. Like other immigrants, their success is due not only to persistence and hard work, but also to the resilience and adaptability of their own culture. Contemporary Chinatown continues on the course set by its earliest residents.

Buddha's Universal Church

Buddha's Universal Church is affiliated with the World Fellowship of Buddhists in Bangkok. This relationship is limited to the exchange of materials and occasional meetings. The church was founded by Mrs. Chee Mar, Mrs. Dick Fung (mother of Dr. Paul Fung, a church leader until his passing some years ago), and Dr. Charles Yick in the late 1920s.

After the San Francisco earthquake and fire of 1906, buildings started to rise as soon as the debris was cleared. Among those to occupy a spot in Chinatown was a wooden structure at 720 Washington Street. Its last tenant was the old Club Mandalay, a nightclub that closed in 1951. The property was then purchased by Buddha's Universal Church. A modest $500 remodeling job was projected, but due to the condition of the structure, which lacked solid walls on three of the four sides, the city required the church to tear it down. This was a big blow for the congregation, which had only $10,000.

After several meetings they decided they had to sacrifice to build the church. One by one, the 300 members pledged to donate thirty to eighty hours and ten to twenty percent of their incomes per month. Then they rolled up their sleeves and went to work demolishing the old building. They gladly accepted all the help offered by people who did not belong to the church. Before long it was common to see a sturdy band of schoolchildren, housewives, grocers, doctors, and many others of all races working together, rain or shine. A brochure distributed by the church describes some of their efforts:

In the spring of 1952, the total assets of the church were . . . one of the largest mud holes in San Francisco, a $20,000 deficit, not a stick of building material, and an inept but willing crew of "church builders." These were lonely and dark hours.

A project of cookie sales was started on weekends by the younger members to raise funds to buy material. Sometimes, because of the total lack of money, construction stopped completely while the whole congregation baked, wrapped and sold cookies. The transformation of cookies to concrete—to church building—was a slow and laborious process. But, nevertheless, the work progressed continuously every evening and every weekend. Occasionally, some city fathers did not quite understand the urgency about the cookie sale, but they became most helpful when they understood that . . . "No cookies—no concrete . . . no concrete—no church."

They raised money every way they could and used it only for materials. All labor was donated. Unions pitched in to help, and Frank Yick contributed liberally, donating the use of all his equipment and shop as well as any labor that could be spared (see Chapter 42). Worley Wong, the architect, had to study Buddhist teachings before he could begin to start the architectural plans.

It took eleven years and four months to complete the five-story church. The *San Francisco Chronicle* estimated that the structure could not be duplicated for less than a million dollars. Dr. Paul Fung, the church leader, described the church as follows during the dedication on March 1, 1963:

Buddhists do not regard Buddha as God, but a great teacher of the moral truths, as the truth revealed in the lotus blossom . . . The main chapel, just inside the entrance, is golden

Hammered bronze bas-relief of the Buddha seated under the Bodhi tree, inside the front entrance of Buddha's Universal Church. [Photo by Nancy Warner.]

colored as Buddha's aura. The altar is shaped like a Dharma Ship. The altar is set off by a six-foot mosaic of Buddha.

A smaller meditation chapel—the Chapel of the Purifying Waters—is across the hallway, with a small fountain. Buddha taught by small streams. On the mezzanine is another chapel, called the Monastery of the Bamboo Grove, modeled after a famous place where Buddha gave lectures 2,500 years ago.

The church has a library, research and translation rooms, and a general assembly room in the basement. The beautiful roof garden has a small grove containing a Bodhi tree, a cutting from the tree under which Buddha sat; and a lotus pool, carved in the shape of a lotus leaf in white terrazzo with a fountain spraying the shape of the blossom.

In recent years Buddha's Universal Church has staged a bilingual play produced and directed by the Research Council of the church. It is given annually around Chinese New Year (generally in February) for several weeks. Each play is based on an ancient story of China and is performed by members of the church. From young to old, the play has a part for all. Rehearsals may take half the year, with everyone partaking in some way: sewing costumes, making scenery, making up, preparing programs, selling ads, selling tickets, and so forth.

The church itself is always busy. It is a popular place for weddings. A Buddhist priest will wed the couple bilingually in English and Chinese, and a piano and an organ together with musicians are available.

In 1988, as this book is being written, the church has embarked upon an expansion program. Around the corner on Kearny Street an old-time theater has been stripped and reinforced with structural steel beams. Toward the rear of the church the building and theater both meet, forming an el around a small corner commercial building. A large opening in the connecting properties will then provide access between the two structures, and the church will be able to enlarge its operation.

Buddha's Universal Church is one of the largest and most modern Buddhist Churches in North America. It can also probably lay claim to being among the first to provide public lectures bilingually in Chinese and English.

71 Chinese Historical Society of America

The idea of recording the experience of the Chinese in America had been floating around in my mind since 1924, when I was sent to China at the age of fifteen to get a Chinese education (see Chapter 37). A couple of sojourners in my father's village regaled me with tales of gold mining, railroad building, and farm work in California at the end of the nineteenth century, and I wished I could write down some of what I heard. Unfortunately, my visit was cut short by my father's death. I returned to China again in 1933 for another unexpectedly brief visit— but long enough to hear more stores and to renew my enthusiasm for the history of the Chinese in America.

Late in 1935 my friend Chingwah Lee agreed to finance the first English-language newspaper for Chinese-Americans, the *Chinese Digest*. (The story of the *Chinese Digest* is told in Chapter 33.) Although it lasted only a short time and was able to record little besides current history in the making, it did encourage the associate editor, William Hoy, to organize some of the first research into the history of the Chinese in America. He and a few friends later organized the California Chinese Pioneer Historical Society, which sponsored many field trips over the couple of years it operated. The society gradually dwindled away as its members were drafted into the armed forces. After the Second World War many of the same people were too busy earning a living and raising a family to do much about their historical interests.

In the fall of 1962, realizing that time was passing and no one in sight had done anything about it, I decided to give it one last try. In spring of 1962 I approached several friends about forming an organization dedicated to the history of the Chinese in America, and got them together for lunch. They were Chingwah Lee, H. K. Wong, Thomas W. S. Wu, D.D.S., and C. H. Kwock. As a result of that luncheon meeting we met many times that year, formulating a plan of organization, a constitution, and a set of bylaws.

The first formal meeting of the Chinese Historical Society of America was held at my home at 1175 Chestnut Street, San Francisco, with thirty-one persons in attendance: Mr. Alessandro M. Baccari, Jr., Mr. John Bransten, Mr. and Mrs. Shuck M. Chan, Mr. and Mrs. Thomas W. Chinn, Mrs. Gladys C. Hansen, Mr. Paul Hong, Mr. Joe Yuey, Mr. C. H. Kwock, Mr. Chingwah Lee, Mr. Edward C. Lee, Mr. and Mrs. Kem Lee, Mr. and Mrs. Lim P. Lee, Mr. and Mrs. Albert C. Lim, Mr. and Mrs. R. Marcus, Mr. and Mrs. J. H. Mohr, Miss Margaret O'Sullivan, Mr. H. K. Wong, Mr. and Mrs. Richard Wong, Dr. Walter M. Wong, Dr. and Mrs. Thomas Wu, and Mr. and Mrs. Jon Y. C. Yu. The date was January 5, 1963.

This first group of people became the charter members of the society. I was named president; H. K. Wong became first vice-president; Dr. Thomas Wu, second vice-president; Jon Y. C. Yu, treasurer; and C. H. Kwock, secretary. The first directors were myself, Gladys C.

President Lyndon B. Johnson accepting honorary membership in the Chinese Historical Society of America, August 2, 1964. He was the first American president to become a member of a Chinese organization. He is accepting an honorary scroll from two founding members: C. H. Kwock (left) and H. K. Wong. [White House photo.]

Hansen, C. H. Kwock, Chingwah Lee, Lim P. Lee, Albert C. Lim, H. K. Wong, Richard Wong, Dr. Thomas Wu, and Jon Y. C. Yu.

I was reelected president each of the next three years, despite my protestations. Those first few years, when the society was just getting off the ground, were especially trying. Among other activities, we began a series of photo exhibitions and field trips. The annual highlight became our anniversary, usually on the third Saturday of January, and a speaker and music became part of the ritual, along with the installation of officers.

On August 2, 1964, a great honor was bestowed on the society. In a brief ceremony at the White House, President Lyndon B. Johnson became an honorary member. He was the first president of the United States to become a member of a Chinese-American organization.

On October 2, 1966, the society opened its new headquarters and a small museum at 17 Adler Place in San Francisco's Chinatown. The building was owned by the Shoong Foundation, and the rent-free lease for a period of fifteen years plus a $25,000 donation for remodeling were arranged by Mr. Milton Shoong, son of Joe Shoong. Many visitors from all over the world have seen the museum, which has always provided free admission for all. The society's monthly bulletin, which has published hundreds of articles about the history of the Chinese in America, has attracted many university libraries as members. The bulletin also keeps members informed of membership activities such as monthly meetings and field trips.

One of the society's most popular early projects was a traveling photography exhibit that provided a brief history of the Chinese in America and was made available free to other organizations. Each recipient paid for shipping and insurance and promised to follow a strict schedule.

On April 19, 1969, the society sponsored a seminar on the subject "A History of the Chinese in California." This was designed as a response to the numerous requests for information the society had received from historians, writers, and educators. The seminar was held at the Chinese-American Citizens Alliance auditorium, and several hundred people attended. A paperback syllabus entitled *A History of the Chinese in California* was published and distributed at the same time. The book is now in its sixth printing.

The formation of the society acted as a clarion call, awakening memories and prompting research from Hawaii to the East Coast. Slowly but surely, the challenge was taken up by interested individuals, academics, and newly formed historical associations. San Francisco State University was one of the first educational institutions to become involved, and asked whether any of our members could teach a course on Chinese-American history. Him Mark Lai and Philip Choy were willing to teach, and they did so for several years. (I later learned, to my pleasure, that they were the first Chinese-American teachers of Chinese-American history.) Other institutions also began to recognize the need for departments of Chinese- or Asian-American studies and libraries to support them.

As time went on the society accumulated a great deal of material on Chinese-American history, and we were constantly having to respond to questions from researchers and others that required us to search through our files. This became a burden to our volunteer staff because our collection was not cataloged and was scattered in the houses of various members who had room for it.

To alleviate this problem, I suggested that we turn over all of our materials to the San Francisco Library as a special collection on long-term loan. Gladys Hansen, the Archivist of the City and County of San Francisco, accepted my proposal, and she and her staff cataloged the collection and housed it so that the public could have access to the material without going through us. This took place in 1971. In April of 1983 the collection was

Ceremony commemorating the centennial of the first transcontinental railroad in the United States, May 4, 1969. Members of the San Francisco Chinese community paid tribute to the Chinese workers who built the Central Pacific Railroad. Two bronze plaques were made for the occasion, one for the west end and one for the east end of the Central Pacific portion of the railroad. Left to right: Chinese Historical Society of America President Philip P. Choy; Chinese Consul General Tung-hua Chou; San Francisco Supervisor Peter Tamaras, representing the mayor; the author's mother (and the daughter of forty-niner Lee Man Bien), Mrs. Chinn Lee Shee Wing, who unveiled the plaque; and the author. [Photo by Kem Lee.]

Left: *Chairpersons and speakers from the First National Conference on Chinese-American Studies, held at the University of San Francisco in July of 1975. This photo was taken during the closing banquet at the Empress of China restaurant. The conference was sponsored by the Chinese Historical Society of America. [Photo by Kem Lee.]*

Below left: *Four of the five founders of the Chinese Historical Society of America, 1983. Left to right:* Thomas W. S. Wu, Thomas W. Chinn, H. K. Wong, and C. H. Kwock. *The fifth founder,* Chingwah Lee, *passed away in January of 1980.*

transferred to the Asian-American Studies Library at UC Berkeley, also on long-term loan, where it remains today.

In 1975 the society sponsored the First National Conference on Chinese-American Studies, held at the University of San Francisco on July 10 through 12, with over 300 persons attending. This was followed by the Second National Conference, sponsored by the Chinese Historical Society and the Chinese Culture Center, held at the Chinese Culture Center on October 9 through 11, 1980.

In 1987 the society began publishing an annual report called *Chinese America: History and Perspectives.* The twenty-fifth anniversary of the society was celebrated on January 16, 1988 at the Empress of China restaurant, with over 450 people in attendance. Highlights of the first quarter century were outlined in a Silver Commemorative Booklet, which I presented as the keynote speaker.

72

Other Nonprofit Organizations

During the period from 1850 to around 1960, new Asian immigrants arriving in San Francisco generally had to fend for themselves. Relatives and family associations could sometimes help ease the shock of adjusting to a new life in a new culture, but many people did not have these resources to fall back on. Language and cultural differences were the major problems for new immigrants, and these barriers exacerbated the problems of finding decent housing and basic medical care.

In 1960, in part because of the growing influence and affluence of the Chinese-American community, nonprofit organizations began forming in Chinatown to address these and other concerns. Today their services have proliferated, to the great benefit of the Asian community. This chapter describes the work of a few of these organizations.

Ping Yuen Public Housing

Although not, strictly speaking, a nonprofit organization like the others in this chapter, the Ping Yuen housing complex is the most visible sign of improvement in Chinatown's treatment of new immigrants. The first buildings for Ping Yuen (which means "Tranquil Garden") were built at Pacific and Powell and at Pacific and Stockton by San Francisco's Housing Authority in 1952. Nine years later, in 1961, Ping Yuen North was built in the area bordered by Broadway, Cordella, and Pacific Avenue, between Stockton and Powell, adding 194 units to the 234 built earlier, for a total of 428 units. These efforts were followed in 1969 by the construction of 92 units of senior citizens' housing at Pacific and Mason Streets. The Ping Yuen complex has done much to alleviate overcrowded living conditions in Chinatown.

Chinese Culture Foundation of San Francisco

The Chinese Culture Foundation of San Francisco had its origin in 1965 with the establishment of the Chinese Culture Center. Founded by J. K. Choy, the center's aim was and continues to be to promote the preservation of the cultural heritage of China among first-generation Chinese and to encourage them to share that heritage with younger Chinese. It also provides public access to the richness and variety of Chinese art and culture through exhibits and other programs.

The Chinese Culture Foundation is located in the heart of San Francisco Chinatown, on the third floor of the Holiday Inn on Kearny Street, and has been at this location since 1972. Since it opened, the center has presented a number of exhibits, lectures, and performances by both local and overseas artists. Research programs devoted to all aspects of Chinese and Chinese-American culture are also conducted through the center.

Self Help for the Elderly

Self Help for the Elderly was founded in 1966 by the Chinatown-North Beach Economic Opportunity Council. With the goal of improving the lives of the elderly, the agency provides social services, meals, and skilled nursing and home health services to the elderly of Chinatown and North Beach. It is licensed by the state as a home health agency and provides care for Medicare and MediCal patients.

1971 marked a memorable year for Self Help; it became incorporated as a nonprofit agency, set up its first meal site, and provided its first home-delivered meals. By 1988, under director Anni Chung, the agency was providing up to 700 lunches and dinners a day at five locations.

Other services include housing, employment assistance, and support services. The housing unit of the agency contracts to manage apartment units for property owners as a means of generating income. There is a critical shortage of housing for seniors in Chinatown. Self Help assists the elderly in locating housing and helps them with applications and problems with landlords. It also works to improve and create affordable housing for seniors. One innovative program in the employment unit trains seniors for jobs as housekeepers and home health aides and develops small business contracts to train and employ older workers. Participants can also make use of counseling, escort, and interpreter services.

Self-Help for the Elderly is funded by the United Way of the Bay Area, the Commission on Aging, city and federal funds, private contributions, and fund-raisers.

Chinese for Affirmative Action

Chinese for Affirmative Action (CAA) was founded in 1969 by a small group of college graduates and community activists who wanted to establish a strong, independent voice for the Chinese-American community. The organization is very active in promoting equal opportunity in education and employment for all persons. Under Executive Director Henry Der, the civil rights organization has worked to eliminate societal conditions that foster bigotry and racial discrimination against Asian-Americans and other minority groups.

In recent years Chinese for Affirmative Action has conducted research studies on a wide range of civil rights activities and has researched public policy issues affecting Chinese-Americans. It has also kept a close eye on legislation and civil rights cases.

The hard-working staff of ten offers several services, including job placement and counseling services for the community. In addition to the staff, CAA has an active volunteer base.

Chinese Newcomers Service Center

The Chinese Newcomers Service Center was founded in 1969 to help monolingual immigrants and refugees from China and neighboring areas to understand and adjust to life and culture in America. It offers a comprehensive array of programs and support services that range from counseling to classes in American history and government aimed at preparing individuals for citizenship.

One widely used and effective service provided by the center is its Chinese Language Mental Health Information and Referral Program, which helps participants cope with "culture shock." The center also offers an Employment Training and Job Placement Program, a joint effort with the California State Employment Development Department. Other employment assistance includes training in resume writing and information on employment laws. In 1986 the organization assisted more than 10,000 people.

Under its current director, Roland Po Wong, the center, with its large staff and several active volunteers, continues to expand its services for a rising tide of Asian immigrants.

Chinatown Youth Center

Since its inception in 1970 the Chinatown Youth Center has provided services for Chinatown and Asian youth with the goal of helping them reach their highest potential and become responsible individuals in their communities. From its initial focus on juvenile crime prevention, the center has expanded to provide personal and family counseling, drug education, employment services, and other assistance needed by youth.

Under the direction of Keith Choy, the center works closely with other youth agencies in San Francisco. It is involved in joint community projects such as youth leadership conferences and a national employment alliance.

An important component of the center is its employment program, begun in 1975, which offers vocational training and counseling to youth. Among other things, it provides an intensive seven-week period of classroom training and on-the-job experience. Employers participating in the program are reimbursed for 50 percent of the cost of training a youth for a specific kind of work.

North East Medical Services, Inc.

North East Medical Services (NEMS) was founded in 1972 to offer comprehensive medical services, ranging from primary health care to dental care, to the Chinatown community. Supplemental services include nutrition and social services. Dr. Thomas Y. Hum, M.D., served as the first chairman of the board of directors.

NEMS accepts patients from all income groups and stresses the importance of preventive medicine. Specialized programs aimed at health, education, and social services seek to minimize the impact of linguistic, cultural, and financial barriers on the health of its patients. A unique feature of its approach is its blend of eastern and western medical practices.

Under the direction of Sophie Wong, NEMS has increased its services as well as the number of patients it serves. The center now offers interpretation, escort, and transportation services in addition to health care.

Other Medical Services

Several small nonprofit health services are located in Chinatown. The *California Chinese Medical Center Corporation*, incorporated in 1978, operates a free clinic on Sundays at the Ping Yuen Association on Pacific Street. Since 1980 the clinic has offered medical attention to the community, with an emphasis on traditional Chinese medical preventive methods. Individuals can visit the center for acupuncture treatment, blood pressure checks, and treatment of minor health problems.

Located on busy Stockton Street in Chinatown are *Chinatown-North Beach Clinical Services* and *North East Community Mental Health Services.* The center's services include help for people with mental health problems that can be treated with rehabilitation or acupuncture, and programs to help people cope with stress.

The *Chinatown Child Development Center* meets the needs of parents who are concerned about their children's behavior or who have questions about parenting. Located on Grant Avenue, its programs include psychological evaluation and psychotherapy. The bilingual staff offers treatment for children as well as adults. The center operates under the direction of Sai-ling Chan-sew.

The *Chinatown-North Beach Community Care Program* is located in the same building as the Chinatown Child Development Center and offers day services for the treatment of mental health and emotional problems on a sliding fee scale. The multilingual staff of the center includes social workers, health workers, and therapists. The director of the program is Lucia Tran.

Chinatown American Cooks School

A nonprofit organization, the Chinatown American Cooks School has prepared immigrants and low-income San Franciscans for employment as cooks since 1972. The school's training period, which lasts nearly six months, combines basic cooking theory with practical application that amounts to a thousand hours of hands-on training, according to founder and current director of the school Sammy Louie.

Its facilities, located in the Salvation Army building on Powell Street, contain a complete instructional kitchen with professional work stations and a dining area where low-cost meals are prepared by cooks in training as a community service.

In addition to the regular curriculum, a catering program is funded by the Mayor's Office of Community Development. Through this program, students prepare and serve entrees for special events and meetings given by nonprofit community organizations. The revenue collected from this program contributes to the school's operating costs.

The school's English training and job placement programs are important adjuncts to its culinary curriculum. These programs contribute to the success students of the school have had in securing jobs with restaurants in the Bay Area.

On Lok Health Services

On Lok Health Services is a pioneer in providing total health care for the frail and elderly. With its emphasis on independent care, the organization offers an alternative to costly nursing homes.

Since it opened in 1973 On Lok has provided the frail and elderly of the ethnically diverse communities of Chinatown, North Beach, and Polk Gulch with medical, nutritional, and social services in a cost-effective manner. Physicians, nurses, therapists, social workers, and support staff assess the need for and deliver these services. The agency includes three adult day-care centers, a home care department, and an apartment building for low-income and elderly persons.

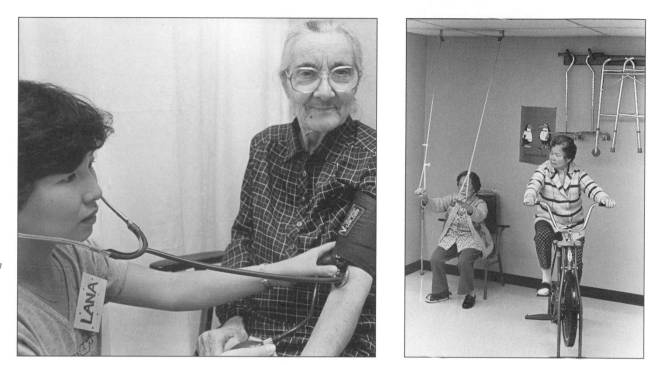

Right: *Blood pressure testing at On Lok. [Photo by Randy Dean, courtesy of On Lok.]*

Far right: *Physical therapy at On Lok. [Photo by Randy Dean, courtesy of On Lok.]*

On Lok's founder, Dr. William L. Gee, started the organization with a $2,000 federal grant. He enlisted the help of social worker Marie Louise Ansak to set up the first center on Broadway. They named it On Lok, which in Chinese means "happy, peaceful abode." Ansak is currently the director of the organization.

A second center was opened in 1979, and the following year a modern facility consisting of a health center and apartments was built on Powell Street. In 1977 On Lok became the official model for the provision of Medicaid benefits in California.

In 1983 On Lok became the first organization in the country to assume responsibility, through HMO-type financing, for the complete care of the frail and elderly. Congress waived certain Medicare and Medicaid regulations, giving On Lok the flexibility to provide a broad range of services. Further growth for the organization in the 1980s was made possible by the addition of a hospital and skilled nursing facilities, as well as forty-five units of housing.

A full range of services, from medical care to counseling, is provided by the staff at each of On Lok's centers.

The organization also offers many kinds of in-home assistance programs. Under contract, On Lok provides professional care in optometry and audiology, as well as medical and transportation services.

In recognition of On Lok's innovative program, the Robert Wood Johnson Foundation awarded the organization a one-year grant in 1985 to study the feasibility of applying the On Lok model to similar services elsewhere in the United States. As a result of On Lok's success, six organizations in the United States are preparing to adopt its system of long-term care for the frail and elderly.

Chinatown Neighborhood Improvement Resource Center

The Chinatown Neighborhood Improvement Resource Center was organized in response to a recognized need for an agency to plan, guide, and expedite physical improvement programs for the community. Dedicated to the physical improvement of Chinatown, the center began in 1977 when five volunteer grassroots organizations joined forces to provide staff and technical assistance for their individual programs. They met as a team to advocate low-income housing, open space in crowded Chinatown, and solutions to traffic problems.

Above left: *Chinatown's Spofford Alley in 1985, before the modernization project by the Chinatown Neighborhood Improvement Resource Center.* Left: *Spofford Alley in 1987, after the modernization project. [Photos courtesy of Chinatown Neighborhood Improvement Resource Center.]*

Chinatown's continued population growth has increased the center's role in advocating, providing technical assistance for, and coordinating projects aimed at achieving specific planning goals. In 1978 the center established the Chinese Community Housing Corporation, with the purpose of exploring opportunities for low-income housing within the North Beach and Chinatown areas. It also works with the Chinatown Coalition for Better Housing and other concerned community groups to advocate tenants' rights to high-quality, affordable housing and expanded housing opportunities.

Another activity of the center has been to draw up, in collaboration with other community groups, a Chinatown Community Plan to serve as a reference point for establishing goals. Balancing the complex and multiple interests of the community, the plan provides for the preservation of Chinatown's historical value, affordable housing, and opportunities for new immigrants.

The center has also provided assistance to and has been instrumental in the expansion of the Geen Mun Center, a multipurpose facility for a variety of service agencies, and has given aid to tenant groups active in the Chinatown area. Under Gordon Chin, its executive director, the center is expanding its programs to serve the thriving community of low-income residents and small business groups that need assistance.

The Northeast Community Federal Credit Union

The Northeast Community Federal Credit Union (NCFCU) was organized in 1981 as a nonprofit, community-chartered financial institution owned by member shareholders. Its membership is drawn from the Chinatown and North Beach areas.

Aside from providing personal and business loans to the residents of these communities, NCFCU is committed to the development and improvement of the areas in which they live. This is achieved through a Community Needs Plan, which identifies specific areas of concern and recommends action to the NCFCU board of directors.

The credit union has recently concentrated on providing financial assistance to the increasing number of Southeast Asians who have settled in the area and want to start their own businesses, initiating a business loan program in conjunction with the Southeast Asian Resettlement Center. The program seeks to help newcomers who are credit-worthy but who lack credit history.

Under the direction of Lily Low, the credit union continues to grow and to seek to enhance the community's development through loans and other assistance to newly forming businesses.

Civic Organizations

The 1986 San Francisco Chinatown Business Telephone Directory gives a very clear picture of the types of civic organizations that have come into being to meet the various social needs of the Chinese community in San Francisco through the years. Under the heading "General Associations" are listed the Chinese Consolidated Benevolent Association, the National Chinese Welfare Council, the Chinese Cemetery Association, the Chinese Hospital, the Chinatown Lions Club, and the Chinese General Peace Association. Under "District Associations" are

73

Chinese Television and Radio

The board of directors of the Chinese Chamber of Commerce, 1986–87. Front row, left to right: *Richard Szeto, Cheung Hon Wah, Sidney Chan, Pius Lee, Philip Lee, Stephen Fong, Robert Yick, James Ho, Cheong K. Lau, Jin Moon Lee.* Center row: *Eric Wu, Sum Y. Siu, Ringo Wong, Lily Chan, James Chow, Peter Yu, Stephen Ng, Victoria F. Wee, Doris Him, James Hall.* Back row: *Richard Chang, Walter Fong, Douglas Wong, Tony Fong, Dr. Shu Wing Chan, Wayne Hu.*

listed thirty-six tongs, benevolent associations, and charity organizations. This list includes the seven district associations that make up the Chinese Consolidated Benevolent Association. The book also lists fifty-two family associations, including the Chins, Gees, Huies, Lees, Tams, Woos, and Yees. Finally, there are ten fraternal organizations, half of which are business associations, the other half being mah-jongg clubs.

Although Chinese television originated in New York, San Francisco was soon to follow. A large portion of the approximately 300,000 Chinese in the Bay Area use the Chinese language predominantly, so entrepreneurs have had good reason to try to reach this audience. The three major sources of Chinese-language television and radio in the Bay Area today are described briefly here.

Overseas Chinese Communication

Franklin Y. Wu founded Overseas Chinese Communication, Inc., in April of 1975. By 1988 he could look back over thirteen years of successful televising to a large portion of the local Chinese population. His company uses Channel 38, and broadcasts Monday through Saturday from 7 to 9 P.M. Both Cantonese and Mandarin are used in the regular format, which consists of a news report covering local, area, state, and national news of Chinese interest, followed by films, plays, dramas, interviews, and so on.

His staff of ten is kept busy at his downtown office and studio at 844 Folsom Street. Wu and his wife, Frances, have raised three children: Sutsen, a business major from S.F. State University; James, a mass communications major also S.F. State; and Jason, a psychology major from UC Davis.

The Chinese Television Co.

The Chinese Television Co. at 2 Waverly Place was founded in June of 1976. It uses Channel 26 and broadcasts ten hours a week, from 7 P.M. to 9 P.M., Monday through Friday. Dr. John Hwang, the founder, is president; his son James is director; and daughter-in-law Jennie is manager. English, Cantonese, and Mandarin are used in their broadcasts.

Sinocast

Sinocast, a company that uses radio, television, and magazines to reach its audience, started operations in February 15, 1977, with radio broadcasting, and within two years had expanded to include cable television. The Sinocast staff grew, and as they became more knowledgeable they entered the third phase of media coverage for their audience. On August 28, 1985, they published the first issue of *Sinocast* magazine, which is thirty-six pages long and is published entirely in Chinese.

For radio broadcasting, Sinocast uses Subsidiary Communications Authorization (SCA) eighteen hours a day, from 6:30 A.M. to 12:30 A.M., Monday through Friday; and fifteen hours a day, from 9 A.M. to 12 midnight, on Saturday and Sunday. For TV they use Viacom Cable 22 and broadcast three and a half hours a day, from 9 P.M. to 12:30 A.M., Monday through Friday; and from 9 to 11 P.M. on Saturday and Sunday. In both radio and television broadcasts Cantonese is used two-thirds of the time, and Mandarin the rest of the time.

The company was founded by Phillip Chan, president. The general manager is his son Charles C. Chan, who majored in business and advertising at San Francisco State University. The entire staff consists of twenty-eight persons.

APPENDIX A: Clan Charts

Historical Development of the
San Francisco Huiguan System

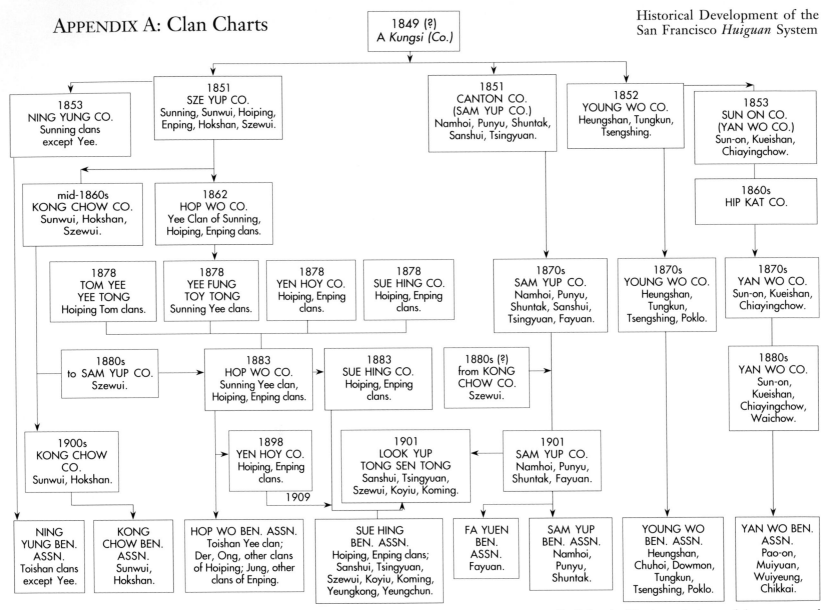

1849 (?)
A *Kungsi (Co.)*

1853
NING YUNG CO.
Sunning clans
except Yee.

1851
SZE YUP CO.
Sunning, Sunwui, Hoiping,
Enping, Hokshan, Szewui.

1851
CANTON CO.
(SAM YUP CO.)
Namhoi, Punyu, Shuntak,
Sanshui, Tsingyuan.

1852
YOUNG WO CO.
Heungshan, Tungkun,
Tsengshing.

1853
SUN ON CO.
(YAN WO CO.)
Sun-on, Kueishan,
Chiayingchow.

mid-1860s
KONG CHOW CO.
Sunwui, Hokshan,
Szewui.

1862
HOP WO CO.
Yee Clan of Sunning,
Hoiping, Enping clans.

1860s
HIP KAT CO.

1878
TOM YEE
YEE TONG
Hoiping Tom clans.

1878
YEE FUNG
TOY TONG
Sunning Yee clans.

1878
YEN HOY CO.
Hoiping, Enping
clans.

1878
SUE HING CO.
Hoiping, Enping
clans.

1870s
SAM YUP CO.
Namhoi, Punyu,
Shuntak, Sanshui,
Tsingyuan, Fayuan.

1870s
YOUNG WO CO.
Heungshan,
Tungkun,
Tsengshing, Poklo.

1870s
YAN WO CO.
Sun-on, Kueishan,
Chiayingchow.

1880s
to SAM YUP CO.
Szewui.

1883
HOP WO CO.
Sunning Yee clan,
Hoiping, Enping clans.

1883
SUE HING CO.
Hoiping, Enping
clans.

1880s (?)
from KONG
CHOW CO.
Szewui.

1880s
YAN WO CO.
Sun-on,
Kueishan,
Chiayingchow,
Waichow.

1900s
KONG CHOW
CO.
Sunwui, Hokshan.

1898
YEN HOY CO.
Hoiping, Enping
clans.

1901
LOOK YUP
TONG SEN TONG
Sanshui, Tsingyuan,
Szewui, Koyiu, Koming.

1901
SAM YUP CO.
Namhoi, Punyu,
Shuntak, Fayuan.

1909

**NING
YUNG BEN.
ASSN.**
Toishan clans
except Yee.

**KONG
CHOW BEN.
ASSN.**
Sunwui,
Hokshan.

HOP WO BEN. ASSN.
Toishan Yee clan;
Der, Ong, other clans
of Hoiping; Jung, other
clans of Enping.

**SUE HING
BEN. ASSN.**
Hoiping, Enping clans;
Sanshui, Tsingyuan,
Szewui, Koyiu, Koming,
Yeungkong, Yeungchun.

**FA YUEN
BEN.
ASSN.**
Fayuan.

**SAM YUP
BEN. ASSN.**
Namhoi,
Punyu,
Shuntak.

**YOUNG WO
BEN. ASSN.**
Heungshan,
Chuhoi, Dowmon,
Tungkun,
Tsengshing, Poklo.

**YAN WO BEN.
ASSN.**
Pao-on,
Muiyuan,
Wuiyeung,
Chikkai.

Based on "Historical Development of the Chinese Consolidated Benevolent Association/Huiguan System" by Him Mark Lai, in the 1987 issue of *Chinese America: History and Perspectives*, published by the Chinese Historical Society of America.

See Appendix G for the Pinyin equivalents of the names used in this chart.

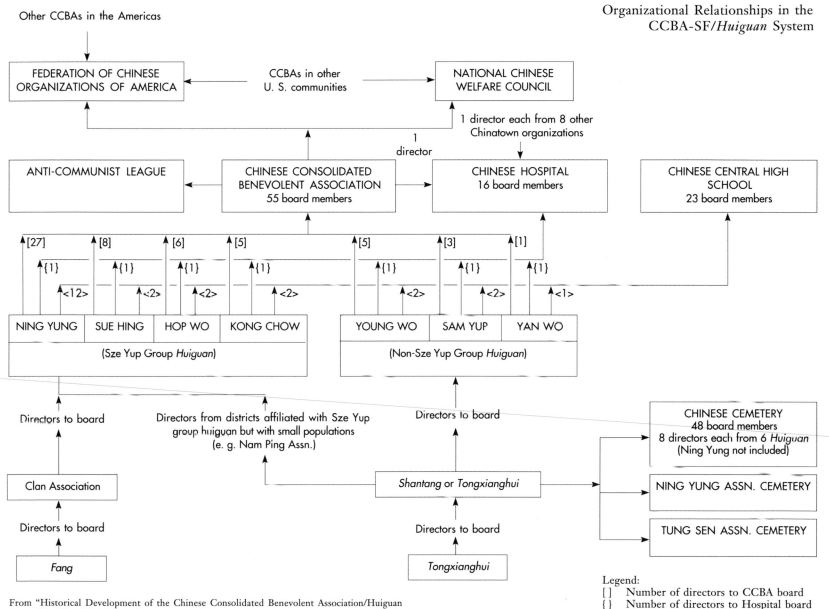

Organizational Relationships in the
CCBA-SF/*Huiguan* System

Other CCBAs in the Americas

FEDERATION OF CHINESE
ORGANIZATIONS OF AMERICA

CCBAs in other
U. S. communities

NATIONAL CHINESE
WELFARE COUNCIL

1 director each from 8 other
Chinatown organizations

1
director

ANTI-COMMUNIST LEAGUE

CHINESE CONSOLIDATED
BENEVOLENT ASSOCIATION
55 board members

CHINESE HOSPITAL
16 board members

CHINESE CENTRAL HIGH
SCHOOL
23 board members

[27] [8] [6] [5]   [5] [3] [1]

{1}   {1} {1} {1}   {1} {1} {1}

<12>   <2> <2>   <2>   <2> <2> <1>

NING YUNG | SUE HING | HOP WO | KONG CHOW   YOUNG WO | SAM YUP | YAN WO

(Sze Yup Group *Huiguan*)   (Non-Sze Yup Group *Huiguan*)

Directors to board

Directors from districts affiliated with Sze Yup
group huiguan but with small populations
(e. g. Nam Ping Assn.)

Directors to board

CHINESE CEMETERY
48 board members
8 directors each from 6 *Huiguan*
(Ning Yung not included)

Clan Association

Shantang or *Tongxianghui*

NING YUNG ASSN. CEMETERY

Directors to board

Directors to board

TUNG SEN ASSN. CEMETERY

Fang

Tongxianghui

Legend:
[ ]   Number of directors to CCBA board
{ }   Number of directors to Hospital board
< >   Number of directors to school board

From "Historical Development of the Chinese Consolidated Benevolent Association/Huiguan
System" by Him Mark Lai in the 1987 issue of *Chinese America: History and Perspectives*, published
by the Chinese Historical Society of America.

APPENDIX B: Some Early Chinese Newspapers

This listing of Chinese newspapers was collected by Yuk Ow in his unpublished manuscript "A Selected List of Published and Unpublished Materials Written by the California Chinese and Brief Biographies of the Authors" (University of California at Berkeley: Bancroft Library, 1960).

Abbreviations:

(AAS) American Antiquarian Society, Worcester, Mass.
(B) Bancroft Library, University of California, Berkeley
(ChiHS) Chicago Historical Society
(CHS) California Historical Society
(ChHS) Chinese Historical Society
(CoU) Columbia University
(F) Fiddletown Preservation Society, Fiddletown, Calif.
(LA) Los Angeles Museum Library
(LC) Library of Congress
(LL) Public Library, Leicester, Mass.
(MHS) Minnesota Historical Society, St. Paul, Minn.
(NJHS) New Jersey Historical Society
(NYHS) New York Historical Society
(NYPL) New York Public Library
(NYSL) New York State Library
(SFL) San Francisco Library
(SFTS) San Francisco Theological Seminary, San Anselmo, Calif.
(S) Stanford University, Hoover Far East Collection
(UC) University of California, Berkeley
(UI) University of Illinois

Nineteenth-Century Newspapers

Tung-Ngai San Luk (*The Oriental*). Published triweekly in Chinese, weekly in English, 1/4/1855 to 7/12/1855; published monthly, 9/1855 to 12/1856. Sacramento and Stockton, San Francisco. Publisher: Rev. William Speer of Chinese Presbyterian Church, S.F. Editors: Lee Kan, Rev. Speer. Contents: bilingual, general news, and special articles connected with local Chinese culture. Speer became ill in 1856, and the paper suspended publication the next year. (AAS) 4-28, 8 1855. (B, CSL, MHS, NJHS, NYHS, NYPL, SFTS)

Chinese Daily News. Started 12/1856. Sacramento. Publisher: Ze Too Yune, alias Hung Tai. Published for almost two years, at first daily, then triweekly, then irregularly, sometimes once per week, sometimes once per month. (Missouri Historical Society)

The California China Mail and Flying Dragon. Monthly, 1/1/1867 to (?). San Francisco. Printer: E. Bosqui. Contents: bilingual, market and prices, shipping, financial. (AAS, B)

San Francisco China News. Weekly, 7/14/1874 to (?). 744 Washington Street, San Francisco. Publisher: Gordon Bocardus. Contents: local and Chinese news, poems, short essays, stories. (B, LA)

War Kee, The Oriental Weekly. Weekly, 9/11/1875 to (?). Name changed in 1875, again on 9/2/1876, and allegedly again in 1900. Publisher: Done Lim. Editor: Ah Fong. Contents similar to *San Francisco China News*. (B, AAS, LL, UC East Asiatic Library, WHS.)

San Francisco Chinese Newspaper. Weekly, 8/26/1876 to (?). Publisher: Hoffmann, Li Mon Ting. Circulation: 800. (B)

The Chinese Record. Semimonthly, 11/13/1876 to (?). 434 California St., later 414 Market St., S.F. Contents: In English with a separate Chinese edition. Publisher: Prof. Augustus Layres. Chinese edition printed by Wen Chi. (B)

Chinese and Foreign News. Weekly, 10/22/1878 to (?). 420 Clay St., S.F. Contents similar to *The Chinese Record*. (B)

Chinese American. 1883(?) to (?). New York City. (LC, NYHS, NYPL, NYSL, WHS)

Suei Kee American and Chinese Commercial Newspaper. Weekly, 1883 to before 1906. 835-1/2 Dupont St. Contents: local and commercial. (B)

San Francisco Chinese Daily Evening News (*Hua-hsi Shen Pao*). Daily, 1883(?) to (?). San Francisco. (CHS)

Mon Hing Yat Bo (*Chinese World*). Weekly, 1891 to 1901; daily, 1901 to (?). 809-1/2 Washington St. Founded by Reformist Group. After 1906 moved to Los Angeles; later returned to S.F. and changed Chinese name to *Chinese World*. (B, ChHS, F)

Chinese Monthly News (*Jui-hsiang Hua-yang Hsin Pao*). 1891(?) to (?). Boston. (Essex Institute)

Chinese American Advocate Weekly (*Hua-mei Tzu Pao*). 1892 to (?). Philadelphia. Bilingual. (Hist. Soc. of Pennsylvania)

Chinese American. Semimonthly, 1893 to 1896(?). Chicago. (ChiHS)

Occidental Daily News. 1894 to (?). Editor: Loo Kum Shu. Mentioned in Lim P. Lee's article in *Chinese Digest*, November 13, 1936.

Chinese News. Semimonthly, 1896 to 1897. Chicago. (ChiHS)

Wah Mei Sun Bo (*Hua-mei Hsin-pao*). 1898 to 1900. Los Angeles. Said to be founded by Ng Poon Chew. Mentioned in first issue of *Chung Sai Yat Bo*, 2/16/1900.

The Daily Occidental. 1900(?) to (?). 731 Washington St., S.F. Publisher: Horn Hong Co. (F, CHS)

Twentieth-Century Newspapers

Chung Sai Yat Bo. Daily. 2/16/1900 to (?). 811 Sacramento St., S.F. Expanded from *Wah Mei Sun Bo*. Printed in Oakland after the earthquake, from 7/2/1906 to 3/28/1908. (B, UC)

The Pacific Coast Chinese War Cry. 1900 to (?), 815 Sacramento St., S.F. Contents: mostly religious activities of the Chinatown Post of the Salvation Army. (B)

Oriental and Occidental Press. 6/9/1900 to (?). 535 Clay St., S.F. Contents: English; assured Californians of loyalty of Chinese during the Boxer Rebellion. Editor and Publisher: Tong King Chong.

The Chinese Free Press (*Tai Tung Yat Bo*). 1902 to 1925. Organ of the Chih-kung T'ang (Chinese Free Masons). Name changed to

Chinese Republic Journal (*Chung Wah Min Kock Kung Bo*) in 1920. In 1925 Chinese name was changed back to *Tai Tung Yat Bo*.

Chinese World. 1906 to 1969. Weekly. See *Mon Hing Yat Bo*, above.

The New Era (*Kuo-huan Pao*). Daily, 1907 to 1909. 740 Sacramento St., S.F. Founded by the Yee Family.

Chinese Defender. Monthly, 8/1910 to (?). English. S. F. Public Library has Vol.I, No. 1-12; Vol.II, No. 1, 8/1910 to 9/1911.

Young China. Weekly, 1909; daily, 1910 to present. Founded by Dr. Sun Yat-sen.

Chinese Times (*Chin-shan Shih Pao*). Daily, 1924 to present. Publisher: Chinese-American Citizens Alliance. Sold August 1988 to independent group. First paper founded by American-born Chinese.

Morning Sun (*Kung-Lun Shen Pao*). 1929 to 1933. Organ of the Chih-kung T'ang (Chinese Free Masons).

Chinese Nationalist Daily (*Kuo Min Yat Bo*). 1/1927 to 1960. Official organ of the Kuomintang. Name changed to *Chinese Daily Post* in 1953.

Chinese Digest. 1935 to 1940. Published weekly for a year, then monthly, then quarterly or less often. First true Chinese-American newspaper in the English language.

Kung-shang Chou-pao. Weekly. 1939 to (?). Shopping newspaper.

California Chinese Press. 1940 to 1952. English-language tabloid-size newspaper. Name later changed to *Chinese Press*.

Chinese News. 1940 to 1942. Chinese-American newspaper.

Chinese Pacific Weekly. 10/1946 to 8/1983. Taken over by *East West* in 1983.

Chinatown Shopper (*Hua-shang Tao-pao*). Weekly, 1948 to (?).

China Weekly (*Chin-men Ch'iao-pao*). 5/1949 to 1951. Tabloid-size newspaper.

Free China Daily. 10/1955 to 1957.

BISHOP

ALPHABETICAL LIST

OF

CHINESE BUSINESS HOUSES

IN SAN FRANCISCO.

ACT

Act Lee, groceries, 741 Sacramento
Ack Lee, laundry, 208 Commercial
Ah Chin, cigars, 811 Market
Ah Chong, laundry, 27 Ellis
Ah King, cigars, 530 Sacramento
Ah Long, interpreter, 439 Bush
Ah Loy, lodgings, 795 Clay
Ah Quing, lodgings, 37 Waverly pl
Ah Quing, cigars, 309 Battery
Ah Sam, barber, 745 Sacramento
Ah Sam, laundry, 1513½ Leavenworth
Ah Sang, laundry, 34 Washington alley
Ah Sing, tailor, 733 Washington
Ah Soung, laundry, 504 Pacific
Ah Wea, barber, 637 Jackson
Ah Wing, laundry, 151 Shipley
Ah Yow, variety, Jackson alley
Ah Yung, laundry, Brannan nr Ninth
Alaska Cigar Co., 29–31 Pacific
Arago & Co., cigar factory, 767 Clay
Aurora Co., cigar factory, 206 Dupont
Bee Woo, laundry, 1136 Folsom
Bing You, cigar manufacturer, 308 and 425 Commercial
Buena & Co., cigar manufacturers, 723 Sacramento
Callao Co., cigar manufacturers, 609 Dupont
Car Lock Hen, restaurant, 629 Jackson
Carolina Co., cigar manufacturers, 617 Commercial
Cascade Co., cigar manufacturers, 223 Dupont
Cerro Gordo Co., cigar manufacturers, 115 Jackson
Chan Ning Tuck Kee, drugstore, 704 Dupont
Chang Sing, laundry, 537 Merchant
Chang Wa Sang, groceries, 943 Dupont
Charley Yow Long, physician, 1017 Dupont
Che Wa, groceries and variety, 723 Jackson
Cheap John, cigarstore, 530 Sacramento
Chee —, carpenter, 809 Washington
Chee Lee & Co., 804 Washington

CHU

Chen Chong & Co., tea, sugar, rice, oil, etc., 714 Jackson
Cheong Leong, Chinese passenger clerk with P. M. S. S. Co.
Chew Fun, watchmaker, 922 Dupont
Chin Chung, jeweler and goldsmith, 716 Jackson
Chin Chong, jeweler, 1011 Dupont
Chin Lee & Co., Chinese and Japanese goods, 521 Kearny
Ching Goy Lang, lodgings, 754 Washington
Ching Tin, drygoods and shoes, 908 Dupont
Ching Wo, tea, sugar, rice and oil, 707 Jackson
Ching Yuen, groceries, 8 Prospect pl
Chip Chong, tailor, 737 Jackson
Choie Tane, clerk with Wells, Fargo & Co., res 933 Dupont
Chong Fook Tong, drugs, 615 Jackson
Chong Hong, laundry, 188 Jessie
Chong Kee, variety, 734 Pacific
Chong Lee, laundry, 741½ Folsom
Chong Wong, laundry, 282 Stevenson
Choy Che Ong, clothing, 726 Dupont
Choy Far Lung, baker, 20 Ross
Choy Sun & Co., shoe manufacturers, 716 Sacramento
Choy Yan Low, restaurant, SE cor Washington alley and Jackson
Chu Lung, laundry, 617 Jackson
Chu Kee, cabinetmaker, 754½ Washington
Chuin Gee, cigars, 741 Pacific
Chun Lee, laundry, 50 Natoma
Chun Yik, sugar, rice and tea, 747 Sac
Chun Wo Tong & Co., Chinese medicines, 933 Dupont
Chung Kee, laundry, cor Drumm and Oregon
Chung Kee & Co., manufacturers and dealers clothing, 841 Dupont
Chung Lee, doctor, 721 Jackson
Chung Lung, variety, 722 Pacific

Chung Sing & Co., groceries and butchers, 741 Sacramento
Chung Un, laundry, 738 Brannan
Chung Wa, laundry, 3 Dodge
Chung Wah, laundry, 829 Vallejo
Chung Yik, laundry, Ellick alley
Chy Lung & Co., importers Canton crape, silk shawls, Chinese and Japanese goods, etc., 640 Sacramento, [see adv. page 29A.]
City Cigar Co., 610 Montgomery
Clind Ayet, laundry, Twelfth nr Market
Col Lo Haein & Co., provisions, 629 Jackson
Colmo & Co., cigar factory, 607 Dupont
Colombo & Co., cigar manufacturers, 715 Dupont
Coly Ying, tea and rice, 938 Dupont
Con Lee, umbrellas, parasols and fans, 756 Clay
Cosmopolitan Sugar Co., (Ke Ying & Co.) 427 Sacramento
Cuba Cigar Co., 25 Dupont
Cum Coch In, restaurant, 17 Jackson
Cun Lung, tailor, 727 Pacific
Cun Yuen, laundry, 818 Mission
Decota Co., cigar and clothing manufacturers, 524 Commercial
Din Lee, laundry, 924 Howard
Do Sar Wing, tea and rice, 721 Jackson
Don Carlos Co., cigar manufacturers, 808 Sacramento
Dye Wo, tea, sugar, rice, oil and merchandise, 725 Jackson
E Key, laundry, 703 Harrison
Eh Lay, laundry, 235 Third
Estella Co., cigar manufacturers, 229 Pacific
Eureka Co., cigars, 1112 Dupont
Fang Chang, laundry, 44 Natoma
Fang Chung Lung, cigar manufacturer, 537 Commercial
Fat Wau, laundry, 777 Folsom
Fat Young, cigar manufacturer, 441 Bush
Florence Co., cigar manufacturers, 115 Oregon
Fong Kee, tailors, 815 Sacramento
Fong Yet, laundry, 756 Bryant
Foo Hidg & Co., umbrellas, parasols and fans, 746 Washington
Foo Lang, merchant tailor, 839 Dupont
Fook Chang Hong, druggist and chemist, 744 Sacramento
Fook Hing, lodgings, Sacramento alley
Fook Long, laundry, 1233 Mission
Fook Woo Tong & Co., general merchandise, 803 Dupont
Fook Yul, boarding, 627 Jackson
Fook Yuen & Co., groceries, 711 Dupont
Foug Yik, sugar, rice and tea, 747 Sac
Fung High, lodgings, 710 Dupont
Fung Kee, rice and tea, 815 Sacramento
Fung Ty, clothing, 712 Dupont
Fur Sing, laundry, 751 Harrison
Ge Loy, laundry, 134 Fifth
Ge Wo Lun, wholesale tea, sugar, rice, oil, opium and provisions, 817 Sacramento

Gee Ashon, laundry, 709 Front
Gee Kee, boarding, 1001, Dupont
Gee Tau Hong & Co., drugs, 740 Commercial
Gee Tuck, tea and rice, 619 Jackson
Gee Wo, barber, 620 Jackson
Gee Wo Sang, tea, sugar, rice, oil and provisions, 1019 Dupont
Gee, Yuen & Co., general merchandise, 22 Ross
Get Lee, cigars, 48 Sacramento
Gim Gou, laundry, 708 Folsom
Gim Hi & Co., manufacturers of jewelry, 804 Dupont
Gim Lee, laundry, 1006 Pacific
Ging Mow, rice and tea, 904 Dupont
Gnip Chong, boarding, 737 Jackson
Goey Hing Kee & Co., merchant tailors and grocery dealers, 738 Dupont
Gong Yune Long, laundry, 441 Guerrero
Goon Chong, laundry, 219 O'Farrell
Guin Chong, laundry, 924 Folsom
Gun Fet & Chim Kee, shoe factory, 311 Pine
Gung Git, slipper manufacturer, junc Sutter and Market
Guy Long, laundry, 818 Greenwich
Hag Kee & Co., boarding, 730 Jackson
Hang Fer Low & Co., Chinese Restaurant, 713 Dupont
Hang Hayn, laundry, 433 Third
Hang Lung & Co., merchant tailors, 829 Dupont
Hang Wo, laundry, 1030 Market
Hasting & Co., cigar manufacturers, 734 Commercial
He Sang Tong, drugs, 650 Jackson
Hee Wau, butcher, vegetables and fish, 735 Commercial
He Yik & Co., tea, sugar, rice, oil and merchandise, 713 Jackson
Hen Lee Lung, laundry, 918 Jones
Hep Yuen, lamps, tinware, etc., 915 Dupont
Hey Wau, laundry, 124 Seventh
Hi Long, laundry, 403 Sutter
Hi Loong, slipper manufacturer, 414 Sacramento
High Sing, laundry, 950 Mission
Hight Sing, laundry, 505 Clay
Him Lung & Co., drapers and tailors, 930 Dupont
Hing Chong, wholesale and retail dealer cigars and tobacco, 504 Clay
Hing Chong, laundry, 730 Pacific
Hing Chung, drygoods, clothing and merchandise, 920 Dupont
Hing Kee, laundry, 726 Jackson
Hing Kee & Co., wholesale tinware, tea, sugar, rice and oil, 716 Commercial
Hing Lee, laundry, 109 First
Hing Yang, clothing, 920 Dupont
Hip Sing, laundry, 315 Tehama
Hip Wo & Co., tea, sugar, rice and oil, 735 Commercial
Ho Chuck Hung, physician, 828 Washington

Ho Tuen & Co., commission merchants and manufacturers of clothing, 909 Dupont
Hog Kee, physician, 730 Jackson
Hou Mon, carver and painter, 805 Dupont
Hong Sing, jeweler, 811 Dupont
Hong Fat, laundry, 555½ Bryant
Hong Goon Loy, laundry, 142 Page
Hong Hen, laundry, 600 Broadway
Hong Sang, laundry, 917 Washington
Hong Sang, laundry, 33 Morton
Hong Sang, laundry, 744 Harrison
Hong Sing, shoe factory, 752 Clay
Hong Sing, laundry, 21 Geary
Hong Soon, laundry, 1049 Howard
Hong Yone, laundry, 809 Sixteenth
Hong Yuen, general merchandise, 825½ Dupont
Hong Yune & Co., wholesale tea, rice, sugar and oil, 731 Commercial
Hop Dack, laundry, cor Twenty-seventh and San Bruno road
Hop Kee & Co., rice, tea, sugar, oil, etc., and boot and shoe factory, 705 Dupont
Hop Kee & Co., shoe factory, 801 Sacramento
Hop Kee, laundry, 413 Broadway
Hop Lee, laundry, 236 Fourth
Hop Lee, laundry, 103 Sacramento
Hop Lee, laundry, 652 Pacific
Hop Lee & Co., preserves, 904 Dupont
Hop Long, laundry, 526 Broadway
Hop Lung & Co., shoe factory, 738 Jackson
Hop Lung, clothing and provisions, 921 Dupont
Hop Moon, laundry, S s Sixteenth nr Valencia
Hop Sang, butcher, 733 Sacramento
Hop Shing & Co., manufacturers clothing, 627 Pacific
Hop Wa, laundry, 1055 Market
Hop Wo, laundry, 518 Pine
Hop Wo Co., joss house, 751 Clay
Hop Yuen & Co., cigar factory, 734 Commercial
Hoy Kee, rice and sugar, 910 Dupont
Hoy Lee, laundry, 231 Fifth
Hoy Yuen, laundry, 520 Clay
Hu Lung, laundry, 617 Jackson
Hung Fat, barber, 729 Sacramento
Hung Fat, laundry, 311 Sixth
Hung Gee, laundry, 737 Sacramento
Hung Gee & Co., boot and shoe factory, 823 Clay
Hung Hine, laundry, 208 Minna
Hung Sang Lung & Co., wholesale and retail Chinese merchandise, 805 Dupont
Hung Shang, butchers, 731 Sacramento
Hung Sing, laundry, 17½ Dupont
Hung Son, butcher, 731 Sacramento
Hung Wing, laundry, 511 Hyde
Hung Wo Tong, Chinese medicines 611 Jackson

Isabella Co., Cigar Manufacturers, 760 Clay
Isabella Cigar Factory, 612 Pacific
Jay Hon Chung, physician, 743 Washington
Jim, physician, 918 Dupont
Jinns, laundry, 829 Clay
Lee John, laundry, 250 Eighth
Lee John, laundry, 403 Brannan
Jim Bruce, laundry, 1122 Mission
Jim Lung, laundry, 1133 Howard
Jim Wing, laundry, 2009 Polk
Kam Lun & Co., tailors and shoes, 722 Dupont
Kan Lee, interpreter, Bank of California, res 721 Commercial
Ke Ying & Co., Cosmopolitan Sugar Co., 427 Sacramento
Kee Sang Tong, wholesale drugs, 742 Sacramento
Kee Wing Fat On, slipper manufacturer, 501 Sacramento
Keng Wha, variety, 711½ Jackson
Kie Wo, employment office, 614 Jackson
Kim Lee, lodgings, 610 Dupont
Kim Lung & Co., drugs and tailors, 728 Dupont
Kim Wa, laundry, 15 Sacramento
Kim Yick, laundry, 517 Fourth
Kin Nam & Co., wholesale dealers, tea sugar, rice, nuts, oil, opium, Chinese, provisions, etc., 1008 Dupont
Kis Long, provisions, 747 Sacramento
Kon Sang, laundry, 810 Union
Kong Choy Asylum, 512 Pine
Kong Sing, laundry, 637 Post
Kong Wing, laundry, 254 Steuart
Kong Woo, pawnbroker, 639 Jackson
Kong Yuen Chong & Co., tea and rice, 728 Commercial
Kum Kee, intelligence office, 711 Sacramento
Kum Kee & Co., drygoods, clothing and merchandise, 912 Dupont
Kum Wo & Co drygoods, clothing and merchandise, 928 Dupont
Kum Yuen, tea, rice, sugar and opium, 711 Jackson
Kung Sung, laundry, 701 Bush
Kwong Chong Kee & Co., tea, sugar, rice, nut oil, opium, and Chinese provisions, 719 Dupont
Kwong Chong Wing Co., wholesale tea, sugar, rice, oil and opium, 733 Commercial
Kwong Choy Yuen & Co., grocery, 29 Sal alley
Kwong Fong Tai & Co., provisions, sugar, tea, rice and oil, 714 Sacramento
Kwong Fook Tong, drug store, 1047 Dupont
Kwong Hang & Co., wholesale tea, sugar, rice and oil, 710 Commercial
Kwong Hing Long, manufacturers and dealers in shoes, balmorals, etc., 734 Sacramento

Kwong Hing Long, shoe manufactory, 531 Sacramento
Kwong Lee, clothing manufactory, 828 Dupont
Kwong Lun Chong & Co., tea, sugar, rice, oil, opium, Chinese provisions, drugs, etc., 714 Dupont
Kwong Lune, clothing, 1013 Dupont
Kwong Mow War & Co., drygoods, 727 Jackson
Kwong On Cheong, tea and rice, 728 Sacramento
Kwong Sam Kee & Co., clothing, 1008 Dupont
Kwong Lung Tai & Co., tea, sugar, rice, oil merchandise, etc., 836 Dupont
Kwong Tai Lung & Co., wholesale tea, rice, sugar, opium, provisions and oil, 719 Commercial
Kwong Waa Tong, Chinese drug store, 801 Dupont
Kwong Wing Sang & Co., (Mon Ting and Yee Mon) provisions, rice, sugar, tea and Chinese dry goods, 750-752 Washington
Kwong Wo Lung & Co., tailors and tea, sugar, rice and oil, 735 Jackson
Kwong Wo & Co., wholesale butchers, 1071 Dupont
Kwong Yue, opium, 627 Jackson
Kwong Yune Sung & Co., teas, sugar, rice, nut oil, etc., 727 Dupont
Laconia Co., manufacturers cigars, 1016 Dupont
La Espanola Co., (Bing You proptr) cigar manfry, 308 and 425 Commercial
Lai Hing Lung & Co., wholesale tea, sugar rice, oil etc., 729 Commercial
Lai Sang & Co., jewelry, 726 Jackson
Lai Yong Portrait and Photograph Gallery, 743 Washington
Lang Con, laundry, 1103 Clay
Lee Fook Hotel, 721 Dupont
Lee Fook, cigar manfr, 406 Battery
Lee Gun, laundry, 525 Valencia
Lee Hop, laundry, 661 Mission
Lee Man Sing, shirt manfr, 832 Washington
Lee Sam, laundry, cor Seventeenth and Dolores
Lee Sing, laundry, 623 Pacific
Lee Toy, meat and vegetables, 719 Sacramento
Lee Ung, laundry, 811 Market
Lee Wing, laundry, 113 Jackson
Lee Yik, laundry, 134 Sacramento
Lee Yeck, slipper manfr, 826 Clay
Lee Ying, oculist and physician, 621 Dupont
Lee Yong Fong, physician, 1021 Dupont
Lee Yuen & Co., tea, sugar, rice and oil, 741 Sacramento
Li Wing Sun Kee, money broker, 737 Jackson
Li Po Tai, physician, 737 Washington
Lin Mau, merchant tailor, 806 Dupont

Lin Tie & Co., merchant tailor, 716 Dupont
Lin Wor, laundry, 1431 Dupont
Lin Wood, cigars, 205 Pacific
Lisle & Co., cigar factory, 824 Clay
Log Gee, laundry, 335 Fourth
Lon Wo, provisions, 711 Sacramento
Long Wou, laundry, 986 Folsom
Loon Chong, laundry, 926 Pine
Loucitat, physician, 14 Brenham pl
Lotus Co., cigars, 620 Pacific
Loy Fook Won, physician, 615 Jackson
Loy Sing, laundry, 320 Hayes
Lum Toan Ke, physician, 742 Sacramento
Lun Chong & Co., butchers, 745 Sacramento
Lun Chong Yuen, clothing, 1014 Dupont
Lun Fat, slipper factory, 745 Commercial
Lun Hing, laundry, 906 Post
Lun Hing, tailor, 644 Jackson
Lun Hop, laundry, 471 Minna
Lun Lay, laundry, 1321 Mission
Lun Sing, laundry, 409½ Fourth
Lun Su Wah, slipper factory, 534 Commercial
Lun Ty & Co., clothing, 716 Dupont
Lun Wah, laundry, 320 Green
Lun Wo & Co., wholesale tea, rice and opium, 711 Sacramento
Lun Wo & Co., wholesale tea, sugar and rice, 716 Sacramento
Lung Chang, laundry, 1011 Jackson
Lung Chung, rice and tea, 720 Dupont
Lung Sang, laundry, 149 Post
Lung Sing & Co., wholesale tea, sugar, oil, etc., 706 Sacramento
Lung Fat, shoe manfr, 745 Commercial
Lung Yik & Co., cigar manfr, 425 Commercial
Lung Wau, laundry, 129¼ Eleventh
Ly Chong, groceries and provisions, 735 Jackson
Ly Chung, jeweler and silversmith, 615 Jackson
Ly Wing, money broker, 636 Jackson
Ly Wo, pawn broker, 1001 Dupont
Man Chong & Co., tea, sugar, and rice, 828 Dupont
Man Fong & Co., bakery, 631 Jackson
Man Lee, provisions, rice, sugar and tea, 709 Dupont
Man Loong & Co., wholesale tea, sugar, rice and oil, 711 Sacramento
Man On Lung, laundry, 1114 Dupont
Man On Tong, drugs, medicines and Chinese goods, 945 Dupont
Mang Shing & Co., tea, sugar, rice and oil, 616 Jackson
Man Tang & Co., butchers, 631 Jackson
Manto Tong, drugs, 617 Jackson
Man Wo & Co., wholesale and retail dealers in pork, tea, sugar, rice, oil and Chinese merchandise, 633 Jackson
Man Wo Cheong & Co., wholesale tea, sugar, rice and oil, 738 Sacramento
Me Nom, tailor, 640 Jackson

Me Wa Chong, carver, 753 Clay
Milo Co., cigar manfrs, 744 Washington
Mong Hong Hu, restaurant, 643 Jackson
Mou On & Co., commission merchants, wholesale and retail dealers in tea, rice, sugar, Chinese merchandise, etc., 934 Dupont
Mun Woa, laundry, Dunbar Alley
Mung Sing, laundry, 22 Clay
Nam Kee, tailor, 825 Dupont
National Co., cigar manfrs, 823 Sacramento
Neblina Co., manfrs and dealers in cigars, 525 Sansome
Ogey Long, grocer, 747 Sacramento
On Chong Long, laundry, Larkin nr Union
On Lang, laundry, SE cor Pacific and Larkin
On Sing, intelligence office, 624 Jackson
On Sing, wood and lumber, 646 Pacific
On Tie & Co., tea and rice, 715 Dupont
On Tie & Co., manufacturers jewelry, 716½ Dupont
On Tsoy, laundry, Sutter nr Sansome
On Wah Long & Co., tailors, 611 Dupont
Ong Wo & Co., general merchandise, 625 Jackson
Oo Lang, merchant tailor, 839 Dupont
Oung Lee, laundry, 1005 McAllister
Onong Wo, laundry, 302 Sutter
Oy Kee, tailor and carver, 916 Dupont
Oy Wo Tong & Co., drugs, 708 Jackson
Pacific Co., manufacturers and dealers in cigars and cigaritos, 537 Commercial
Palmer Co., cigars, 646½ Pacific
Partagos A. & Co., cigarmakers, 730 Jackson
Pay Kee, shoemaker, 310 Pine
Paw Chong, tailor, 1015 Dupont
Pioneer Cigar Co., 24 Dupont
Pon Jib, manager Kwong On Cheong, 728 Dupont
Qui Sung, laundry, 1022 Kearny
Qung Chong Long, groceries, 740 Sacramento
Qung Hain Chung, dry goods, 716 Dupont
Qung Hong Ching, groceries, 803 Sacramento
Qung Wa, lodgings, 801 Sacramento
Quon Gun, laundry, 20 Stockton
Quon Ohu, groceries, 1005 Dupont
Quoug —, laundry, 1512 Mason
Quong Chan Chung, boarding, 753 Clay
Quong Chong Yee & Co., tea and rice, 761 Clay
Quong Chune, cigar manufacturer, 152 Steuart
Quong Chung Lung & Co., importers and wholesale dealers sugar, rice, oil, opium and peanuts, 717 Sacramento
Quong Chung Shing & Co., wholesale tea, sugar, rice and oil, 724 Commercial
Quong Chung Yee & Co., clothing, rice and tea, 761 Clay

Quong Fat ...
Quong Fook ...
728 Commercial
Quong Fook Sing & Co., tea, sugar, rice oil, and Chinese provisions, 1013 Dupont
Quong Hang A Co., tea and rice, 710 Commercial
Quong Hing, butcher, 711 Sacramento
Quong Hing & Co., provisions, 713 Sacramento
Quong Hing, lodgings, 838 Dupont
Quong Lee, tailor, 828 Dupont
Quong Ling Lung, laundry, 722 Vallejo
Quong Lung, Chinese dry goods, 813½ Dupont
Quong Lung Chung & Co., manufacturers and dealers in ladies', misses' and childrens' shoes, 219 Commercial
Quong Marn Long, groceries and provisions, 623 Dupont
Quong Moon, cabinetmaker, 708 Dupont
Qung Sam Lung & Co., tea, sugar rice, nut oil and provisions, 706 Dupont
Quong Sang Lung, confectioner, 733 Washington
Quong Sing, laundry, 814 Folsom
Quong Sing Tai Kee, wholesale sugar, tea, rice, provisions and opium, 717 Commercial
Quong Son & Co., pork, sausage and provisions, 751 Sacramento
Quong Tuck, jeweler, 640 Jackson
Quong Wah Ying, merchant tailor and dealer in dry goods, etc., 940 Dupont
Quong Wan Lung & Co., tea and rice, 741 Commercial
Quong Wing, laundry, 939 Clay
Quong Wing Chong & Co., tea, sugar, rice, oil and Chinese merchandise, 809 Dupont
Quong Wing Lung & Co., groceries and provisions, 619 Dupont
Quong Wo Chong & Co., China clothing and silk dry goods, 904 Dupont
Quong Wong Lung, tea and rice, 619 Dupont
Quong Yee On & Co., wholesale and retail dealers in Chinese merchandise, 910 Dupont
Quong Yek Chong & Co., tea, sugar, rice and oil, 835 Dupont
Quong Yik Lee, laundry, 455 Stevenson
Quong Ying Kee & Co., wholesale tea, sugar, rice, oil, opium and provisions, 718 Commercial
Quong Yune At, pawnbroker and lodgings, 1006 Dupont
Quong Yune Sang & Co., tea and rice, 727 Dupont

Qun Fod, laundry, 816 Jackson
Qung Shung Lung, laundry, 1521 Folsom
Racine Co, wholesale and retail cigar factory, 1106 Dupont
Ramirez & Co., manufacturers and dealers in cigars, 425 Commercial
Rolema Co., cigars, 611½ Jackson
Royal Chinese Theatre, Yu Henn Choy, 626 Jackson
Sallie Hart Co., cigar manufactory, 633 Pacific
Sam, laundry —, 209 Sansome
Sam, laundry, 621 California
Sam Cheen, laundry, 738 Commercial
Sam Gee, laundry, 2515 Bush
Sam Hing, laundry, 122 Dupont
Sam Kee, grocer, 807 Sacramento
Sam Kee, wholesale tea, sugar and rice, 723 Sacramento
Sam Kee, employment office, 511 Bush
Sam Kee, laundry, Laguna nr Buchanan
Sam Kee, laundry, 1318 Dupont
Sam Kee, laundry, 1509 Mission
Sam Lee, laundry, 607 Grove
Sam Lee, laundry, NE cor Seventeenth and Dolores
Sam Lung, laundry, SW cor Clara and Fifth
Sam Lung, laundry, 1406 Stockton
Sam Lung, laundry, 525 Howard
Sam Nan Long, laundry, 805 Washington
Sam Sing, laundry, 1845 Bush
Sam Sing, manufacturer, and dealer in cigars, 631 Pacific
Sam Wo, laundry, 529 Stevenson
Sam Wing, laundry, 1320 Pine
Sam Yung, tea and rice, 623¼ Jackson
Sam Yik, clothing, 747 Sacramento
Sam Yik, ivorycarver, 805 Dupont
San Lee, laundry, 17 Everett
San Nam Long, laundry, 807 Washington
San Wo Lee, laundry, cor Ninth and Brannan
Sang Hong, laundry, 106 Jessie
Sang Lung, laundry, SW cor Maraposa and Tennessee
Sang Lung, laundry, 147 Post
Sang Lung & Co., slipper manufacturers, 826 Dupont
Sang Lung, tea, sugar and rice, 826 Dupont
Sang Yune & Co., tinsmith, 819 Dupont
See Chung, tea, sugar, rice, oil, Chinese merchandise, etc., 625 Dupont
See Hop & Co., butchers, 1009 Dupont
See Lee, broker, 620 Jackson
See Lee, clothing, 814 Dupont
See Wo Lung & Co., wholesale and retail dealers sugar, tea, rice, oil and Chinese merchandise, 621 Dupont
Sein Gung, laundry, 711 Union
Sen Kee, barber, 642 Jackson
Seu Lung, variety store, 718 Jackson
Shang Lee, laundry, 1510 Stockton
Shang Tin, laundry, 504 O'Farrell
Shang Wa Sang, tea and rice, 913 Dupont

Shay Woo, butcher, 720 Jackson
Sheang Sai Shong, physician, 705 Jackson
Shee Chong, tailor, 713 Jackson
Shee Chong & Co., tea and rice, 709 Jackson
Shee Kee Co., wholesale tea, sugar, rice and oil, 810 Sacramento
Shee Lee, clothing, 816 Dupont
Sheridan Company cigar manufacturers, 413 Davis
Shew Wa, varieties, 711 Jackson
Shing Yick & Co., wholesale Chinese goods and provisions, 722 Jackson
Shing Yung, laundry, 8 Washington
Shu Lee, lodgings, 709 Jackson
Shee Woo, tea and rice, 707 Jackson
Shun Yik & Co., grocery, 723 Dupont
Shung Sing, tea and rice, 617 Jackson
Sic Kee, merchant tailor, 715¼ Dupont
Sin Kee, laundry, 906 Larkin
Sin Kwong Lun & Co., clothing, silk, tea, opium, etc., 813 Dupont
Sin Long One, laundry, 1106 Folsom
Sin Shing, laundry, 234 Turk
Sin Chin, wood engraver, 708 Dupont
Sing Chong & Co., tea, sugar, rice, oil and merchandise, 823 Dupont
Sing Chung, restaurant, 734 Jackson
Sing High, laundry, 505 Clay
Sing Kee, rice, sugar, tea, etc., 809 Sacramento
Sing Kee, laundry, 904 Pacific
Sing Ky, grocer, 1013 Dupont
Sing Lee & Co., manufacturer clothing, 814 Clay
Sing Mee Tong, tea and rice, 822 Dupont
Sing Mow, clothing, 902 Dupont
Sing Ping Yuen, New Chinese Theatre, 623½ Jackson
Sing Quong Lung, laundry, 233 Jackson
Sing Sang, laundry, 45 Sacramento
Sing Shong, carpenter, 734 Jackson
Sing Yuen, tinsmith, 1018 Dupont
Sing Wa, laundry, 300 O'Farrell
Sing Wo & Co., merchants, 639 Jackson
Sing Yik, grocer, 722 Jackson
Sik Kee, tailor, 713 Dupont
Siong Lee, laundry, 1016 Dupont
Skue Long, laundry, 521 Bush
Soi Bun, laundry, 32 Steuart
Soi Chin, goldsmith, 747 Commercial
Song Sing, laundry, 504 Post
Song Yuen, tinsmith, 819 Dupont
Soon Hung, laundry, 764 Clay
Soon Sing John & Co., cigars, 716 Pacific
Soong Chong & Co., merchant tailors, 812 Dupont
St. George Joss House, 731 Jackson
St. Lucie Co., cigar manufacturers, 639 Commercial
St. Louis Cigar Manufacturing Co., 520 Clay
Su Wah Lung, silk factory, 531 Commercial
Sue Lee, fruit and nuts, 623 Jackson
Sue Wo, tea, rice and Chinese goods, 720 Jackson

Sue Wo, wholesale and retail dealer in Chinese merchandise, 911 Dupont
Suey Quong, laundry, 138 Minna
Sui Lung, laundry, 660 Harrison
Sun Chin, variety store, 709 Jackson
Sun Chong & Co., clothing, 717 Sacramento
Sun Chong Wo & Co,. wholesale sugar, tea, rice and oil, 710 Sacramento
Sun Chong, Yuen & Co., rice, tea, oil, opium and Chinese provisions, 1014 Dupont
Sun Fun & Co., shoe manufacturers, 709 Commercial
Sun Hung, laundry, 764 Clay
Sun Kam Wah, clothing and fancy goods, 714 Dupont
Sun Lee, laundry, 12 Commercial
Sun Quong Lun & Co., clothing, 813 Dupont
Sun Tong Sang, laundry, 260 Brannan
Sun Ty Chong, boarding, 638 Jackson
Sung Chong, laundry, 702 Mission
Sung Sing Kee, butcher, 733 Sacramento
Sung Wa, grocer, 641 Jackson
Tai Sing & Co., manufacturers and tailors, 732 Jackson
Tai Yuen Cheong & Co., wholesale tea, sugar, rice and opium, 721 Commercial
Tam Chung, missionary, res 8½ Prospect pl
Tan Hing, laundry, 519 Dupont
Tan Lee, laundry, S s Filbert nr Mason
Tang Gee, laundry, 128 Geary
Tapes Lee, laundry, 2 Dodge
Tay Ghong & Co., Chinese provisions, 20 Washington alley
Tay Wang, laundry, 621 Mission
Ti Loey & Co., wholesale and retail dealer in Chinese provisions, 911 Dupont
Tia Wo & Co., shoe factory, 534 Commercial
Tie Sang Tong, wholesale and retail dealer in Chinese drugs, 929 Dupont
Tie Wing & Co., merchants, 737 Washington
Tie Yuen, manufacturer of jewelry, 1008 Dupont
Tin Hop & Co., wholesale and retail dealers in teas, rice, sugar, oil, Chinese merchandise, etc, 936 Dupont
Tin Wo Tong & Co., drugs and medicines, 622 Jackson
Tin Yuen, jewelers, 710 Jackson
Ton Lee, laundry, 128 Hayes
Tong Chong & Co., merchants, 743 Sacramento
Tong Chong Loong, general merchandise, 14 Brenham pl
Tong Chung, laundry, 714 Green
Tong Gim, laundry, 573 Mission
Tong Lee, laundry, 158 Steuart
Tong Luno, restaurant, 636 Jackson
Tong San & Co., slipper manufacturers, 216 Sansome

Tong Sang & Co., shoe manufacturers, 419 Commercial
Tong Sing & Co., cigars, 807½ Washington
Tong Tie & Co., tea, rice, oil and dried fish, 728 Sacramento
Tong Tuck, cigar factory, 837 Dupont
Tong Wan, laundry, 622 Third
Tong Wo, barber, 736 Jackson
Tong Wo, laundry, 812 Pacific
Tong Wo & Co., groceries, 722 Sacramento
Tong Wo & Co., tea and rice, 721 Sacramento
Tong Ying Chung, clothing, 717 Jackson
Tong Yoong & Co., sugar, tea, rice, oil, dried fish, etc., 736 Sacramento
Too Long Ah Jo, boarding, 747 Clay
Took Wo Tong, drugs, 803 Dupont
Toon Fot, shoe manufacturer, 328 Pine
Toy Cheong, merchant tailor, 626 Dupont
Toy Hung Lou, boarding, 612 Jackson
Tsau Kee, hotel, 621 Jackson
Tsue Chong Wing, wholesale, tea, rice, sugar, oil and opium, 711 Commercial
Tsun Kee, laundry, 807 Sacramento
Tuck Chong & Co., tea, rice, sugar and nut oil, 789 Sacramento
Tuck Chong Wo & Co., wholesale tea, sugar, rice and oil, 627 Dupont
Tuck Hop, manufacturer of clothing, 614 Dupont
Tuck On Yuen, wholesale pork, sausage, tea, sugar, rice and oil, 727 Sacramento
Tuck Sing Tong & Co., wholesale and retail dealer Chinese merchandise, 1021 Dupont
Tuck Wo, wholesale and retail dealer Chinese provisions, 685 Jackson
Tun Kee, laundry, 807 Sacramento
Tung Chong & Co., wholesale tea, sugar and rice, 743 Sacramento
Tung Foo & Co., pork butchers and provisions, 729 Sacramento
Tung Hing, laundry, 950 Howard
Tung Hop & Co., shoe manufacturers, 832 Washington
Tung Kee, lodgings, 615 Jackson
Tung Ling & Co., wholesale tea, rice, sugar and oil, 732 Sacramento
Tung Wa, boarding, 709 Commercial
Tung Ye Tong & Co., wholesale general merchandise, 710 Dupont
Tung Ye Tong, tea and rice, 911 Dupont
Tung Yet, barber, 745 Sacramento
Tuno Thai, laundry, 829½ Clay
Ty Loen, tea and rice, 911 Dupont
Ty Loie, laundry, 25 Pacific
Ty Wing & Co., wholesale tea, sugar, rice, drygoods, etc., 737 Washington
Ung Lee, laundry, 811 Market
Ung Yik, barber, 413 Geary
Ung Wa, laundry, 2742 Mission
Ung Wing, laundry, 934 Harrison
Union Cigar Co., 17 Dupont

Wa Kee, carpenter, 752 Washington
Wa Lung & Chung Kee, slipper manufacturers, 641 Commercial
Wa Sing, manufacturing tailor, 735 Jackson
Wa Sing, laundry, 652 Pacific
Wa Sing, laundry, 1338 Pacific
Waa Yek, laundry, 319 Third
Wah Kee, laundry, 1125 Sutter
Wah Ye, laundry, 666 Howard
Wah Yee, laundry, SW cor Geary and Leavenworth
Wah Ying Lung, merchant tailor, 824 Dupont
Waign Hoign, laundry, 23½ Geary
Wau Kee, laundry, 803 Howard
Wang Yuan & Co., provisions, 806 Sacramento
Wau Yunt Lung Kee, whoesale tea, sugar, rice, oil and opium, 739 Commercial
We Lee, laundry, 368 Minna
We Wo, laundry, 505 Minna
We Sang, laundry, 25 Folsom
Wee Sin, restaurant, 808 Dupont
Why Chong, retail butcher, and dealer in groceries, 615 Dupont
Win Hy, carpenter, 618 Dupont
Win Lung Sin, laundry, 105 Austin
Wing Chin, jeweler, 811½ Dupont
Wing Fat, laundry, 524 East
Wing Fong, laundry, 53 Clementina
Wing Fung & Co., tea, sugar, rice, oil and opium, 745 Sacramento
Wing Gin, tea and rice, 811½ Dupont
Wing Guen, laundry, 561 Howard
Wing Hi, laundry, 14 Fourth
Wing Hing Lung & Co., shoe factory, 708 Sacramento
Wing Hong, laundry, 209 Stevenson
Wing Hop & Co., wood and lumber, 732 Jackson
Wing Hop Long & Co., grocery and fish, 737 Sacramento
Wing Lee, woodyard, Brooklyn pl nr Sacramento
Wing Lee, laundry, 536 Folsom
Wing Lee, laundry, 317 Davis
Wing Lee, laundry, 126 Berry
Wing Lee, laundry, 282 Minna
Wing Mo Hie, laundry, 609 Post
Wing Sing, laundry, 1618 Sacramento
Wing Song, laundry, 609 Stockton
Wing Tie Jan & Co., importers tea, rice, oil, sugar and opium, 734 Sacramento
Wing Tong, laundry, 811 Dupont
Wing Tong & Co., merchants, 745 Sacramento
Wing Wa, barber, 709½ Jackson
Wing Wo Sang & Co., rice, sugar, and agents challenge tea, 720 Sacramento
Wing Yik, barber, 812 Dupont
Wing Yik, laundry, 24 Taylor
Wing Yu Tong, drugs, 715 Jackson
Wo Hop & Co., laundry, 1879 Mission

Wo Kee & Co., wholesale and retail dealers in teas, rice, sugar. opium, Chinese merchandise, etc., 930 Dupont
Wo Lee, slipper manufacturer, 421 Commercial
Wo Lee & Co., tea, sugar, rice, oil and provisions, 743 Sacramento
Wo On Chung & Co., manufacturers shoes and gaiters, 411 Commercial
Wo Sing, slipper manufacturer, 409 Commercial
Wo Shing, tailor, 736 Jackson
Wo Sing & Co., cheese factory, 708½ Dupont
Wo Sun, laundry, 927 Dupont
Wo Yuen, tinsmith, 1018 Dupont
Wo Yune, laundry, S s Francisco nr Mason
Wong Kee, laundry, 533 Geary
Wong Mook, editor, China News, 744 Washington
Wong Poo Ling Qua, laundry, 24 Mason
Woo Sin Lung, provisions, 808 Dupont
Woo Yik, laundry, 213 Sixth
Wood & Co., cigars, 614½ Jackson
Woodland Co., cigars, 1320 Stockton
Wung Wa Ying, tailor, 940 Dupont
Wung Yu, tea and rice, 627 Jackson
Yam Kee, dealer in shelled peanuts, 721 Jackson
Yan Wo Tong & Co., drugs, 705 Jackson
Ye Chung, grocer, 6 Jackson alley
Ye Kee, laundry, 336 Bush
Ye Wa, laundry, 495 Brannan
Ye Wah, laundry, 459 Jessie
Yee Chin, restaurant, 650 Jackson
Yee Chung & Co., variety, 709 Jackson
Yee Chung Weng & Co., wholesale and retail dealers in Chinese drygoods, 818 Dupont
Yee Chy Lung & Co., wholesale and retail dealers in tea, sugar, rice, oil, Chinese drugs and drygoods, 810 Dupont
Yee Shung Tong Kee & Co., drugs and general provisions, 650 Jackson
Yee Yune, tea, sugar and rice, 822 Clay
Yek Hing, laundry, 325 Third
Yek Kee, clothing, 906 Dupont
Yek Woo, laundry, 1211 Pacific
Yet Kee, tinstore, plumbing and gasfitting, 913 Dupont
Yet Lee, rice, tea, sugar and produce, 735½ Sacramento
Yet Lee & Co., wholesale rice, tea and oil, 719 Sacramento
Yet Lung, laundry, cor Haight and Gough
Yik Foo, laundry, 612 Commercial
Ying Sing & Co., tea, sugar, rice, oil and dried fish, 726 Sacramento
Yin Song Tong, drugs, 741 Commercial
Yit Chong & Charley, laundry, 624 Minna
Yong Wo Tong Kong Kee & Co., tea, sugar, rice, oil, etc., 725 Dupont
Yop Sing, laundry, 769 Mission

Yot Long, laundry, SW cor Montgomery av and Jackson
Yot Loy, laundry, 502 Hyde
You Hop & Co., wholesale tea, rice, sugar and opium, 825 Sacramento
You Kee, carpenter, 718 Clay
You Kee, merchant tailor, 919 Dupont
You Long, clothing, 621 Jackson
Yout Sien, laundry, 522 Green
Young & Co., cigar manufacturers, and clothing, 707 Dupont
Yu Wo & Co., wholesale tea, sugar, rice, oil and clothing, 717 Dupont

Yu Yuen Ching Kee & Co., tea, sugar, rice, etc., 730 Sacramento
Yue Wo, laundry, 47 Minna
Yuen Hang, groceries, 624 Jackson
Yuen Tsun, physician, 606 California
Yuen Wo & Co., groceries, 1001 Dupont
Yune Foong, restaurant, 710 Jackson
Yune Yune, laundry, 715 Lombard
Yung Gee, boarding and intelligence office, 825 Clay
Yung Thung, laundry, 811 Dupont
Yut Loy, barber, NW cor Sacramento and Dupont

CLASSIFIED
CHINESE BUSINESS DIRECTORY.

Asylums.
Kong Choy, 512 Pine

Bakers and Confectioners.
Choy Far Lung, 20 Ross
Man Tong & Co, 631 Jackson
Quong Sang Lung, 733 Washington

Barbers.
Ah Sam, 745 Sacramento
Ah Wea, 637 Jackson
Gee Wo, 620 Jackson
Hung Fat, 729, Sacramento
Sen Kee, 642 Jackson
Tong Wo, 736 Jackson
Tang Yet, 745 Sacramento
Wing Wa, 707½ Jackson
Wing Yik, 812 Dupont
Yut Loy, NW cor Sac and Dupont

Broker—Merchandise,
See Lee, 620 Jackson

Brokers—Money.
Li Wing Sun Kee, 636 Jackson
Ly Wing, 636 Jockson

Butchers.
Hee Wau, 735 Commercial
Hop Sang, 733 Sacramento
Hung Shang, 731 Sacramento
Hung Son, 731 Sacramento
Kwong Wo & Co, 1071 Dupont
Lee Toy, 719 Sacramento
Lun Chong & Co, 745 Sacramento
Man Tang & Co, 631 Jackson
Quong Hing, 711 Sacramento
See Hop & Co, 1009 Dupont
Shay Woo, 720 Jackson
Sung Sing Kee, 733 Sacramento
Why Chong, 615 Dupont

Carpenters.
Chee —, 809 Washington
Quong Woon, 708 Dupont
Sing Shong, 734 Jackson
Wa Kee, 752 Washington
Win Hy, 618 Dupont
You Kee, 718 Clay

Carvers and Engravers.
Hon Mon, 805 Dupont
Me Wa Chong, 753 Clay
Oy Kee, 916 Dupont
Sam Yik, 805 Dupont
Sing Chin, 708 Dupont
Sing Chung, 734 Jackson

Cheese Manufacturers.
Wo Sang & Co, 708½ Dupont

Cigar Manufacturers.
Ah Chinn, 811 Market
Ah King, 530 Sacramento
Ah Quing, 309 Battery
Alaska Cigar Co, 29, 31 Pacific
Arago & Co, 767 Clay
Aurora Co, 206 Dupont
BING YOU, 308 and 425 Commerc'l
Buena & Co, 723 Sacramento
Callao Co, 609 Dupont
Carolina Co, 617 Commercial
Cascade Co, 223 Dupont
Cerro Gordo Co, 115 Jackson
Cheap John, 530 Sacramento
City Cigar Co, 610 Montgomery
Colmo & Co, 607 Dupont
Colombo Co, 715 Dupont
Cuba Cigar Co, 25 Dupont
Decoto Co, 524 Commercial
Don Carlos Co, 808 Sacramento
Estella Co, 229 Pacific
Eureka Co, 1112 Dupont
Fat Young, 441 Bush
Fang Chung Lung, 537 Commercial
Florence Co, 115 Oregon
Get Lee, 48 Sacramento
Hasling & Co, 734 Commercial
Hing Chong, 504 Clay
Hop Yuen & Co, 734 Commercial
Isabella Co, 760 Clay
Isabella Factory, 642 Pacific
Laconia Co, 1016 Dupont
La Espanola Co, 308, and 425 Comcl
Lee Fook, 406 Battery
Lin Wood, 205 Pacific
Lisle & Co, 824 Clay
Lotus Co, 620 Pacific
Lung Yik & Co, 425 Commercial
Milo Co, 744 Washington
National Co, 823 Sacramento

Neblina Co, 525 Sansome
Pacific Co, 537 Commercial
Palmer Co, 646½ Pacific
Partagos A & Co, 730 Jackson
Pioneer Cigar Co, 24 Dupont
Quong Chune, 152 Steuart
Quong Lee, 729 Pacific
Racine Co, 1106 Dupont
Ramirez & Co, 425 Commercial
Rolema Co, 614½ Jackson
Sallie Hart Co, 653 Pacific
Sam Sing, 631 Pacific
Sheridan Co, 413 Davis
Soon Sing John & Co, 716 Pacific
St Lucie Co, 639 Commercial
St Louis Co, 520 Clay
Tong Sing & Co, 807½ Washington
Tong Tuck, 837 Dupont
Union Co, 17 Dupont
Wood & Co, 614½ Jackson
Woodland Co, 1320 Stockton
Young & Co, 707 Dupont

Clothing Manufacturers.
Choy Che Ong, 726 Dupont
Decoto Co, 524 Commercial
Fung Ty, 712 Dupont
Hing Chung, 920 Dupont
Hing Yang, 900 Dupont
Ho Tuen & Co, 909 Dupont
Hop Lung, 921 Dupont
Hop Shing & Co, 627 Pacific
Kum Kee & Co, 912 Dupont
Kwong Lee, 828 Dupont
Kwong Lune, 1013 Dupont
Kwong Sam Kee & Co, 1003 Dupont
Lun Cheong Yuen, 1014 Dupont
Lun Ty & Co, 716 Dupont
Quong Chung Yee & Co, 761 Clay
Quong Wo Chong & Co, 904 Dupont
Sam Yik, 747 Sacramento
See Lee, 814 Dupont
Shee Lee, 816 Dupont
Sin Quoug Lun & Co, 813 Dupont
Sing Leo & Co, 814 Clay
Sing Mow, 902 Dupont
Sun Chong & Co, 747 Sacramento
Sun Kam Wah, 714 Dupont
Sun Quong Lung, 813 Dupont
Tong Ying Chung, 717 Jackson
Tuck Hop, 614 Dupont
Yet Kee, 906 Dupont
You Long, 621 Jackson

Drugs and Medicines.
Chang Wing Tuck Kee, 704 Dupont
Chong Fook, 615 Jackson
Fook Chang Hong, 744 Sacramento
Gee Tau Hong & Co, 740 Commerc'l
He Sang Tong, 650 Jackson
Hung Wo Tong, 611 Jackson
Kee Sang Tong, 742 Sacramento
Kim Lung & Co, 728 Dupont
Kum Wo & Co, 928 Dupont
Kwong Lung Chong & Co, 714 Dpnt
Kwong Fook Tong, 1017 Dupont
Kwong Waa Tong, 801 Dupont
Man On Tong, 945 Dupont
Munto Tong, 617 Jackson
Oy Wo Tong & Co, 708 Jackson
Tie Sang Tong, 929 Dupont
Tin Wo Tong & Co, 622 Jackson
Took Wo Tong, 803 Dupont
Wing Yu Tong, 715 Jackson
Yan Wo Tong & Co, 705 Jr. son
Yin Song Ton, 744 Commercial
Young Wo Tong Kong Kee & Co, 725 Dupont

Dry Goods.
Ching Tin, 908 Dupont
Kum Kee & Co, 912 Dupont
Kum Wo & Co, 928 Dupont
Kwong Mow War & Co, 727 Jackson
KWONG WING SANG & CO, 750, 752 Washington
Qung Hain Chung, 716 Dupont
Quong Lung, 813½ Dupont
Quong Wah Ying, 440 Dupont
Quong Wo Chong & Co, 904 Dupont
Tong Chong Loong, 14 Brenham pl
Yee Chung Weng & Co, 818 Dupont
Yee Chy Lung & Co, 810 Dupont

Employment Offices.
Ki Wo, 614 Jackson
Kum Kee, 711 Sacramento
On Sing, 624 Jackson
SAM KEE, 511 Bush
Sue Lee, 623 Jackson
Yung Gee, 825 Clay

Groceries and Provisions.
Act Lee, 741 Sacramento
Chang Wa Sang, 943 Dupont
Che Wa, 723 Jackson
Chen Chong & Co, 714 Jackson
Ching Wo, 707 Jackson
Ching Quen, 8 Prospect pl
Col Lo Hacin & Co, 629 Jackson
Coly Ying, 938 Dupont
COSMOPOLITAN SUGAR CO, 427 Sacramento
Do Sar, 721 Jackson
Dye Wo, 725 Jackson
Fook Yuen & Co, 711 Dupont
Foug Yik, 747 Sacramento
Fung Kee, 815 Sacramento
Gee Tuck, 619 Jackson
Gee Wo Sang, 1019 Dupont
Ging Mow, 904 Dupont
Hee Yik & Co, 713 Jackson
Hing Kee & Co, 716 Commercial
Hip Wo & Co, 735 Commercial
Hop Kee & Co, 705 Dupont
Hop Lee & Co, 904 Dupont
Hop Lung, 921 Dupont
Hoy Kee, 910 Dupont
KE YING & CO, 427 Sacramento
Kis Long, 747 Sacramento
Kong Yuen & Co, 728 Commercial
Kum Yuen & Co, 711 Jackson
Kwong Choy Yuen & Co, 29 Sal aly
Kwong Fong Tai & Co, 714 Sac'nto
Kwong Lung Cheng & Co, 714 Dupt
Kwong Ou Cheong, 728 Sacramento
Kwong Sung Tai & Co, 636 Dupont
KWONG WING SANG & CO, 750, 752 Washington

Kwong Yune Sung & Co, 727 Dupnt
Lee Yuen & Co, 741 Sacramento
Lon Wo, 711 Sacramento
Lun Chung, 720 Dupont
Ly Chong, 735 Jackson
Man Chong & Co, 825 Dupont
Man Lee, 700 Dupont
Man Shing & Co, 616 Jackson
Man Wo & Co, 633 Jackson
Mou On & Co, 934 Dupont
Ogey Long, 747 Sacramento
On Tie & Co, 715 Dupont
Qung Chong Long, 740 Sacramento
Qung Hong Ching, 803 Sacramento
Quon Ohn, 1005 Dupont
Quong Chong Yee & Co, 761 Clay
Quong Chung Yee & Co, 761 Clay
Quong Fook Sing & Co, 1013 Dupnt
Quong Hang & Co, 710 Commercial
Quong Hing & Co, 713 Sacramento
Quong Mann Long, 623 Dupont
Quong Sam Lung & Co, 706 Dupont
Quong Son & Co, 751 Sacramento
Quong Wan Lung & Co, 741 Com
Quong Wing Chong & Co, 809 Dupt
Quong Wing Lung & Co, 761 Clay
Quong Wong Lung, 619 Dupont
Quong Yee On & Co, 910 Dupont
Quong Yek Chong & Co, 835 Dupont
Quong Yune Sang & Co, 727 Dupont
Sam Kee, 807 Sacramento
San Lung, 826 Dupont
See Chong, 625 Dupont
See Wo Lung & Co, 621 Dupont
Shang Wa Sang, 943 Dupont
Shee Chong & Co, 709 Jackson
Shu Woo, 707 Jackson
Shung Sing, 617 Jackson
Shun Yik & Co, 723 Dupont
Sin Kwong Lun & Co, 813 Dupont
Sing Chong & Co, 823 Dupont
Sing Kee, 809 Sacramento
Sing Ky, 1013 Dupont
Sing Mee Tong, 822 Dupont
Sing Yik, 722 Dupont
Sue Lee, 623 Jackson
Sue Wo, 720 Jackson
Sun Chong Yuen & Co, 1014 Dupont
Sung Wa, 641 Jackson
Tay Ghong & Co, 20 Wash alley
Tin Hop & Co, 936 Dupont
Tong Tie & Co, 728 Sacramento
Tong Wo & Co, 722 Sacramento
Tong Wo & Co, 727 Sacramento
Tong Yoong & Co, 736 Sacramento
Tuck Chong & Co, 739 Sacramento
Tuck Wo, 635 Jackson
Tung Foo & Co, 729 Sacramento
Ty Loen, 911 Dupont
Wan Yuen & Co, 806 Sacramento
Why Chung, 615 Dupont
Wing Fung & Co, 745 Sacramento
Wing Gin, 811½ Dupont
Wing Hop Long & Co, 737 Sac
Wing Tie Jan & Co, 734 Sacramento
Wing Wo Sang & Co, 750 Sacramto
Wo Kee & Co, 939 Dupont
Wo Lee & Co, 743 Sacramento
Woo Sin Lung, 808 Dupont
Wung Yu, 627 Jackson
Yam Kee, 721 Jackson
Ye Chung, 9 Jackson alley
Yee Chy Lung & Co, 810 Dupont
Yee Shung Tong Kee & Co, 650 Jack
Yee Yune, 822 Clay
Yet Lee, 735½ Sacramento
Yim Sing & Co, 726 Sacramento
Yong Wo Tong Kong Kee & Co, 725 Dupont
Young Wo Tong Kong Kee & Co, 725 Dupont
Yu Yuen Hang Tong & Co, 730 Sac
Yuen Hang, 624 Jackson
Yuen Wo & Co, 1001 Dupont

Hotels.
Lee Fook, 721 Dupont
Tsau Kee, 624 Jackson

Interpreters.
Ah Long, 439 Bush
Kan Lee, 721 Commercial

Japanese and Chinese Fancy Goods.
Chin Lee & Co, 521 Kearny
CHY LUNG & CO, 640 Sacramento [see adv, p 29 A]
Man On Tong, 945 Dupont
Sue Wo, 720 Jackson
Sue Wo, 941 Dupont

Watchmakers and Jewelers
Cheu Fun, 922 Dupont
Chin Chung, 716 Jackson
Chin Chong, 1011 Dupont
Gin Hi & Co, 804 Dupont
Hong Sing, 811 Dupont
Lai Sang & Co, 726 Jackson
Ly Chung, 615 Jackson
Ou Tie & Co, 716½ Dupont
Quong Tuck, 640 Jackson
Soi Chin, 747 Commercial
Tie Yuen, 1008 Dupont
Tin Yuen, 710 Jackson
Wing Chin, 811½ Dupont

Laundries.
Ack Lee, 208 Commercial
Ah Chong, 27 Ellis
Ah Sam, 1513½ Leavenworth
Ah Sang, 34 Washington alley
Ah Soung, 504 Pacific
Ah Wing, 151 Shipley
Ah Yung, Brannan nr Ninth
Bee Woo, 1136 Folsom
Chang Sing, 537 Merchant
Chong Hong, 188 Jessie
Chong Lee, 711½ Folsom
Chong Wong, 282 Stevenson
Chu Lung, 617 Jackson
Chun Lee, 50 Natoma
Chung Kee, cor Drumm and Oregon
Chung Un, 738 Brannan
Chung Wa, 3 Dodge
Chung Wah, 829 Vallejo
Chung Yik, Ellick alley
Clind Ayet, Twelfth nr Market
Cun Yuen, 818 Mission
Din Lu, 924 Howard
E Key, 703 Harrison
Eh Lay, 235 Third
Fang Chong, 44 Natoma
Fat Wau, 777 Folsom
Fong Yet, 756 Bryant
Fook Long, 1223 Mission
Fur Sing, 751 Harrison
Ge Loy, 134 Fifth
Gee Ashon, 709 Front
Gim Gou, 708 Folsom
Gim Lee, 1006 Pacific
Gong Yune Long, 441 Guerrero
Goon Chong, 219 O'Farrell
Guin Chong, 924 Folsom
Guy Long, 818 Greenwich
Hen Lee Lung, 918 Jones
Hey Wau, 124 Seventh
Hi Long, 403 Sutter
High Sing, 950 Mission
Hight Sing, 505 Clay
Hung Ku, 776 Pacific
Hing Lee, 109 First
Hip Sing, 315 Tehama
Hong Fat, 555½ Bryant

Hong Goon Loy, 142 Page
Hong Hen, 630 Broadway
Hong Sang, 917 Washington
Hong Sang, 33 Morton
Hong Sang, 744 Harrison
Hong Sing, 21 Geary
Hong Soon, 1049 Howard
Hong Yone, 803 Sixteenth
Hop Dack, cor Twenty-seventh and San Bruno Road
Hop Kee, 413 Broadway
Hop Lee, 236 Fourth
Hop Lee, 103 Sacramento
Hop Lee, 652 Pacific
Hop Long, 526 Broadway
Hop Moon, Sixteenth nr Valencia
Hop Way, 1055 Market
Hop Wo, 518 Fifth
Hoy Yuen, 520 Clay
Hu Lung, 617 Jackson
Hung Fat, 341 Sixth
Hung Gee, 737 Sacramento
Hung Hine, 208 Minna
Hung Sing, 17½ Dupont
Hung Wing, 514 Hyde
Jim ——, 829 Clay
John Lee, 250 Eighth
John Lee, 403 Brannan
Jim Bruce, 1122 Mission
Jim Lung, 1133 Howard
Jim Wing, 2000 Polk
Kim Wa, 15 Sacramento
Kim Yick, 517 Fourth
Kon Sang, 810 Union
Kong Sing, 637 Post
Kong Wing, 254 Steuart
Kung Sung, 704 Bush
Lang Con, 1103 Clay
Lee Gun, 525 Valencia
Lee Hop, 661 Mission
Lee Sam, cor Seventeenth & Dolores
Lee Sing, 523 Pacific
Lee Ung, 811 Market
Lee Yik, 134 Sacramento
Lin War, 1431 Dupont
Log Gee, 335 Front
Long Won, 986 Folsom
Loon Chong, 926 Pine
Loy Sing, 320 Hayes
Lun Hing, 906 Post
Lun Hop, 471 Minna
Lun Lay, 1321 Mission
Lun Sing, 402½ Fourth
Lun Wah, 320 Green
Lun Chang, 1011 Jackson
Lun Sang, 19 Post
Lung Wan, 120½ Eleventh
Man On Lung, 1114 Dupont
Mun Sing, 22 Clay
Mun Woa, Dunbar alley
On Chong Long, Larkin nr Union
On Lang, SE cor Pacific and Larkin
On Tsoy, Sutter nr Sansome
Oung Lee, 1005 McAllister
Ouong Wo, 302 Sutter
Qui Sung, 1022 Kearny
Quon Gun, 20 Stockton
Quong ——, 1512 Mason
Quong Ling Lung, 722 Vallejo
Quong Sing, 814 Folsom
Quong Wing, 939 Clay
Quong Yik Lee, 455 Stevenson
Qun Fod, 816 Jackson
Qung Shung Lung, 1521 Folsom
Sam ——, 269 Sansome
Sam ——, 621 California
Sam Cheen, 738 Commercial
Sam Gee, 2515 Bush
Sam Hing, 122 Dupont
Sam Kee, Laguna nr Buchanan
Sam Kee, 1318 Dupont
Sam Kee, 15 9 Mission
Sam Lee, 607 Grove

Sam Lee, NE cor Seventeenth and Dolores
Sam Lung, SW cor Clara and Fifth
Sam Lung, 1406 Stockton
Sam Lung, 525 Howard
Sam Nam Lang, 805 Washington
Sam Sing, 1845 Bush
Sam Wo, 529 Stevenson
Sam Wing, 1320 Pine
Sam Lee, 17 Everett
Sam Nam Long, 807 Washington
San Wo Lee, cor Ninth and Brannan
Sang Hong, 106 Jessie
Sang Lung, SW cor Mariposa and Tennessee
Sang Lung, 147 Post
Sein Gung, 711 Union
Shang Lee, 1510 Stockton
Shang Tin, 504 O'Farrell
Shing Yung, 8 Washington
Sin Kee, 906 Larkin
Sin Long One, 1106 Folsom
Sin Ching, 234 Turk
Sing Kee, 904 Pacific
Sing Quong Lung, 233 Jackson
Sing Sang, 45 Sacramento
Sing High, 505 Clay
Sing Wa, 300 O'Farrell
Siong Lee, 1016 Dupont
Skue Lung, 521 Bush
Soi Bun, 32 Steuart
Song Sing, 503 Post
Soon Hung, 764 Clay
Suey Quong 138 Minna
Sui Lung, 660 Harrison
Sung Hung, 761 Clay
Sun Lee, 12 Commercial
Sun Tong Sang, 260 Brannan
Sun Chong, 702 Mission
Ten Hing, 519 Dupont
Tan Lee, S s Filbert nr Mason
Tang Gee, 128 Geary
Tapes Lee, 2 Dodge
Tay Wong, 621 Mission
Ton Lee, 128 Hayes
Tong Chung, 714 Green
Tong Gin, 573 Mission
Tong Lee, 158 Steuart
Tong Wan, 622 Third
Tsun Kee, 607 Sacramento
Tung Hing, 950 Howard
Tuno Thai, 829½ Clay
Ty Loie, 25 Pacific
Ung Lee, 811 Market
Ung Sing, 413 Geary
Ung Wa, 2742 Mission
Ung Wing, 934 Harrison
Waign Hoign, 23½ Geary
Wa Sing, 652 Pacific
Wa Sing, 1339 Pacific
Waa Yek, 349 Third
Wah Ye, 666 Howard
Wah Yee, SW cor Geary and Leavth
Wau Kee, 1125 Sutter
Wau Kee, 803 Howard
We Lee, 308 Minna
Wee Wo, 505 Minna
We Sang, 25 Folsom
Wiu Lung, 95 Austin
Wing Fat, 521 East
Wing Fong, 53 Clementina
Wing Guen, 561 Howard
Wing Hi, 14 Fourth
Wing Hong, 203 Stevenson
Wing Lee, 536 Folsom
Wing Lee, 317 Davis
Wing Lee, 126 Barry
Wing Lee, 282 Minna
Wing Mo Hie, 609 Post
Wing Sing, 1618 Sacramento
Wing Song, 709 Stockton
Wing Tong, 811 Dupont
Wing Yik, 24 Taylor
Wo Hop & Co, 1879 Mission

Wo Sun, 927 Dupont
Wo Yune, S s Francisco nr Mason
Wong Kee, 533 Geary
Wong Po Ling Qua, 24 Mason
Wook Yip, 213 Sixth
Ye Kee, 336 Bush
Ye Wa, 495 Brannan
Ye Wah, 459 Jessie
Yek Hing, 325 Third
Yek Woo, 1211 Pacific
Yet Lung, cor Haight and Gough
Yik Foo, 642 Commercial
Yit Chong & Charley, 624 Minna
Yop Sing, 769 Minna
Yot Long, SW cor Mont av and Jksn
Yot Loy, 502 Hyde
Yout Sien, 522 Green
Yue Wo, 47 Minna
Yune Yune, 715 Lombard
Yung Thung, 811 Dupont

Lodgings.

Ah Loy, 795 Clay
Ah Quing, 37 Waverly pl
Chin Goy Lang, 754 Washington
Fook Hing, Sacramento alley
Fook Yue, 627 Jackson
Fung High, 710 Dupont
Gee Kee, 1001 Dupont
Gimp Chong, 737 Jackson
Hag Kee & Co, 730 Jackson
Kim Lee, 616 Dupont
Quing Wa, 801 Sacramento
Quon Chan Chung, 735 Clay
Quong Hing, 838 Dupont
Shu Lee, 709 Jackson
Sun Ty Cheong, 638 Jackson
Too Long, 749 Clay
Toy Hung Lou, 612 Jackson
Tung Kee, 615 Jackson
Tung Wa, 700 Commercial
Yung Gee, 825 Clay

Merchants.

Chee Lee & Co, 804 Washington
Chy Lung & Co, 640 Sacramento
Fook Wo Tong & Co, 803 Dupont
Ge Wo Lun, 817 Sacramento
Ge Quen & Co, 22 Ross
Ho Tuen & Co, 909 Dupont
Hong Quen, 825½ Dupont
Hong Yune & Co, 731 Commercial
Hung Sang Lung & Co, 805 Dupont
Kin Nam & Co, 1008 Dupont
Kum Kee & Co, 912 Dupont
Kum Wo & Co, 928 Dupont
Kwong Chong kee & Co, 710 Dupont
Kwong Chong Wing & Co, 731 Com
Kwong Harg & Co, 710 Commercial
Kwong Tai Lung & Co, 719 Com
Kwong Wo Lung & Co, 735 Jackson
Lai Hing Lung & Co, 729 Com
Lun Wo & Co, 711 Sacramento
Lun Wo & Co, 716 Sacramento
Lung Sing & Co, 706 Sacramento
Man Loong & Co, 711 Sacramento
Man Wo & Co, 633 Jackson
Man Wo Cheong & Co, 738 Sac
Mou On & Co, 934 Dupont
Ong Wo & Co, 625 Jackson
Quong Chung Sung & Co, 717 Sac
Quong Chung Shing & Co, 724 Com
Quong Fook On & Co, 728 Com
Quong Sing Tai Kee, 717 Com
Quong Gee On & Co, 910 Dupont
Quong Ying Kee, 718 Commercial
Sam Kee, 723 Sacramento
See Wo Lung & Co, 621 Dupont
Shee Kee Co, 810 Sacramento
Shing Yik & Co, 722 Jackson
Sing Wo & Co, 639 Jackson
Sue Wo, 911 Dupont
Sun Chong Wo & Co, 710 Sac
Tai Yuen Cheong & Co, 721 Com
Ti Loey & Co, 911 Dupont

Tie Wing & Co, 737 Washington
Tin Hop & Co, 936 Dupont
Tong Chong & Co, 743 Sacramento
Tsuo Chong Wing, 714 Commercial
Tuck Chong Wo & Co, 627 Dupont
Tuck On Yuen, 727 Sacramento
Tuck Sing Ton & Co, 1021 Dupont
Tuck Wo, 635 Jackson
Tung Chong & Co, 743 Sacramento
Tung Sing & Co, 732 Sacramento
Tung Ye Tong & Co, 710 Dupont
Ty Wing & Co, 737 Washington
Wau Yune Lung Kee, 739 Com
Wing Tong & Co, 745 Sacramento
Wo Kee & Co, 939 Dupont
Yet Lee & Co, 719 Sacramento
You Hop & Co, 825 Sacramento
Yu Wo & Co, 717 Dupont

Opium.

Kwong Yue, 627 Jackson

Painter.

Hon Mon, 805 Dupont

Pawn Brokers.

Kong Wo, 639 Jackson
Ly Wo, 1001 Dupont
Quong Yune At, 1006 Dupont

Photographer.

Lai Yong, 743 Washington

Physicians.

Charley Yon Long, 1017 Dupont
Ho Chuck Hung, 828 Washington
Hog Kee, 730 Jackson
Jay Hon Chung, 743 Washington
Jim ——, 918 Dupont
Lee Ying, 621 Dupont
Lee Yong Fong, 1021 Dupont
LI PO TAI, 737 Washington
Loucitat ——, 14 Brenham pl
Loy Fook Won, 615 Jackson
Lun Toan Ke, 742 Sacramento
Sheang Sai Shong, 705 Jackson
Yuen Tsun, 606 California

Restaurants.

Car Lock Hen, 629 Jackson
Choy Yan Low, SE cor Washington and Jackson alley
Cum Coch In, 17 Jackson
Hang Fer Low & Co, 713 Dupont
Mong Hong Yu, 643 Jackson
Tong Lum, 636 Jackson

We Sin, 808 Dupont
Yee Chin, 650 Jackson
Yoone Foong, 710 Jackson

Shirt Manufacturers.

Lee Man Sing, 832 Washington

Shoe Manufacturers.

Choy Sun & Co, 716 Sacramento
Gun Fet & Chin Kee, 311 Pine
Hong Sing, 752 Clay
Hop Kee & Co, 705 Dupont
Hop Kee & Co, 804 Sacramento
Hop Lung & Co, 738 Jackson
Houg Gee & Co, 823 Clay
Kam Lun & Co, 722 Dupont
Kwong Hing Long, 734 Sacramento
Kowong Hing Long, 534 Sacramento
Lung Tat, 745 Commercial
Pay Kee, 310 Pine
Quong Eat Chong, 407 Commercial
Quong Lung Chung & Co, 419 Com
Sun Fun & Co, 709 Commercial
Tong Sang & Co, 419 Commercial
Toon Fot, 308 Pine
Tung Hop & Co, 832 Washington
Wing Hing Lung & Co, 708 Sac
Wo On Chung & Co, 411 Commercl
Wo Tia & Co, 534 Commercial

Silk Factory.

Su Wah Lung, 534 Commercial

Slipper Manufacturers.

Gung Git, junc Sutter and Market
Hi Loong, 414 Sacramento
Kee Wing Fat On, 501 Jackson
Lee Yeck, 826 Clay
Lun Fat, 745 Commercial
Lun Su Wah, 534 Commercial
Sang Lung & Co, 826 Dupont
Tong San & Co, 216 Sansome
Wa Lung & Chung, 641 Commercial
Wo Lee, 401 Commercial
Wo Sing, 409 Commercial

Tailors.

Ah Sing, 733 Washington
Chip Chong, 737 Jackson
Cun Lung, 727 Pacific
Fong Kee, 815 Sacramento
Foo Lang, 839 Dupont
Goey Hing Kee & Co, 738 Dupont
Hang Lung & Co, 809 Dupont
Him Lung & Co, 930 Dupont
Kam Lun & Co, 722 Dupont

Kim Lung & Co, 728 Dupont
Lin Man, 806 Dupont
Lin Tie & Co, 716 Dupont
Me Nom, 64 Jackson
Me Nom, 67 Jackson
Nam Kee, 825 Dupont
On Wah Long Co, 611 Dupont
O'O'Lang, 839 Dupont
Oy Kee, 916 Dupont
Pau Chong, 1015 Dupont
Quong Lee, 828 Dupont
Shee Chong & Co, 713 Jackson
Sie Kee, 715½ Dupont
Sik Kee, 713 Dupont
Soong Chong & Co, 812 Dupont
Tai Sing & Co, 732 Jackson
Toy Cheong, 726 Dupont
Wa Sing, 735 Jackson
Wah Ying Lung, 824 Dupont
Wo Shing 736 Jackson
Wung Wa Ying, 940 Dupont
You Kee, 919 Dupont

Theatres.

New Theatre, Sing Ping Yuen, 623½ Jackson
Royal Theatre, Yu Henn Choy, 626 Jackson

Tinsmiths.

Hep Yuen, 915 Dupont
Hing Kee & Co, 716 Commercial
Sang Yune & Co, 819 Dupont
Sing Yuen, 1018 Dupont
Song Yuen, 819 Dupont
Wo Yuen, 1018 Dupont
Yet Kee, 913 Dupont

Umbrellas and Fans.

Con Lee, 756 Clay
Foo Hing & Co, 746 Washington

Varieties.

Ah Low, Jackson alley
Cho Wa, 723 Jackson
Chong Kee, 704 Pacific
Keng Wha, 711½ Jackson
Seu Lung, 718 Jackson
Shew Wa, 711 Jackson
Sun Chin, 709 Jackson
Yee Chung, 709 Jackson

Wood and Lumber.

On Sing, 640 Pacific
Wing Hop & Co, 732 Jackson
Wing Lee, Brooklyn pl

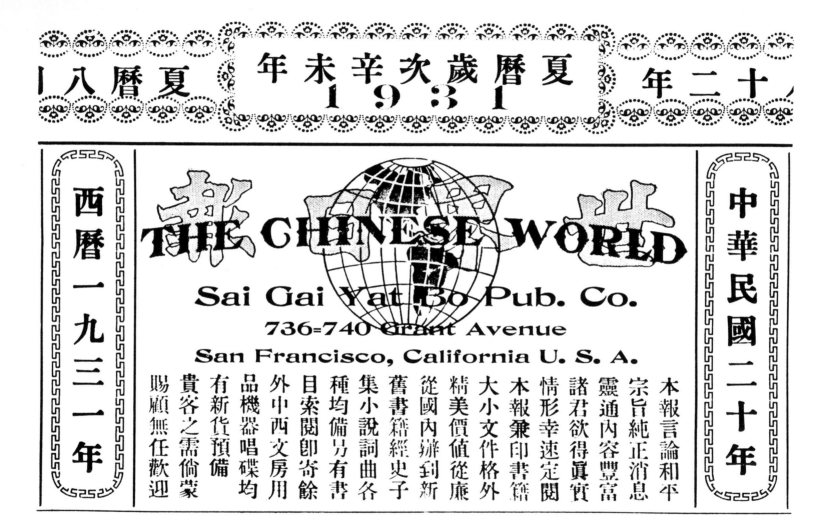

金山正埠 San Francisco, Cal.

都板街 Grant Avenue

Business	Number
City of Hankow Co.	405
Suey Chung	415
Duklap Co.	444
New Shanghai	453
Shanghai Low	532
Chang On Co.	564
Grand View Hotel	605
Tiu Yuen Woey	613½
Sang Chong Lung	616
Sam Sing Tong	617
Yuen Tung Low	635
Postal Telegraph	669
Chew Jan	700
Fookwah	701-705
Kwong Shing Lung	702
Republic Drug Co.	704
Republic Hotel	706
Tin Wo	716
Jing Chong	717
Hop Wo Lung	718
Hang Far Low	723-25
Quong Yuen Hing	727
Lai Jan Co.	729
Mow Lee	730
Him Yick Lung	733
THE CHINESE WORLD	736
Chun Fook	741
Sun Tai Chong	742
Tai Ping Young	744
Suey Don Tong	745
Tung Fong Lo	747
Kwong Hong Fat Co.	751
Wing Wah Sing	754
Chan Ning Tong	755
Yick Sue Tong	756
Tie Yick	757
Shing Chong	800
Yee & Co.	801
S. T. Lok	803
Choy Jee Tong	804
Loy On & Co.	805
Yan Nin Tong	807
Western Co.	808
Lun Chong & Co.	815
Wing Hop & Co.	819
Yee Chong Lung	824
Wing On	826
Tin Suie Tong	827
Yick Sang Tong	829
Service Supply Co.	831
Shew Hing Lung	832
Sam Yup Assn.	835
Yet Wah Lung Co.	837
Shun On & Co.	839
Dan Sang Tong	842
W. Young	843
Doap Leun Hong	844
Kung Yick Wing	845
Ti Hang Lung	846
Quong Lee & Co.	848
Shun Yuen Hing	849
Shiu Tai & Co.	852
Mow Wo & Co.	853
Wing Chin Co	857
May Sang	860
Suey Lee	864
Sang Wo & Co.	867
Wing Lee Co.	900
Fook Sang Tong	901
Fat Ming	903
Chew Chong Tai	905
Shing Shun & Co.	909
Tai Quong Co.	910
Wing Hing Chong	911
Lee Ass'n	913
Wong Nam Kee	914
Bow Tsee Tong	915
M. Theatre Office	915A
Hong Yan Tong	916
Wing Mow Co	917
Ginn Wall	919
Man Fung Wo	921
Foo Kee Co.	922
Long Kong Assn.	924
Suey Sing Tong	925
Him Sang Chong	928
Chong Jan & Co.	930
Son Loy & Co.	932
Chung Hing Hotel	933
Bank of America	939
Fook Wo Tong	940
Kwong Yick	941
Golden Gate Hotel	942
Van Wo Assn.	945
Farley & Co.	946
Tin Bow Tong	947
Quong Lun & Co	950
Wo Kee & Co.	951
Ching Loy Co.	952
Sue Wo & Co.	953
Kwong Chong Sing	955
Lai Hing & Co	956
Fong Tai & Co	957
Wah Sun	962
Fung Chong	1001
Tin Yuen & Co	1005
Quong Fat	1009
Chun Wo Tong	1012
Kung Yuen & Co.	1013
Yuen Hing	1016
Wing Sun Lung	1019
M. Theatre	1025a
Hong Sang	1026
Chung Wah	1029
Wah Ting	1030
Yee Sang Yuen	1033
Wo Yuen	1037
San Hing	1040
San Lung & Co.	1050
Quan Hing	1051
Lee Yuen	1066
Bow Sang	1067
Wo Lung Co	1103
Hee Tai Wo & Co	1105
Pekin Rest.	1111½
Nam Lung Co	1123
Kwong Fat	1129
Sai Woo Hotel	1133
Kwong Lung	1142

唐人街 Sacramento St.

Business	Number
White & White	
Shee Jun Co.	660
D. Woo	704
Wing Shoy Wo & Co.	708
Suey Fung Yuen	709
Chung Sai Yat Bo	716
Asia Com. Co.	722
Mer Chin	727
Lincoln Clam & Co.	728-34
Tong Chun Gauk	729
Chin Cham Com.	730
Quong On Lung Co	736
Yeong Wo Assn.	750
Jay On Tong	755
Kwock Man	760
Nam Kue School	761
Sing Kee Co.	762
Kwong Lee Chong	766
Lun On	771
Kun Wo Chong	759
Quong Ham Wo Co.	775
Sun Yuen Hing	776
Shang Git	781
Kuo Min Yat Po	809
Hong On Wo Co.	823

企李街 Clay Street

Business	Number
Man Chong Yuen	
Ng Gee Co.	663
John Chong	715
Nam On Chong	719
Num Ping Assn	721
Soy Sang Lung	725
Wing Chong & Co	733
Kwong On & Co	735
Qung Sang Lung	737
Wing Fat Chong	745
On Yick Tong	747
Sun Sun Co	753
Sun Quong Wing	771
Hip Sing Tong	761
Young Yuen Tong	766
Wah Chong	770
Mee Lee	775
Sue Yuen Tong	805
Bow On Tong	808
Chin Kee	813
Joseph Tape & Co.	814
C Wing Chen Co	815
Tom Family	817
Ngs Family	824
Tong Hing	824
Foo Wing Co	825
Yut Tun Hotel	841
Kay Sang Co.	843
Quong Yuen Shing	846
Sai Fook Tong	847
Kee Yee	847
Nom Sang Long	851
Lew G. K. S.	854
New China Hotel	857
San San Guy	858
Tai Sun Co	865
Mon Hing Hotel	868
The Young China	881

花園角 Brenham Place

Business	Number
Suey Ying Tong	15
Wing Sang	17

嘩盛頓街 Washington St.

滿 利	Moon Lee	445
壇 豐	King Fong	534
多 利 房	Geo Bros.	642
仁安藥房	Yan On	727
茂廣 祀昌	Mow Fong	733
榮瑞 受杏	Quong Kee Jan	736
新話簡 隆香	Tsue Chong Wing	737
德 公司	Suey Hai Lung & Co.	742
悅 興	Sun Hang Hong	744
美三 生	Pac. Tel. & Tel. Co.	743
廣 安	Tuck Hing & Co.	746
永 和	Yut Sing Co.	754
見孔 隆	May On	812
麗如 郡	Sam Wo	813
奇 會	Quong Yee Lung Co.	815
和 陳	Wing Hong Sing	816
仁 珍	Shun Hop Kin Kee	818
大 奇	Confucial Society	820
胡 生	Lai Wah Lung	824
篤 和	Yee Jun	834
福 堂	K. K. Rest	835
逢 公	Wo Sang	836
大 所	Yen Wo Co.	837
余 降	Tai Sang Tong	838
裕 閣	Woo Family Soc.	840
公 來	Oak Chun Tong	840
同 豐	Fook Lung Co.	845
泗 公	Fung Loy Restaurant	848
永 所	Tie Fung Wo & Co.	857
聚 牛	Yee G. K. S.	858
諒 論	Yee Sang Tong & Co.	864
廣 美	Kung Lun Bo	867
尊 理	Kwong Mee Hing	870
勝 髮	Tong Lee Barber S.	872
合 生	Su Wa Sang & Co.	872
	Wing Tai Lung	873
	Gai On	876
	Leong Kee	879
	Quong Yick Wo	886
	Po Wuh Co.	898
	Sing Hop	903

裕尾慎街 Commercial St.

均 源	Quon Yuen	658
陳天 一	TIN YUT	690
廣 生	Quong Sang	708
廣祥 隆	K. Chung Lung	741
廣昌 和	Kwong Chong Wo	764
四邑客商	Chinese Com'l Co.	769
台山公司	HOY SUN CO	774
寧臨公會	NING KAU	778

昃慎街 Jackson St.

	HIGH LOY	134
	Quong Tai	436
泰密鉅大生興行成醉薄生蘭醉成會至梁不大同廣天天瑞均麗天貞德茶利貞和愛泰泰聯義所伯揚公司新同僑棧	Guey Lung	622
來泰隆華源發堂祀園際庄亭樓發居聖天館新珍生隆生福祥隆香司堂生源影所和英	Tai Jung Wah	630
	Sang Yuen	641
中安春華月	Hing Fat	655
	Hong On Tong	657
	SING KEE	661
來德別	Joy Chan Yuen	662
忠芳	Po Wah Lung	665
	Shanghai	672
夜	Lun Hing	670
	Joy Yet Low	675
	Shing Fat	677
	Woey Loy Guey	699
	Gee Tuck	701
	Lang Jung H T	703
	Moonlight Inn	704
	Tai Shing Hotel	706
	H. W. Sun	707
	Quong Chun	708
	Tin Sang	714
	Tin Sing	716
	Suey Sang	710
	Quan Lung	720
	Lai Sang & Co	724
	Tin Fook & Co	727
	Ching Chung	728
	Tuck Long	731
	Char Hong	732
	Lee Jing	733
	Oy Wo Tong	734
	Tie Sang & Co	737
	Tai Yuen	740
	Tai Chong & Co	743
	Lun Yee	750
	Bok Young Co.	751
	Sun Tong Wo	765
	Kiu Ying Mak	838

天后廟街 Waverly Place

裕大公司裕安堂記根東黃寧永甜錦悅寶	Yee Tai Co.	28
大安堂記公云陽會豐溪昌隆事	Yee On Tong	16
	Kin Kee	3.
	Bing Kong Tong	35
	Wong Wun Sun	39
	Ning Yung Assn.	41
	Wing Fung	45
	Heam Kay	48
	Kam Fung	51
	Yut Lung	52
	Bow Wah & Co.	56

天后廟街 Waverly Place

祥 利	Chong Lee & Co.	57
同 義和	Tong Ye Wo	101
朱家公所	Gee Family Assn.	105
李麗西堂	Lee Lung Si Tong	109
生 記	Sing Kee	112
金山南報堂	Chinese Times	119
肇慶會館	Tong Hing Assn	124
聯成	Seu Hing Assn.	125
五福堂濟孔	Lin Hop Co.	132
廟廣	Ng Fook Tong	127
余風采堂	Fong Quong Jai	128
合勝堂堂	Yee Fung Toy Assn.	131
至德政黨	Hop Sing Tong	137
惠和	S. K. Building	140
黃江夏堂	Chinese Ref. Party	142
金生	Chinese Peace Soc.	142
瑞芝和	Wong's Ben. Assn.	143
高密公所	Gim Sing	145
同和	Suey Jee Wah	150
中國車房	Ko Met Assn.	154
盛	Tong Wo Hing	155
同昌富源桑源	China Draying Co.	156
	Tong C. Shing	157
	Foo Yuen	159
	Chey Yuen	166

舊呂宋巷 Ross Alley

榮 利	Wing Lee	14
利源押	Lee Yuen Art	24
林家公所	Lums Family	30
趙家公所	Chews Family	35
深光濟	Leong Quong Gai	37
蕭 祿	Sue Luke	53
耀	Yew Kee	61

新呂宋巷 Spofford Alley

海宴公所	Hoy Yin Kong Saw	4
堂 記	Hong Kee	5
岡陵公記	Kong Ling Co.	28
祥 記	Chong Kee	33
致公黨	Chee Kung Tong	36
永和	Wing Wo Chong	43
奇 芳	Kay Fang	48

德和街 Wentworth Place

協義堂	Hip Yee Tong	19
英源發京	Ying Chong	28
南新	Yuen Fat	30
一	Nam King	35
禹山信局	Yut Sun	54
俊英學	Yee Shan Co.	60
	Jing Ying Tong	65

士作頓街 Stockton St.

周梯雲	Chow Hai Won	815
中華會舘	C.Consol.Ben.Ass'n	843
中華學堂	Chinese School	843
遠東旅舘	Oriental Hotel	856
百草堂	Bock Toa Tong	859
利	Lee Chong	860
滇市公司	Oriental Co.	864
中華藥房	China Pharmacy	868
廣隆會舘	Quong Wah Lung Co.	901
合和會舘	Hop Wo Assn.	913
南	Nam Sing	917
利勝	Lee Chong Lung	937
酒和明	See Wo Sang	940
同	Hong On	944½
萬壽谷	Man Sang Yuen	948
牛豐	Man Fong Lung	949
日光公司	Quong Yick Wing Co	952
龍岡公所	Yut Quong	1010
廣怡同	Lung K. K. S.	1034
永肇明	Quong Yee Chong	1036
	Wing Hong Yick	1039
	Chew Ming	1043
同源純舘房	United Par N.S.G.S	1044
乾坤藥奇	Kin Quon Herb Co.	1049
	Kay Chong	1051
膝氏	Dun Chun	1053
中美洋箱	C. & A. Trunk Co.	1076
永源泰	H. William & Co.	1114
共和麵厰	Republic N. F.	1117
亞洲	He Shin Ass'n	1123
漢陽公司	H. Young	1125
永同昌	WING HONG CHONG	1131
廣東礮艇	Canton N. F.	1135
同 堂牛	Tong Sen Assn.	1137
麗民公司	Lai Mun	1140
和 勝	Wo Sing Co.	1143
忠義堂牛	Cheung Yu Tong	1150
源	Yuen Sing & Co.	1197
上海洋箱	Shanghai Co.	1210
廣利	K. L. Yuen	1222

怕思域街 Pacific St.

新華	Sun Wah Yuen	631
廣福生	Quong Fook Sang	758
瑞生昌	Suey Sang Chong	767

孟甘街 Montgomery St.

鶯咕銀行	Anglo Cal. Bank	
中華領事	Chinese Consul	617
廣東銀行	Bank of Canton	555

APPENDIX E: 1988 Business Directory

BROADWAY

843	(No name)	Sewing factory
835	Tam's Beauty House	Beauty salon
831	On Lok	Senior health center
807	Broadway Laundromatic	Laundry
801–03	Poon Lung	To-go food/restaurant
799	Benny Yee and Associates	Real estate
787	Golden Key Restaurant	Restaurant
785	Wing Wah Restaurant	Restaurant
781	Chinese Mercantile Co.	General merchandise
750	Ping Yuen	Housing project
715	Silver Star Sports Square	Sportswear
711	Chi Shing Co.	Clothing
691	James Lee Realtor	Realty
683	Mon Kiang Restaurant	Restaurant (Hakka)
677	AKO Store Branch	Grocery
675	Fortune Restaurant	Restaurant (Chiu Chow)
671	VIP Coffee & Cake Shop	Restaurant
	Royal Pacific Motor Inn	Motor inn
641	Metro Food Co.	Grocery
631	Sweet Fragrance Cafe	Bakery
621	Oriental Arts Co.	Art
619	Mai Ling Trading Co., Inc.	Grocery
617	K & P Co.	Clothing
615	Sam Wong Hotel	Hotel
611	Columbus Italian Food	Restaurant
607	Lee Poy, Watches & Repair	Watches
601	Gifts Bazaar	Bazaar

PACIFIC AVENUE

620	Pacific Avenue Market	Food, produce
628	(No name)	Produce store
638	Cam Ky Restaurant	Restaurant
642	New China Bookstore	Chinese books
648	(No name)	Restaurant, bakery
714A	Sing Sang Jewelry	Jewelry
718	Wing On Trading Inc.	Chinese herbs
720	D.I.M. Fashions	Clothing
728	Miriwa Center	Shopping mall
750	Lop Keung Trading Co., Inc.	Chinese grocery
758	Capitol Kim Tar Restaurant	Restaurant
772	New Asia Restaurant	Restaurant

PACIFIC AVENUE

774	Lee Home Furnishings	Furniture
	Pacific Wearhouse Sales	Toys, gifts
808	Tong Fong Restaurant	Restaurant
822–56	Ping Yuen North	Housing project
874	New Hong Kong Noodle Co., Inc.	Noodles
914	Chow's Co.	Wholesale
918	Wong Chong Kee Jewelry	Jewelry
942	Mayanne Beauty Salon	Beauty salon
948	San Francisco Senior Escort Office	Outreach program
945	Ben L. Yep Furs	Furs
923	(No name)	Sewing factory
917	Kwong's Barber & Beauty Shop	Barber
917A	Burma Overseas Friendship Office	Association
895	Ping Yuen West	Housing project
835	Hong Kong Tea House	Restaurant
831	Chinese Books and Arts	Chinese books, arts
829	Cal Trade International	
	C & Y Construction Co.	
	Imperial United Enterprises, Inc.	
	Ott Wong Investment, Inc.	
	Western Electronics Co.	
827	Pacific Postal Box	
	BTO Bottling & Distributing Co. Inc.	
	Phillip Advertising Service	
825	Taj of India	Restaurant
821A	Anita Hair Design	Beauty salon
821	Wah Fat Fish Market	Fish market
795–99	Ping Yuen Central	Housing project
655	Ping Yuen East	Housing project
609	New City Hardware Store	Hardware

JACKSON STREET

907	Mee Mee Beauty Salon	Beauty salon
899	California Petite	Clothing
865	Cumberland Presbyterian Chinese Church	
845	Chinese Hospital	Hospital
835	Chinese Hospital Medical Offices	Medical office building
823	Chinatown Medical Pharmacy	Pharmacy
803	James Watch Shop	Watch repair
777	Dick Lee Pastry	Bakery
765	Garden Bakery	Bakery
761	Feng Huang Pastry Shop	Bakery
759	Great China Trading Co.	Import/export
755–57	Chinese Herbs Co.	Herbs

JACKSON STREET

753	Wing Hong Ning Trading Co.	Import/export
751	New Hoa Thai Trading Co.	Import/export
749	Gold Fortune Jewelry	Jewelry
743	Tin Fook Jewelry	Jewelry
741	Frank's Trading Co.	Arts, crafts
737	Lai Wah Flowers	Arts, crafts
735	Ocean Garden Restaurant	Restaurant
731	Royal Jade House	Jewelry
727	Yu Yee Jewelry Co.	Jewelry
707–09	(No name)	Jewelry, records
699	New Woey Loy Goey Restaurant	Restaurant
675	Tao Tao Restaurant	Restaurant
667	Golden Flower Vietnamese	Restaurant
665	Soon Kee Chung	Import/export
661	I–Chong Art Gallery	Art gallery
657	Hang On Benevolent Assn.	Association
655	Sam Lok Restaurant	Restaurant
649	Great Eastern Restaurant	Restaurant
647	Fah Yuen Chong Sen Assn.	Benevolent association
641	Ocean Sky Restaurant	Restaurant
631	Mei Wo Florist	Florist
627	Universal Photographic	Photographers
617	Tsung Tsin Benevolent Assn.	Association
615	Wah Do Restaurant	Restaurant
609	Mon Lee Laundry	Laundry
607	Lin Trading Co.	Import/export
	Lin Tours	Tours/travel
605	Star Lunch	Restaurant
601	Supreme Electric	Electronics
606	Chung King Restaurant	Restaurant
608	Tung Hwa Assn.., Inc.	Association
614	Ti Sun Hardware	Hardware
622	Hunan Home's Restaurant	Restaurant
626	Heng Loong Foreign Exchange	Foreign exchange
636	Great Star Theater	Chinese movies
648	Shew Kee Grocery	Grocery
650	Ping Yuen Bakery	Bakery
662–64	New Maxim's Bakery No. 2	Bakery
670	New Lun Ting Cafe	Restaurant
672	Red's Place	Cocktails/bar
710	Bow Hing Jewelry	Jewelry
714	Sun Light Tradings	Import/export
716	Royal Jewelry Co.	Jewelry
720	Wo Chong Co.	Produce/bean sprout mfg.

JACKSON STREET

724	Ng Hing Kee Co.	Chinese books
728	Hoa An Jewelry	Jewelry
732	Yong Kee Meat Co.	Food
734	Shew Wo Meat Co.	Meat market
740	Tai Yuen & Co.	Import/export
750	H.K. Allan Hair Treatment	Design & beauty salon
752	Jay's Chee Kay	Bakery
756	Chinatown Theatre	Chinese theatre
768	Min Hing Co.	(not known)
772	Kong Chong Wing	(not known)
776	(For lease)	
780	Man Lai Boutique	Boutique
	Vicki Tam Translation & Office	Editing Services
784	Tai Sung Jewelry	Jewelry
788	Tai Wing Trading Co.	Import/export
818	Medical-Dental Building	Offices
830	J. C. Market	Meat market, produce
834–38	Hang Seng Meat Market	Meat market
844	Four Seasons Produce Co.	Produce
848	Sun Chong Co.	Produce
864	Lotus Beauty Salon	Beauty salon
868	Yau Hing Co.	Chinese herbs
870	Kai Mee, Leather Tailor	Tailor
872	Mandarin Jewelry	Jewelry
890	Medical-Dental Building	Offices
	Jackson-Powell Pharmacy	Pharmacy
	(No stores on 900 block)	

WASHINGTON STREET

981	Chinese Independent Baptist Church	Church
	Commodore Stockton School	Elementary School
903	American Pacific Trading Co.	Meat, food
899	Mandarin Tower Arcade	Shopping mall
895	Mandarin Pharmacy	Pharmacy
869	Lucky Jewelry Co.	Jewelry
867	Leung Wah Sang Jewelers	Jewelry
863	Tong Hing Pastry	Bakery
857	Great China Art Co.	Art, gifts, herbs
851	Tien Vang Kim Do Jewelry Co	Jewelry
849	Tin Cheung Co.	Herbs, import/export
845	Sang Sang Jewelry Co.	Jewelry
839	Superior Trading Co.	Import/export
835	M&B Associates	Offices

WASHINGTON STREET

833	Golden Dragon Restaurant (take-out)	Restaurant, meat market
819	Red Dragon Cocktails	Restaurant, bar
815	(To lease: formerly Great Wall Restaurant)	
813	Sam Wo Restaurant	Restaurant
743	Bank of Canton	Bank
739	All Seasons Hibachi Restaurant	Restaurant
737	Silver Restaurant	Restaurant, meat market
733	Mow Fung Co.,Inc.	Wholesale produce
729	Che Sun Tong Co.	Herbs, ginseng
727	Hi-Q Photo	Photo developing
	PORTSMOUTH SQUARE	Park
720	Buddha's Universal Church	Church
728	Golden Phoenix Restaurant	Restaurant
732	Henry's Sportswear	Clothing
	Public Parking	Parking
736	Golden Sun Tours	Tours
738	Vincent M. Chinn, CPA	Accountant
	Arthur B. Chinn, PA	Accountant
740	Nam Yuen Restaurant (For lease)	Restaurant
744	Sun Hung Heung Restaurant	Restaurant
746	Hanson Fong Photography	(Since 1988 - Photo Studio)
750	Kow Kong Benevolent Assn.	Association
754	Louie Bros. Book Store	Chinese books
802	(No name)	Art, Chinese magazines
812	Mee On Co.	Grocery
816	Golden Dragon Restaurant	Restaurant
824	Hip Sen Benevolent Assn.	Association
826	King Tin Restaurant	Restaurant, meat market
834	Kam Lok Restaurant	Restaurant
836	Chan Ning Tong Co.	Herbs, delicatessen
838	Chinese Center Employment Agency	Employment agency
848	Sun Wah Kue	Restaurant, bakery
852	Foo Wah Cheung Jewelry Co.	Jewelry
854	Mr. Martin Restaurant	Restaurant
860	Paul's Jewelry Co.	Jewelry
864	Chat Hai Co.	Jade jewelry
870–72	Tong Kee Restaurant	Restaurant
859	Tai Fung Wo Bargain Market	General merchandise
878	Regal Jewelry	Jewelry
894	Yun Kee	Toys, candy, etc.
920	Chinese Methodist Church	Church
940	Gum Moon Women's Residence	Women's residence
	Community services: Oriental Home and School	
	of the W.H.M.S. of the Methodist Church	

WASHINGTON STREET

940	Asian Women's Resource Center	
949	Commodore Stockton School Annex	School
990	Jupie Multique	Clothing
1080B	Leanna Hair Design	Beauty salon

CLAY STREET

979–65	YWCA	Association
929	Clay Medical Center	Medical offices
919	Medical offices	
881	The Celadon	Restaurant
857	(Remodeling)	
855	Van's Fashions	Clothing
	Linda's Hair Salon	Beauty salon
853	Hong Kong Monica Hair Design	Beauty salon
851	Hong Kong Co.	Import/export
843	Rever Hair Styling	Beauty salon
839	Capital Restaurant	Restaurant
835	Offices	
825	Gin Hing Co.	Jewelry
819	Sun Ya Restaurant	Restaurant
817	Tom Family Assn.	Association
815	Chin Family Assn.	Association
813	Dick Chin Realtors	Realty
811	Kum Tai Jewelry Co.	Jewelry
805	Medical offices	
783	Art's Trading Co.	Grocery
779	King of B.B.Q.	Restaurant
775	Chuck Lee's Produce	Produce
761	Hip Sing Assn.	Association
759	Golden City Market	Meat market
757–61	Hip Wah Hing Assn.	Association
753	GP Bridal Co.	Bridal clothing
751	Offices	Realty, insurance, business counselor
749	Canited Video	Chinese videos
749A	Chinese Newcomer Health Assn.	Offices
747	Chin Family Assn.	Association
745	Wong, Yan, & Associates	Insurance, accounting
745A	Man Chi Records	Chinese records
735	Dragon Plaza, Inc.	Clothing, gifts
733	Pacific Printing Co. Inc.	Printing, books
729	Pacific Rubber Stamps & Signs	Signs
727	Wah Ying Club	Social club
723–25	Ho Tai Printing, Bookstore & Art Goods Co.	Printing, books

CLAY STREET

719	Victor's T.V.	Electronic goods
715	Superior Bakery	Bakery
709	Sun Chi Book Store	Chinese books
	PORTSMOUTH SQUARE	Park
760	Hy Lo Ry Restaurant	Restaurant
762	Sun House	Clothing
764B	Gong Sun Shoe Repair	Shoe repair
764	Jewelry Arts	Jewelry
766	(No name)	Clothing
768	(No name)	Clothing, gifts
800	King Wah Co.	Magazines, newspapers
806	Sun Yue Kuen (?) Assn.	Association
	Louie Fong Kwong Assn.	Association
810	Hong Chun Co.	Chinese dresses
818	Great China, Inc.	
	Acupuncture Clinic	Acupuncture
	Pacific Travel Service	Travel
	Mee Chong Realty	Realty
	Lemuel Jen, Real Estate Broker	Realty
820	Wei-Ping Wu Acupuncture	Acupuncture
	Ze-Xian Wu Chinese Medicine	Chinese medicine
822	(For lease)	
824	May's Fashions	Clothing
840	Golden Star Travel Service	Travel
	Golden Star Co.	Records, television
	Golden Star Printing Co.	Printing
852	Tin Shung Trading Co.	Grocery store
858	Grand Century Enterprise, Inc.	Chinese herbs
860	Bangkok Import and Export, Inc.	Import/export
868	Oscar Hair Design	Beauty salon
912–14	American Chinese Presbyterian Missionary Society offices	
916	China Cultural Printing Co.	Printing
	Pacific Rim Enterprises	Offices
	Commodore Stockton Elementary School	

SACRAMENTO STREET

700	Kitman Chan, C.P.A.	Accounting
706	Hi-Times	Stationery
708	Ky Cleaners & Laundry	Cleaners
716	K. Y. Impression	Clothing
720	Council of State Governments	Offices
722	CT Dental Group	Dentist
728	Chinatown Printing Center	Printing
730	Chinese Chamber of Commerce	Association

SACRAMENTO STREET

732	Chase Development & Trading Co.	Hardware
736	Wing Chong Jewelry Co.	Jewelry
748	Alfred T. Lee, O. D.	Optometrist
750	Gway Sen Assn.	Association
752	Hong Kong Boutique	Clothing
756	Dowd Bros. Real Estate	Realty
758	Starlite Travel Service	Travel
760	Nissan Reishi	Chinese videos
766	Hoi's Art Wholesaler	Art, framing
770	China's Antique Arts Wholesale	Import/export
776	A Nice Fair	Import/export
800	Gold Mountain Monastery	Monastery
	Dharma Realm Buddhist Assn.	Buddhist association
816	Excelsis Music/Clarion Music Center	Musical instruments
	Chinese Playground	Public playground
872	May's Flower Shop	Florist
874	Don Fung Literary Society	Offices
878	Rainbow Kids Boutique	Children's clothing
920	Cameron House	Chinese Social Center
729	Woo & Co.	Realty, investments
731	Hoy Ping Benevolent Assn.	Association
755	Nam Kue Chinese School	School
767	Happy Times Travel	Travel
771	Lun On Co.	Furniture, antiques
773	Chinese Sportsmen's Club of San Francisco	
775	Ralph & Sons Wholesale	Wholesaler
779	Wei Ping Wu/Chie Mie Chuan Wu	Chinese medicine
781	Victory Realty	Realty
	Victory International Trading Co.	Import/export
809–11	Grant Printing Co.	Printing
819	Jack Look	Contracting
819A	Y.C. Wong Kung Fu Studio	Martial arts
821	China News	Newspaper
823	Caesar's World International	Caesar's Tahoe
825	Sun Hing Printing Co., Inc.	Printing
827	Ming's Hair Design	Beauty salon
829	Overseas Fukienese Assn.	Association
855	YMCA	Association
891	Little House Coffee Shop	Asian/American food
901–13	Geen Mun Neighborhood Center	Cmmunity services

MASON STREET

1200	Wen Hwa Co.	Grocery
1206	Fashion Laundry	Laundromat

MASON STREET

1208	(No name)	Sewing factory
1242	(No name)	Sewing factory
1248	Golden Peacock Beauty Salon	Beauty salon
1250	Junior Co.	Beef jerky mfg.
1256	Standard Grocery	Grocery
1262	(No name)	Flour wholesale
1300	Eastern Bakery	Bakery
1352	(No name)	Sewing factory
1356	(No name)	Sewing factory
1358	Chinese Kitchen	Restaurant
1430	True Sunshine Episcopal Church	Church

POWELL STREET

999	Chuck's Chinese-American Food	Restuarant
1001	(No name)	Laundromat
1003	Industrial Sewing Machine Co.	Sewing machine repair
1003A–05	Mayway Trading Co.	Chinese herbs
1015	William C. Lee, D.D.S.	Dentist
1047	Wah Wai Dry Cleaners	Cleaners
1049	Citi Sin Buddhist & Temple	Taoist association
	Harry Huey & Co.	Accounting
1069	Triangle Investment Co.	Realty
1077	Jung & Jung	Law offices
1099	Cable Car Corner	Groceries
1101	James Laundromat	Laundromat
1117	Paris Beauty Salon	Beauty salon
1123	San Francisco Korean Methodist Church	
1135	Chinatown Branch Library	Public library
1149	Fans Trading Co.	Wholesaler
1165	Richard Lee's Tours	Tours
1201	Seng On Market	Grocery, produce
1213	Cathay (Wah Sang) Mortuary	Mortuary
1241	Hon's Tailor	Chinese dresses
1299	Mobil	Gas station
1301	Welcome Supermarket of California	Grocery, produce
1315	Kam Po (H.K.) Kitchen	Meat market
1321	Hong Kong Biklaikung Beauty Salon	Beauty salon
1321A	Tung Shing Trading Co.	Import/export, herbs
1329F	Pack Cheong Tong	Chinese herbs
1329	Georgia's Beauty Salon	Beauty salon
1362	Hotel Du Midi	Apartments
1350	Golden Key Restaurant & Cocktail Lounge	
1344	Asia Co.	Gifts
1336	United 6 Meat Market	Meat market

POWELL STREET

1326	Chew Chow Restaurant	Restaurant
1300	Mei Chow Trading Co.	Produce
1234	Duck Sin Benevolent Assn.	Association
1232	Kong Ming Co.	Art
1230	Powell Florist	Florist
1224	Irving Enterprises, Inc., Korea Ginseng Center	
1216	(No name)	Sewing factory (?)
1212	(No name)	Sewing factory
1188	Asian V.I.P. Tours	Tours
1140	Gold Hill Garage	Garage
	Automotive Service Center	Garage
1122	Crystal Aquariums	Aquariums, fish
1104	Quong Ming Buddhism & Taoism Society	
1100	Marathon Sport	Clothing
	Maybellein Hair Design	Beauty salon
1038	Venus Unisex Hair Design	Beauty salon
958	Powell Grocery	Grocery
956	Man Lai Beauty Center	Beauty salon
954	Nob Hill Cleaners	Cleaners

STOCKTON STREET

1262	Best Food	Grocery, market
1254	Camtau Jewelry	Jewelry
1252	Dr. Alvin Yee	Optometrist
1250	Wee Wah Co.	Market
1242	(Chinese name)	Meat, dim sum
1230	May Wah Trading Co.	Market
1226	Bank of the Orient	Bank
1222	Junmae Guey Restaurant	Restaurant
1216	Little Saigon Coffee Shop	Coffee shop
1210	Wo Soon Produce Co.	Produce market
1206	Top Quality Meat Co.	Meat market
1120	The Ying Co.	Chinaware
1118	Golden World Enterprise	Market
1108	Canton Tea House & Restaurant	Restaurant
1102	Tai Wing Trading	Bazaar
1100	Photo Focus	Film developing
1076	American Asian Bank	Bank
1074	Chinese Community Cultural Service Center	
1068	ABC Bakery	Bakery
1060	Tune Get Jewelry	Jewelry
1044	CACA Grand Lodge	Association
1040A	Sandy's Restaurant	Restaurant
1038	Gum Sum Jewelry	Jewelry

1032	Tai Chong Co.	Clothing
1028	Golden Star	Shoes, toys
1024	Mandarin Delight	Food, grocery
1018	Tai Sang Co.	Import/export
1016	Tam's Wing Wah Jewelry	Jewelry
1014	Li's Trading	Clothing
1012	Tai Chong Co.	Clothing
1000?	Lee's Boutique	Clothing
1000	Jade Galore Jewelry Co.	Jewelry
946	Mandarin Tower	Apartments
944	Bank of America/Mandarin Towers Branch	
902	St. Mary's Chinese Catholic Center	
844	(Chinese Name)	Chinese school
830	Rainbow Photo	Film developing
824	World Journal	Books
820	Chinatown Real Estate Co.	Realty, insurance
814	Wonkow Food Produce Co.	Grocery
810	Hanayome Beauty & Figure Salon	Beauty salon
806	Hap Yuen Jewelry	Jewelry
802	(Chinese Name)	Import/export
800	Art's Co.	Carpet, flooring
770	Foon P. Chin, M. D.	Doctor
758	Ping's Beauty Salon	Beauty salon
740	S. Lee & Co.	Clothing, shoes, gifts
Bdwy./Stock.	May Wah Market	Grocery, fruit
1261	Hing Lung Co.	Meat market
1251	Lun Sang Market	Meat and fish market
1249	New Maxim's Bakery	Pastry
1247	Kum Yuen Restaurant	Restaurant
1241	Pacific Coast Savings & Loan Assn.	Bank
1239	Chinatown Medical Lab	Laboratory
1235	Suppertime Travel	Travel
	Yick Electric Co.	Electronics
	Royal Electric Inc.	Electronics
1231	Dr. Sonia L. Yick	Optometrist
1215	Sun Fat Market	Meat, grocery
1213	Louie's Produce Co.	Produce
1211	Li's Trading Co.	Clothing
1207	Lee Sang Fish Market	Fish
1205	Sun Sang Market	Meat, grocery, to-go food
1201	Wing Sun Co.	Fruits
1199	Hop Sang Co.	Meat market
	(No name)	Magazine stand
1151	Shew Wo Meat Co.	Meat, pastry

1145	Clothing Market of Chinatown	Clothing
1143	Sun Sang Market	Fish
1135	Canton Market	Fish, meat, to-go food
1131	Lee Yuen Market	Grocery
1129	Tung Sen Benevolent Assn.	Association
1125	New Ping Yuen Bakery & Restaurant	Bakery, restaurant
1123	Hee Shen Assn.	Association
1121	(No name)	Housewares
1117	(Chinese Name)	Grocery, fruit
1115	Silk H. Chan, Real Estate Broker	Realty, insurance
1111	Russell Sit Lew, D.D.S.	Dentist
1107	Sun Duck Market	Poultry, fish, produce
1101	Golden Gate Meat Market	Meat market
1055	Orange Land	Fruits
1053	Wellman's Pharmacy	Pharmacy
1051	Gourmet Chicken	To-go foods
1049	Lee Chong Co.	Grocery
1045	On Ning Tong Co.	Herbs, ginseng
1043	King Seng Market	Grocery
1041	Golden Daisy	Delicatessen, food to-go
	(No name)	Magazine stand
1039	Stockton Street Bakers	Pastry shop
1037	(Chinese Name)	Grocery, vegetables
1035	Chinatown Coalition for Better Housing	
1027	Chat Hoi Jewelry & Goldsmith Co.	Goldsmith
1025–23-21	Flea Market	Clothing
1017	Home Federal Savings & Loan Assn.	Bank
1001	Chinese United Methodist Church	Church
949	Hogan & Vest Real Estate	Realtor, insurance
947	Chung Mee Co.	Chinese antiques, imports
945	Shing Hing Co. #2	Grocery
943	Hopkins Real Estate	Realty
941	May Garden Restaurant	Restaurant (Vietnamese)
937	Hee Chan's Tours	Tours to Reno
935	Fong Bros. Distributor	Wholesaler, milk distributor
929	Little Paris	Coffee shop, pastries
925	Chinese Presbyterian Church	Church
915–17	Kong Fai Trading Co.	Clothing
913	Hop Wo Benevolent Assn.	Association
	John Yehall Chin	Public accountant
905	Kim Chau	Goldsmith
903	Sun Wah Lee Co.	Grocery
901	Jack Jair Realty	Realty
867	United States Post Office	

STOCKTON STREET

855	Kong Chow Benevolent Assn.	Association
855B	American Chinese Acupuncture Clinic	Acupuncture
843	Chinese Parents Committee English School	
	Chinese Six Companies	Association
837	China Import and Export Co.	Import/export
833	Raymond Gee Hair & Beauty Center	Beauty salon, clothing
	Central Chinese High School	Chinese school
815	Kee Photo	Photography
811	Anky Hair Design	Beauty salon
805	Ellison Enterprises, Inc.	Grocery
801	Thing Wan Printing Co.	Printing
777	Chinatown Neighborhood Center	Community Center

GRANT AVENUE

	Old St. Mary's Catholic Church	Church
614	Old St. Mary's Paulist Center	Books
616	Canton Bazaar	Bazaar
626	Canton Building	Attorneys, insurance
656	Mimi Jewelry	Jewelry
658	Lee's & Mei Ling Jewelry	Jewelry
662–70	Gifts Paradise	Gifts
700	Kun Wah Co.	Art, jewelry
702	A Nice Fair	Import/export
704	Republic Pharmacy	Pharmacy
708	Kan's Restaurant	Restaurant
710	Republic Hotel	Hotel
712	World of Pastry	Bakery
716	Hang Fat Co.	Import/export
718	Grant Avenue San Francisco	Gifts
720	Eastern Bakery	Bakery
730	K. S. Co.	Jewelry
734	K. S. Tsien, M. D.	Doctor
736	Chinatown Import/Export	Import/export
738	Asia Society of Arts of America/Asia Art Insitute	Art society
742	Twan Kee Co., Inc.	Jewelry
752	T. S. Trading Co.	Jewelry
754	Long Boat Jewelry	Jewelry
756	Photo Dynamics	Photo developing
800	Gifts & Linen	Import/export
804	The Wok Shop	Cooking utensils
808–10	Tai On	Import/export
814	Lai On Co.	Import/export
826	China Bazaar	Bazaar
832	Jade Empire	Jewelry

GRANT AVENUE

838	Empress of China Restaurant	Restaurant
	China Trade Center	Stores/bazaars
848	Dan Fook Jewelry	Jewelry
850	Bow Hon Restaurant	Restaurant
854	Yee Shew Yan Assn.	Association
	Kang Nam Yue	Acupuncturist
864	Damon Market	Grocery
900	(Chinese Name)	Import/export
904	Hing Wah Art Co.	Import/export
910	The Art Co.	Jewelry
914	(Chinese Name)	Clothing
916	Li-Po Cocktails	Cocktail lounge
918B	L&S Fashions	Clothing
918	Wing Wah Fine Jewelry	Jewelry
924	Jade Beauty Salon	Beauty salon
928	Goldmine Travel Agency	Travel
	Amerasian Fashion Gift Shop	Gifts
	Amerasian Investment Realty Co.	Realty
930	Kent's Trading Co.	Import/export
932	American Export Import Corp.	Import/export
950	Grand Palace	Restaurant
	Little Palace	Restaurant
952–54	Jen Ju & Co., Inc.	Jewelry, souvenirs
956	Sun Hai Jewelry Co.	Jewelry
960	Golden Pagoda	Restaurant
966	(formerly) Italian Market	T-shirts, clothing
1000	1st Nationwide Bank	Bank
1014	Louie's of Grant Avenue	Restaurant
1016	Ginn Wall Co.	Hardware
1024	Tip Top Fashions	Clothing
1040–42	Great Western Bank	Bank
1044	Elegance Fashion House	Clothing
1050	Javin Market	Chinese grocery
1056	Dennis Yabumoso, D.D.S	Dentist
	Charles L. Chin, M.D.	Doctor
1066	United Savings Bank	Bank
	United Savings Bank Real Estate Loans Dept.	
1100	Canton Market	General market
1114	On Sang Poultry Co.	Poultry market
1116	Man Sung Market	Poultry market
1118	New World Travel Service	Travel
1122	Wing Yuen Co.	Chinese grocery
1126	(No name)	Records, tapes
1128	Wing Hing Trading Co.	Chinese grocery

1136	Hong Kong Market	General food market
1142	Clearance Center	Gifts
1160	Wells Fargo Bank	Bank
601	McDonald's	Fast food, hamburgers
607	Empire Cameras	Cameras, shirts
615	Chinatown Gallery	Gallery
	Lee Tours	Travel
	Chinatown Child Development Center	
	Chinatown North Beach Community Care Center	
627	Gin Ling Arts	Bazaar, import/export
631	Far East Cafe Restaurant	Restaurant
645	Shanghai Bazaar	Bazaar
667	Bargain Bazaar	Bazaar
701	Bank of America	Bank
717	Chinatown Kites	Kites, shirts
719	Ong Ko Met Benevolent Assn.	Association
	Chinn Accountancy Corporation	Accountants
725–29	Far East Flea Market	Bazaar
731	Four Seas Restaurant	Restaurant
733	Royal House	Bazaar
737	National Chinese Welfare Council	Organization
739	Song Kee Co.	Clothing
745	Ying On Labor & Merchant Benevolent Assn.	
747	Dock Wah Co.	Linens, bazaar
749	Gold Wing Imports	Goldsmith
751	Cathay Fashion	Clothing
757	Kee Fung Ng Gallery	Paintings
801	The Empress	Jewelry, antiques
803	Moon John	Clothing
805	Bow Chong Co.	Jewelry
807	Tai Li Co.	Antiques
815	Hong Kong Gifts-Souvenirs	Souvenirs
819	Wing Hop Hing Kee Co.	Bazaar
827	Tin Shew Tong	Bazaar
829	Wai Hing Ivory & Imports Inc.	Import/export
831	Yau Hing Co.	Ginseng, herbs
835	Sam Yup Benevolent Assn.	Association
837	Gifts Unlimited	Bazaar
839	Arts of China	Ivory, jewelry, wares
843	Arts of China	Furniture, jewelry
845	Citicorp Savings	Bank
857–67	Shanghai Imports	Bazaar
901	Buddha Lounge	Bar

903	Fat Ming Co.	Stationery
905	Chew Chong Tai & Co.	Stationery
909	Kowloon Pastries	Pastries
911	Wo Yick Co.	Jewelry
913	Gong Num Camera Shop	Cameras
915	Lee Family Assn.	Association
915A	Sars All Coverage Insurance Company	Insurance
	Lee Noy Cho Acupuncturist	Acupuncture
	Chow Chin Hun Associates	Antiques
	NE Community Federal Credit Union	Credit union
	Occidental Life Insurance	Insurance
	Chinese-American Voters Education Comm. Office	
919	Imperial Palace	Restaurant
921	Chung Fat & Co.	Clothing
925	Suey Sing Chamber of Labor & Commerce	
933	Central Bank	Bank
941–43–47	Kwong Sang Lung Co.	Bazaar, herbs
949	Ten Ren	Ginseng, tea
953	Far East Fashion	Clothing
955	Asia Jewelry Co.	Jewelry
957	Hop Lee	Bazaar
1001	Bank of Trade	Bank
1019	Li John	To-go foods
1021	Mall (Old Sun Sing Theatre)	Jewelry, clothing, magazines
1029	Golden Gate Bakery	Bakery
1039	Oriental House of Beauty	Beauty salon
	Medical/dental offices	
1043	Kayes Footware	Shoes
1047	Johnson Imports	Bazaar
1051	Mee Shing Radio Co.	Electronic, watches
1055	Grant Pacific Imports	Jewelry
1101	New May Wah	Grocery, produce
1105	Universal	Clothing, grocery, to-go food
1109	Ping Yuen Drug Store	Pharmacy
1111	Ping Yuen Market	Market
1123	Hong Kong Center	Clothing, miscellaneous
	Shoe House	Shoes
	Jade Fashions	Clothing
1131	Yuen's Garden Restaurant	Restaurant, pastry, to-go food
1143	International Gifts	Bazaar
1147–49	New Hop Yick Meat Market	Meat market
1151	International	Clothing
1155	Bow Bow	Bar
1157	Kwong Jow	Chinese sausage maker

KEARNY STREET

943	Coin-Operated Laundry	Laundry
941	Great Hunan No. 2	Restaurant
939	Franthai Restaurant	Restaurant
935	Hotel St. Paul	Hotel
925	Phuong's Vietnamese Restaurant	Restaurant
923	Joe's Bar-B-Q	Restaurant
919	Kong's Restaurant	Restaurant
915	Sai's Deli (French-Vietnamese)	Restaurant
911	Far East Travel Service	Travel
905	Grassland	Bar
901	DPD Restaurant	Restaurant
861	Jay's Grocery	Grocery
859	Wayne's Liquors	Grocery
855	Baby Hunan	Restaurant
853	Original Hunan	Restaurant
849	Hofina	Bazaar
839	Hunan Village	Restaurant
835	Golden Coin Savings & Loan	Bank
829	Hsu & Co.	Chinese art
827	Alan Chan, O. D.	Optometrist
809	Kaman Shoe Co.	Shoes
801	World Ginseng Center	Herbs
733	Portsmouth Square Garage	Public garage
653	Chinatown TV, Inc.	Televisions
651	Hong Kong TV Video Programs, Inc.	Chinese videos
633	Thomas Wong, O. D.	Optometrist
631	Y-Pay-More Cleaners	Cleaners
	Happy Fast Photo	Photo developing
	BR & G Lounge	Restaurant
625	Sing Tao Newspapers, Ltd.	Newspaper office
619	Jack Sen Tong Assn.	Association
615	Hans J. Wong	Herbalist, chiropracter
	Sarah E. Wong, D.D.S.	Dentist
605	Mini Market	Grocery
601	Young's Cafe	Restaurant

ALLEYS

WETMORE STREET
Residences only

JOICE STREET

210	Back of Cameron House (Basketball courts, side entrance)

STONE STREET

(odd)	Kai Ming Head Start	Community services
(even)	Side of Commodore Stockton School Annex, Side of Chinese Hospital	

TRENTON STREET

(Between Jackson and Washington—Chinese Hospital parking)
(Between Jackson and Pacific—Houses, side of Ping Yuen West)

DUNCOMBE ALLEY

6,8,10	(No names)	Sewing factories

JASON COURT

1	Far East Aquarium	Aquarium
9	Erwin Jong Signs	Signs
19	Lucky Travel	Travel
34	Chinese Cemetery Assn.	Association

ST. LOUIS PLACE

7	Chung Fat Sausage Co.	Meat
12	Ming Yeh	(Unknown)
19	(No name)	Sewing factory
20	Yook Ying Assn.	Association
21	(No name)	Sewing factory

ROSS ALLEY

56	French Adult Fortune Cookie	Fortune cookies
32	Mr. Alan Gin	Barber
24	(No name)	Sewing factory
22	Chinatown Dry Cleaning & Laundry	Dry cleaners
20	Tong Kee Food Products, Inc.	Food import/export
14	Sam Bo Trading Co.	Import/export
12	Canton Flower Shoppe	Florist
10	Wong's TV-Radio Service	TV/Radios
21	(No name)	Sewing factory
23,25,27	(No name)	Sewing factory
29,29A,31	(No name)	Sewing factory
41	(No name)	Sewing factory
53	(No name)	Sewing factory

OLD CHINATOWN LANE

1	ABC Knitting Co.	Sewing factory
9	(No name)	Chinese herbs
11	Mabel Y. Kao, M.D.	Obstetrics/gynecology

OLD CHINATOWN LANE

10	M.K. Lee Public Accountant	Accountant
	Juanita Lee's Tours	Tours
8	Raymond Chu Hair Design	Beauty salon
4,6	(No name)	Sewing factory

SPOFFORD ALLEY

54	Chan Y.D. Printing Center	Printing
50	Chin Kuo San	Social hall
48	Szeto Chun Yun Tong	Association office
44	Mou Young	Association
36	Chinese Free Masons	Association meeting hall
34B	Chu Hai University Assn.	Alumni office
32	(No name)	Sewing factory
24	(No name)	Sewing factory
5	(No name)	Florist
33	Chinese Laundry Assn., Inc.	Association
43,45	(No name)	Sewing factory

WAVERLY PLACE

155	Furama Jewelry Co.	Jewelry
153	Ken's Barber Shop	Barber
145	Anthony Wong's Beauty Salon	Beauty salon
141	Hop Sing Tong	
133	Wonder Food Co.	Produce, grocery
127	S. Lam Chan	Jewelry, art
125	Tin How Temple	Temple
117	Anthony's Beauty & Hair Center	Beauty salon
115 ½	Tai Canton	Social hall
115	(No name)	Laundromat
111	Culture-Lite Printing	Printing
109	Norras Temple	Buddhist temple
105	Gee Poy Kuo Assn.	Association
103	Pacific Hobby & Toys	Toys
101	Yick Gee Book Co.	Book store
65	Uncle's Coffee Shop	Restaurant
61	His 'n Hers Unisex Hairstyling Salon	Beauty salon
59	Franklin M. Lam	Tax and accounting service
45	West Coast Life Insurance Co.	Insurance
43	N.Y. Chi-Am Tours, Inc.	Travel
	Clay Realty	Realty
41	Hoy-Sun Ning Yung Benevolent Assn.	Association
39	Wong Family Benevolent Assn.	Association
37	Mun Sek Kee Loo	Meeting room, social hall
35	Bing-Kong Tong Free Masons	Meeting hall

WAVERLY PLACE

35	Oliver C. Chang Recreation Center	Backside, playground building
15	First Chinese Baptist Church	Church
2	Chinese TV Co.	Showroom
	Chinese Television Production Co.	Production office
18	(No name)	Sewing factory
28	Four Seas Restaurant (rear entrance)	Restaurant
30	(No name)	Sewing factory
36	Asian Law Caucus	Offices
40	(No name)	Chinese bookstore
44	Daily Travel Service, Inc.	Travel
46	Ying Fat Yuen Club	Club room
56	(No name)	Martial arts studio
	Lee, Wong & Leong Insurance	Insurance office
100	Jeanette's Travel Service, Inc.	Travel
112–14	Ming's Travel, Inc.	Travel
118–20	Quong Shing Co.	Produce
	Quong Shing Co.	Candy
126	Kay Sun Cleaners-Laundry	Laundry
128	The Light Co.	Import/export
132	Chinatown Photographic Society	Offices
	Hwang Pu Alumni Assn.	Association
	Hoy Sun Normal School Alumni Assn.	Association
138	Gee Tuck Sam Tuck Assn.	Association
150	The Pot Sticker	Restaurant
160	Lee T. Tan, D.D.S	Dentist
	William H. Yim, D.D.S	Dentist
	Choy Won Beauty Salon	Beauty salon

HANG AH STREET

49–51	Young China Daily	Newspaper office
33	Postal Chinese Club	Club
31	Kong Fung Club	Club
29	Lee Ming Sewing Co.	Sewing factory
27	Cathay Times	Newspaper office
1	Hang Ah Tea Room	Restaurant

COMMERCIAL STREET

(Between Grant and Kearny Streets)

779	Kar Mee Hair Design	Beauty salon
777	Unified Financial Services	Income tax
775	Ted Chew Community Center, Inc.	Community center
	The Newcomer News	News offices
825	Express Chinese Photo-Typesetting Co.	Typesetting
755	(No name)	Sewing factory

COMMERCIAL STREET

751	(No name)	Sewing factory
747	(No name)	Sewing factory
739–41	National Noodle Co.	Noodles
735	(No name)	Sewing factory
731	American Asia Trading Co., Inc.	Import/export
725	Ampac Trading (U.S.A.) Co.	Ginseng export
723	Law Offices	Offices
721	International Daily News	Newspaper office
711	C.P.A. Offices	Offices
700	Henry Hung Construction Co., Inc.	Office
708	(No name)	Rice distribution
730	(No name)	Sewing factory
740	Shew Kee Assn.	Association
754	Steve M. Jeong Realty	Realty
	Rodney K. Jeong	Attorney-at-law
756	(No name)	Income tax service
758	Calvin L.Y. Chan	Notary
772	Cathay Club	Social club
774	Mow Lee Co.	Chinese grocery
776	Hoy Sun High School Alumni Assn.	Association
650	Chinese Historical Society of America (between Kearny and Montgomery)	Society/museum

WALTER U. LUM PLACE

(Formerly Brenham Place)

13	Hair of Fashion	Beauty salon
	Lien-Ying Tai-chi Chuan Academy	Tai-chi school
17–19	Chinese for Affirmative Action	Reading room, office

WALTER U. LUM PLACE

21	Chinese Congregational Church	Church
35	China Trade Center	Shops, bazaars
49	Golden Gate Trading Co.	Import/export
57	Salon Studio	Photography
61	William (Bill) Wong & Associates	Sales, life insurance
63	Yarn Boutique	Yarn shop
	PORTSMOUTH SQUARE	Public park

WENTWORTH STREET

20	Y.K. Lau Co.	Picture framing and furniture repair
30	Oriental Arcade	Yarn
42	Anthony Wong's Beauty Salon	Beauty salon
	Union Fashion	Clothing
60	Pon Yup Chong How Benevolent Assn.	Association
64	Wan Hua Co.	Chinese herbs
?	Trophy Co.	Jewelry
39	Union Fashion Knit Unlimited	Clothing
37	Package Tours (U.S.A.) Limited	Travel
	Goldmine Travel Agency (928 Grant)	Travel
	Amerasia Investment Rty. (928 Grant)	Realty
	Amerasia Import-Export (928 Grant)	Import/Export
	Jade Beauty Salon	Beauty salon

BECKETT STREET

8?	Kay Leung & Co. Noodles	Noodle manufacturer
26	(No name)	Sewing factory

APPENDIX F: Maps of Chinatown

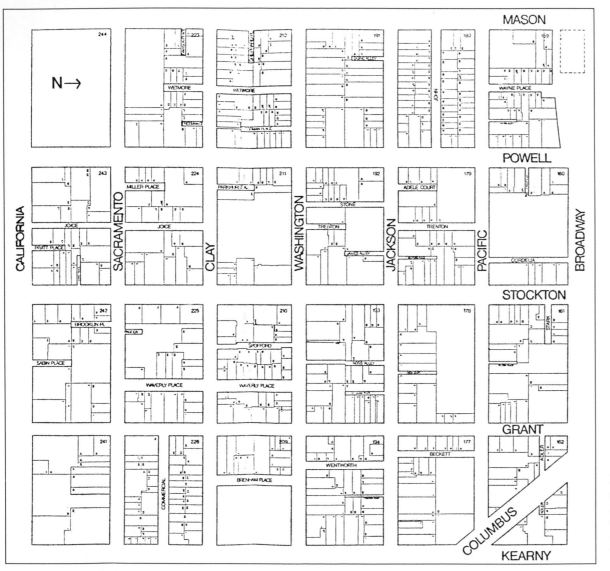

Left: *Core area of San Francisco China-town.* Right: *Northeast corner of San Francisco, showing core area (solid line) and extended area (dashed line) of China-town. [Maps courtesy of Chinatown Neighborhood Improvement Resource Center.]*

APPENDIX G: Notes on Transliteration

The Chinese place names used in this book are spelled according to the Wade-Giles system of transliteration. The more recently developed Pinyin system of transliteration is based on the Mandarin dialect and is currently used by the Chinese government and many western scholars. However, most of the people described in this book trace their ancestry to South China, and are accustomed to using the more traditional spellings.

The following reference table is provided for the convenience of readers who may be familiar with Pinyin.

Place names

A = area, C = city, D = district, P = province, V = village

Wade-Giles	Pinyin
Canton (C)	Guangzhou
Chiayingchow (D)	Jianyingzhou
Chikkai (D)	Qixi
Chuhoi (A)	Zhuhai
Chungshan Yuan (D)	Zhongshanxian
Dowmon (A)	Dumen
Fa Yuan (D)	Huaxian
Fukien (P)	Fujian
Hakka (A)	Kejia
Heungshan, Hangshan (D)	Xiangshan
Hoiping (D)	Kaiping
Hokshan (D)	Keshan
Hong Kong (C)	Xianggang
Hunan (P)	Hunan
Kiangsi (P)	Jiangxi
Koming (D)	Kaoming
Kong Yick Fou (C)	Jiangyifu
Koyiu (D)	Gaoyao
Kueishan (D)	Guishan
Kwangsi (P)	Guangxi
Kwangtung (P)	Guangdong
Macao (C)	Aomen

Wade-Giles	Pinyin
Muiyuan (D)	Meixian
Namhoi (D)	Nanhai
Pao-on (D)	Baoan
Peking (C)	Beijing
Poklo (D)	Boluo
Punyu (D)	Panyu
Samshui (D)	Sanshui
Sam Yup (3 districts)	Sanyi
Shanghai (C)	Shanghai
Shek Gong (A)	Xijiang
Shing Hong Lea (V)	Xinghongli
Shuntak (D)	Shunde
Sunning (D)	Xinning
Sun-on (D)	Shunan
Sunwui (D)	Xinhui
Sze Yup (4 districts)	Siyi
Szewui (D)	Sihui
Tientsin (C)	Tianjin
Toishan (D)	Taishan
Tsengshing (D)	Zhengcheng
Tsingyuan (D)	Qingxian
Tungkun (D)	Tongkun
Waichow (A)	Huizhou
Wuiyeung (D)	Huiyang
Yanping (D)	Yangping
Yeungchun (D)	Yangcun
Yeungkong (D)	Yangjiang

Family Names

Chan, Chin	Chen
Cheung	Zhang
Der, Tse	Xie
Jang, Jeung	Zhang
Lai	Li
Loy, Louie	Lei
Ng	Wu
Ong	Deng, Weng
Toy	Cai
Wu, Woo	Hu

Names of Companies and Benevolent Associations

Wade-Giles	Pinyin
Canton Co.	Guangdong Gongsi
Hip Kat Co.	Xie Kai Gongsi
Hop Wo Co. (Hop Wo Ben. Assn.)	He He Gongsi
Kong Chow Co. (Kong Chow Ben. Assn.)	Gangzhou Gongsi
Look Yup	Liu Yi
Ning Yung Co. (Ning Yung Ben. Assn.)	Ning Yang Gongsi
Sam Yup Co. (Sam Yup Ben. Assn.)	San Yi Gongsi
Sue Hing Co. (Sue Hing Ben. Assn.)	Rui Xing Gongsi
Sun On Co.	Shun An Gongsi
Sze Yup Co.	Si Yi Gongsi
Tah Yuen Ben. Assn.	Da Yuan Gong Suo
Tom Yee	Tang Yi
Tong Sen Tong	Tong Shan Tang
Toy Tong	Cai Tong
Yan Wo Co. (Yan Wo Ben. Assn.)	Ren He Gongsi
Yee Tong	Yi Tang
Yee Fung Toy Tong	Yu Feng Cai Tang
Yen Hoy Co.	Yan Hai Gongsi
Young Wo Co. (Young Wo Ben. Assn.)	Yang He Gongsi

Bibliography

Ira B. Cross. *Financing an Empire: History of Banking in California*. Chicago: S. J. Clarke, 1927.

Charles Caldwell Dobie. *San Francisco Chinatown*. New York: Appleton-Century, 1936.

John Hittel. *The Commerce and Industries of the Pacific Coast of North America*. San Francisco: Bancroft, 1882.

William Hoy. *The Chinese Six Companies*. San Francisco: Chinese Six Companies, 1942.

Rose Hum Lee. *The Chinese in the United States of America*. Hong Kong: Hong Kong University Press, 1960.

Him Mark Lai. "Historical Development of the Chinese Consolidated Benevolent Association/Huigan System," in *Chinese America: History and Perspectives 1987*. San Francisco: Chinese Historical Society of America, 1987.

Him Mark Lai, Genny Lim, and Judy Yung. *Island: Poetry and History of Chinese Immigrants on Angel Island, 1910–1940*. San Francisco: HOC DOI (History of Chinese Detained on Island), 1980.

Victor Low. *The Unimpressible Race: A Century of Educational Struggle by the Chinese in San Francisco*. San Francisco: East/West, 1982.

Chih Meng. *Chinese American Understanding: A Sixty-Year Search*. New York: China Institute in America, 1981.

J. S. Tow. *The Real Chinese in America*. New York: Chinese Consulate General, 1923. Tow was a secretary of the New York Chinese Consulate, with the rank of consul-élève.

Index

Page numbers in italics refer to illustrations.

Production director and designer: Nancy Warner
Editors: Rebecca Pepper and Sean Cotter
Typesetter: Warner-Cotter Company
Linotronic output: Pinnacle Type
Jacket printer: Lithocraft, Santa Rosa, California
Printer: Malloy Lithographing, Ann Arbor, Michigan
Binder: John H. Dekker & Sons, Grand Rapids, Michigan
Marketing: Butterfield Associates, Emeryville, California

Text: Jansen Text
Display: Futura